# JUDAEA AND ROME IN COINS
## 65 BCE – 135 CE

# JUDAEA AND ROME IN COINS 65 BCE – 135 CE

Papers Presented at the International Conference Hosted by Spink,
13th – 14th September 2010

*edited by*

David M. Jacobson and Nikos Kokkinos

LONDON 2012

First Published 2012
by Spink & Son Ltd.
69 Southampton Row
Bloomsbury
London WC1B 4ET

ISBN 978-1-907427-22-0

© 2012
David M. Jacobson & Nikos Kokkinos

All rights reserved. No part of this publication may be reproduced, stored in a retrieval system, or transmitted, in any form or by any means, without the prior permission in writing of Spink & Son Ltd.

Typeset by Design to Print UK Ltd., Forest Row, East Sussex, RH18 5FS.
Printed and bound in Malta by Gutenburg Press Ltd.

# CONTENTS

Foreword (by Markham J. Geller) ............................................................................. vii

Preface (by the Editors) ............................................................................................. ix

Andrew BURNETT ........................................................................................................1
    The Herodian Coinage Viewed against the Wider Perspective of Roman Coinage

Rachel BARKAY ..........................................................................................................19
    Roman Influence on Jewish Coins

Anne LYKKE ................................................................................................................27
    The Use of Languages and Scripts in Ancient Jewish Coinage: An Aid in Defining the Role of the Jewish Temple until its Destruction in 70 CE

Danny SYON ................................................................................................................51
    Galilean Mints in the Early Roman Period: Politics, Economy and Ethnicity

Robert BRACEY ..........................................................................................................65
    On the Graphical Interpretation of Herod's Year 3 Coins

Nikos KOKKINOS ........................................................................................................85
    The Prefects of Judaea 6-48 CE and the Coins from the Misty Period 6-36 CE

Robert DEUTSCH ......................................................................................................113
    The Coinage of the Great Jewish Revolt against Rome: Script, Language and Inscriptions

David HENDIN ..........................................................................................................123
    Jewish Coinage of the Two Wars: Aims and Meaning

David M. JACOBSON ................................................................................................145
    The Significance of the Caduceus between Facing Cornucopias in Herodian and Roman Coinage

Ted V. BUTTREY ........................................................................................................163
    Vespasian's Roman Orichalcum: An Unrecognised Celebratory Coinage

Marius HEEMSTRA ....................................................................................................187
    The Interpretation and Wider Context of Nerva's Fiscus Judaicus Sestertius

Kevin BUTCHER ........................................................................................................203
    The Silver Coinage of Roman Arabia

Boaz ZISSU and David HENDIN ..............................................................................215
    Further Remarks on Coins in Circulation during the Bar-Kokhba War: Te'omim Cave and Horvat 'Ethri Hoards

Larry J. KREITZER ....................................................................................................229
    Hadrian as Nero *Redivivus*: some supporting evidence from Corinth

List of Contributors ..................................................................................................243

Group Photograph ....................................................................................................245

# FOREWORD

The *Judaea and Rome in Coins* Conference was co-sponsored by the Institute of Jewish Studies (IJS) at University College London, as part of its programme to promote 'Jewish scholarship and civilisation at the highest level of academic excellence.' The two editors of this volume, David Jacobson and Nikos Kokkinos, who are Honorary Research Fellows of the Department of Hebrew and Jewish Studies at UCL, are to be commended for initiating this successful conference, and the IJS is pleased to be associated with this volume and the impressive scholarship on ancient coins which it has to offer.

Markham J. Geller
*Director, Institute of Jewish Studies, UCL*

# PREFACE

The papers in this volume are based on presentations at an international two-day conference entitled *Judaea and Rome in Coins, 65 BCE to 135 CE*, held at Spink & Son in London on 13-14 September, 2010. The event followed two earlier London conferences (*The World of the Herods and Nabataeans* in 2001 and *Herod and Augustus* in 2005). The proceedings of the earlier conferences, both of which attracted large audiences, were also published and they have become since reference points.

The original list of speakers at Spink included Professor Dan Barag, a teacher, colleague and friend to many of the contributors, who sadly passed away in mid-November 2009, and to whose memory we dedicate this volume. Dan's intended paper was entitled 'Jewish Coinage of two Wars – Aims and Meaning', and it is not coincidental that David Hendin adopted that name for his paper.

The period covered in the present collection spans the Roman conquest of Judaea by Pompey through to the last major Jewish uprising against Rome under Simon Bar-Kokhba, encompassing the age of the Herods and the birth of Christianity. The past few decades have seen considerable advances in numismatic scholarship dealing with this period, stimulated by archaeological exploration and important coin finds, which have shed new light on the historical events and associated political, social and economic issues.

The authors of the papers are well-known names in the fields of Roman and Jewish numismatics, who have pooled their specialist knowledge to illuminate important issues in the history of Judaea and its relationship to Rome. As is often the case, scholarly enquiry throws up more questions than it is able to answer with total confidence. But the aim throughout has been to bring clarity to those problems which have been difficult to interpret. An attempt has been made to set the papers in chronological order, though this has only been possible to some degree. Aspects of the Herodian coinage and its Roman influence are dealt with by Andrew Burnett and Rachel Barkay. Anne Lykke has explored what she perceives as a link between the languages and scripts on Jewish coins to 70 CE, on the one hand, and the Temple, on the other. Danny Syon has concentrated on Jewish Galilee and its boundary to the outbreak of the First Jewish Revolt. Robert Bracey has analysed the die links of Herod's largest coin, while Nikos Kokkinos has covered the coins struck when Judaea was governed by Roman prefects. There follow two papers on the coinage of the First Revolt by Robert Deutsch and David Hendin, with Hendin also examining that of the Bar Kokhba Revolt. Next are a pair of papers by David Jacobson and Ted Buttrey on the winged caduceus and crossed cornucopias motif, which frequently recurs on Judaean issues, their studies intersecting at the time of Vespasian. Marius Heemstra then addresses Nerva and his Fiscus Iudaicus sestertius, followed by a study of the silver currency of Arabia under Trajan by Kevin Butcher. Boaz Zissu and David Hendin describe a sensational find of a hoard of Bar Kokhba coins and its significance. Finally, Larry Kreitzer completes the volume with a study of the provincial issues of Corinth in relation to the persecution of 'God's people' by Nero and Hadrian, as recorded in some classical Jewish and Christian sources.

Annotation has followed the hybrid version of the British-Harvard bibliographical systems, as used in many learned journals and books. This allows the use of notes (as in the British system), freeing the text from lengthy modern references, while at the same time employs the style of referring to author, date and page number (as in the Harvard system) within these notes. But the classical references, unless there is a series of them, are kept in the main text. An alphabetical bibliography (preceded by abbreviations other than those of journals) appears at the end of each paper. Abbreviations of academic journals in the bibliography have adopted the standard listing in the latest volume of the *Année Philologique*. Archaeological journals not listed there have followed the list published in the *American Journal of Archaeology* 111 (2007). Numismatic journals not listed there are to be found in the latest volume of the *Numismatic Chronicle*. All three lists may also be consulted on the websites of these journals. Although there is no total consistency among scholars, the Loeb Classical Library provides most of the preferred abbreviations of classical authors. Biblical references have adopted those listed in the introduction to the latest edition of the Nestlé-Aland *The Greek New Testament*. Rabbinical references followed the tractates as abbreviated in Danby's *The Mishnah*. Ancient names of places and people in their English spelling follows the index of the revised edition of E. Schürer's *The History of the Jewish People in the Age of Jesus Christ*, or occasionally the latest edition of *The Oxford Classical Dictionary*. The spellings of modern sites adopted those in the *New Encyclopedia of Archaeological Excavations in the Holy Land*.

The Editors would like to extend our thanks to Spink and Son Ltd. and the Institute of Jewish Studies for sponsoring this undertaking. Our gratitude goes to Amelia Dowler, Curator of Greek coins in the Department of Coins and Medals at the British Museum and her colleagues for welcoming the idea of the conference and staging a special exhibition on Jewish coins. The British Museum is acknowledged for allowing reproduction of its coin images in this scholarly publication. Last but not least, was it not for the steadfast support and encouragement of Philip Skingley, and his indefatigable efforts as co-organiser on behalf of Spink & Son, the conference and its volume would not have easily become a reality. We also wish to express our appreciation to Catherine Gathercole of Spink for her assistance with the arrangements for the event.

David M. Jacobson<br>
Nikos Kokkinos

# THE HERODIAN COINAGE VIEWED AGAINST THE WIDER PERSPECTIVE OF ROMAN COINAGE

Andrew Burnett

## Jewish Numismatic Scholarship

The coinage of Herodian rulers of Judaea has attracted the attention of collectors and scholars for many years, and the coins continue to generate an interest that always seems disproportionately large. Vast amounts are paid for the coins in the saleroom, since they are rare and potential collectors many; and catalogues and discussions are published with what sometimes seems a wearying frequency. Yet, in comparison, the coinage of vast areas of the ancient world remains, even today, little studied and indeed relatively undervalued in monetary terms in the saleroom. The reason is easy enough to understand, since the possibility that archaeological evidence of any sort might throw light on the Bible has an obvious enough appeal.

It would be a limitless, and perhaps pointless, task to review the relevant literature, stretching back for over 150 years, at least to the excellent work of Madden.[1] But the story of the modern study on the Herodian coinage is indissolubly linked with the name of the late Ya'akov Meshorer.[2] He was one of the great figures of modern numismatics, and archaeology, and he was one of the most brilliant speakers one might ever encounter at a conference. Yet publications in Meshorer's name are surprisingly unreliable, especially the earlier ones, in part because the great amount of new discoveries of new material were not made till the very end of the 20th century, and in part because the coins of the Agrippa I, at least, are usually very poorly preserved. So his 1967 and 1982 handbooks could not be regarded as very reliable; it was only his *Treasury* of 2001 that attained an accuracy that does anything like justice to the surviving evidence.[3]

Other scholars have, of course, contributed greatly to our recent understanding of Jewish coinage of the first century CE. Although it is perhaps invidious to single any out, I would mention the work of Arie Kindler, not least because his attention to the detail of provenance has helped solved several problems of mint attribution, and of Alla Stein (later Kushnir-Stein), who has contributed a series of fundamental articles, especially on matters of chronology.[4]

Most scholars have tended to focus entirely on particular aspects of the Jewish or Herodian coinage, so it may therefore be useful to provide some sort of overview, and to set the coinage in its wider Syrian and imperial context, enabling us to see just how different from other contemporary coinages it was.[5]

---

[1] Madden 1864; 1881.
[2] Meshorer 1967; 1982; 1990/1; 2001.
[3] And even the *Treasury* needs to be used with care.
[4] See, for example, Kushnir-Stein 2007.
[5] My remarks build on my earlier publications: Burnett 1987; *RPC* 1; *RPC* 2; Burnett 2002.

## Overview of Herodian Coinage

Hasmonean coinage began in the late second century BCE under John Hyrcanus I (**Fig. 1**), and continued until the reign of Mattathias Antigonus, the last Hasmonaean king and high priest (40-37 BCE). It consisted entirely of small bronze coins minted in Jerusalem. Neither Hasmonaean coinage, nor the succeeding coinage of Herod and the Herodian dynasty, was ever of any economic significance. Herod (40-4 BCE) himself issued only one set of coins with different designs for different denominations. Some are dated to his third year (**Fig. 2**), and these coins and the more plentiful undated coins with the same designs are analysed by R. Bracey elsewhere in this volume.[6] The coinage of his three sons made in his divided kingdom was episodic and small scale, though, as well as being made in Jerusalem by Archelaus (**Fig. 3**), it was also produced at Caesarea-Philippi/ Panias by Philip (**Fig. 4**) and Tiberias by Antipas (**Fig. 5**). Their successor Agrippa I (37-44 CE) (**Figs 6-8**) made coinage at first at Panias, but, as the size of his kingdom of Agrippa expanded due to the favourable regard in which he was held by the emperors Caligula and Claudius, so too the number of mints expanded. As well as Panias, he also minted at Jerusalem (**Fig. 9**), Tiberias and Caesarea-on-sea (**Figs 10-11**). The dates on the coins show that they were minted only intermittently, and all but one of these coinages are very rare today and must have been made in very small quantities, as we can see from the die statistics given by J.-P. Fontanille on his website:[7]

|  | Meshorer 2001/RPC | Specimens | Obv. dies |
|---|---|---|---|
| Caligula/Germanicus | 116/4976 | 21 | 2 |
| Agrippa/Agrippa | 113/4974 | 13 | 3 |
| Caesonia/Drusilla | 117/4977 | 10 | 2 |
| Agrippa/corncucopia | 119/4979 | 19 | 2 |
| Claudius/temple    LZ | 121/4983 | 9[8] | 3 |
| LH | 125/4984 | 10 | 3 |
| Claudius/Tyche | 122/4985 | 32 | 13 |
| Clasped hands | 124/4982 | 6 | 4 |

Only the prutah from Jerusalem were made in large quantities; even with them, the low face value implies that they were of little economic importance.

---

[6] See also Fontanille and Ariel 2006.

[7] www.menorahcoinproject.org/. In the table I omit the specimens he found too worn to classify. The identification of dies is very difficult as the specimens are always in poor condition.

[8] Fontanille lists 32 specimens but for most he says 'Most of the following specimens seem to present a different die on obverse. But the precise identification and classification is extremely difficult for this type'. My table includes only the 9 specimens for which he gives greater certainty.

# THE HERODIAN COINAGE VIEWED AGAINST THE WIDER PERSPECTIVE OF ROMAN COINAGE

**Fig. 1:** John Hycanus. Bronze.

**Fig. 2:** Herod. Bronze dated to year 3.

**Fig. 3:** Archaelaus. Bronze. Minted at Jerusalem.

**Fig. 4:** Philip. Bronze of year 34. Minted at Caesarea-Philippi/Panias.

**Fig. 5:** Antipas. Bronze of year 24. Minted at Tiberias.

**Fig. 6:** Agrippa I: Agrippa I/Agrippa II. Year 2. Minted at Panias.

**Fig. 7:** Agrippa I: Caligula/Germanicus. Year 5. Minted at Panias.

**Fig. 8:** Agrippa I. Caesonia/Drusilla. Year 5. Minted at Panias.

**Fig. 9:** Agrippa I. Year 6. Minted at Jerusalem.

**Fig. 10:** Agrippa I: temple. Year 8. Minted at Caesarea-on-sea.

**Fig. 11:** Agrippa I: Tyche. Year 7. Minted at Caesarea-on-sea.

**Fig. 12:** Agrippa I: clasped hands/coronation scene. Year ?8. Minted at Caesarea-on-sea.

The coinage of Agrippa II (c. 50- c. 90 CE) included some early small bronze issues from a Neronias (**Fig. 13**), sometimes identified with Sepphoris,[9] and Panias. His main coinage, struck under the Flavian emperors (**Figs 14-15**), has, however, always been something of a *crux*, since the dates for his regnal years implied by some coins which also refer to Domitian's consulships imply that other coins he made in Vespasian's name were posthumous; implausibly so. I believe the solution to this *crux* has been found by Kushnir-Stein, though not all have accepted her view, which involves dividing the coinage between two mints, each of which used a different dating era.[10] But her proposal provides a very seductive solution to a very puzzling phenomenon. If there were indeed two mints, then one was at Panias (a few rare coins have a figure of Pan) and the other somewhere else, as yet uncertain.[11] Finally, the coins which refer to Domitian's consulships are of a very different style and appearance from the other coins of Agrippa II, and a case can certainly be made for regarding them as minted in Rome or from dies engraved at Rome **(Fig.16)**.[12]

**Fig. 13:** Agrippa II: Nero/wreath. Minted at 'Neronias'.

**Fig. 14:** Agrippa II: Vespasian/Tyche. Year 14.

**Fig. 15:** Agrippa II: Titus/Nike. Year 26.

**Fig. 16:** Agrippa II: Domitian/altar. Year 26.

Intertwined among the Herodian coinage are some other coin issues from the region, of two main sorts. The first is what we might call standard Roman provincial coins. The Claudian coins of Gaba (**Fig. 17**) and Tiberias, or Neronian coins of Sepphoris and Caesarea-on-sea (**Fig. 18**), are good examples: an imperial bust and inscription on the obverse, with a design of local reference and the ethnic on the reverse (*RPC* 1, 4856-7; 4851-3; 4849-50; 4862-65).

---

[9] But, as N. Kokkinos has kindly pointed out, Sepphoris was outside Agrippa II's kingdom, and he had little or nothing to do with this city (see Kokkinos 1998, 317-41).
[10] Kushnir-Stein 2002; not accepted by Kokkinos 2003.
[11] Hendin attributes them to Caesarea-on-sea, but Caesarea was not part of Agrippa's kingdom. Also it would seem unlikely that Caesarea would have produced both coinage for Agrippa II and for the newly founded colony (and perhaps the 'provincial coinage', unless one believes – as I do – that this is really colonial coinage of Caesarea lacking the city's name). So maybe a mint elsewhere should be sought. A. Kushnir-Stein has been collecting provenances. See also Burnett, forthcoming 1.
[12] The anomalous (for Syria and Judaea) use of a 6 o'clock die axis convinces me that the coins were also made at Rome.

# THE HERODIAN COINAGE VIEWED AGAINST THE WIDER PERSPECTIVE OF ROMAN COINAGE

**Fig. 17:** Claudius I. Minted at Gaba.     **Fig. 18:** Nero. Minted at Caesarea-on-sea.

The second consists of more enigmatic coins. The earlier ones were produced in the reigns of Claudius and Nero, and are sometimes in Greek but sometimes in Latin, and once even bilingual (*RPC* 1, 4858). They lack an ethnic, and so are hard to attribute to a mint and interpret:

– the Latin 'family' coins of Claudius, which depict Britannicus and his siblings, probably from Panias in the late 40s (**Fig. 19**) (*RPC* 1, 4842-4).
– the Latin coins of Agrippina and Octavia, Nero's mother and wife, presumably made between Nero's marriage to Octavia in 53 and Agrippina's death in 59 and probably minted from Panias (*RPC* 1, 4845).
– the Latin coins of Diva Poppaea and Diva Claudia, Nero's later wife and daughter, also from Panias, and minted after Poppaea's death in 65 (**Fig. 20**) (*RPC* 1, 4846).[13]
– the Latin coins of Claudius with reverses of a rudder or an anchor, minted at Panias or Caesarea-on-sea (**Fig. 21**) (*RPC* 1, 4847-8)
– the coins of Claudius with Greek obverses, and with with OB C S in wreath or Agrippina in Greek, from Caesarea-on-sea (*RPC* 1, 4858-9)
– the Greek coins of Nero and Agrippina from Caesarea-on-sea (**Fig. 22**) (*RPC* 1, 4860-1).

**Fig. 19:** Claudius/Britannicus, Octavia and Antonia. Perhaps minted at Panias.     **Fig. 20:** Diva Poppaea and Diva Claudia. Perhaps minted at Panias.

**Fig. 21:** Claudius. Minted at Panias or Caesarea-on-sea.     **Fig. 22:** Nero and Agrippina II. Perhaps minted at Caesarea-on-sea.

The coins are hard to interpret and the phrase 'Roman administration' is often used. I suppose the analogy may be with the so-called procurator coins of Jerusalem, which, made after Archelaus' death in 6 CE, just refer to the emperor and have his regnal year, and

---

[13] N. Kokkinos points out that if *RPC* 1, 4846 and 4847-8 were minted at Panias, then they would fall under Agrippa II.

reflect the fact that Jerusalem was directly controlled by the Romans at the time. We have to choose whether the coins listed above are some such 'Roman' issue or whether they are just city coins which lack an ethnic, as we might assume elsewhere in the empire.[14] Normally I would be tempted to conclude the latter, but the (irregular) appearance of Latin is so unexpected that it perhaps encourages us to think of the former. But this cannot be regarded as at all certain.

The later coins of this more enigmatic group were made in the reign of Agrippa II:
- the Greek *Judaea capta* coinage, minted c. 71-73, from Caesarea-on-sea (**Fig. 23**) (*RPC* 2, 2310-13)
- the Latin 'provincial Judaean coinage', made in three groups during the reign of Domitian (**Fig. 24**) (*RPC* 2, 2300-09).

**Fig. 23:** Vespasian: 'Judaea capta'. Minted at Caesarea-on-sea.

**Fig. 24:** Domitian: 'provincial Judaean coinage'. Minted at Caesarea-on-sea.

The 'Judaea capta' coins were presumably minted by the Romans at Caesarea-on-sea just before Agrippa II started to mint there (see above). However, the 'provincial Judaean coinage' seems more likely to me to be from the newly founded colony at Caesarea-on-sea (hence the Latin inscriptions), which omit the city's name.[15]

**Silver and Gold Minted at Caesarea-on-sea?**

It was argued in *RPC* 2 that a small group of early Flavian aurei (**Fig. 25**) and silver tetradrachms (**Fig. 26**) were minted at the same place as the *Judaea capta* coinage, and so presumably at Caesarea-on-sea, in c. 70-3 (*RPC* 2, 1908-13; 1963-9).[16]

**Fig. 25:** Vespasian. Aureus. Perhaps minted at Caesarea-on-sea.

**Fig. 26:** Vespasian. Silver tetradrachm. Perhaps minted at Caesarea-on-sea.

---

[14] E.g. the question of the Nicopolis coins under Nero (*RPC* 1, 1371-77, with discussion there).
[15] But see Hendin 2007.
[16] Previously, I have wondered if the enigmatic Nero/Claudius tetradrachms once attributed to Caesarea in Cappadocia (*RPC* 1, 4122-3), but apparently Syrian in terms of circulation, might also have been minted here. But recent analytical work indicates that, after all, they were made in Caesarea, and presumably transported from there to Syria (see Butcher and Ponting 2009).

## Tyre

One of Meshorer's more persistent ideas has been that some of the later silver shekels of Tyre (**Figs 27-28**: years 158 and 172) were minted at Jerusalem. This is not convincing, but seems to persist because the notion of silver coins minted at Jerusalem is somehow attractive (certainly to those who wish to buy and sell coins!).[17]

**Fig. 27:** Tyre. Silver shekel. Year 158.    **Fig. 28:** Tyre. Silver shekel. Year 172.

From the late second century BCE Tyre had produced a series of shekels or tetradrachms dated according to the city's era, and from the late first century it represented one of the two principal silver currencies of Syria, the other being the silver from Antioch. Meshorer found it hard to believe that the Jewish kingdom might have produced only low value bronze coinage, especially as the Tyrian shekel and half shekel played such an important role in Judaea, for example being the medium in which the annual temple tax was paid by all Jews. For that reason, not least, many of them are found in Judaea, and they certainly seem to have represented the principal silver coin in Judaea.

He adduced several supporting arguments, none of which has any great strength. First, he identified a roughening of style and the introduction of a new monogram, consisting of the Greek letters KP or KPA. He interpreted these as representing a transfer of minting from Tyre to Jerusalem and an abbreviation for KPATOC, power, which he took to be as a reference to Roman power. He also regarded the cessation of minting in 66 as caused by the outbreak of the Jewish War, an event that directly affected Jerusalem but only indirectly Tyre.[18]

The question has also been discussed by *RPC* 1, p. 656, and more fully by B. Levy,[19] and comprehensively refuted by Weisser.[20] Many arguments can be deployed against the hypothesis, of which the most telling seems to me the impossibility of one city (Jerusalem) using another's (Tyre) city era. There would have to be compelling evidence to cast any doubt at all on the obvious interpretation (that the later coins are also coins of Tyre), and there is no such evidence. The notion of any Jewish silver coinage under the Herodians should firmly be resisted.

## The Context of Herodian Coinage

The coinage of early imperial Syria followed, in general, the pattern of provincial coinage in other parts of the empire, though there were differences and geographical exceptions, of

---

[17] So a coin of year 159 may be advertised as a coin of the year of the crucifixion: e.g. *CNG* 64 (2003) lot 411, and many others – see Coin Archives, when searched (in August 2010) for 'Tyre' and 'crucifixion': 14 examples were found!

[18] He is correct in his view of the date of the end of the Tyrian coinage, *pace RPC*, which dates it to mostly 60 and connects it with Nero's reforms of the silver coinage of Antioch (following, in general, the views of Walker 1976, 58). Even though shekels are now known for years 60/1, 61/2, 62/3, 63/4 and 64/5 (*RPC Supplement* 1, 4680B; *RPC Supplement* 2, S2-4680Ba; *RPC Supplement* 1, 4680C-E) and half shekels for 65/6 (*RPC* 4706), they are still very rare after 60.

[19] Levy 2007.

[20] Weisser and Cotton 2002.

which Judaea was one. The differences and exceptions can be understood best in the light of a description of the coinage as a whole, and its background.

In the Hellenistic period the area was part of the Seleucid Empire. The Seleucid kings made coinage in silver and bronze. There was some rare gold, but they minted none in the first century BCE. But, as the power of the Seleucid kings declined, that of the cities increased. This is reflected in the coinage. The royal coinage was supplemented with increasing amounts of civic silver and bronze; for the silver, the most important mint was Tyre, but other mints like Laodicea and Sidon also produced silver.

**Fig. 29:** Antioch. Silver tetradrachm, minted by the governor Aulus Gabinius.

**Fig. 30:** Cleopatra and Mark Antony. Silver tetradrachm.

After the Roman conquest by Pompey, coinage was provided principally by the mint of Antioch. In line with the conservatism visible in other areas which were annexed by the Romans, there was no sudden imposition of a Roman style coinage – quite the reverse, since for the first 40 years (from 56 to 16 BCE) the silver coinage consisted of posthumous silver tetradrachms made in the name of Philip Philadelphus (**Fig. 29**), one of the last Syrian kings. The Roman pieces can be distinguished by the presence of a monogram of a Roman official's name, or later, a year date in the reverse exergue based on a Caesarian Era. The only interruption was, perhaps, the tetradrachms of Cleopatra and Antony (**Fig. 30**), though their mint is a matter of dispute and was probably not Antioch (see commentary on *RPC* 1, 4094-6).

**Fig. 31:** Augustus. Silver tetradrachm. Minted at Antioch.

**Fig. 32:** Augustus. Bronze coin. Minted at Antioch.

**Fig. 33:** Nero. Silver tetradrachm. Minted at Laodicea.

In the last decade of the first century BCE, the coinage of Antioch was reformed, probably by the Roman governor Varus, and portraits were introduced on both the silver and the bronze (**Figs 31-32**). The coinage was somewhat unusual, however, since, while the silver was in Greek, the bronze was mostly (but not exclusively!) in Latin. Other silver was produced principally at Tyre, discussed above, and there were also small issues of civic silver from Laodicea (**Fig. 33**), Apamea and Sidon, but these all petered out in the first half of the first century CE.[21] These coinages were of differing weights and fineness. A reform of the silver coinage of the region was undertaken in the reign of Nero, in about 60 CE, as part of the empire-wide changes made to the silver coinage; this saw the improvement of the silver fineness.

The events of 66-70 saw further changes to the silver. I continue to believe that all of the silver of Nero (**Fig. 34**), Galba and Otho was made there, rather than the more dispersed minting which has been suggested in the past (see *RPC* 1). The early tetradrachms of Vespasian were also mostly made at Antioch, although sometimes from dies cut at Alexandria, but one group is alike the *Judaea capta* coins, and so, like them, was probably made at Caesarea-on-sea (**Fig. 25**) (for all this, see above, and *RPC* 2, pp. 273-7).

Some gold has probably been minted in Syria during the triumviral period, by Antony, but it is always difficult to be sure of the exact place of minting. Thereafter gold was not made in Syria until the Flavian period, when we find aurei made very early in Vespasian's reign at Antioch and, as discussed above, probably also at Caesarea-on-sea (*RPC* 2, 1901-35).[22]

As well as the bronze of Antioch, a number of cities also produced bronze coinage, such as Seleucia or Apamea in the north, but their output was much less, and one can see that it was the coinage of Antioch that dominated, even for example at Palmyra.[23] Coinage in Syria, however, differed from other parts of the empire in several respects.

First, the physical size of the coinage, especially the bronze coinage, remains much more constant than in other parts of the empire, and there is little sign of the introduction of coins with larger modules, copying the Roman sestertius, as one finds elsewhere, such as in Asia or Egypt. The only exceptions to this are the large module coins of Agrippa II, dated to years 26-27 (**Fig. 35**) (and so datable to either 74/5 and 75/6 or 85/6 and 86/7),[24] and the coins of Domitian and *Divos Vespasianvs* (*RPC* 2, 2300), probably coins of the colony of Caesarea-on-sea and dating to 81/2 CE. Both of these are strongly Roman contexts (as I shall argue for Agrippa II later), and it is the context that presumably provides the explanation.

**Fig. 34:** Nero. Silver tetradrachm. Perhaps minted at Antioch.

**Fig. 35:** Agrippa II: Vespasian/Pan. Minted at Panias.

---

[21] In parallel to the Antioch coinage, a series of silver tetradrachms with a seated Zeus were minted at an uncertain mint (*RPC* 1, 4108-21), perhaps in Cilicia rather than Syria.

[22] The attribution is repeated by Carradice and Buttrey 2007, 175-6 (see also 46), with an extended list: nos. 1530-38.

[23] Burnett 2002, 116.

[24] *RPC* 2, 2282. For the coin of year 26, see Hendin 2009 = Hendin 2010, no. 1281. It has a diameter of 35mm and a weight of 28.66g

A second difference is in language, and I have already briefly commented on the surprisingly common use of Latin, especially in a province where probably only a tiny proportion of the resident population consisted of Latin speakers.[25] There are a surprising number of issues minted in Latin, and, although some were small, the cumulative impact could have been quite substantial, especially given the prevalence on the bronze coinage of Antioch.

A third difference concerns designs. In general Syrian coinage was characterised by a slowness to adopt the imperial portrait. At Antioch it did not appear on the coinage until the reforms of 5 BCE, so probably some 20 years after its appearance elsewhere in the empire. The same holds true for many of the city coinages: not at Seleucia until 6 CE, Apamea until 4/3 BCE or at Laodicea until the reign of Claudius.

Syrian mints do not, very often, portray members of the imperial family other than the emperor himself, although the depiction of family members was widespread in other areas, such as Asia.

As for the reverse designs, we find the widespread depiction of figures or aspects of local cults, but, again unlike Asia, we do not find the introduction of a more diverse choice of designs or, for example, any of the buildings that start to appear on other provincial coinages.

All these difference make Syrian coinage stand out from that of other parts of the empire. And, although the use of Latin is hard to explain, one can see that the other differences, both of module and design, express a visual conservatism that somewhat isolates Syria from the changes to provincial coin design that were affecting other areas, as they became more reflective of their Roman context.

Against this general pattern of Syrian coinage, two areas stand out. One, Phoenicia, is even more conservative; but the other, Judaea, is much more innovative.

In Phoenicia the dominant mint was, as has been observed, Tyre (**Fig. 36**). Its coinage and that of other cities like Sidon retained their earlier, Hellenistic identity even more strongly than the rest of Syrian coinage. They used the same designs as before, and retained elements of Phoenician in their inscriptions, such as at Tyre, Aradus or Sidon (**Fig. 37**). By the time of the empire, Phoenician was a language long since effectively dead, so its retention on these coinages is a symbol of the way the cities wanted to continue to define their identity in terms of their Phoenician past, rather than in terms of the reality of the Roman world in which they found themselves.

**Fig. 36:** Tyre. Bronze coin.  **Fig. 37:** Augustus. Minted at Sidon.

The other exceptional area was Judaea. In the Hellenistic period, under the Hasmonaeans, it had like Phoenicia looked elsewhere than the Greek roots of urban civilisation to choose its designs (**Fig. 1**). Figural designs based Jewish iconography, most notably the menorah, were combined with Jewish names and titles written in palaeo-Hebrew characters – a dead script by the first century BCE. Just like the choice of Phoenician letters in Phoenicia, this choice intentionally sets the coinage aside from the mainstream of regional coinage and must have been intended, in a similar but different way, to stress the distinct Jewish identity.

---

[25] See also Burnett 2002, 119-20.

# THE HERODIAN COINAGE VIEWED AGAINST THE WIDER PERSPECTIVE OF ROMAN COINAGE

Greek (or indeed Aramaic[26]) does, however, start to be used on some coins of the Hasmonaean period and is found on coins of Alexander Jannaeus (103-76 BCE) and Mattathias Antigonus (40-37 BCE), but it became standard on Jewish coinage only from the time of Herod, from whose accession it became the only script to appear on Jewish coins (**Fig. 2**). This represents a change of focus, on the part of Herod and his successors. It marks a shift away from cultural separation and a shift towards a more standard Graeco-Roman outlook. It is a reflection of the way that members of the Herodian dynasty were closely integrated into Roman elite society, an inevitable consequence of their need to adopt the *Realpolitik* of the day. Herod's choice of designs, however, was still conservative and he made no attempt to recognize the superior power of the Roman Emperor, either by inscription or design (including a portrait). Yet, as Barkay argues elsewhere in this volume, many of the designs he uses can be regarded as derived from Roman denarii.[27]

Herod's choice of designs may in part be influenced by the mint which made his coins – which remains uncertain.[28] The importance of the mint certainly becomes clear with the coinage of his divided kingdom, as the coins produced by each of his sons show a striking difference, largely as a result of the location of their mints. The coins of Archelaus, from Jerusalem (**Fig. 3**), are much in the tradition of Hasmonaean coinage from the same mint, since they avoid the use of any human (or indeed, animal) images. Those of Antipas were made as his newly founded capital at Tiberias, and show a similar conservatism, using only a reed or a palm and a wreath. But the coins of Philip from Panias show a very different approach, depicting both the emperor and his family (Livia), and the tetrarch himself. This was the first time that a Jewish ruler had depicted any person, such as the emperor, let alone himself, on his coins. In addition, the reverse designs include, famously, a depiction of the 'beautiful temple of white marble' that he erected in honour of Augustus (Josephus, *Ant.* 15.363) (**Fig. 4**). The use of ruler portraits and the choice of a building stands in sharp contrast to the coins of his brothers, and places his coinage very much at the front end of innovation in the provincial coinage as a whole. It is much more innovative, for example, than the bulk of Syrian coinage and more in line with what we find in the province of Asia. The general explanation given is that the inhabitants of his territory were non-Jewish, and so less likely to be offended by this approach to iconography.[29]

Very much the same pattern holds true for Agrippa I, perhaps even more so, unsurprisingly in view of the close links he had with the emperors and the imperial family. He was educated in Rome and was intimate with many members of the imperial household, including Antonia, the grandmother of Caligula. Agrippa had taken his side against Tiberius, and so was well rewarded on Caligula's accession with Philip's tetrarchy and the title of king. He later played a crucial role in the accession of Claudius, and was again rewarded with a very much enlarged territory and the title of great king.

All this is well reflected in his coinage. His coins minted in Jerusalem continue the restrained conservatism of earlier times (**Fig. 9**), but the coins he minted at Panias and Caesarea-on-sea have very striking designs. The coinage of Agrippa I even copied bronze coins minted at Rome: both the portraits of Caligula and Claudius, and reverse designs depicting Caligula's sisters or Germanicus in a triumphal quadriga (**Figs 6-7**).[30] They also

---

[26] Aramaic characters are used for the coins of Alexander Jannaeus (Meshorer 2001, 210-11).
[27] See R. Barkay in this volume. See also Ariel 2008.
[28] Jerusalem is considered as a possibility by Meshorer (2001, 62ff.). As he points out, the problem with Jerusalem for the coins dated 'year 3' is the likelihood (not certainty) that they were minted before he held Jerusalem, which was occupied by Mattathias Antigonus until 37 BCE.
[29] E.g. Meshorer 2001, 86.
[30] Burnett 1987; cf. *RPC* 1, 4973-87.

depict unexpected members of the imperial family,³¹ such as Caesonia the wife of Caligula, the fourth and last wife of the emperor, and their daughter Julia Drusilla (**Fig. 8**).³² In the case of the designs he employed for the coins from Caesarea-on-sea in the reign of Claudius (**Figs 10-12**), the focus on Rome is even tighter: an inscription including the detailed terminology in the swearing of the treaty oath between Claudius and Agrippa (**Fig. 12**), and, I believe, a depiction of the Capitoline Temple of Jupiter showing the sanctification of the treaty and its deposit in that temple (**Fig. 10**). I have previously suggested that the crouching figure in front of the temple is sacrificing a pig, the normal way in which Roman treaties were sanctified. Unsurprisingly this idea has not found favour with Jewish numismatists,³³ but I continue to believe it is likely. Unfortunately, although a number of new specimens have been discovered over the last 20 years, none of them is well enough preserved to resolve the question.

Agrippa II was also bought up in the Roman court, and although many uncertainties surround him and his coinage (e.g. the era(s) used on his coins,³⁴ or the date of his death³⁵), his coinage is also very Roman in character, although it is unclear why Agrippa II did not follow his predecessor's example and depict himself. Mention has already been made of the production of a large bronze coin like the Roman sestertius, one of only two examples from Flavian Syria. If the figure of Tyche on the largest coins is somewhat idiosyncratic (**Fig. 14**), the two versions of Nike – advancing r. with palm and wreath (**Fig. 15**); and standing l. inscribing shield which rests on her knee – are both derived from Roman coins.³⁶

As with the coins of Agrippa I, the inscriptions on the coins of Agrippa II are also derived from Roman models:

Reign of Vespasian

ΑΥΤΟΚΡΑ ΟΥΕСΠΑСΙ ΚΑΙСΑΡΙ СΕΒΑСΤΩ

ΑΥΤΟΚΡ ΤΙΤΟС ΚΑΙСΑΡ СΕΒΑС

ΔΟΜΙΤΙΑΝΟС ΚΑΙСΑΡ

These inscriptions are very like – and so presumably derived from - those used on the 'Judaean' aurei, discussed above (*RPC* 1530-38): they use a lot of abbreviations and have a word order whereby *Caesar* follows Vespasian as a *nomen* rather than preceding Vespasian as a *praenomen*, as was normal at Rome. The way the inscriptions are long and have several elements is also a 'Latin' rather than a 'Greek' characteristic. The reverse designs are also nearly all 'Roman in essence' (*RPC* 2, p. 309), especially the depictions of Victoria/Nike, both

---

[31] Women appear from the reign of Philip, in 30/1 CE (*RPC* 1, 4949, cf. 4951).

[32] Misidentified by Meshorer (2001, 95), partly because he mistranslates the inscription as 'daughter of the Caesar' when it is 'daughter of the Emperor'. The identification as Caesonia has been contested by Kokkinos (2002, 101-3, 265-7), who prefers to retain an identification as Antonia. But is accepted by others, and I hope to return to the point in due course: see Burnett, forthcoming 2.

[33] Meshorer 2001, 98: 'We are not enthusiastic about this proposal ... but we are unable to offer a better suggestion'.

[34] See above note 9.

[35] Although the literary evidence implies he died c. 100 CE, none of the coinage may be any later than 88/9 on Kushnir-Stein's chronology (the coins of year 29 on an era of 60: see above). That does not of itself proved he died then, since he made no coinage for most of his reign. The supposed reading on a weight of year 43 is actually of 23: Kushnir-Stein, 2002.

[36] See, e.g., *RPC* nos. 14, 47-8, 361, etc.

advancing with wreath and palm or inscribing a shield, both of which are derived from the bronze coinage minted at Rome.[37]

The final element of the coinage of Agrippa II, the 'Latin series' coins of Domitian, dated to years 25 and 26 of Agrippa's reign (*RPC* 2, 2265-6, 2269-72), are exact copies of contemporary asses minted in Rome: MONETA AVGVST (*RIC* 207) and SALVTI AVGVST (**Fig. 16**) (*RIC* 209). The exact details of obverse inscription and portrait as well as reverse design and inscription are all exactly the same. This is perhaps not surprising, since, as discussed above, the dies were clearly made in Rome and the coins were probably also minted there.[38] They make a neat contrast with the coins of Agrippa I: the coins of Agrippa I show a very detailed knowledge in Judaea of bronze minted in Rome, whereas the coins of Agrippa II show the reverse, a knowledge in Rome of bronze minted in Judaea. And, of course, in neither case did the relevant coins circulate in the other area.

## Conclusion

This investigation of Judaean and Herodian coinage enables us to see just how different Jewish coinage was, compared with the mainstream of coinage in Syria, itself different from that encountered in other parts of the Roman Empire. Apart from the puzzling use of Latin, Syrian coinage was conservative in terms of module and, especially, designs. 'Conservative' in the sense that it did not look to the reality of the new Roman world and its coinage as a source of innovation, as other areas of the empire did. Even so, some areas were even more 'conservative': Phoenicia both in the Hellenistic and the early Roman periods; Judaea during most of the Hasmonaean period. But the Herodian coinage swings right in the other direction and to an extreme. It is more 'romanised' even than the coinage produced in other areas like Asia or Egypt. This can be seen most clearly on the coinage of Philip, Agrippa I and Agrippa II. The contrast with the rest of Syria is explicable, since the coinage of a 'client king' would naturally focus on the city of Rome and the emperor. But, although that is true, the Herodian coinage is much more 'romanised' than the coinage of any other kingdom. No other such coinage embraces Roman ideology, members of the imperial family and Roman coinage itself in the way that the Herodian coinage does, especially that of Agrippa I. As a recent commentator has put it: 'only the Herodian kings and tetrarchs performed the role of super-Romans'.[39]

The position of 'client kings' was entirely dependent on Rome,[40] and the iconography used in the Herodian world reflected the connections with, and dependence on, the imperial court. This is the context to understand the extraordinary (by Jewish and other standards!) iconography of the Warren silver cup of Neronian date, found, as it was, in the territory of

---

[37] The exception is the design on the largest denomination, often called a Tyche. But it seems rather to be Demeter: the head seems to wear a *kalathos* (I don't think it is ever veiled, as Meshorer suggests is sometimes the case) and holds corn ears and a cornucopia. There seems no obvious 'Roman' (or indeed any other) significance in the use of Demeter/Ceres – the design remains unexplained.

[38] For other provincial Flavian silver and bronze coins made in Rome for circulation in the eastern Mediterranean (Cappadocia, Syria, Cyprus, Asia and Lycia), see Carradice and Buttrey 2007, 4.

[39] See the survey by Dahmen 2010. Thanks to H. Gitler for pointing out this article to me.

[40] And in the case of Agrippa he had of course been brought up there.

the Herodian kings (**Fig. 38**).[41] The Herodian kings built a spectacular temple at Caesarea for the cult of Roma and Augustus (Jos., *Ant.* 15.339), and in their sphere of influence too one can see indications of Italian influence on architecture.[42] So it is understandable that their coinage, too, falls at the opposite end of the spectrum from the situation I have described for the coinage of Phoenicia, whose coinage is the least Romanised in Syria, and indeed in all the Roman Empire. The tragedy of the Jewish revolt was, perhaps, that the zealots did not understand the Romans in the way that their kings did, nor, unlike their kings, did they wish to make any attempt to appease or embrace them.

**Fig. 38:** The 'Warren Cup'. First century AD.
British Museum

[41] The Warren Cup was said to have been found at Bittir, 6 miles SW of Jerusalem, together with coins of Claudius. It was acquired by the British Museum in 1999, and has the registration number is GR 1999.4-26.1. See now Williams 2006. Little or no attention has been paid to the provenance.

[42] Boëthius and Ward-Perkins 1970, 416: e.g. the use of *opus reticulatum* at Jericho or concrete in the theatre at Caesarea.

# APPENDIX: CONSPECTUS OF MINTING IN HERODIAN JUDAEA[43]

Red means coins with no overt reference to Jewish rulers; underlined (or underlined) means inscriptions in Latin (all or part)

| | | | Jerusalem | Caesarea Panias | Tiberias | Caesarea-on-sea | other |
|---|---|---|---|---|---|---|---|
| Hasmonean | 132/1 BCE – 37 BCE | | X | | | | |
| Herod | 40 - 4 BCE | | undated coins? | | | | ?Samaria Year 3 = ? 40 BCE |
| Herodians: | | 4/3 BCE | Archelaus 4BCE - 6 (undated coins) | Philip 4 BCE-34 | Antipas 4 BCE-39 | | |
| | | | X? | | | | |
| | | | X? | | | | |
| | | | X? | | | | |
| | | CE 1/2 | X? | Ph 1/2[1] | | | |
| | | 5/6 | Aug CE 6 | | | | |
| | | | Aug 8/9 | Ph 8/9 | | | |
| | | | Aug 9/10 | | | | |
| | | 10/11 | Aug 10/11 | | | | |
| | | | | Ph 12/3 | | | |
| | | 15/6 | Tib 15/6 | Ph 15/6 | | | |
| | | | Tib 16/7 | | | | |
| | | | Tib 17/8 | | | | |
| | | | Tib 18/9 | | **founded 19** | | |
| | | 20/1 | | | Antipas 20/1 | | |
| | | | Tib 24/5 | | | | |
| | | | | Ph 26/7 | | | |
| | | | Tib 29/30 | Ph 29/30 | Antipas 29/30 | | |
| | | 30/1 | Tib 30/1 | Ph 30/1 | Antipas 30/1 | | |
| | | | Tib 31/2 | | | | |
| | | | | Ph 33/4 | Antipas 33/4 | | |
| | | 35/6 | | | | | |
| Agrippa I | 37 – 43 | | | | | | |
| | | | | Ag I 37/8 | | | |
| | | | | | Antipas 39 | | |
| | | 40/1 | | | Ag I 40/1 | | |
| | | | Ag I 41/2 | | | | |
| | | | | | | Ag I, 42/3 | |

[43] See also Kushnir-Stein 2009

[1] From this point in the table, each row represents one year.

|  |  |  | Jerusalem | Caesarea Panias | Tiberias | Caesarea-on-sea | other |
|---|---|---|---|---|---|---|---|
| Agrippa I (Cont.) |  |  |  |  |  | Ag I, 43/4 |  |
|  |  | 45/6 |  |  |  |  |  |
|  |  |  |  | Cl c 47[2] |  | Cl c.47[3] |  |
|  |  | 50/1 |  | Cl c 50[4] |  |  |  |
| Agrippa II | 50-90/100[5] |  |  | Ner c 54[6] | Cl 53/4[7] |  |  |
|  |  |  | Cl 54[8] | Ner c 55[9] |  |  |  |
|  |  | 55/6 |  | (era of 49) |  |  |  |
|  |  |  | Ner 58/9[10] |  |  |  |  |
|  |  | 60/1 |  |  |  |  |  |
|  |  | 65/6 |  | c 65[11] |  |  |  |
|  |  |  | Coins of Jewish revolt |  |  |  |  |
|  |  |  | Coins of Jewish revolt | ??66/7[12] |  |  |  |
|  |  |  | Coins of Jewish revolt |  |  | Ner 67/8[13] | 'Neronias'[14] 67/8 |
|  |  |  | Coins of Jewish revolt |  |  |  |  |
|  |  | 70/1 |  |  |  | 70-1: Ioudaias Ealokias AV, Ag Tetras[15] |  |
|  |  |  |  |  |  |  | Ag II, 73/4 (14) |
|  |  |  |  |  |  |  | Ag II, 74/5 (15) |
|  |  | 75/6 |  | Ag II, 75/6 (26)[16] | 75/6[17] |  |  |
|  |  |  |  | Ag II, 76/7 (27) |  |  |  |
|  |  |  |  |  |  |  | Ag II, 77/8 (18) |
|  |  |  |  | Ag II, 78/9 (29) |  |  | Ag II, 78/9 (19) |
|  |  |  |  | Ag II, 79/80 (30) |  |  |  |

[2] *RPC* 1, 4842-4 (Claudius/Antonia, Britannicus, Octavia; Claudius/Britannicus; Britannicus).
[3] *RPC* 1, 4847-8 (Claudius/rudder; /anchor) (but mint not certain)
[4] *RPC* 1, 4858-9 (Claudius/OB C S or /Agrippina).
[5] Date of death uncertain.
[6] *RPC* 1, 4845 (Agrippina/Octavia).
[7] *RPC* 1, 4851-3 (Claudius/ΤΙΒΕΡΙΑΣ in wreath; year 13).
[8] *RPC* 1, 4970-1 (procurators).
[9] *RPC* 1, 4860-1 (Nero/Agrippina)
[10] *RPC* 1, 4972 (procurators).
[11] *RPC* 1, 4846 (Diva Poppaea/Diva Claudia)
[12] *RPC* 1, 4991-2 ('year 11 and 6'). Meshorer, *Treasury*, p. 233 no. 132 dates it to 67/8.
[13] *RPC* 1, 4862-5 (Nero, year 14).
[14] *RPC* 1, 4988-90: Panias according to Meshorer, Treasury p. 105; but see RPC p. 685
[15] *RPC* 2, 1908-13, 1963-69, 2310-13.
[16] For this and the next entries, I follow Kushnir-Stein's view of chronology. Hendin attributes the coins of her Mint 2 to Caesarea Maritima, but it was not in his territory; so the coins are listed under 'Other'.
[17] *RPC* 2, 2242 (ΤΙΒΕΡΙΑC, 'year 15')

| | | | Jerusalem | Caesarea Panias | Tiberias | Caesarea-on-sea | other |
|---|---|---|---|---|---|---|---|
| Agrippa II (Cont.) | | 80/1 | | | | 81-3: Caesarea, Domitian's 'provincial'[18] | |
| | | | | Ag II, 83/4 (34)[19] | | | Ag II, 83/4 (24) Ag II, 84 (Rome) |
| | | | | Ag II, 84/5 (35) | | | Ag II, 84/5 (25) |
| | | 85/6 | | | | | Ag II, 85/6 (26) Ag II, 86 (Rome) |
| | | | | | | | Ag II, 88/9 (29) |

## Acknowlegements

The illustrations are drawn from a mixture of the British Museum collection and a variety of auction sales; thanks also to David Hendin for his help.

## Bibliography

The following abbreviations (other than journals) are used in this paper:
*CNG* = Classical Numismatic Group (Lancaster PA and London); *RPC* 1 = A. Burnett, M., Amandry and P. P. Ripollès, *Roman Provincial Coinage* Vol. I (London/Paris: British Museum Press/Bibliothèque Nationale, 1992); *RPC Supplement* 1 = A. Burnett, M., Amandry and P. P. Ripollès, *Roman Provincial Coinage Supplement* 1 (London/Paris: British Museum Press/Bibliothéque Nationale, 1998); *RPC Supplement* 2 = A. Burnett, M. Amandry, P.P. Ripollès, I.A. Carradice, *Roman Provincial Coinage. Supplement* 2 (www.uv.es/~ripolles/rpc, 2006); *RPC* 2 = A. Burnett, M. Amandry, and I. A. Carradice, *Roman Provincial Coinage* Vol. II (London/Paris: British Museum Press/Bibliothèque Nationale, 1999).

Ariel, D. T., 2008. 'The Coins of Herod the Great in the Context of the Augustan Empire', in D. M. Jacobson and N. Kokkinos (eds.), *Herod and Augustus. Papers Read at the Institute of Jewish Studies Conference, 21st-23rd June 2005* (IJS Studies in Judaica 6; Leiden/Boston: Brill Academic Publishers), 113–127.
Boëthius, A. and Ward-Perkins, J. B., 1970. *Etruscan and Roman Architecture* (Harmondsworth: Penguin).
Burnett, A., 1987. 'The Coinage of Agrippa I of Judaea and a New Coin of Herod of Chalcis', in H. Huvelin *et al.* (eds.), *Mélanges de numismatique offerts à Pierre Bastien* (Wetteren: Numismatique Romaine), 25–38.
Burnett, A., 2002. 'Syrian Coinage and Romanisation from Pompey to Domitian', in C. Augé and F. Duyrat (eds.), *Les Monnayages Syriennes. Quel apport pour l'histoire du Proche-Orient hellénistique et romain? Actes de la table-ronde de Damas 10-12 Novembre 1999,* (IFAPO Bibliothèque Archéologie et Historique 162; Beirut), 115–122.

---

[18] *RPC* 2, 2231, 2300-8.
[19] Assuming coins of years 34 and 35 were made according to the era on 49/50; if, of course, they were on the era of 60, then they would be eleven years later.

Burnett, A., forthcoming 1. 'Wife, sister or daughter?', *INR* 6
Burnett, A., forthcoming 2. 'The coinage of Agrippa I', in *Essays Barag* (Jerusalem: *INJ*).
Butcher, K. and Ponting, M., 2009. 'The Silver Coinage of Roman Syria under the Julio-Claudian Emperors', *Levant* 41, 61–80 (pdf available at www2.warwick.ac.uk/fac/arts/classics/staff/butcher/levant_article.pdf).
Carradice, I. A. and Buttrey, T. V., 2007. *The Roman Imperial Coinage. Vol. II – Part 1: From AD 69-96 Vespasian to Domitian* (London, 2007).
Dahmen, K., 2010. 'With Rome in Mind? Case Studies in the Coinage of Client Kings', in T. Kaizer and M. Facella (eds.), *Kingdoms and Principalities in the Roman Near East* (Stuttgart: Franz Steiner Verlag), 99–112.
Fontanille, J.-P. and Ariel, D. T., 2006. 'The Large Dated Coin of Herod the Great: The First Die Series', *INR* 1, 73-86.
Hendin, D., 2007. 'Echoes of "Judaea Capta": The Nature of Domitian's Coinage of Judea and Vicinity', *INR* 2, 123–130.
Hendin, D., 2009. 'A New Medallion of Agrippa II', *INR* 4, 57–61.
Hendin, D., 2010. *Guide to Biblical Coins*, 5th ed. (New York: Amphora).
Kokkinos, N., 1998. *The Herodian Dynasty: Origins, Role in Society and Eclipse* (JSPSS, no 30; Sheffield: Sheffield Academic Press).
Kokkinos, N., 2002. *Antonia Augusta. Portrait of a Great Roman Lady* (enlarged paperback ed.: London: Libri).
Kokkinos, N., 2003. 'Justus, Josephus, Agrippa II and his Coins', *SCI* 22, 163–180.
Kushnir-Stein, A., 2002a. 'The Coinage of Agrippa II', *SCI* 21, 123–131.
Kushnir-Stein, A., 2002b. 'Two Inscribed Lead Weights of Agrippa II', *ZPE* 141, 295–297.
Kushnir-Stein, A., 2007. 'Coins of the Herodian Dynasty: The State of Research', in N. Kokkinos (ed.), *The World of the Herods. Volume 1 of the International Conference* The World of the Herods and the Nabataeans *held at the British Museum, 17–19 April 2001* (Oriens et Occidens 14; Stuttgart: Franz Steiner Verlag), 55–60.
Kushir-Stein, A., 2009. 'Editors' Note', *INR* 4, 5–7.
Levy, B., 2005. 'Later Tyrian Shekels: Dating the "crude" issues; Reading the controls', in C. Alfaro *et al.* (eds.), *XIII Congreso Internacional de Numismática – Madrid 2003 – Actas* (Madrid: Ministerio de Cultura), 885–890.
Madden, F. W., 1864. *History of Jewish Coinage, and of Money in the Old and New Testament* (London: Bernard Quaritch).
Madden, F. W., 1881. *Coins of the Jews* (London: Trübner & Co.).
Meshorer, Y. 1967. *Jewish Coins of the Second Temple Period* (Tel Aviv: Am Hassefer andd Massada) – English and revised edition of the Hebrew original published in 1966.
Meshorer, Y. 1982. *Ancient Jewish Coinage*, vols. 1-2 (New York: Amphora Books).
Meshorer, Y. 1990/1. 'Ancient Jewish Coinage: Addendum I', *INJ* 11, 104–32.
Meshorer, Y. 2001. *A Treasury of Jewish Coins* (Jerusalem: Ben-Zvi Press) – English and revised edition of the Hebrew original published in 1997.
Walker, D. 1976. *The Metrology of the Roman Silver Coinage*, Vol. I (Oxford: British Archaeological Reports S5).
Weisser W. and Cotton, H. M., 2002. 'Neues zum "Tyrisches Silbergeld" herodianischer und römischer Zeit', *ZPE* 139, 235–250.
Williams, D., 2006. *The Warren Cup* (London: British Museum Press).

# ROMAN INFLUENCE ON JEWISH COINS

## Rachel Barkay

Roman influence on Jewish coins applies mainly to those minted by the Herodian dynasty, from 40 BCE to 100 CE. Some rulers were granted the title of king and others had lower titles, but all were appointed by the Romans and so they had to show gratitude and loyalty to the Roman Emperor. This was the atmosphere in which the Herods chose motifs and inscriptions to put on the coins they minted. As offspring of king Herod the Great and some of the Hasmonaeans as well, they were considered Jewish, and when they ruled over a Jewish population it was appropriate to have kept to the Jewish traditions, avoiding the use of any motifs such as portraits or deities that would be in conflict with Jewish law.

**Herod the Great** (40–4 BCE) was the founder of the dynasty. The coins he minted in Samaria (40–37 BCE) are different from those he minted in Jerusalem (37–4 BCE). Herod had arrived in Samaria from Rome in 40 BCE and minted coins, if only to counterbalance those of Antigonus the Hasmonaean. On his Samarian coins he copied symbols from Roman coins, thus expressing his gratitude to his Roman sponsors, while and flattering them for granting him his title and dominion. Most symbols were taken from contemporary Roman coins or other Roman contexts.

The four types minted at Samaria (**Figs 1-4**) featured Roman motifs, such as an *apex*, the ceremonial cap of Roman augurs, a crested helmet with cheek pieces and a shield reflecting the Roman way of showing power; the tripod, the *aphlaston* placed at the stern of the ship and the winged caduceus appeared on Roman coins of that period.

**Fig. 1:** Herod The Great,
Tripod and helmet,
Year 3 = 40 BCE

**Fig. 2:** Herod The Great,
Crested helmet and shield,
Year 3 = 40 BCE

**Fig. 3:** Herod The Great,
Winged caduceus and poppy,
Year 3 = 40 BCE

**Fig. 4:** Herod The Great,
Aphlaston and palm branch,
Year 3 = 40 BCE

In 37 BCE Herod overthrew Mattathyah Antigonus and so ruled also over Judaea. He struck his new coins in what had been the Hasmonaean mint in Jerusalem. These issues of Herod showed minimal Roman influence. King Herod, the great builder of Masada, of the port of Caesarea, of the Temple in Jerusalem, of Herodium and more, minted relatively poor quality coins in Jerusalem. It was as though he chose to minimise the efforts he put into issuing coins in that city. They were minted in low denominations of one half, one and two *pruthot* only, although some of his Samarian coins were of higher denominations – 1, 2, 4 and 8 *pruthot* (**Figs 5-6**).[1] This decision may have been related to his position under the Romans. Herod knew that he would not be able to issue coins appropriate to his status as king: he could not put his own portrait on the coins; nor perhaps could he mint in silver or gold – presumably a privilege of the Emperor, though arguably client kings were not prohibited in doing so. Thus, although issuing coins was not only a monetary need but also a statement of autonomy and sovereignty, it seems that he decided not to flex his muscles in this field. As a client king of the Romans, he was submissive to his patrons, and at the same time did not provoke his Jewish population. Nevertheless, he could not avoid some Roman influence.

**Fig. 5:** Herod The Great, Diadem and tripod, 37-4 BCE

**Fig. 6:** Herod The Great, Anchor and galley, 37-4 BCE

Single and double cornucopias on Herod's coins resembled the Hasmonaean coins, and thus seem a rather naïve motif, but they also appeared on Roman coins of the period.[2] The double cornucopia with the caduceus between the horns instead of the Hasmonaean pomegranate (**Fig. 7**) was reminiscent of Mark Antony's denarii minted in 40 BCE.[3] The same applies to the anchor appearing on the obverse of this coin, which also resembled the Hasmonaean *pruta*, and Mark Antony's denarii. These were tolerable to the Jews, unlike the reverse motif of the half *pruta* with the one cornucopia on its obverse (**Fig. 8**). The reverse of this small coin depicted an eagle. Meshorer suggests that it was meant to show the golden eagle that, as Josephus (*Ant.* 17.150-52) tells us, Herod donated to the Jewish temple in Jerusalem as a 'holy gift'.[4]

**Fig. 7:** Herod The Great, Anchor and cornucopiae, 37-4 BCE

**Fig. 8:** Herod The Great, One cornucopiae and eagle, 37-4 BCE

---

[1] Meshorer 2001, 71
[2] Crawford 1974, no. 494/14.
[3] Crawford 1974, no. 520/1.
[4] Meshorer 2001, 67-9.

This gift to the temple, reminiscent of the Roman eagle, caused great anger among the Jews, and we can only assume that they were not happy to see the eagle on Herod's coins even when it appeared on a very low denomination.

It seems that Herod did make an effort to minimise Roman influence on his coins, and when it did appear, it usually played a supporting, not leading, role. After King Herod died in 4 BCE, three of his sons ruled in his stead: Herod Archelaus, Philip and Herod Antipas. None of them was granted the title of king.

**Herod Archelaus** (4 BCE–6 CE) ethnarch of Judaea, Samaria and Idumaea, ruled over a majority of Jewish population, and thus showed no Roman symbols on his coins. Yet, he could not avoid some Roman influence, in his depiction of a galley. On his father's coins, a galley was struck to mark the foundation of the harbour at Caesarea. The galleys on the coins of Herod Archelaus could have been interpreted in the same way. But there was another reason for the appearance of maritime symbols on the coins of Archelaus (**Figs 9-11**). Archelaus made a sea voyage to Rome in connection with his struggle against Herod Antipas over King Herod's will.[5] On his trip to Rome Archelaus hoped to convince Augustus to raise his rank and extend his powers. Depicting ships on coins to commemorate an event connected to a sea voyage was common in antiquity. It was a tradition which did not break any Jewish law, though influenced by foreign customs.

**Fig. 9:** Herod Archelaus, Two cornucopiae and galley, 4 BCE – 6 CE

**Fig. 10:** Herod Archelaus, Anchor and double cornucopiae 4 BE – 6 CE

**Fig. 11:** Herod Archelaus, Prow of galley and wreath, 4 BCE – 6 CE

---

[5] Meshorer 2001, 79.

**Philip** (4 BCE–33 CE) ruled as tetrarch over the former domain of Zenodorus the Ituraean (Paneas, Gaulanitis, Trachonitis, Aurranitis and Batanaea), north-east of the Land of Israel. Most of the population under his rule was pagan, and he could therefore allow himself to put Roman portraits on the obverse of most of his coins. The emperors Augustus (**Fig. 12**) and Tiberius (**Fig. 13**), as well as Livia, were depicted on his coins. Livia appeared once together with Augustus as his wife, and later, alone on a lower denomination, as the mother of Tiberius (**Fig. 14**). Philip, however, went one step further, and was the first Jewish ruler to depict his own portrait on his coins (**Fig. 15**). Showing respect to his Roman patrons, his head appeared on lower denominations than those on which the emperors appeared.

**Fig. 12:** Philip, Head of Augustus and temple, Year 12 = 8/9 CE

**Fig. 13:** Philip, Head of Tiberius and temple, Year 37 = 33/34 CE

**Fig. 14:** Philip, Bust of Livia and hand with ears of grain, Year 34 = 30/31 CE

**Fig. 15:** Philip, Head of Herod Philip and temple, Year 5 = 1 CE

**Herod Antipas** (4 BCE–39 CE) was tetrarch over the Galilee and the Peraea (in the Transjordan) and he, too, ruled over a Jewish population. Accordingly, his coins were only decorated with neutral symbols, with one exception, minted in 39 CE. This issue of four denominations had a new reverse inscription. Instead of the usual legend 'Tiberias' it reads ΓΑΙΩ ΚΑΙΣΑΡ(Ι) ΓΕΡΜΑΝΙΚΩ (**Figs 16-17**). The legend was obviously meant to flatter Caligula, and the occasion marked the visit of Antipas to the Emperor in Rome (Jos., *Ant*. 18.240-56). The aim of the visit was to win Caligula's favour against Agrippa I concerning the rule over the tetrarchy after the death of Philip. The new legend reflected both the wish of Antipas to flatter the Emperor, and to avoid using any non-Jewish motifs, such as the emperor's portrait. Unfortunately the visit was not a success and Antipas was exiled.

**Fig. 16:** Herod Antipas, Palm tree and wreath, Year 43 = 39 CE

**Fig. 17:** Herod Antipas, Cluster of dates and wreath, Year 43 = 39 CE

**Agrippa I** (36/37–44 CE), grandson of Herod the Great, was educated in Rome and supported Caligula against Tiberius. When Caligula ascended the throne, he granted Agrippa the territories of both Philip and Antipas. In Agrippa's sixth year, 41/42 CE, the Emperor Claudius added Judaea and Samaria to Agrippa's domain. Thus, Agrippa minted coins in three different places: Paneas, Jerusalem and Caesarea-on-sea.[6]

With the exception of his Jerusalem issue, all his coins show a strong Roman influence. On the high denominations, he put the heads of Caligula and later of Claudius. Agrippa also copied Roman coins in order to honour the Emperor and his family, including one showing Caligula's sisters, Agrippina, Drusilla and Julia, and one with Germanicus, Caligula's father, in a *quadriga* (**Fig. 18**). As did Philip before him and following Roman tradition, Agrippa I minted coins depicting his own head (**Fig. 19**) and he added also that of his wife and of his son. In 42/43 CE, in his seventh year, in order to flatter the Emperor Claudius, and to manifest his love and friendship, Agrippa used the legend: ΒΑΣΙΛΕVC ΜΕΓΑC ΑΓΡΙΠΠΑC ΦΙΛΟ(ΚΑΙCΑΡ) (**Fig. 20**). The following year, 43 CE, he put on the coins the legend reading: "a vow and treaty of friendship and alliance between the great king Agrippa and Augustus Caesar [Claudius] and the people of Rome" (**Fig. 21**). This was to commemorate a ceremony held in the forum of Rome on the occasion of Claudius signing a treaty of friendship with the Jewish kings, Agrippa I and his brother Herod, King of Chalcis (Jos., *Ant.* 19.274-9).

**Fig. 18:** Agrippa I, Head of Caligula and Germanicus in quadriga, Year 5 = 40/41 CE

**Fig. 19:** Agrippa I, Bust of Agrippa and Tyche, Year 7 = 42/43 CE

**Fig. 20:** Agrippa I, Bust of Claudius and temple with two figures, Year 7 = 42/43 CE

**Fig. 21:** Agrippa I, Agrippa, Claudius and Herod of Chalcis and clasping hands; Year 8 = 43 CEE

---

[6] Agrippa's first two issues, Year 2 (= 37/38 CE) and Year 5 (= 40/41 CE), were minted in Paneas, or one in Paneas and the other in Tiberias. Year 6 (= 41/42 CE) was minted in Jerusalem, and Year 7 (= 42/43 CE) and Year 8 (= 43/44) in Caesarea-on-sea.

**Agrippa II** (60/61-94/95 [100] CE) son of Agrippa I ruled over the kingdom of Philip, with a part of Galilee and a part of Peraea. He was raised at the court of Claudius and his roots were deep in the Roman world, so he was committed to the Roman emperors Nero, Vespasian, Titus and Domitian (**Figs 22-25**). He was very loyal to the Romans, but he avoided depicting his own portrait.

Fig. 22: Agrippa II, Bust of Nero and wreath, c. 67/68 CE

Fig. 23: Agrippa II, Bust of Vespasian and Tyche-Demeter, Year 14 = 74/75 CE

Fig. 24: Agrippa II, Bust of Titus and Nike, Year 26 = 74/75 (era of 49 CE)

Fig. 25: Agrippa II, Bust of Domitian and wreath, Year 24 = 84/85 CE

In the Jewish War, Agrippa II took a clearly pro-Roman stand. The great bond with the Roman world is seen on his coins, which show not only the heads of emperors, but also of Nike, which could easily be interpreted as symbolising the Roman victory over Judaea. He also depicted the deities Tyche and Pan, and other motifs from contemporary Roman coins (**Fig. 26**). On his issue of Year 19 (78/79 CE), Agrippa II commemorated a sea voyage to Rome, as had Herod Archelaus before him, by using maritime symbols (**Fig. 27**). The voyage of Agrippa and his sister Berenice to Rome had taken place on the occasion of the completion of the Temple of Peace in 75 CE. Dio (65.15.4) and Tacitus (*Ann.* 2.2) mentioned that Agrippa and Berenice hoped that the new emperor would marry her. The higher denomination shows the portrait of Titus on the obverse and a galley on the reverse; a similar but lower denomination

Fig. 26: Agrippa II, Bust of Domitian and Altar, Year 25 = 85/86 CE

Fig. 27: Agrippa II, Bust of Domitian and galley, Year 19 = 79/80 CE

shows the head of Domitian, and the smallest denomination bears the head of a woman (**Fig. 28**), interpreted by Meshorer as the portrait of Berenice.[7] The hope that she would become empress did not materialise as Titus realised that the Romans were against the match.

**Fig. 28:** Agrippa II,
Head of Livia and anchor,
Year 19 = 79/80 CE

**The First Revolt Against Rome** (66-70 CE) saw coinage minted by the Jewish authorities in Jerusalem, bearing only Jewish symbols. These coins were minted in bronze and silver. This was the first Jewish issue in silver (**Figs 29-30**), and most probably a statement by the Jews for their independence.

**Fig. 29:** The First Revolt Against Rome, Cup and stem of pomegranates, One shekel, Year 3 = 68/69 CE

**Fig. 30:** The First Revolt Against Rome, Cup and stem of pomegranates, Half shekel, Year 3 = 68/69 CE

**The Second Revolt Against Rome** (132-135 CE) saw again the minting of silver coins. The issues of Bar Kokhba were struck over coins that were already in circulation. In the minting process, the Jewish motifs obliterated the original Roman designs, covering the emperors' portraits. The dominant Jewish motif on Bar Kokhba's coins was the facade of the Jerusalem Temple minted on a large silver coin (**Fig. 31**). Depictions of temples during the Roman period were popular, usually showing the deity's statue between the front columns of the temple in order to identify it. On the Bar Kokhba tetradrachms, the deity was replaced by a holy object. Following the concept of depicting pagan temples, the object had to have been something which stood in the Holy of Holies of the Jewish Temple; it is usually identified as the Ark of the Covenant or the showbread table.[8]

**Fig. 31:** The Second Revolt Against Rome,
The Temple of Jerusalem and bundle of *lulav*
with *ethrog*, Year 2 = 133/4 CE

[7] Meshorer 2001, 110.    [8] Romanoff 1944, 40; Barag 1987, 22-5.

To summarize, Roman influence on Jewish coins can be divided into two main categories:
1. The use of Roman motifs for political reasons.
2. The use of elements inspired by the Roman world.

Most instances of the Roman influence on Jewish coins belong to the first group, mainly because the Herodian dynasty were client kings of Rome, and thus wished to please the emperors and the Roman administration in the province. These rulers were therefore Rome-oriented in choosing the motifs for their coins. Their identification with the Romans was expressed by depicting elements copied from Roman coins, portraits of the emperors and their families and even Roman deities. The fact that many of the subjects of the Herods were not Jews made such a strong Roman influence on the coins possible. Yet, it should be stressed that the Jerusalem coins almost always strictly followed the Jewish tradition and avoided any direct Roman influence.

**Bibliography**

Barag, D., 1987. "The Shewbread Table and the Facad of the Temple on the Coins of the Bar Kokhba War", *Qadmoniot* 20 (77-78), 22-25 (Hebrew).
Crawford, M.H., 1974. Roman Republican Coinage I-II (Cambridge).
Meshorer, Y., 2001. A Treasury of Jewish Coins (Jerusalem).
Romanoff. P., 1944. Jewish Symbols on Ancient Jewish Coins (Philadelphia).

# THE USE OF LANGUAGES AND SCRIPTS IN ANCIENT JEWISH COINAGE: AN AID IN DEFINING THE ROLE OF THE JEWISH TEMPLE UNTIL ITS DESTRUCTION IN 70 CE

Anne Lykke

## 1. Introduction

The use of different languages and scripts in ancient coinage was always meant to pronounce and underline official statements of a political nature and at the same time emphasise the cultural-religious context of the coinage produced. Scripts and languages were never applied randomly, but according to deliberate considerations and intentions as well as predetermined by the context of the political actors using this medium. This article will examine aspects of the different languages and scripts used in ancient Jewish coinage and take a closer look at the connection between the ancient institution of the Jewish temple in Jerusalem, the political environment and intentions of individual Jewish rulers on the basis of the use of the different coin legends at different times.

## 2. Early Jewish Coinage in the Province of Judah and the Palaeo-Hebrew Script

Minting of coins in the Persian province of Judah was probably initiated at the very beginning of the 4th century BCE, most likely due to a conjunction of different historical circumstances. Egypt had by the end of the 5th century BCE regained its independence from the Persian Empire, which necessitated structural changes to the southern border of the 5th Persian satrapy, appearing in form of building activities in a chain of administrative and military sites south of Judah around 400 BCE, and a close involvement of the Persian government in the local provincial administration of the Jewish temple state. This development led to noticeable changes in the material culture, amongst others visible in the form of the use of more standardised stamped seal impressions – which probably constitute the closest comparable group of material in relation to the iconography and legends of the coinage – than during the previous centuries.[1]

The YHD (*yehud*) coins, primarily found within the borders of the Jewish province (**Fig. 1**),[2] were minted under the Persian administration during the 4th century BCE and under Ptolemaic rule to at least the middle of the 3rd century BCE.[3] They display a combination of iconographic elements which can specifically be attributed to the material culture of Persian, Greek, or Jewish dominated areas, characteristic of this small province (e.g. **Figs 2-3**).[4] The coins carry the Persian name of the province of Judah, which at the same time was possibly also the name of the city of Jerusalem.[5] In the beginning it was written only in Aramaic as YHD, but later under Ptolemaic rule also in Hebrew as YHDH (*yehudah*), almost always using the palaeo-Hebrew script.[6] In addition a few personal Hebrew names and titles have

---

[1] Fantalkin and Tal 2006, 167-97; Lipschits 2006, 19-52; Lipschits and Tal 2007, 45-46; Vanderhooft and Lipschits 2007, 12-37; Lipschits and Vanderhooft 2007, 77-84.
[2] Weippert 1988, 691; Lipschits and Tal 2007, 36-38.
[3] Gerson 2001, 111.
[4] Mildenberg 1998a, 72, ns. 28, 75; Gerson 2006, 34.
[5] This is also evident in the case of the name of Samaria, where the designation refers both to the province and to the city, Meshorer and Qedar 1999, 19.
[6] Barag 1986-1987, 4-5; Mildenberg 1998b, 56; Ronen 1998, 125.

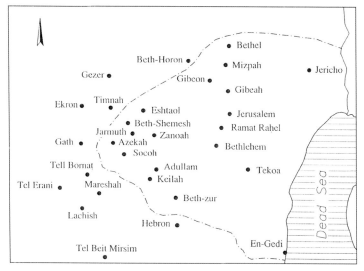

**Fig. 1:** The borders of the Persian province of Judah.
Reprinted from Lipschits, O., 2005. *The Fall and Rise of Jerusalem: Judah under Babylonian Rule* (Winona Lake, IN), 183, map 6; © 2005 Eisenbrauns; reprinted with permission.

**Fig. 2:** YHD coin (1:2) (ca. 400-350 BCE).
AR Gerah (ca. 0.46g)., Obv.: Head of Athena r., Rev.: Owl standing, head facing; left lily, crescent, right legend YHD. © David Hendin, reprinted with permission.

**Fig. 3:** YHD coin (1:2) (ca. 400-330 BCE).
AR Half gerah (ca. 0.26g)., Obv.: Head of Persian King r., Rev.: Falcon with wings spread, head l.; left legend YHD. © David Hendin, reprinted with permission.

**Fig. 4:** YHD coin (1:2) (ca. 360-340 BCE).
AR Half gerah (0.16g)., Obv.: Facing head in circle, Rev.: Owl standing, head facing; legend upwards left YWḤNN, downwards right HKWHN.
© David Hendin, reprinted with permission.

**Fig. 5:** YHD coin (1:2) (ca. 340-320 BCE).
AR Half gerah/obol (ca. 0.26g)., Obv.: Facing head in circle of dots.,
Rev.: Owl standing r., head facing; legend left HPḤH, right YḤZQYH.
© David Hendin, reprinted with permission.

**Fig. 6:** YHD coin (1:2) (ca. 300-285 BCE).
AR Triobol (1.66g)., Obv.: Diademed head of Ptolemy I r., Rev.: Eagle with Fulmen, turned l.; legend left YHDH. © David Hendin, reprinted with permission.

been identified on these coins (e.g. **Figs 4-5**).[7] Uncertainties still remain concerning the exact chronology of the coins – with the exception of the more securely identified Ptolemaic issues (e.g. **Fig. 6**), which parallel the official royal silver coin issues minted in Alexandria during the first part of the 3rd century BCE.[8] The main focus of interest is here the use of the palaeo-Hebrew script.

Hebrew had until the time of the Babylonian exile (598-538 BCE)[9] and the destruction of the first Jewish temple in 586 BCE been the primary language in the kingdom of Judah, but it had already from the late 8th century BCE largely been restricted to this area.[10] During the time of the exile Jews adopted the Aramaic language and by the end of the 4th century BCE this language had to a large extent superseded Hebrew in Judah not only as the colloquial language, but also as the lingua franca.[11] The lack of documents written in Hebrew and the few probably early dating seals and stamp impressions found bearing this language show that Hebrew should not be considered a common everyday language past the early days of the Persian period.[12]

The letters of the palaeo-Hebrew script were introduced into epigraphic sources and coinage during the 4th century BCE.[13] From this time onwards Hebrew and the palaeo-Hebrew script apparently remained in use as a liturgical language and it was continuously used in religious literature, exemplified by many of the Qumran texts written and used long after the Persian period.[14] The Hebrew language was explicitly used to emphasise Jewish national and religious identity, as can be observed by the specific use of Hebrew for texts with a religious or national content in contrast with secular texts in neighbouring Samaria.[15] The main sources for the active use of the Hebrew language from the 3rd century BCE to the 2nd century CE are the Qumran texts, those found at Masada or from the documents of Bar Kokhba from different sites in the Judaean Desert – not to mention the early Hebrew inscriptions from Jerusalem and its environs, such as that on the façade of the Bene Hezir tomb overlooking the Kidron

---

[7] Lykke 2010, 77-80.
[8] Gitler and Lorber 2006, 1-25; Lykke 2010, 80-81.
[9] Weippert 1988, 687-91.
[10] Naveh 1970, 278-79; Naveh 2009a, 4-5.
[11] Naveh 1970, 279; Kottsieper 2007, 97-102; Naveh 1998, 91-92; Naveh 2009a, 5; Naveh 2009b, 34-35.
[12] Levine 1998, 74; Kottsieper 2007, 104.
[13] Lipschits and Vanderhooft 2007, 78-79.
[14] Naveh 1998, 92; Kottsieper 2007, 97-102, 104, 109-10; Naveh 2009, 35.
[15] Naveh 1998, 92; Naveh 2009, 35.

Valley (1st century BCE),[16] or the Nash Papyrus from Egypt dated variously from between the 2nd century BCE to the 1st century CE.[17] These texts may suggest that the Hebrew language was mainly used within circles of well-educated members of the Jewish society or among specific groups with highly developed religious-nationalistic ideologies.[18] The development of Rabbinic Hebrew is a result of the continued use of the Hebrew language. It is very difficult to ascertain where and exactly to what extent the languages were used during the preceding centuries, since neither the dominant Aramaic, nor Hebrew or the various dialects of both were used exclusively at any point in time.[19]

Considering that Hebrew should not be regarded the official language at the beginning of the 3rd century BCE, except perhaps within the context of the temple cult and certainly within religious literature, the introduction of the Hebrew word YHDH on coins of the Ptolemaic period must have held a specific meaning. Their attribution as YHD coins is secured by their legends, either by the use of the Aramaic inscription YHD, or the Hebrew YHDH, generally without including any written reference to the Ptolemaic rulers.[20] Under the rule of Ptolemy I Soter the standard type displays the diademed head of Ptolemy I on the obverse and the Ptolemaic eagle with spread wings and clutching a thunderbolt on the reverse (**Fig. 6**). Rarer variations of this type and other types were also issued, which will not be discussed here.[21]

The preceding use of the Aramaic word YHD is not surprising, considering that this was the official language of the Persian administration at the time. The use of the palaeo-Hebrew script is noticeable, but it is difficult to judge the significance of this. It should be taken into consideration that the priestly administration of the Jewish temple was indeed the minting authority, since already all other monetary matters were verifiably dealt with within the temple administration.[22] It is more than likely that the use of this script was determined by this connection and by extension, perhaps, with the actual place of minting. The use of the palaeo-Hebrew alphabet and the continued use of the Hebrew language would reflect its importance within the temple administration, at the same time probably mirroring continued use of Hebrew among the literate members of the Jewish society. It does however not immediately explain the addition of YHDH on some of the provincial coins during the period of Ptolemaic rule. What was or were the reasons for this change? The answer to this can only be assumed, but it must have been a deliberate choice made by the minting authorities. The minting of the early Jewish coins probably continued within the priestly administration of the Jewish temple between the Persian and Ptolemaic periods of rule; at least there is no evidence for any immediate changes at that time. The iconography of the YHD coins minted under Ptolemaic rule were close imitations of the royal Ptolemaic coinage, but the word YHDH was used to specify their place of origin and area of use. But the word did more than specify geography. The use of the Hebrew language, with the palaeo-Hebrew script, was simultaneously a conscious religious and national statement, that these coins were truly Jewish, combining land, people and religion in one,[23] a tradition which was carried into the following periods.

---

[16] Levine 1998, 75. The use of Hebrew in the Dead Sea Scrolls cannot be seen as immediately mirroring the use of Hebrew as a colloquial language, although to some extent this was the case within the various religious groups, as different traditions of Hebrew have been identified in these writings; see Sáenz-Badillos and Elwolde 1996, 132.

[17] See, e.g., Albright 1937, 145-76.

[18] As pointed out by L. Levine (1998, 74-75).

[19] Sáenz-Badillos and Elwolde 1996, 170-71.

[20] Meshorer 2001, 20, no. 31. A prominent exception are the imitations of the Ptolemaic *theōn adelphōn* type displaying the jugate heads of Ptolemy II and Arsinoe II on the obverse and the jugate heads of Ptolemy I and Berenike I on the reverse with the legend YHD, Barag 1994-1999, 29-32.

[21] Kindler 1974, 73-76; Jeselsohn 1974, 77-78; Barag 1994-1999, 29-32; Lykke 2010.

[22] Kottsieper 2007, 109.

[23] Also stated by Kottsieper 2007, 109.

## 3. The Development of the Jewish Temple as a Financial Institution

The introduction and development of coinage in Judah was probably directly related to the rebuilding of the temple in Jerusalem and reinstatement of the cult during the early Persian period after the return from the Babylonian exile,[24] and its establishment as a financial institution. The payment of the taxes – especially the poll tax – to the temple can be traced in Biblical sources and through epigraphic evidence throughout approximately five centuries.[25] The poll tax was possibly institutionalised in Judah by Ezra (Ezr 7) during the late 5th or very early 4th century BCE, with the introduction of new Persian regulations issued under the Achaemenid king Artaxerxes II (404-359 BCE).[26] The Biblical text states that the priests and other servants of the Jewish temple were to be exempted from paying this tax (Ezr 7:24), an arrangement later revived respectively by Antiochus III (Jos., *Ant.* 12.142-4) and Antiochus VII (1 Macc 15:5-6).[27] According to Matthew 17:24, the payment of this tax was continued into the 1st century CE, until the destruction of the Jewish temple in 70 CE.[28] The monetary development in Judah was probably a direct response to the institutionalisation of these fiscal laws centred on the administration of the temple state in Jerusalem.

The strong connection between the Jewish temple and the minting of coinage during this time is probably best illustrated by the coin of YWḤNN HKHN (*Yoḥanan ha-kohen*),[29] who has convincingly been identified with the high priest Yoḥanan II of the mid 4th century BCE.[30] It should be taken into consideration that under the Persian administration the office of the governor, the HPḤH (*ha-pechah*) known from the coins of YḤZQYH (*Yeḥezqiyah*) and stamped seal impressions, and the position of the Jewish high priest at least in some instances were combined in one person.[31] This would be in conformity with the appointment of Persian governors during the previous centuries, where individuals from local aristocratic dynasties – to which also the Jewish high priests belonged – had been selected to hold these positions.[32] A merging of the political positions of the high priest and the governor, however, does not have to be the only explanation for the appearance of the title HKHN on this coin. With the establishment of the new Persian regulations at the beginning of the 4th century BCE and probably also the implementation of a local coinage in Judah from this time, the Jewish temple apparently came simultaneously to function as a treasury, bank, and possibly also as a mint – most likely under the supervision of the high priest, who also – at times if not always – acted as the appointed Persian provincial governor.[33] Taxes were not only collected and administrated here, but perhaps also the metal was melted down before being sent as tribute to the Achaemenid king, according to the standard practice of other ancient Near Eastern palaces and temples,[34] corresponding with the Achaemenid practice of handling and refining

---

[24] Del Omo Lete 2009, 54-55.
[25] Lemaire 2007, 56-62.
[26] The dating of Ezra has been subject to extended discussion. Arguments have been put forward for a dating of his activity to the reign of Artaxerxes I (465-424 BCE) and Artaxerxes II (404-359 BCE). The dating of Ezra is examined by Avishur and Heltzer 2005, 17-8, n. 1 with further references. The later date of the scribe to Artaxerxes II is discussed by Lemaire 1995, 56-61 and Lemaire 2007, 55, with further references.
[27] Bickerman 1988, 146; Schäfer 1995, 56-58.
[28] Lemaire 2007, 59-60.
[29] Mildenberg 1998a, 71-2; Barag 1985, 166-68; Barag 1986-1987, 7-21; Ronen 1998, 125; Meshorer 2001, 14. The same is probably also true in the case of YḤZQYH / YḤZQYH HPḤH, Lykke 2010, 78-79.
[30] Barag 1986-1987, 10-17.
[31] J. Schaper offers the possible explanation that both the high priests and the Persian governors minted coins, therewith deducing the rule of Judah to be a diarchy of sorts (Schaper 2002, 157-59).
[32] Also Vanderkam 2004 and Brutti 2006 (dealing with the time from the beginning of the Ptolemaic rule of Palestine until the beginning of the Hasmonaean Dynasty).
[33] This would conform to the conception of the high priest acting as the leader of the Jewish people also during subsequent periods; see Zeitlin 1957, 3-4.
[34] Schaper argues against the concept of Judah being a temple state according to the model of the Mesopotamian temple states (Schaper 2002, 165).

silver and gold, as attested by Herodotus (3.96.2), even if the specific details concerning these procedures are still largely unknown.[35] The high purity of the silver used for the YHD coins conformed to the demands for a high metallic purity by the Persian administration.[36]

The foundation for the increasing political and economic power of the high priests established during this time, in line with the practices found in temples and sanctuaries in other parts of the Persian Empire,[37] was probably a result of the overall development of the Jewish temple as a financial institution, which included the development and use of its semi-autonomous coinage.[38] A comparable example is the local silver coinage minted during the early Hellenistic period (c. 340-300 BCE) in Bambyce (later Hierapolis).[39] According to their Aramaic legends, those coins were first issued by the priests 'BD HDD (*Abd-hadad*) and 'BY'TY (*Abyati*).[40] On the obverse of the coins the facing or profile head of Atargatis with a crown or a female head without headgear is displayed, on the reverse a priest with one hand raised in the fashion of praying figures known from Achaemenid iconography standing below a canopy or a chariot carrying a figure (the high priest?) with one hand raised and in front of him a charioteer is included in the composition on the coin.[41] The names of the priests were later replaced by the Hellenised ones, *Alexandros* and *Se(leukos)*.[42] The sacred iconography used here unquestionably also had specific political implications namely, the enactment of a certain amount of local independence within the Seleucid Empire, but not quite reaching full autonomy,[43] as was the case with Jewish coinage at this time.

In all likelihood, the importance of the Jewish temple as the financial centre of the Jewish province did not diminish during the succeeding Hellenistic period. The continuity found in the settlement patterns of Judah between the Persian period and the early Hellenistic period provides revealing evidence for not only understanding the rural nature of the Persian province, but also the political administration of the area. Contrary to the discontinuity of many settlements noticeable between the late Iron Age and the Persian period, the continuity between late Persian period and Hellenistic period sites – regardless of the character of the settlements as residential, administrative or military sites – seems to have been the rule, with few or no noticeable changes in the structures and the material culture of these settlements. This continuity is equally visible in sanctuaries and cultic installations in Palestine in general between the periods.[44] The same picture is reflected in the material of the Judahite seal impressions and coins, pointing towards continuity in the administrative system between the late 4th century and early 3rd century BCE in Judah.[45] This continuity is probably also reflected in the epigraphic evidence on tax collection from the 4th century, as for example it has been revealed by Aramaic ostraca from Khirbet el-Qom in Idumaea,[46] where the same set phrases were used into the early Hellenistic period, only replacing the Persian names with Greek ones of the officials. It is not unreasonable to deduce that the same practice could have applied to the taxation system of neighbouring Judah.[47]

---

[35] Zournatzi 2000, 242-52.
[36] Zournatzi 2000, 256-64. The coins would have been eligible for the payment of the annual temple-tribute (Ex 30:13 and 30:15), Gitler and Lorber 2006, 15, 20-25. According to the Hebrew text, the tax of half a shekel paid to the temple was to be equivalent to the weight of half a shekel according to the standard of the temple shekel, without specifying the use of coins. In the Greek Septuagint version however, the payment of the temple tax is specified to be the half of a didrachm. As in Hebrew, in the Vulgate the payment is specified to be a *dimidium sicli iuxta mensuram templi* or *sanctuarii* (Ex 30:13). From this it is not possible to deduce anything about the early coins having been minted as the one-to-one equivalent of the required tax of half a shekel. It seems more likely that the payment was measured according to the weight of half a shekel, rather than coin type – although this later changed.
[37] Blenkinsopp 2001, 61-68.
[38] Lemaire 2007, 60 – with further references.
[39] Seyrig 1971, 11-21; Zahle 1996, 128-29.
[40] Seyrig 1971, 16 no. 1-3d (*Abd-hadad*), 19 no. 4a-b (*Abyati*).
[41] The reverse type is an imitation of the royal Sidonian coinage of the 4th century BCE; Betlyon 1976, 11-35.
[42] Seyrig 1971, 20-21 no. 8-13 (*Alexander*), 21 no. 14.
[43] Zahle 1996, 129-30.
[44] Tal 2008, 165-83.
[45] Lipschits and Tal 2007, 36, 47; Lykke 2010, 81.
[46] Aḥituv and Yardeni 2004, 8.
[47] Lemaire 2007, 56.

The fact that apparently the administration in Judah was allowed to continue the production of their fractional silver coins under Ptolemaic rule is noteworthy, contrasting with the coinage issued in most other places under the highly centralised Ptolemaic monetary administration and coinage monopoly.[48] The strong economic position of the Jewish temple might have been crucial for its continued existence as a financial centre, as can also be found in the Seleucid period, where the appointment of the Greek *epistatēs* Philip as the administrator of the Jewish temple in 169 BCE by Antiochus IV (2 Macc 5:22-3) not only meant the loss of its self-government for the Jews, but also placed the administration of the temple under direct Seleucid control.[49]

## 4. The Use of Legends in Hasmonaean Coinage

The fact that during the Hasmonaean period Jewish coins were minted primarily with Hebrew, Greek as well as briefly with Aramaic legends not only reflects the diversity of the cultural context in which they were issued, as well as the historic circumstances of the individual rulers under which they were minted, but also of the increasing Hellenisation of the Hasmonaean kingdom and Jewish society as a whole. It is to be expected that among the literate population of this period Hebrew, Aramaic and Greek were understood and used and that while Hebrew was still maintained as a liturgical language, and was, to some extent, spoken as well. The different languages and scripts offered the Hasmonaean rulers a tool to express religious and national sentiments similar already to the YHD coinage of the Persian and early Hellenistic period, as well as their individual political aspirations.[50] Furthermore, the development of Hasmonaean coinage seems equally to have been based on the administrative traditions of the Jewish temple already established during the previous centuries, as reflected in the wording of the Hasmonaean coins legends.

It is well-known that according to the First Book of Maccabees (15:6) the third of the Maccabaean brothers Simon (142-135 BCE) was granted the right to mint coins by Antiochus VII Sidetes (138-129 BCE) in his function as *hiereus megalos* and *ethnarchēs* (according to 1 Macc 15:1-2), in addition to concessions of amnesty, tax exemptions, and the recognition of the Jewish de facto sovereignty of Judaea (1 Macc 15:5-8), reconfirming the rights and privileges previously bestowed on the Jews.[51] Bearing in mind that in the Greek text no clear distinction is made in the wording of Simon's political role, it has to be considered whether the minting rights were given to Simon as Jewish ruler (*ethnarchēs* and *stratēgos*) or if all the rights were bestowed on Simon as high priest (*hiereus megalos*). It is of course clear that during this time religion and politics were not separable entities, hence Simon was not functioning either as *the* secular ruler or *the* high priest, but a closer examination of the ancient use and understanding of these terms in the source texts might cast some additional light on this issue.

Of the designations used in connection with Simon the title of *hiereus megalos* comes first and the title of *ethnarchēs* has a secondary position in the ancient texts. His role as *stratēgos*

---

[47] Lemaire 2007, 56.
[48] Mørkholm 1991, 70; Mildenberg 2000, 94.
[49] Hengel 1988, 486-95; simultaneously with the appointment of Philip, the *epistatēs* Andronicos had been appointed to the temple in Samaria (2 Macc 5:23), which lends credibility to the idea that the temple there was of an equally high (economic) importance to the Seleucid government; see Schäfer 1995, 43.
[50] Barag 1986-1987, 18; Gerson 2001, 118.
[51] Schürer 1973, 182-83, 189-91; Schäfer 1995, 54, 56, 58. These rights were possibly reconfirmed in the later alliance between Antiochus VII and John Hyrcanus I; see Hoover 2003, 31-34.

is only emphasised in connection with his appointment as the official Jewish leader by the Jewish *synedrion*[52] and people (1 Macc 14:42-47), which was also subsequently recognised by the Roman Senate (1 Macc 15:15-24).[53] During the early Roman period the title *ethnarchēs* was assigned as an official title to both the high priest John Hyrcanus II, as well as to the Herodian Archelaus by the Romans, not only with intention to avoid the use of the title of king, but also – in the case of Hyrcanus II – to politically degrade the official position of the Hasmonaean ruler.[54] This title conferred essentially the same status as provincial rulers/governors, and according to Josephus formally still recognising his role as high priest.[55] The question is if it is valid to assume the similar use of this title to Simon.

It is no longer possible to determine the exact Semitic title(s) originally held by Simon, which corresponded to the Greek *ethnarchēs*.[56] During his time the title of *ethnarchēs* does appear to have been equivalent to the Hebrew title NŚY' (*nasi*),[57] and a direct translation of NŚY' to *ethnarchēs* in the Greek text should probably be considered correct.[58] The term NŚY' was applied with many variations[59] and apparently underwent some changes over time. It ranged between being the honorary title of a *primus inter pares* to that of a king until it later finally became the title of the head of the Rabbinic Sanhedrin.[60] When exactly the title actually came to refer to the head of the Jewish *synedrion* – and later the Sanhedrin – in Jerusalem is however disputed.[61] It has been suggested that this term was in fact already applied as a honorary title to the leader of the office of the high priest during the Persian period, which carried through the Ptolemaic and Seleucid periods as well, during which the high priest acted as the highest Jewish ruler under the different foreign authorities until the establishment of the Hasmonaean rule.[62]

The hereditary titles and privileges bestowed on Simon which shaped the high priestly ruler dynasty of the Hasmonaeans[63] feature in the legends of the Hasmonaean coinage, although neither of the honorary titles *ethnarchēs* nor NŚY' appear in the Hebrew legends on the Hasmonaean coins. Instead, the Hebrew titles or designations HKHN HGDWL (*ha-kohen ha-gadol*) (the high priest), R'Š (*roš*) (head) or HMLK (*ha-mælæk*) (the king) were used and, from the time of Alexander Jannaeus, also the Greek title *basileus*. The title of the high priest and the institution of the ḤBR HYHWDYM (*ḥever ha-yehudim*), which is possible to equate with the *synedrion*, are the only recurrent terms in the palaeo-Hebrew legends. This is reasonably consistent with the picture gained from the use of titles in connection with Simon. John Hyrcanus I (135-104 BCE), who was the first to implement the titles or designations

---

[52] The term *synedrion*, i.e. the Jewish council, is here understood to have preceded the Sanhedrin, an expression confined to literary sources of the Roman Imperial period, see *ABD* 5, 977 s.v. Sanhedrin (A.J. Saldarini); Grabbe 2008, 13-15; Other Greek terms were also applied to this institution: *gerousia* (council of elders), *boulē* (advisory council), inter alia summarised by Grabbe 2008, 3-13, 17.

[53] Schürer 1973, 194-97.

[54] Also Sharon 2010, 479.

[55] Jos., *Ant.* 14.192-98, Jos., *Ant.* 17.317; *DNP* 4 (1998) 165-66.

[56] Sharon 2010, 474-78, 489-90, argues that the title *ethnarchēs* was erroneously attributed to Simon (caused by the translator of the original text into Greek) and in extension to John Hyrcanus I and that the title in fact "was probably an invention of the early Roman period" (p. 490).

[57] Alon 1984, 622-24; Samuels 2000b, 87-88.

[58] *EncJud* 14., 784 s.v. NASI (G. Y. Blidstein); Contrary to Alon 1984, 622, Meshorer is of the opinion that the Greek title *ethnarchēs* was not the translation of NŚY', but the translation of the title of the *head* of the Jewish council, Meshorer 2001, 141. The one does not exclude the other.

[59] See especially Botterweck, Ringgren and Fabry 1986, 647-57 s.v. נָשִׂיא (H. Niehr), for a comprehensive survey of the use of the title NŚY'.

[60] Gesenius, s.v. נָשִׂיא; Koehler – Baumgartner, s.v. נָשִׂיא; EncJud 14., 784-85 s.v. NASI (G. Y. Blidstein); Botterweck, Ringgren and Fabry 1986) 647-57 s.v. נָשִׂיא (H. Niehr).

[61] *EncJud* 14., 784 s.v. NASI (G. Y. Blidstein).

[62] Zeitlin 1957, 3-4; Alon 1984, 623-24; Grabbe 1998, 5-7. This is although not without controversy, Bickerman 1988, 142-43.

[63] Schürer 1973, 193-94.

inherited from Simon, is titled the *R'Š ḤBR HYHWDYM*, i.e. the *head* of the Jewish council, on coins displaying a crested helmet belonging to one of the rarest Hasmonaean coin series (**Fig. 7**).[64] This could possibly correspond with the title *ethnarchēs* accorded to John Hyrcanus' father, mentioned in I Maccabees – if the attribution of the coins to John Hyrcanus I is correct.[65] However, a combination of the designation R'Š and the depiction of the helmet is not repeated in other Hasmonaean coins.

**Fig. 7:** AE Double prutah (1:2), John Hyrcanus I (135-104 BCE).
Obv.: Double cornucopiae with ribbons; Palaeo-Hebrew legend YHWḤNN HKHN HGDWL R'Š ḤḤBR HYHWDWM; border of dots. Rev.: Crested helmet, r.; border of dots.
© David Hendin, reprinted with permission.

The possibility of a continuous administrative structure of the Jewish temple established during the Persian period may be reflected indirectly in the use of the titles that appear on the Hasmonaean coins. Even if the right to mint coins was not put into practice during Simon's brief rule under Antiochus VII,[66] this is not to say that the process, although no longer discernible, may have been put into motion – despite Antiochus' later withdrawal of these rights – within the framework of the existing temple administration. Another archaeological indication of administrative continuity, preceding the minting of the Hasmonaean coins, can be found in the group of the late YHD stamp impressions, which seem to have directly preceded Hasmonaean coinage.[67] It should be taken into consideration that the old administrative tool of the YHD stamps which were continuously in use during the previous centuries extended to the early part of the Hasmonaean period, but ceased with the expansion of the Hasmonaean kingdom and the emergence of the coinage carrying the same palaeo-Hebrew script.[68] It is likely that the minting of Hasmonaean coinage was established within the existing administrative structure of the temple. The equal weight given in the coin legends to the political and religious roles of the Hasmonaean leadership should be noted; this situation continued at least until the reign of Alexander Jannaeus.

---

[64] Meshorer 2001, 207 Group H.
[65] An attribution of these coins to John Hyrcanus II has also been suggested. In this case the helmet could have functioned as a sign of the authority of the *Ethnarch* bestowed on him by Caesar in 47 BCE, Hübner 2005, 181; an earlier bestowal of the title under Pompey in 63 BCE has also been argued; on this possibility, see Sharon 2010, 479-81.
[66] The main reason for this was probably the fact that Antiochus VII did not adhere to his initial promises, and after having established his position as the new Seleucid ruler, Antiochus apparently did not see the necessity to keep the support of the Jews and his alliance with them (1 Macc 15:27-35; Jos., *Ant.* 13.226; cf. Hendin 2007-2008, 83). The fact that Simon only ruled for approximately three years under Antiochus VII, during which time he had to consolidate his rule and fight against Antiochus, before he was insidiously killed in Jericho by his son-in-law Ptolemy (1 Macc 16:11-16; Jos., *Ant.* 13.228), would have left him only a brief span of time to develop and establish the minting of his own coinage.
[67] Lipschits and Vanderhooft 2007, 85; Geva 2007, 92-101.
[68] Geva 2007, 99-101.

## 4.1 The use of the palaeo-Hebrew script in Hasmonaean coinage

The palaeo-Hebrew script employed on Hasmonaean coins from the start makes a statement that the minting authority was truly Jewish, combining land, people and religion in one. Through the use of this script, both the supplying authorities and the primary users were characterised as Jews, thereby firmly establishing their cultural-religious identity and context. Since the script itself was no longer widely used except for some of the Qumran texts already mentioned and very occasionally in funerary inscriptions,[69] as it has been noted time and again, it is not to be considered self-evident that many of the general public could read and understand these coin legends, by the beginning of the 1st century BCE.[70] The immediate reason for the ongoing use of the script can be explained by the placing of the mint of the Hasmonaean coins in the hands of the administration of the Jewish temple, where the ancient script was still in use. Via this context, it is probable that the script itself in time came to hold a sacred meaning, based on its history of use and its association with the temple, which made it more than a political symbol.

A certain degree of epigraphic change in the palaeo-Hebrew script on the coins of the Hasmonaeans occurred during the course of that dynasty, which does offer some basis for comparisons and analysis. Not only do the letters vary in form and style, which can help to arrive at a classification into different groups,[71] also the accuracy – through the omission of certain letters – and the quality of the extended palaeo-Hebrew legends is also variable. The differences accounted for in the script and the completion of the legends can be explained by the varying skills of the individual die-engravers and their understanding – or lack of understanding – of the old script.[72] Accordingly, it does seem reasonable to refrain from attempting to establish a relative chronology of the Hasmonaean coinage or groups based on script types,[73] since different styles of letters can be found together and over a longer period of time.[74]

A stylistic comparison between the Greek and Semitic letters used on the Hasmonaean coins furthermore shows that two different techniques apparently were put to use simultaneously. In contrast to the Semitic letters, the Greek letters were executed as points connected through straight lines, a technique familiar from the Seleucid coinage.[75] Evidently, a well-known technique was imitated in the Greek legends on the Hasmonaean coins and two different palaeographic traditions were deliberately used simultaneously.

## 4.2 The Greek legends on Hasmonaean coins

The additional parallel use of Greek, and partly Aramaic, legends on the Hasmonaean coins was more consistent with the actual everyday linguistic requirements, where the coins were put to use also by non-Jews.[76] It is noticeable that only Alexander Jannaeus (103-76 BCE) and later Mattathias Antigonus (40-37 BCE) made use of Greek legends – in addition to the standardised palaeo-Hebrew legends – designating themselves as kings, and that only certain coins of Alexander Jannaeus bear legends in Aramaic script. In both cases the explanations for the varying use of languages and scripts should most likely be sought in their individual political aspirations and the historical circumstances affecting the rule of both rulers.

---

[69] E.g. the tomb inscription from Givʻat Hamivtar, Naveh 1975, 73-74; Levine 1998, 74.
[70] Meshorer 2001, 40-41, 48.
[71] As done by Meshorer 2001, 42-48.
[72] Meshorer 2001, 48-49; Hendin 2010, 36.
[73] As done by Kindler 1954, Pl. 14.
[74] Meshorer 2001, 49.
[75] Kindler 1968, 190.
[76] Hübner 2005, 178-79.

The simultaneous use of the Hebrew and Greek legends – the latter introduced for the first time on the coins of Alexander Jannaeus – presented him both as priest and as king, a title which had not been used earlier on the Hasmonaean coins. Not only do the Greek legends on the coins of Alexander Jannaeus show how he conceived himself part of the Greek Hellenistic ruler tradition.[77] He clearly followed iconographic traditions found in the coinage of the Greek Hellenistic kings, as it is evident from a comparison with Seleucid coins evidently minted in Jerusalem before and around the time of the emergence of Hasmonaean coinage.

**Fig. 8:** AE Prutah (ca. 15mm/2.50g) (1:2), Antiochus VII Sidetes (138-129 BCE) or John Hyrcanus I (135-104 BCE).
Obv.: Anchor; left Greek legend ΒΑΣΙΛΕΩΣ ΑΝΤΙΟΧΟΥ, right ΕΥΕΡΓΕΤΟΥ, date below anchor ΑΠΡ (181 = 132/131 BCE). Rev.: Lily. Reprinted from Meshorer, Y., 2001, 30,
© 2001 Amphora Books; reprinted with permission.

It has been suggested that the bronze coin type displaying the images of the lily and the anchor (**Fig. 8**), two motifs with long traditions in Palestinian coinage, was minted by or in the name of Antiochus VII Sidetes (138-129 BCE) in the years 181 and 182 of the Seleucid era (131/130 and 130/129 BCE).[78] This would place the coin type either as one of the latest Seleucid coin series minted in Jerusalem,[79] or as the first coin series issued in the mint established in Jerusalem under John Hyrcanus I.[80] This coin series would have functioned as a transitional coin between the Seleucid and the Hasmonaean period of rule and marked the beginning of Hasmonaean coin minting.[81]

The obverse-reverse combination of the lily and the anchor, together with the Greek legend *Basileōs Antiochou Euergetou*, on this late Seleucid coin series does point towards mutual interaction taking place, which evidently did not limit itself to the Jewish coins.[82] The meaning of the motif of the lily as a symbol for Judaea (or Jerusalem) and/or the Jewish temple was presumably maintained on these locally minted Seleucid coins, as well as on the Jewish coins, and the anchor was used in imitation of royal Seleucid iconography.[83] This image seems to have functioned widely as an iconographic means of monetary authorisation within the Seleucid Empire, judging from its appearance as a countermark on foreign coins of the appropriate metal and of a weight suitable with the uniformity of the Seleucid monetary weight system, as well as on Seleucid coins;[84] through the use of the anchor as countermark

---

[77] Hübner 2005, 181; Ostermann 2005, 27 Fig. 10; Lykke 2011, 135-36.
[78] Meshorer 1982, 62-63; Meshorer 2001, 8-10, 34-35; Fischer 1984, 48; Hoover 2003, 30-33; Hübner 2005, 180; Hendin 2007-2008, 84; SC II, 2008, 391-92, no. 2123.
[79] Hübner 2005, 172.
[80] Kindler 1968, 190 Pl. 20B no. 7-9; Meshorer 1982, 39 Fig. 1; Jacobson 2000, 74-76; Meshorer 2001, 30; Hübner 2005, 181; a monogram is rendered on two series of tetradrachms minted by Antiochus VII, which has been suggested to refer to the name Hyrkanos (*hyrkan[ou]*), Fischer 1975, 194.
[81] Meshorer 2001, 31; Hendin 2007-2008, 83-84; Hendin 2010, 181.
[82] Also Hoover 2003, 32-33.
[83] Meshorer 2001, 37; Jacobson 2000, 74-80; Hoover 2003, 32-37.
[84] Zahle 1996, 127; Hoover 2007, no. 110-11 (Antiochus I), no. 172 (Seleucus II), no. 248, 250 (Antiochus III), no. 319 (Antiochus IV), no. 830-32 (Aspendus), no. 833 (Side); SC I, 2002, no. 1184 (Antiochus III, Uncertain mint).

the coins were legitimised. It is also found as a reverse type in different locally minted minor Seleucid coin series attributed to different Eastern mints.⁸⁵ In these cases the motif seems generally to have functioned as an iconographic recognition of the Greek sovereign. This iconographic language was transferred into the Hasmonaean coinage at its very beginning and was especially implemented by Alexander Jannaeus imitating the preceding Seleucid coin iconography (**Fig. 9**).⁸⁶

**Fig. 9:** AE Prutah (ca. 1.0g) (1:2), Alexander Jannaeus (103-76 BCE).
Obv.: Anchor; Greek legend ΒΑΣΙΛΕΟΣ ΑΛΕΞΑΝΔΡΟΥ. Rev.: Star in diadem; palaeo-Hebrew legend Y H N T N H M L K between rays. © David Hendin, reprinted with permission.

**Fig. 10:** AE Prutah (ca. 2g) (1:2), Alexander Jannaeus (103-76 BCE).
Obv.: Wreath with legend YHWNTN HKHN HGDL WḤBR HYHWDYM, tied at bottom., Rev.: Double cornucopiae with inserted pomegranate and ribbons; border of dots.
© David Hendin, reprinted with permission.

**Fig. 11:** AE Prutah (ca. 1.40g) (1:2), Alexander Jannaeus (103-76 BCE).
Obv.: Star in dotted circle; Aramaic legend MLK' 'LKSNDRS ŠNT KH. Rev.: Anchor in circle; Greek legend ΒΑΣΙΛΕΩΣ ΑΛΕΞΑΝΔΡΟΥ, date flanking anchor L KE (Year 25).
© David Hendin, reprinted with permission.

---

⁸⁵ Hoover 2007, no. 97 (unattributed Eastern mint), no. 116 (uncertain Eastern mint), no. 139 (Antiochus II, Cabyle or uncertain mint in Western Asia Minor), no. 705 (Alexander II Zabinas, Antioch-on-the-Orontes); numerous examples are listed in *SC* I, 2002 & *SC* II, 2008, e.g. no. 26 (Seleucus I, Antioch-on-the-Orontes), no. 283-89 (Seleucus I, Aï Khanoum), no. 364 (Antiochus I, Europus (Dura)), no. 2230 (Alexander Zabinas, Antioch-on-the-Orontes); miscellaneous types are unattributed or of uncertain mints.
⁸⁶ Also Hoover 2003, 32-35.

THE USE OF LANGUAGES AND SCRIPTS IN ANCIENT JEWISH COINAGE 39

Alexander Jannaeus was clearly a Jewish ruler who followed his royal Hellenistic predecessors, as well as adhering to his positions in Jewish society as high priest and presumably his role in the *synedrion*, judging by his continued use of the legend YHWNTN HKHN HGDWL WḤBR HYHWDYM (Yehonatan the High Priest and the Council of the Jews) (**Fig. 10**). The implicitness with which he initially displayed and consolidated himself as a Hellenistic ruler, highlighted through the addition of his name and title written in Greek, seems to have changed during the later part of his reign. The diadem, which initially framed the star, disappears on the later coins minted from 79/78 BCE and was replaced by a dotted circle (**Fig. 11**). The palaeo-Hebrew legend was detached from the rays of the star and replaced by an Aramaic legend positioned around the new beaded circle. Through this the direct connection between the ruler and the star (and the diadem of the ruler) was eliminated.[87] This could very well have been a reaction to the ongoing internal political differences with the Pharisees that had come to a head during his period of rule, which, according to Josephus (Jos., *Ant*. 13.403-4) allegedly upon the advice of Alexander Jannaeus, were reconciled during the time of rule of Salome Alexandra (76-67 BCE).[88]

**Fig. 12:** AE Eightfold prutah (ca. 14g) (1:2), Mattathias Antigonus (40-37 BCE).
Obv.: Double cornucopiae; Hebrew legend MTTYH KHN GDL ḤBR YDM around and between.
Rev.: Wreath with ribbons; legend ΒΑCΙΛΕΩC ΑΝΤΙΓΟΝΟΥ
© David Hendin, reprinted with permission.

**Fig. 13:** AE Prutah (1.85g) (1:2), Mattathias Antigonus (40-37 BCE).
Obv.: Showbread table; Hebrew legend (*reconstructs as: Mattathya kohen gadol*); border of dots.
Rev.: Menorah; Greek legend [ΒΑΣΙΛ]ΕΩΣ ΑΝΤ[ΙΓΟΝΟΥ].
BM Reg. No.: 1888,0512.29 © The Trustees of the British Museum.

---

[87] Meshorer 2001, 41, 47.    [88] Schäfer 1995, 75-76; Meshorer 2001, 41.

Despite his additional use of the Greek title *Basileus Antigonos*, Mattathias Antigonus basically remained faithful to the Hasmonaean coin legends developed and used previously through his use of the legend MTTYH KHN GDWL WḤBR HYHWDYM (Mattathias High Priest and the Council of the Jews) (**Fig. 12**).[89] It is noticeable that he, as the only Hasmonaean ruler, used the Greek title of king and the Hebrew words for high priest on the same coins. His was furthermore the first and only Jewish minting authority to use depictions of the seven-branched Menorah and the shewbread table on ancient Jewish coins (**Fig. 13**).[90] Through the bold use of both legends and depictions he was as ruler able to refer directly to the temple in Jerusalem and the temple cult and along with this his role as high priest. This stands in stark contrast to his political opponent the half-Jew Herod, who – as the descendant from an Idumaean family and with a Nabataean mother – would never be able to occupy the position of the high priest due to this deficiency in his genealogy.[91] Mattathias probably resorted to the use of these iconographic elements in combination with the acclaimed legends as a last attempt to appeal to the Jewish population for support as both the legitimate religious and secular leader of the Jewish people.[92]

## 5. The Coin-Legends in Herodian Coinage

Compared with the previous coinage of the Hasmonaeans and the coinage of the two Jewish wars, the coins minted by Herod the Great and his dynastic successors represent a completely different convention within ancient Jewish coinage, primarily relying on the Graeco-Roman traditions.[93] The exclusive use of Greek in the legends of the coins of all the Herods has to do with the origins and political agendas of the members of this dynasty,[94] which is also increasingly reflected in the iconography of their coins. The coinage of Herod the Great and his successors bore little in common with other ancient Jewish coins, apart from those of the contemporary Roman Prefects and Procurators. Regard for religious sensibility does seem to have played a role in certain coin series minted by some of these rulers, but the general picture gained from this coinage is that it was produced by thoroughly Hellenised rulers, although they show independent traits in their choices of coin iconography, use of wording of the legends and reasons for their issue, where these are known.[95] Viewed against this contemporary setting, the contrast between the coinage of the Herodian dynasty and the Jewish coinage minted previously and later, during the *Bellum Judaicum*, appears even sharper.

## 6. The First Jewish War

The resumption of the old script during the time of the first Jewish War (66-70 CE) – after a gap of approximately 100 years since the last Hasmonaean coins were minted – is noticeable and the reasons for this development might seem self-evident. The Jewish state was threatened and the natural reaction to this was to demonstrate and promote what was surely to bring victory, in this case the true faith and the temple. The declarations mediated by the images

---

[89] E.g. the coin hord from 'Ein Feshkha, Bijovsky 2004, 75-76.
[90] Amar 2010, 48-55, with a new discussion of the realism of the depiction of the shewbread table.
[91] Meshorer 2001, 54, 56, 220 no. 41; Hübner 2005, 182.
[92] Meshorer 2001, 56-57.
[93] Jacobson 1986, 145-65; Jacobson 2007, 97-99.
[94] 1998, 360-61.
[95] Lykke 2011, 138-42.

and legends of the coins of the first Jewish War represent a completely new development within Jewish coinage, as an immediate response to the circumstances under which they were produced. Contrary to Jewish coins minted earlier these coins were not issued in the name of any individual. Rather, they demonstrate a collective Jewish identity focused on the Jewish cult and the land of the Jewish people, both severely threatened by the oppressive Roman rule. The legends, the images, and the different iconographic elements were used to display not only fundamental elements of the Jewish cult, including possibly actual utensils used within the temple, but also to communicate the desired messages for freedom and redemption for the Jewish land and people as an entity. Given the acceptance of the premise that the mint of these coins was placed under the high priestly authorities of the temple,[96] at least during the first part of the war,[97] the use of the script appears even clearer.

It is more than likely that the legends written in the old script could not be read and understood by the general population at this time,[98] as it had already been the case during the later Hasmonaean period, since it by now had been out of common use for well over a century and had been replaced by the use of the Aramaic square script. As it was the case with the palaeo-Hebrew epigraphy on the Hasmonaean coins, variations in the form and style of the letters of the coins of the first Jewish War have been established.[99] Particularly noticeable are changes in the coin legends between the bronze coins of the 3rd and the 4th year, which have led to a suggestion that the minting of the bronze coins should be ascribed to a different mint, possibly that of Simon bar Gioras,[100] but this has not been universally endorsed by scholars.

The general impression gained from the coins is that the minting authorities must have understood the script and language perfectly well and used it in the legends intentionally. The most likely explanation for this is that the ancient script had been maintained continuously by the temple administration and/or for the temple cult. If this assumption is valid its long use would by now have lent it a distinct recognisable symbolic value, even if the actual written words were not widely understood.[101] The financial functions of the temple administration of tax-collection and treasury did apparently not completely cease at any point throughout the previous centuries – although the importance of the temple as an institution probably underwent considerable changes, especially during the rule of Herod the Great and his successors as other mints were developed and used alongside. Considering that during the war many of the motifs of the coins can be connected with the temple or are related to the temple cult, the use of the ancient script should probably be viewed in the same light.

---

[96] Rappaport 2007, 108-09.
[97] Goldstein and Fontanille 2006, 15-16, 24.
[98] Also noted by Goldstein and Fontanille 2006, 23.
[99] Meshorer 2001, 131-32.
[100] Rappaport 2007, 103, 111-14.
[101] The same can be said of the use of the Phoenician inscriptions on the Tyrian coins minted during the early Roman Imperial period onwards, demonstrating a continued positive awareness of the Phoenician culture, Lichtenberger 2009, 152.

**Fig. 14:** AR Shekel (22mm, 14.15g) (1:2), First Jewish War (66/67 CE).
Obv.: Cup, pellet below handle on each side; palaeo-Hebrew inscription ŠQL YŠR'L, date (Year 1) in field above cup; border of dots. Rev.: Sprig with three pomegranates; palaeo-Hebrew inscription YRWŠLM QDŠH; border of dots.
BM Reg. No.: 1927,1219.1 © The Trustees of the British Museum.

In addition to the numbering of the coins according to the years of their issue and the references to their denominational value different keywords and expressions were put to use on the coins. Of these, the legend YRWŠLM QDŠH (Jerusalem the holy) used on the reverse of the silver shekels, carrying the image of a branch or sprig with three pomegranates (**Fig. 14**), reveals some information regarding the development and continuity in the administration of the Jewish temple. The explanation for the wording used is well-known.[102]

The payment of the tributes and taxes to the temple had for centuries been made with Tyrian silver shekels with their assured high silver content necessary for this purpose,[103] in spite of the distinctive pagan iconography displaying the patron god of the city of Tyre, Heracles/Melqart (MLK QRT = *king of the town* in Phoenician)[104] on the obverse of these coins and the eagle of Zeus on the reverse, surrounded by the legend *tyrou hieras kai asylou* and the date of the coin (**Fig. 15**).[105] According to the testimony of the coinages and inscriptions found, several Greek cities in the East were granted the status of holy and inviolable – as well as autonomous – during the second half of the 2nd century BCE, amongst others Ascalon, Ptolemais-Akko, Seleuceia in Pieria, Sidon and Tripolis, but no other cities kept the titles as long and continuously as Tyre in their coinage and none of these cities coinages' enjoyed the same close relationship with Jerusalem.[106]

---

[102] Summarised in Meshorer 2001, 78.
[103] As discussed by R. Deutsch in his lecture held at the conference *Judaea and Rome in Coins* held at Spink in London, September 2010; outlined in the religious requirements of the later *m. Shek.* 2.4.
[104] *DNP* 7 (1999) 1198-99.
[105] Seyrig 1939, 35-39; Rigsby 1996, 481-85.
[106] *RPC* I, 655; Rigsby 1996, 485-96, 519-21.

**Fig. 15:** Tyre (123 BCE), AR Shekel (13.93g) (1:2).
Obv.: Laurated head of Herakles-Melqart r. Rev.: Eagle on prora l.; Greek legend ΤΥΡΟΥ ΙΕΡΑΣ ΚΑΙ ΑΣΥΛΟΥ, left field date ΡΚΓ and club, right field palm branch, ΚΡ and monogram. BM Reg. No.: 1909,0304.3 © The Trustees of the British Museum.

Two facts ostensibly tie the Tyrian shekel and the Jewish shekel together. First of all, the minting of the silver Jewish War shekel appears to have superseded the minting of the Tyrian silver shekel, which had been minted since Tyre was established as an autonomous city in 126/25 BCE, at which time the head of the Seleucid king on the obverse was replaced by the city's main deity, with the royal eagle preserved on the reverse.[107] So far, the last clearly legible dating on a Tyrian shekel Year 191, corresponds with the year 65/66 CE and thus with the beginning of the first Jewish War against Rome and the minting of the new Jewish silver shekel.[108] Some readings of the latest coin date on the Tyrian shekels have been questioned and in accordance with this the cessation of the production of the silver shekels and half-shekels tentatively tied with the Roman reform of the Antiochene tetradrachm in c. 59 CE, which may have replaced the Tyrian silver coinage.[109] However, no explanation is offered regarding the latest date identified on a Tyrian silver half shekel to the year 65/6 CE.[110] Secondly, without regard to any discussion of the end date and reason of the cessation in production of the Tyrian shekels, the similar wording of the legend YRWŠLM QDŠH on the Jewish shekels indicates a specific connection between the Tyrian and the Jewish shekel. The Hebrew designation QDŠH (holy) is most likely to have imitated the comparable use of the Greek term *hiera* on the Tyrian shekels.[111]

The possibility that the production of the Tyrian silver shekel may have ceased at the same time as the production of the Jewish silver shekel began, although from time to time Tyre continued to produce bronze coins,[112] highlights some important points. First of all, the production of the Tyrian silver shekel had probably to some extent been continued to accommodate the payment of taxes in the Jewish temple, as the only coins proper for this purpose,[113] since their general importance was decreasing during the 1st century CE.[114] In this period, city silver coinages well-known from the Hellenistic period were being replaced by

---

[107] Rigsby 1996, 482-83; Meir 2008, 119.
[108] *RPC* I, 655-56; Samuels 2000a, 65; Meshorer 2001, 73-78; Weiser and Cotton 2002, 235, 237, 243; Hendin 2010, 482.
[109] *RPC* I, 52-53, 607, 655-56.
[110] *RPC* I, 655, no. 4706 (silver half shekel).
[111] The term *sacred money* (ἱερὰ χρήματα) is used by Josephus (e.g. *Ant*. 16.166-171), on this point, see Hendin 2010, 479.
[112] Rigsby 1996, 483; Syon 2004, 253-58, 263.
[113] Rappaport 2007, 107; Syon 2004, 164.
[114] Although they were still in use and circulating at that time; see the survey by D. Syon (Syon 2004, 60-61 fig. 29, 65-68, 113, 256). In the only reference made by Josephus directly to the use of Tyrian money (τοῦ Τυρίου νομίσματος) (Jos., *War* 2.592) in connection with John of Gischala it is explicitly stated that Tyrian money of the value of 4 Attic drachmas were put to use.

Roman Imperial coinage,[115] such as the Neronian tetradrachms from the mint of Antioch.[116] In general, the epithet *tou Tyriou nomismatos* seems increasingly to have established itself as an overall reference to silver coins of an equivalent value.[117] Secondly, the Jewish silver shekel may have been introduced to serve cultic needs. This would be consistent with the conclusions drawn by Fontanille and Goldstein in their examination of production of First Revolt shekels, which suggests that they were minted and issued to harmonise with the ritual needs of the Jewish seasonal festivals.[118] Thirdly, this required a continuous administration within the Jewish temple also during the Roman period, which demanded maintaining of the production of Tyrian shekels to provide the necessary means to pay the temple taxes, but without any visible involvement in or influence on their production. It has been suggested that the letters KP, found on the Tyrian shekels beginning with the year 14/13 BCE, should be interpreted as *kata rhōmaious* (in accordance with the Roman), hence the coin legend would have read *Tyrou hieras kai asylou kata rhōmaious*, implying an official involvement of the Roman imperial administration in the issuing of these coins.[119]

The political importance of the Jewish temple lessened with the increasing direct involvement of the Roman government in Palestine from the time of the late Hasmonaean period onwards, beginning with the appointment of Hyrcanus II as *ethnarchēs*. This shift in power did not only diminish the political role of the Hasmonaean ruler, but also reduced the status of the Jewish temple under Roman domination. Considering the political changes taking place in Palestine under Herod and the subsequent subdivision of Palestine among his successors, the central political position of the Jewish temple must have changed accordingly. The religious function of the Temple and the collection of taxes probably remained unaffected until the end of the first Jewish War and the destruction of the temple,[120] but changes to its standing as a financial institution did take place, as it can be seen from the fact that during the 1st century CE the authority of the temple treasury was transferred into the hands of non-priestly officials, of which two were known members of the Herodian family.[121] The brief revival of the temple as an active political factor during the first Jewish War and the coinage of this war only serve to underline this.

With regard to the language and iconography used the coins of the first Jewish War addressed the Jewish users in much stronger nationalist and religious tones than any Jewish coins produced previously, with the one exception of the menorah / table of showbread coin of Matthias Antigonus, which also happened to have been produced at a time of considerable stress. In the coins of the first Jewish War the palaeo-Hebrew script had developed into a visual expression of Jewish values, a reason why it was also employed in the later Bar Kokhba coinage, where the recognisability of the old language and script was probably enough to gain acceptance of the coinage among the supporters of the revolt. The palaeo-Hebrew script was used on the Bar Kokhba coins because of its longstanding association by Jews with their ancient Temple cult.

## 7. Concluding Remarks

The reasons why specific languages and scripts were put to use at certain times and not at others, over the lifetime of ancient Jewish coinage, should be sought in the identity of the

---

[115] Levy 1993, 267, 272; Lichtenberger 2009, 155; some Tyrian silver coins may have circulated, although this does not seem to have been the rule, see Weiser and Cotton 2002, 243.
[116] *RPC* I, 607; Syon 2004, 164-65.
[117] Weiser and Cotton 2002, 238, 243-48.
[118] Goldstein and Fontanille 2006, 20.
[119] Weiser and Cotton 2002, 240.
[120] The continued levying of taxes was at least confirmed by Augustus (Jos., *Ant.* 16.166-171), also Hendin 2010, 478-79.
[121] The names of two secular Herodian treasurers are known by name: Helcias II and Antipas III. On this point, see Kokkinos 1998, 200, 201 ns. 104, 232, 360.

minting authorities and their relation to the administration of the Jewish temple. The legends would vary, with their changing contexts, but essentially the use of this script held specific nationalistic and religious connotations,[122] hence its use also on amongst others the pre-Hasmonaean stamped seals.

The Jewish temple appears to have played a central role in the history of the Jews and on their coinage in antiquity, of which particularly the persistent use of the palaeo-Hebrew script provides some evidence. The use of the different scripts and languages very much bear witness to the varied cultural influences at work in Judaea and the political changes constantly taking place within it, but whereas the Greek language and script reflected the temporal milieu, the palaeo-Hebrew script increasingly came to represent an elusive ideal.[123]

## Acknowledgement

I want to express my gratitude towards Marion Meyer (Vienna), Michael Alram (Vienna), Achim Lichtenberger (Bochum) and especially David Jacobson (London) for their critiques and advice on this article.

## Bibliography

*ABD*     Freedman (ed.), D.N., 1992. *The Anchor Bible Dictionary* (New York: Doubleday).

*ANAJ*     *American Numismatic Association Journal: Advanced Studies in Numismatics*

*BAIAS*     *Bulletin of the Anglo-Israel Archaeological Society* (since 2009: *Strata*)

*DNP*     Cancik, H., Schneider, H. and Landfester, M., (eds.), 2003. *Der Neue Pauly. Enzyklopädie der Antike* (Stuttgart: J. B. Metzler).

*EncJud*     Skolnik, F., and Berenbaum, M., (eds.), 2007. *Encyclopaedia Judaica*, vol. 14, Second Edition (Jerusalem: Keter).

*FAT II*     *Forschungen zum Alten Testament*, 2. Reihe (Tübingen: Mohr Siebeck).

Gesenius     Buhl (ed), F., 1962. *Wilhelm Gesenius' Hebräisches und aramäisches Handwörterbuch über das Alte Testament* (Berlin/Göttingen/Heidelberg: Springer-Verlag).

*INR*     *Israel Numismatic Research* (Jerusalem: Israel Numismatic Society)

Koehler – Baumgartner
    Koehler, L., and Baumgartner, W., 1983. *Hebräisches und aramäisches Lexikon zum Alten Testament*, vol. 3, Third Edition (Leiden: Brill).

*Maarav*     *Maarav. A Journal for the Study of the Northwest Semitic Languages and Literatures* (Rolling Hills Estates, CA: Western Academic Press).

*NTOA*     *Novum testamentum et orbis antiquus* (Göttingen: Vandenhoeck & Ruprecht).

*RPC* I     Burnett, A., Amandry, M., and Ripollès, P., 1992. *Roman Provincial Coinage, Vol. I (in 2 parts): From the Death of Caesar to the Death of Vitellius (44 BC – AD 69)*, (London: British Museum Press / Paris: Bibliothèque nationale de France).

*SC* I     Houghton, A., Lorber, C., and Hoover, O. D., 2002. *Seleucid Coins. A Comprehensive Catalogue Part 1*, Vol. I-II (New York: American Numismatic Society).

*SC* II     Houghton, A., Lorber, C., and Hoover, O. D., 2008. *Seleucid Coins. A Comprehensive Catalogue Part 2*, Vol. I-II (New York: American Numismatic Society).

*SHC*     *Studies in Hellenistic Civilization* (Aarhus: Aarhus University Press)

---

[122] Also Hendin 2007-2008, 85.

*Trans*         *Transeuphratène. Recherches pluridisciplinaires sur une province de l'empire achéménide*, Paris 1, 1989ff.
TSAJ         Texte und Studien zum antiken Judentum (Tübingen: Mohr Siebeck)
*WUB*         *Welt und Umwelt der Bibel*.
WUNT II    Wissenschaftliche Untersuchungen zum Neuen Testament 2. Reihe (Tübingen: Mohr Siebeck).

Aḥituv, S., and Yardeni, A., 2004. 'Seventeen Aramaic Texts on Ostraca from Idumea. The Late Persian to the Early Hellenistic Periods', *Maarav* 11, 7-23.

Albright, W. F., 1937. 'A Biblical Fragment from the Maccabean Age: The Nash Papyrus', *JBL* 56, 145-76.

Alon, G., 1984. *The Jews in Their Land in the Talmudic Age (70-640 CE)* (Jerusalem: Magnes Press, Hebrew University).

Amar, Z., 2010. 'The Shewbread Table on the Coins of Mattathias Antigonus: A Reconsideration', in D. Barag and B. Zissu (ed), *Studies in Honour of Arnold Spaer*, *INJ* 17, 48-58.

Avishur, Y., and Heltzer, M., 2005. 'The Scribe and Priest Ezra: A Leader under Achaemenian Rule', *Trans* 29, 17-36.

Barag, D., 1985. 'Some Notes on a Silver Coin of Johanan the High Priest', *BiblArch* 48, 166-68.

Barag, D., 1986-1987. 'A Silver Coin of Yohanan the High Priest and the Coinage of Judea in the Fourth Century B.C.', *INJ* 9, 4-21.

Barag, D., 1994-1999. 'The Coinage of Yehud and the Ptolemies', *INJ* 13, 27-38.

Barag, D., 2002. 'The Two Mints of the Bar Kokhba War', *INJ* 44, 153-56.

Benoit, P., Milik, J. T. and de Vaux, R., 1961. *Discoveries in the Judaean Desert II. Les Grottes de Murabba'at* (Oxford: Clarendon Press).

Betlyon, J. W., 1976. 'A New Chronology for the pre-Alexandrine Coinage of Sidon', *ANSMN* 21, 11-35.

Bickerman, E. J., 1988. *The Jews in the Greek Age* (Cambridge, Mass.: Harvard University Press).

Bijovsky, G., 2004. 'A Hoard of Coins of Mattathias Antigonus from 'Ein Feshkha'', *IEJ* 54, 75-76.

Blenkinsopp, J., 2001. 'Did the Second Jerusalemite Temple Possess Land?', *Trans* 21, 61-68.

Botterweck, G. J., Ringgren, H., and Fabry, H.-J., (eds), 1986. *Theologisches Wörterbuch zum Alten Testament*, vol. 5 (Stuttgart / Berlin / Köln/Mainz: W. Kohlhammer).

Brutti, M., 2006. *The Development of the High Priesthood during the pre-Hasmonean Period: History, Ideology, Theology*, JSJ 108 (Leiden: Brill).

Del Omo Lete, G., 2009. 'The Redaction of the Hebrew Bible: its Achaemenid Persian Setting', *Trans* 37, 53-79.

Fantalkin, A., and Tal, O., 2006. 'Redating Lachish Level I. Identifying Achaemenid Imperial Policy at the Southern Frontier of the Fifth Satrapy', in O. Lipschits and M. Oeming (eds.), *Judah and the Judeans in the Persian Period* (Winona Lake: Eisenbrauns), 167-97.

Fischer, T., 1975. 'Johannes Hyrkan I. auf Tetradrachme Antiochos' VII.? Ein Beitrag zur Deutung der Beizeichen auf hellenistischen Münzen', *ZDPV* 91, 191-96.

Fischer, T., 1984. 'Another Hellenizing Coin of Alexander Jannaeus?', *IEJ* 34, 47-48.

Gerson, S. N., 2001. 'Fractional Coins of Judea and Samaria in the Fourth Century BCE', *NEA* 64/3, 106-21.

Gerson, S. N., 2006. 'A Transitional Period Coin of Yehud. A Reflection of Three Cultures', in D. Barag (ed), *Studies in Memory of Ya'akov Meshorer*, *INJ* 15, 32-34.

Geva, H., 2007. 'A Chronological Reevaluation of Yehud Stamp Impressions in Palaeo-Hebrew Script, based on Finds from Excavations in the Jewish Quarter of the Old City of Jerusalem', *TelAviv* 34, 92-103.

Gitler, H., and Lorber, C., 2006. 'A New Chronology for the Ptolemaic Coins of Judah', *AJN* 2nd Series, 1-41.

Goldstein, I., and Fontanille, J. P., 2006. 'A New Study of the Coins of the First Jewish Revolt against Rome, 66-70 C.E.', *ANAJ*, 9-32.

Goodman, M., 2007a. *Rome and Jerusalem. The Clash of Ancient Civilizations* (New York: Vintage Books).

Goodman, M., 2007b. 'Coinage and Identity. The Jewish Evidence', in Chr. Howgego, V. Heuchert and A. Burnett (eds.), *Coinage and Identity in the Roman Provinces* (Oxford: Oxford University Press), 163-70.

Grabbe, L. L., 2008. 'Sanhedrin, Sanhedriyyot, or Mere Invention?', *JSJ* 39, 1-19.

Hendin, D., 2007-2008. 'Numismatic Expressions of Hasmonean Sovereignty', *INJ* 16, 76-91.

Hendin, D., 2010. *Guide to Biblical Coins*, fifth edition (New York: Amphora).

Hendin, D., 2010. 'Hasmonean Coin Chronologies: Two Notes', in D. Barag and B. Zissu (eds.), *Studies in Honour of Arnold Spaer*, *INJ* 17, 34-38.

Hengel, M., 1988. *Judentum und Hellenismus. Studien zu ihrer Begegnung unter besonderer Berücksichtigung Palästinas bis zur Mitte des 2. Jh.s v. Chr.*, 3rd Edn. (Tübingen: Mohr Siebeck)

Hoover, O. D., 2003. 'The Seleucid Coinage of John Hyrcanus I: The Transformation of a Dynastic Symbol in Hellenistic Judaea', *AJN* 2nd Series 15, 29-39.

Hoover, O. D., 2007. *Coins of the Seleucid Empire from the Collection of Arthur Houghton Part II, Ancient Coins in North American Collections 9* (New York: American Numismatic Society).

Hübner, U., 2005. 'Die Münzprägung der Hasmonäer des 2. und 1. Jahrhunderts v. Chr. als Massenmedium', in Chr. Frevel (ed), *Medien im antiken Palästina. Materielle Kommunikation und Medialität als Thema der Palästinaarchäologie*, FAT II 10 (Tübingen: Mohr Siebeck) 171-88.

Jacobson, D. M., 1986. 'A New Interpretation of the Reverse of Herod's Largest Coin', *ANSMN* 31, 145-65.

Jacobson, D. M., 2000. 'The Anchor on the Coins of Judaea', *BAIAS* 18, 73-81.

Jacobson, D. M., 2007. 'Military Helmet or Dioscuri Motif on Herod the Great's largest coin?', *INR* 2, 93-101.

Jacobson, D. M., 2008. 'The Roman *corona civica* (Civic Crown) on Bar-Kokhba's Silver Coins', *NCirc* 116/2, 64-66.

Jeselsohn, D., 1974. 'A New Coin Type with Hebrew Inscription', *IEJ* 24, 77-78.

Kanael, B., 1971. 'Notes on the Dates Used During the Bar Kokhba Revolt', *IEJ* 21, 39-46.

Kaufman, J. C., 2004. *Unrecorded Hasmonean Coins from the J. Ch. Kaufman Collection* (Jerusalem: Israel Numismatic Society).

Kaufman, J. C., 2007-2008. 'Additions to the Corpus of Leo Mildenberg's Coinage of the Bar Kokhba War (Second Addendum)', *INJ* 16, 136-39.

Kindler, A., 1954. 'The Jaffa Hoard of Jannaeus', *IEJ* 4, 170-85.

Kindler, A., 1968. 'Addendum to the Dated Coins of Alexander Jannaeus', *IEJ* 18, 188-91.

Kindler, A., 1971. 'A Coin of Herod Philip – the Earliest Portrait of a Herodian Ruler', *IEJ* 21, 161-63.

Kindler, A., 1974. *Coins of the Land of Israel. Collection of the Bank of Israel, a Catalogue* (Jerusalem: Keter).

Kindler, A., 1987. 'Coins and Remains from a Mobile Mint of Bar Kokhba at Khirbet el-ʿAqd', *INJ* 9, 46-47.

Kokkinos, N., 1998. *The Herodian Dynasty: Origins, Role in Society and Eclipse* (Sheffield: Sheffield Academic Press)

Kottsieper, I., 2007. '"And They Did Not Care to Speak Yehudit". On Linguistic Change in Judah during the Late Persian Era', in O. Lipschits, G. N. Knoppers and R. Albertz (eds.), *Judah and the Judeans in the Fourth Century B.C.E.* (Winona Lake: Eisenbrauns), 95-124.

Lemaire, A., 1995. 'La fin de la première période perse en Égypte et la chronologie judéenne vers 400 av. J.-C.', *Trans* 9, 51-62.

Lemaire, A., 2007. 'Administration in Fourth-Century B.C.E. Judah', in O. Lipschits, G. N. Knoppers and R. Albertz (eds.), *Judah and the Judeans in the Fourth Century B.C.E.* (Winona Lake: Eisenbrauns), 53-74.

Levine, L., 1998. *Judaism and Hellenism in Antiquity. Conflict or Confluence?* (Washington: University of Washington Press)

Levy, B., 1993. 'Tyrian Shekels and the First Jewish War', in *Proceedings of the XIth International Numismatic Congress Organized for the 150th Anniversary of the Société Royale de Numismatique de Belgique, Brussels, September 8th-13th 1991* (Louvain-la-Neuve: International Numismatic Commission), 267-74.

Lichtenberger, A., 2009. 'Tyros und Beritus. Zwei Fallbeispiele städtischer Identitäten in Phönikien', in M. Blömer, M. Facella and E. Winter (eds.), *Lokale Identitäten im Römischen Nahen Osten. Kontexte und Perspektiven*, Oriens et Occidens 18 (Stuttgart: Franz Steiner Verlag), 151-75.

Lipschits, O., 2006. 'Achaemenid Imperial Policy, Settlement Processes in Palestine, and the Status of Jerusalem in the Middle of the Fifth Century B.C.E.', in O. Lipschits and M. Oeming (eds), *Judah and the Judeans in the Persian Period* (Winona Lake: Eisenbrauns), 19-52.

Lipschits, O., and Tal, O., 2007. 'The Settlement Archaeology of the Province of Judah', in O. Lipschits, G. N. Knoppers and R. Albertz (eds), *Judah and the Judeans in the Fourth Century B.C.E.* (Winona Lake: Eisenbrauns), 33-52.

Lipschits, O., and Vanderhooft, D., 2007. 'Yehud Stamp Impressions in the Fourth Century B.C.E.', in O. Lipschits, G. N. Knoppers and R. Albertz (eds.), *Judah and the Judeans in the Fourth Century B.C.E.* (Winona Lake: Eisenbrauns), 75-94.

Lykke, A., 2010. 'Proto-jüdische Münzprägung in Palästina. Zu den Namen und Identitäten der münzprägenden Autoritäten', *Schild von Steier* 23 (Graz: Universalmuseum Joanneum), 74-86.

Lykke, A., 2011. 'Politische und religiöse Identitäten auf jüdischen Münzen (bis 66 n. Chr.)', in A. Lykke and F. Schipper, *Kult und Macht. Religion und Herrschaft im syro-palästinischen Raum. Studien zu ihrer Wechselbeziehung in hellenistisch-römischer Zeit*, WUNT II (Tübingen: Mohr Siebeck), 127-57.

Meir, C., 2008. 'Tyrian Sheqels and Half Sheqels with Unpublished Dates from the ʿIsfiya Hoard in the Kadman Numismatic Pavilion', *INR* 3, 117-23.

Meshorer, Y., 1982. *Ancient Jewish Coinage, vol. 1. Persian Period through Hasmonaeans* (New York: Amphora).

Meshorer, Y., 1984. 'One Hundred Ninety Years of Tyrian Shekels', in A. Houghton, S. Hurter, P. E. Mottahedeh and J. A. Scott (eds), *Studies in Honor of Leo Mildenberg. Numismatics, Art History, Archaeology* (Wetteren: Cultura Press), 171-80.

Meshorer, Y., 2000. *Antike Münzen erzählen* (Jerusalem: Israel Museum).

Meshorer, Y., 2001. *A Treasury of Jewish Coins. From the Persian Period to Bar Kokhba* (Jerusalem: Yad Ben-Zvi Press).

Meshorer, Y., and Qedar, S., 1999. *Samarian Coinage* (Jerusalem: Israel Numismatic Society).

Mildenberg, L., 1984. *The Coinage of the Bar Kokhba War* (Aarau: Sauerländer).

Mildenberg, L., 1998a. 'Yehud: A Preliminary Study of the Provincial Coinage of Judaea', in U. Hübner and E. Knauf (eds.), *Vestigia Leonis. Studien zur antiken Numismatik Israels, Palästinas und der östlichen Mittelmeerwelt*, NTOA 36 (Freiburg: Universitätsverlag; Göttingen: Vandenhoeck & Ruprecht), 67-76.

Mildenberg, L., 1998b. 'Palästina in der persischen Zeit', in U. Hübner and E. Knauf (eds.), *Vestigia Leonis. Studien zur antiken Numismatik Israels, Palästinas und der östlichen Mittelmeerwelt*, NTOA 36 (Freiburg: Universitätsverlag; Göttingen: Vandenhoeck & Ruprecht), 54-58.

Mildenberg, L., 2000. 'On Fractional Silver Issues in Palestine', *Trans* 20, 89-100.

Mørkholm, O., 1991. *Early Hellenistic Coinage* (Cambridge: Cambridge University Press).

Naveh, J., 1970. 'The Scripts in Palestine and Transjordan in the Iron Age', in J. A. Sanders (ed.), *Near Eastern Archaeology in the Twentieth Century. Essays in Honor of Nelson Glueck* (New York: Doubleday), 277-83.

Naveh, J., 1975. 'A new tomb-inscription from Giv'at Hamivtar', in Y. Yadin (ed.), *Jerusalem Revealed* (Jerusalem: Israel Exploration Society), 73-74.

Naveh, J., 1998. 'Scripts and Inscriptions in Ancient Samaria', *IEJ* 48, 91-100.

Naveh, J., 2009a. 'The Scripts in Palestine and Transjordan in the Iron Age', in J. Naveh, *Studies in West-Semitic Epigraphy. Selected Papers* (Jerusalem: Magnes Press), 3-9.

Naveh, J., 2009b. 'Scripts and Inscriptions in Ancient Samaria', in J. Naveh, *Studies in West-Semitic Epigraphy. Selected Papers* (Jerusalem: Magnes Press), 34-100.

Ostermann, S., 2005. *Die Münzen der Hasmonäer. Ein kritischer Bericht zur Systematik und Chronologie* (Fribourg: Academic Press Fribourg / Göttingen: Vandenhoeck & Ruprecht).

Rappaport, U., 2007. 'Who Minted the Jewish War's Coins?', *INR* 2, 103-16.

Rigsby, K. J., 1996. *Asylia. Territorial Inviolability in the Hellenistic World* (Berkeley, CA: University of California Press).

Ronen, Y., 1998. 'The Weight Standards of the Judean Coinage in the Late Persian and Early Ptolemaic Period', *NEA* 61, 122-26.

Samuels, C. W., 2000a. 'The Jewish War', in P. Rynearson (ed.), *The Numismatic Legacy of the Jews. As Depicted by a Distinguished American Collection* (New York: Stack's Publications), 59-82.

Samuels, C. W., 2000b. 'The Bar Kokhba War', in P. Rynearson (ed.), *The Numismatic Legacy of the Jews. As Depicted by a Distinguished American Collection* (New York: Stack's Publications), 83-100.

Sáenz-Badillos, A., and Elwolde, J., 1996. *A History of the Hebrew Language* (Cambridge: Cambridge University Press).

Schaper, J., 2002. 'Numismatik, Epigraphik, alttestamentliche Exegese und die Frage nach der politischen Verfassung des achämenidischen Juda', *ZDPV* 118, 150-68.

Schäfer, P., 1981. *Der Bar Kokhba-Aufstand. Studien zum zweiten jüdischen Krieg gegen Rom*, TSAJ 1 (Tübingen: Mohr Siebeck).

Schäfer, P., 1995. *The History of the Jews in Antiquity* (Luxembourg: Harwood Academic Publishers).

Schwarz, D., 1990. *Agrippa I. The last King of Judaea*, TSAJ 23 (Tübingen: Mohr Siebeck).

Schürer, E., 1973. *The History of the Jewish People in the Age of Jesus Christ*, vol. 1. Revised edn. by G. Vermes, F. Millar and M. Black (Edinburgh: T. & T. Clark).

Sear, D. R., 1970. *Roman Coins and Their Values* (London: Seaby).
Seyrig, H., 1939. 'Les rois Séleucides et la concession de l'asylie', *Syria* 20, 35-42.
Seyrig, H., 1971. 'Le monnayage de Hiérapolis de Syrie à l'époque d'Alexandre', *RN* 13, 11-21.
Sharon, N., 2010. 'The Title Ethnarch in the Second Temple Period Judea', *JSJ* 41, 472-93.
Syon, D., 2004. *Tyre and Gamla. A Study in the Monetary Influence of Southern Phoenicia on Galilee and the Golan in the Hellenistic and Roman Periods*, Dissertation submitted to the Hebrew University (Jerusalem 2004).
Tal, O., 2008. 'Cult in Transition from Achaemenid to Greek Rule: The Contribution of Achaemenid-Ptolemaic Temples of Palestine', *Trans* 36, 165-84.
Vanderhooft, D. S., and Lipschits, O., 2007. 'A New Typology of the Yehud Stamp Impressions', *TelAviv* 34/1, 12-37.
Vanderkam, J. C., 2004. *From Joshua to Caiaphas. High Priests after the Exile* (Minneapolis: Fortress Press).
Villeneuve, E., 2008. 'Wenn Münzen erzählen. Eine kleine Geschichte des Geldes im antiken Judäa', *WUB* 47/1, 22-26.
Weippert, H., 1988. *Palästina in Vorhellenistischer Zeit* (München: Beck).
Weisser, W., and Cotton, H. M., 2002. 'Neues zum 'Tyrischen Silbergeld' herodianischer und römischer Zeit', *ZPE* 139, 235-50.
Wroth, W., 1899. *British Museum Catalogue of the Greek Coins of Galatia, Cappadocia and Syria* (London: British Museum).
Zahle, J., 1996. 'Religious Motifs on Seleucid Coins', in P. Bilde, T. Engberg-Pedersen, L. Hannestad and J. Zahle, *Religion and Religious Practice in the Seleucid Kingdom*, SHC 1 (Aarhus: Aarhus University Press), 125-39.
Zeitlin, S., 1957. 'The Titles High Priest and the Nasi of the Sanhedrin', *JQR* 48.1, 1-5.
Zournatzi, A., 2000. 'The Processing of Gold and Silver Tax in the Achaemenid Empire. Herodotus 3.96.2 and the Archaeological Realities', *StIr* 29/2, 241-71.

# GALILEAN MINTS IN THE EARLY ROMAN PERIOD: POLITICS, ECONOMY AND ETHNICITY

Danny Syon

## 1. Introduction

This paper examines in some detail the circulation pattern of coins in the Galilee in the Early Roman Period that come from mints situated within or on the borders of the Galilee itself.[1] As I will suggest, this pattern can mostly be explained through political, economic and ethnic considerations. Naturally, other coins circulated in Galilee as well in the Early Roman period, most notably coins of the Jewish rulers and the Roman governors from the mint of Jerusalem and the coins of the Phoenician cities of Tyre and Sidon. Moreover, the patterns observed in this period are a development of patterns that crystallized in the Hasmonaean period (late 2nd –1st centuries BCE). Thus, for the details to make sense it is necessary to first present the full coin distribution patterns in Galilee, in both the Hasmonaean and the Early Roman periods.

## 2. Materials and Methods

The data used here is taken from my doctoral dissertation, in which I examined coin finds from 186 sites throughout Galilee and the Golan Heights.[2] The source of the data is from published excavation reports, The Israel Antiquities Authority coin database, unpublished excavation data (with full permission of the excavators and respective numismatists) and collections kept in kibbutzim throughout the area, for which the provenance is known.[3] The data was partially updated to reflect some major discoveries since the original period of data collection in 2001–2002.

## 3. The Study Area

The geographical limits of the study include modern day Galilee and the Golan Heights. To the north and east I was unfortunately limited by the modern political borders and the paucity of published data from south Lebanon and Syria.

To the south, the limit is the Jezre'el and Bet She'an valleys, the traditional borders of the historical Galilee. According to Josephus the Jezre'el valley was not included in Galilee in his time, the border passing near Xaloth, at the foot of the Nazareth mountain range (*War* 3.39), rabbinic sources however state that in the Roman period the border was at Legio, near Megiddo (*b. Git.* 7.3; *j. B.M.* 7.7). Bet She'an and its immediate vicinity are included as well, because in the Hasmonaean period it was part of the Hasmonaean state, as evidenced also by the coin finds from the city itself and nearby sites (see below). Since Jewish settlement continued there until the Jewish War and after, as evidenced by Josephus (*War, passim.*) and

---

[1] This paper is an abridged version of the presentation given in the *Judaea and Rome in Coins* conference in that it presents in detail only the circulation of coins from the mints of Galilee, and not that of the mints outside of it. This and the rest of the material will be part of a forthcoming monograph.

[2] Syon 2004.

[3] It is impossible to credit here all the individuals involved. For full details see Syon 2004, 167–190.

rabbinic sources, its inclusion is warranted throughout the chronological range of this study.

Certainly in the Roman period, and most probably as early as latter part of Jannaeus' reign, the central Golan Heights—Gaulanitis—was considered to be part of Galilee by the Jewish population. This affinity of the Gaulanitis to Galilee is shown first in the main literary source of the period, Josephus, where "Judas the Galilean" (Jos., *War* 2.118) and then "Judas the Gaulanite, from a city whose name was Gamala"[4] (Jos., *Ant.* 18.4) are mentioned, and the fact that Josephus himself was appointed by the Jerusalem council to be the governor of both Galilee and Golan (Jos., *War* 2.568). The rabbinic literature too refers to Gamla as being in Galilee (*Safra*, *Behar* 4.1; *b. Arak.* 32.2–3). From an archaeological perspective, Eric Meyers, studying Upper Galilean sites of Ḥ. Shemaʻ, Gush Ḥalav and Meron, stressed the very strong geographical, administrative—and certainly cultural—ties of the Jews in Galilee to the Jews in the Golan.[5] Ceramic evidence also tends to support the continuity between Gaulanitis and Galilee in the Second Temple and later periods.[6]

The northern Golan that was the territory of Paneas, a pagan and later Christian area, is relevant for inclusion in this study because it formed part of the areas under the Herodians. The territory of ʻAkko-Ptolemais, though historically part of southern Phoenicia, always played and important rôle in relation to Galilee.

For clarity, only the major settlement points are indicated on the maps accompanying this paper. These maps are provided for visual impact; the individual sites are unimportant.

There are two fundamental but insurmountable flaws inherent in the data. First, it is not a random sample of the 'population' of coins in antiquity, which statistically could be thought as giving a fair representation of the original population, but rather a fortuitous assemblage, dependent on the keenness of vision of the workmen in the excavation, the availability of a metal detector, my ability to locate the collectors through personal connections and the willingness of the collectors to share the information. The second problem is the use, in any one period, of coins from preceding periods; in other words, coins that circulated for decades. This issue could not be isolated in a study of this scope, partly because of the lack of stratigraphic data for most of the sites and partly because it would have made the presentation very cumbersome. Thus, for each period the coins presented are those that were *minted* and presumably arrived at the site during the period.

## 4. Interpretation of Coin Finds and Circulation

### 4.1 Local economy

The mints of Galilee produced only copper-alloy coins.[7] One of the basic tenets of numismatics states that copper-alloy coins of a local mint would be found predominantly in it and its *chora*, *i.e.* its agricultural hinterland and the villages which were administratively subordinate to it.

### 4.2 Army

Military actions and troop movements are considered to have had an impact on coin circulation. Payments to soldiers could arrive from a central mint or coins could travel with mercenaries and enter the local economy. Though mostly silver coins are considered in this respect, anomalous concentrations of copper-alloy coins, far from their mint, should probably be associated with troop movements as well.[8]

---

[4] Not all accept this equation. For a different view see Smith 1971 and Goodman 1999, 615.
[5] Meyers 1976, 99–100.
[6] Adan-Bayewitz 1993, 247–249; *idem.* 2003; Meyers 1985, 127.

[7] Though most coins discussed are presumably bronze, I prefer this term, which relieves me of the burden of proof. ʻAkko (Ptolemais) is the only mint that struck silver in the Seleucid period and billon and gold in the Crusader period.
[8] Butcher 1988, 27.

## 4.3 Mint output

Mint output naturally affects the circulation and quantity of coins found. Since there is no historical evidence for outputs for the mints under discussion (nor for any ancient mint, for that matter), coin finds are the only way to estimate it.

## 4.4 Trade patterns

It is most often assumed that in an open monetary economy it is trade patterns that were mainly accountable for monetary circulation and vice versa—that coins found at a site or region, by necessity, reflect the trade patterns of that site or region.

Roman Galilee has received disproportionate attention in relation to earlier periods, primarily due to the interest of New Testament scholars, and the availability of the rabbinic sources. In fact, the study of Galilee is dominated even today by Biblical and New Testament scholars trying to reconstruct the economical realities of the Galilee of Jesus, based on anachronistic data, which more often than not are irrelevant.

Based mostly – but not exclusively – on coin finds, we find the following diverse statements concerning Galilee in the Roman period:

> "It is obvious that some residents of Upper Galilee/Golan chose to trade via those gentile cities which encircled it and influenced trade and economy. Chief was Tyre, whose influence is disproportionately well reflected in the coins found in both Galilees".[9]

and

> "The definitive urban influence in this region, especially in the north (near Meron, Gush Halav, and H. Shema') is Tyre".[10]

Z. Safrai, speaking of the Roman period after 70 CE states:[11]

> "Finding foreign coins in the Land of Israel and coins from the Land of Israel abroad might serve as a good indication of foreign trade, as well as of those countries engaging in commerce with the land of Israel".

Further on he states, based on several hoards from Galilee that:

> "Most of the trade and commerce in the rural sector of Northern Israel was with cities outside the Land of Israel".

Horsley[12] is among the first to question the absolute validity of the equating coin circulation with trade patterns, though on the wrong grounds:

> "It seems highly unlikely that one can move directly from the incidence of Tyrian coinage to trade with Tyre. ... Overland trade was expensive".

---

[9] Meyers 1997, 58.
[10] *Ibid.*, 61.
[11] Safrai 1994, 399–400. Safrai's section 'Numismatic Evidence' (pp. 399–404) should be used with caution; the numbers of coins he quotes are often incorrect, and the totals of the percentages add up to over 100%. He uses copper-alloy city coins and provincial silver tetradrachms indiscriminately, even after having stated (p. 399) that for imperial coins, the mint which supplied them was of no economic implications and was related only to matters of administration.
[12] Horsley 1995, 11.

This statement concerns the middle Roman period, when overland trade is actually very well attested in the rabbinic literature and appears to have been widespread.

Lapin[13] also raises questions in this regard:

"The connection between the distribution of coins and 'markets' is far from simple, but the extent that coins circulated or were hoarded at the village level seems a rough index of the extent to which at least some members of the village population made use of money either for storing wealth or for exchange".

Along a different line, Goodman[14], speaking of the Middle Roman period (132–212 CE), tends to see very little interaction between the 'self sufficient' villages of Galilee and the cities therein, and believes that he underscores this view by stating that:

"It would seem that even villages in the immediate vicinity of Sepphoris and Tiberias felt no necessity to rely on the coinage of those cities, but preferred the products of Tyre and elsewhere".

A rapid economic change is postulated for Palestine in the Herodian period by Freyne[15], seeing increased specialization and more sophisticated exchange mechanisms, and hence a more widespread use of money. According to him, this change, induced by Roman rule, was fully felt only from the reign of Antipas onward.

Let us now turn to the coins themselves for their evidence.

## 5. The Mints

*'Akko-Ptolemais*, in Phoenicia. This is the oldest mint, having struck its first coins apparently under Alexander the Great. In the Roman Period it struck only copper-alloy coins. Autonomous and civic coins, possibly dated by a Pompeian, then by a Caesarean era, followed by issues by Antony's regnal years, and back to the Caesarean era until Claudius, when it minted provincial issues.[16] It became a colony apparently in 54 CE, from which year it produced undated colonial issues until the reign of Gallienus (253–268 CE).[17] Its output seems to have been relatively high, but not constant.

*Paneas*. The cultic site of Paneas was refounded as Caesarea Philippi in 2/1 BCE by Philip, son of Herod, who made it his capital. Philip struck his own Roman-style civic and provincial coinage in the city intermittently between 1/2 CE and 33/4 CE dated by his regnal years. Some issues were large, while others small. Later two series of Roman-style coins were struck there by Agrippa I in 38/9 and 40/1 CE.[18] The Roman administration issued four coin types there under Claudius and Nero[19], and one series of Agrippa II was struck in the city during the Jewish War, possibly in 67/8 CE[20] followed by other series under the Flavians.[21] Provincial coinage dated by the era of the city was issued intermittently from the reign of Marcus Aurelius to Elagabalus.[22]

---

[13] Lapin 2001, 119.
[14] Goodman 1983, 133.
[15] Freyne 2000.
[16] For the latest arrangement of the city's pre-colonial coinage, see Syon 2004, 80–85.
[17] The now outdated work by Kadman (1961) is still the most comprehensive on the colonial coins of the city.
[18] I believe the 'year 5' series is from Paneas, not Tiberias, *contra* Meshorer (*TJC*, 230–231).
[19] *TJC*, nos. 350–354.
[20] *TJC*, nos. 129–131.
[21] Kushnir-Stein 2002.
[22] Meshorer 1985b.

*Hippos*. A city founded in the Hellenistic period and conquered (only according to Syncellus, *Chronographia*, ed. Dindorf: 558–559) by Alexander Jannaeus. It was later 'liberated' by Pompey and counted its era from this event. It was given to Herod by Augustus but after Herod's death became an autonomous city. Its minting history is brief and its output apparently small. Hippos minted a single issue in 38/7 BCE[23], and again in 67/8 CE, during the Jewish War. After small issues under Titus and Domitian it minted occasional provincial issues from Antoninus Pius to Elagabalus.[24]

*Nysa-Scythopolis*. This important city was part of Judaea under the Hasmonaeans, but was liberated by Pompey and inaugurated a Pompeian era. It remained autonomous under the Herodians. Considering its importance, its minting history is not very impressive. It inaugurated its civic coinage under the first Roman governors (c. 57–44 BCE) and issued a trickle of dated civic and provincial coins under emperors Caligula, Claudius and Nero, including one large series during the Jewish War (66/7 CE). From Antoninus Pius to Gordian III it issued occasional dated and undated provincial series.[25]

*Sepphoris*. This Jewish town became the capital of Galilee under Antipas in 4 BCE, only to lose the title to Tiberias when the latter was founded in 20 CE. A unique coin may have been minted here by Antipas in 1 BCE/CE.[26] Sepphoris did not participate in the Jewish War and issued a civic series in honour of Vespasian in 67/8 CE. Sepphoris issued a large series of provincial coins under Trajan and was renamed Diocaesarea. Its later provincial issues begin under Antoninus Pius and end under Ealgabalus.

*Tiberias*. Tiberias was founded by Antipas in 20 CE as capital of Jewish Galilee. Antipas issued there intermittent but large series of non-figurative civic coins from 20 CE until 39/40 CE. The Roman administration issued similar coins at the mint in 53/4 CE and Agrippa II in (probably) 63/4. Under Trajan and Hadrian large issues of Roman-style provincial coins were struck at Tiberias dated by the era of the city, but later only a very small trickle of issues appeared under Antoninus Pius to Elagabalus.

*Gam(a)la*. This Jewish town was the capital of Gaulanitis district in the first century CE and fell to the Romans in the Jewish War. A single issue of crude coins was struck during the siege of Agrippa II, shortly before the arrival of Vespasian's legions.[27]

## 6. The Hasmonaean Period (c. 125–63 BCE)

In spite of economic relations that never ceased, beginning in the Hasmonaean period the relationship between Jews and pagans in Galilee was one of deep mistrust and hatred, rooted in the Hasmonaean takeover of the agricultural hinterland the Phoenician cities depended on. This animosity can be traced in the coin circulation patterns as well. **Fig. 1** shows the distribution of coins in the study area. The pattern for the Hasmonaean coins (red) shows in effect the boundaries of the Hasmonaean state in Galilee at its peak. Excepting a few anomalous areas, the almost complete exclusion of 'foreign' coins from the Hasmonaean controlled areas – and vice versa – is very striking. Apart from the logical assumption that

---

[23] Meshorer 1985a, 74, no. 197.
[24] Spijkerman 1978, 168–179.
[25] Barkay 2003.
[26] Hendin 2003–2006.
[27] Syon, forthcoming; Arbel, forthcoming.

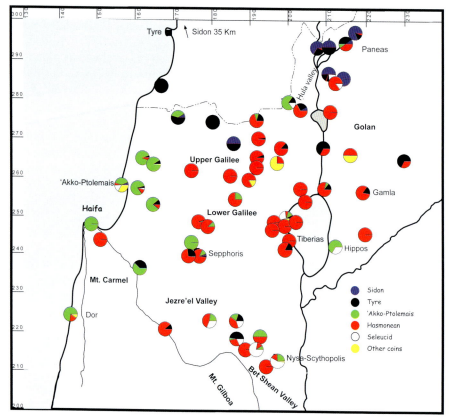

**Fig. 1:** Coin distribution in the Hasmonaean period (125–63 BCE). Only sites with at least ten coins from the period are shown. The miniature pie charts indicate only relative quantities at a site, not absolute numbers.

Hasmonaean currency was expected by the state to be the main currency within its domains, the sharp boundaries seems to be also a reflection of preference/rejection on ethnic grounds. This map is further evidence that Hasmonaean coinage, all of it minted in Jerusalem, was not a local, but a 'national' coinage.

The picture around Scythopolis appears distorted because of the choice of the beginning date of the period in 125 BCE. In addition to Hasmonaean coins, a variety of late Seleucid coins from 'Akko, Antioch and Damascus and autonomous and civic coins of Tyre and 'Akko turn up here, but practically all *predate* the Hasmonaean conquest of the city, which took place probably in 109 BCE.[28]

The coins of 'Akko behave like a local mint supplying its hinterland and the concentration of Sidonian coins near Paneas likewise reflect the fact it is on the border of Sidonian territory and possibly also reflect Ituraean presence.

## 7. From Pompey to the Jewish War (63 BCE–70CE)

**Fig. 2** shows the entire coin distribution in the study area in the Early Roman period. During most of this period Judaea no longer had sovereignty over Galilee as it had under the Hasmonaeans,

---

[28] Barag 1992–93, 11, n. 41

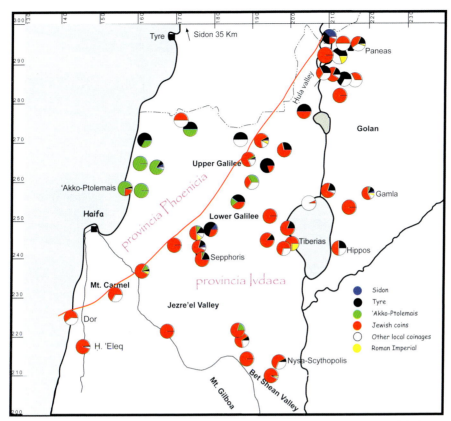

**Fig. 2:** Coin distribution in the Early Roman period (63 BCE–70 CE) with the provincial boundary. The miniature pie charts indicate only relative quantities at a site, not absolute numbers.

so the sharp boundary between areas with 'Jewish' coins (red) and Phoenician territory is all the more striking. In fact, this coin distribution pattern is the strongest visual evidence for the creation of *provincia Ivdaea* under Augustus along ethnic dividing lines. The sites along the provincial boundary show a marked mixing of currencies, not only with coins of 'Akko, but of other local coinages as well. It is reasonable to assign this isolated phenomenon to factors of local economy.

Chronologically this map also includes the time of Jesus. The relatively small number of coins from the mint of Tyre shows that the various assertions (above) about the influence of the coins of Tyre on the economy of Galilee in the time of Jesus are certainly exaggerated.[29]

'Jewish coins' here comprise all coinages of Herod and his sons, those of Agrippa I and the coins of the Roman governors issued in Jerusalem and Tiberias. This time however, the presence in Galilee of large quantities of coins from Jerusalem is not simply a matter of a 'national' currency, but of an obvious preference by the Jewish population to use coins minted by and/or for the Jews. The most striking evidence for this is in the rural area surrounding Scythopolis, which from Pompey's time onwards was no longer under Jewish control, yet the vast majority of coins in the area are 'Jewish' coins, showing that these settlements continued to be inhabited by Jews.

---

[29] The Middle Roman period is outside the scope of this paper, but observations made by the various scholars is certainly valid in the 2nd–3rd centuries, when the coins of Tyre definitely dominated the circulation patterns of Galilee (Syon 2004, 258, Map 34).

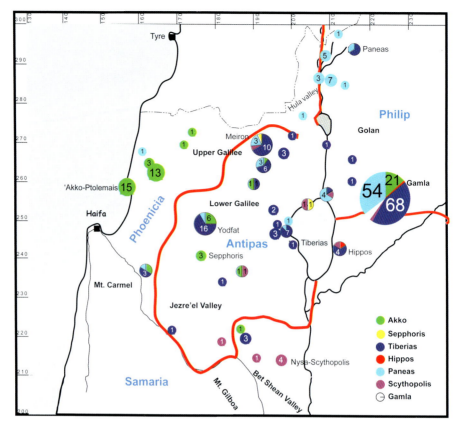

**Fig. 3:** Galilean mints in the Early Roman period (63 BCE–70 CE). The size of the pie charts approximates relative coin numbers. The numbers indicate quantities of coins.

**Fig. 3** shows the distribution of the coins of the mints under discussion in the period from Pompey to the end of the Jewish War.

There is not much we can say about the circulation of the coins of Hippos whose early issue was apparently very small. Hippos only shows two coins of the early series (37 BCE) at Hippos itself and at not too distant Gamla. Coins of Jewish Sepphoris from 67/8 CE were found only in Meiron and Capernaum, rather distant for a local issue, though both sites are Jewish sites. At Gamla seven coins of its ephemeral rebel mint were found and not surprisingly nowhere else in Galilee.[30] Coins of Scythopolis are slightly more numerous, but with one exception at Meiron, stay in the city's vicinity and in Eastern Galilee, behaving in effect as a local issue. The coins of 'Akko-Ptolemais are most abundant in its own territory, but show up in the western part of Jewish Galilee as well, no doubt indicating trade relations. The large number of its coins at Gamla is rather surprising and I cannot offer a plausible explanation for their presence in this period.[31]

In addition to the coins from Jerusalem, the main supplier of coins for Jewish Galilee was unquestionably the mint of Tiberias, mostly issuing under Antipas. The coins of this mint cover

---

[30] A further specimen was found at Sartaba overlooking the Jordan valley, probably lost by a refugee from Gamla on his way to Jerusalem (Syon, forthcoming).

[31] The huge number of coins from Gamla (altogether some 6,400) are the result of meticulous sifting during the excavations.

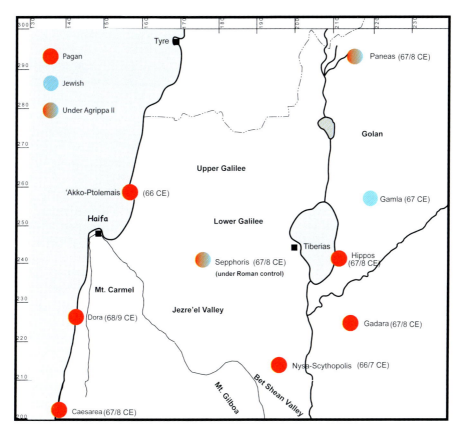

**Fig. 4:** Galilean and neighboring mints during the Jewish War (66–70 CE).

the entire territory of Antipas and only strays are found outside the Jewish areas. Likewise, the mint of Paneas (mostly coins of Philip) supplies mostly its own territory, but with the exception of Gamla, its coins hardly reach its southern border. The interaction between the coins of Paneas and Tiberias is instructive. Few of the Roman-style coins of Philip are found in Antipas' territory, yet the Jewish-style coins of Tiberias penetrate to the southern reaches of Philip's tetrarchy, which was the Jewish Gaulanitis. The Jews of Gaulanitis evidently preferred the coins of Tiberias over those of Paneas, and I would suggest this preference had a religious and ethnic rather than economic rationale.

## 8. The Jewish War (66–70 CE)

In this section I examine the coins minted in Galilee in the course of the Jewish War (**Fig. 4**) and their possible connection to the fighting. Of the pagan cities on the borders of Galilee, 'Akko and Scythopolis served as bases for the Roman legions and isssued military types to commemorate these events. Vespasian assembled his legions in 'Akko in the summer of 66 (Josephus, *War* 3.409). I think it is possible that the municipal authorities, planning to

---

[32] *RPC* 1, nos. 4749–4750. The standards remained on some subsequent issues of this 'founder' type minted under Hadrian and Geta (Kadman 1961, *passim*).
[33] Barkay 2003, nos. 12, 13; *RPC* 1, nos. 4834–4835.

issue a Latin-language imperial 'founder' type coin to commemorate the founding of *Colonia Ptolemais* some twelve years before, seized the opportunity to commemorate both events, and added the legionary standards that were to march on Galilee.[32]

Scythopolis issued one local and one military type coin in 66/7, probably in connection with the billeting of the fifteenth legion in the city for the winter (Josephus, *War* 3.412).[33] Moreover, both 'Akko and Scythopolis (or at least their territories) were attacked by rebellious Jews in the early phases of the revolt (Josephus, *War* 2.458) so they had more reasons to flatter the legionaries who for them meant protection. The cities of Hippos and Gadara were attacked too, so it is possible that the non-military types issued by them in 67/8 were intended to show their support of the Roman legions.[34] Caesarea Maritima, which hosted some of the Roman legions together with Scythopolis (Jos., *War* 3.412), and was also the provincial capital, we would expect to have issued a military type in support of the war effort, but instead it issued a two-denomination provincial series in 67/8 with non-military, local iconography.

On the purely Jewish side we have the rebel issues of Gamla, minted in 67 CE. This town, in the territory of Agrippa II, had not had any Roman presence in it before Vespasian marched on it in September 67. The legend on these coins—written in a mixture of Paleo-Hebrew, Aramaic and retrograde letters—has not yet been satisfactorily read[35], but it probably conveys a messianic or propagandistic text, directly connected with the war and similar to the legends on the contemporaneous Jewish War coins minted in Jerusalem, which served as their prototype.

The two remaining mints, Caesarea Paneas and Sepphoris, have different histories during this turbulent period and it seems their coin issues were motivated by slightly different reasons.

Caesarea Paneas was a pagan city (with a Jewish demographic component) ruled by the Jewish king Agrippa II and obviously did not revolt. The king hosted Vespasian and his legions in the city for a brief 20 day 'rest' in the summer of 67, and this may have been the occasion for the minting of an undated royal coin of Agrippa II that commemorated the city's refounding as *Neronias*.[36]

Sepphoris was the only Jewish city that opened its gates to the Romans right at the start of the hostilities and asked for Roman protection against Josephus and his Jewish army (Josephus, *War* 3.30–34). In 67/8 the Jewish city council minted a Greek language series of two coins that the same time honored Vespasian and proclaimed Sepphoris as *Eirenopolis*, the city of peace. The coins are aniconic, as expected from a Jewish issue.[37]

## 9. From the Jewish War to the Bar-Kokhba Revolt (70–135 CE)

So far, no definite evidence of any kind has been discovered to confirm the participation of the Galilee in the Bar-Kokhba revolt (132–135 CE). Thus, the chronology imposed by the above heading is seemingly an artificial constraint. As it turns out however, the date of 135 CE is close enough to the death of Hadrian in 138, forming a rather clear-cut end point to a numismatically distinct period.

---

[34] Hippos issued a single local type coin (*RPC* 1, nos. 4807–4808), while Gadara issued a three denomination series with a local type and the imperial portrait (*RPC* 1, nos. 4822–4824).

[35] Farhi 2006, Syon 2007.

[36] *TJC*, nos. 129–131; *RPC* 1, nos. 4988–4990.

[37] *TJC*, nos. 127–128; *RPC* 1, nos. 4849-4850. See also Meshorer 1979, Kushnir-Stein 2008.

[38] In Fig. 5 I have inserted two important copper-alloy coin hoards: the one from Migdal (Meshorer 1976) and an unpublished hoard found recently at Wadi Ḥammam. I thank the excavator, Uzi Leibner (Hebrew University, Jerusalem) and the numismatist Gabriela Bijovsky (Israel Antiquities Authority) for allowing me to use the data.

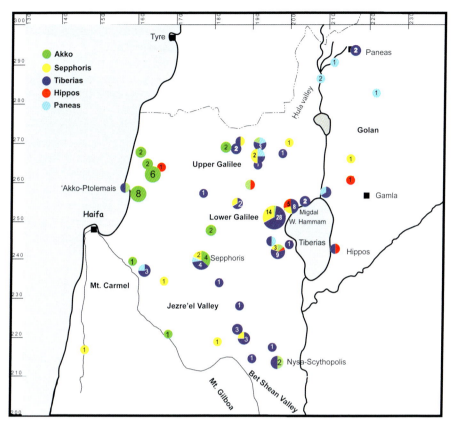

**Fig. 5:** Galilean mints between the Jewish revolts (70–135 CE). The size of the pie charts approximates relative coin numbers. The numbers indicate quantities of coins

Following the devastation caused by the Jewish War, Galilee fared better than Judaea and its economy rebounded rather quickly. Numismatically, the immediately visible change was the complete cessation of Jewish coinage of any kind, in the sense of non-figurative coins aimed at the Jewish population. Thus, ostensibly one can no longer use coin distribution to map the extent of the Jewish settlement. I will show however that indirectly this ethnic group is still 'visible' through the coin distribution. **Fig. 5** shows the five mints active in this period (Scythopolis did not mint during this period and the ephemeral mint at Gamla was destroyed).[38]

As before, the mint of 'Akko produced colonial issues that did not stray too far from the city and served the local economy. However, one enigmatic issue of the city deserves comment. It has a 'Victory with palm branch and wreath' obverse and a 'cornucopia with caduceus' reverse. The OVI AVGVS obverse inscription is not much help in dating it or otherwise, and *RPC* suggests it was minted under Nero.[39] While this may be true, thus making it a Jewish War issue, I think it is more in line with a 'victory' issue *following* the Jewish War and fits better under the Flavians. The enigmatic OVI might be a blundered OYE, the first three letters of Vespasian's name in Greek, cut by a confused local celator.

In this period Hippos issued just a few provincial issues, under the Flavians only, but none shows any connection to the Roman victory. At Paneas, Agrippa II issued a long series

---

[39] *RPC* 1, no. 4751.

of coins of under the Flavians between 74 and 84 CE. Some are victory types but, as **Fig. 5** shows, the issues were apparently small and with a few exceptions stayed near Paneas and within the Upper Galilee, being in effect a 'local economy' currency.

The major 'players' during this period were undoubtedly the mints of Tiberias and Sepphoris. Though Agrippa II apparently issued several series in Tiberias under the Flavians,[40] the mint became really prolific under Trajan and Hadrian. Sepphoris did not issue coins under the Flavians, but it had a large issue under Trajan.

Although all these coins are 'Roman style' in that they bear the bust of the emperor, they were issued by cities governed at the time by a Jewish council. The coins of Sepphoris have a decidedly Jewish, aniconic reverse.[41] The distribution pattern of the coins of these two cities as seen in **Fig. 5**, as well as the relatively large quantities of them in this period strongly suggests that they were the replacement for the 'Jewish' coins in the areas of Jewish Galilee and were preferred over the coins of the neighboring mints.[42] After Hadrian's reign the minting efforts of Sepphoris and Tiberias are few and far between. From the time of Antoninus Pius and onwards, coin circulation in Galilee reflects only local economic and trade needs.

## 10. Conclusions

I have shown that distribution of coin finds based upon large quantities can suggest circulation patterns. Circulation patterns in turn can be used to make inferences about diachronic regional processes.

Though not showing the entire body of coins circulating in Early Roman Galilee but only that of a small number of mints, the regional pattern presented in this paper, when combined with historical information, can provide insights into these processes better than by employing data from single sites.

Coin circulation patterns are dynamic. Not only do they vary over time and space, they depend on mint output, trade patterns, political and administrative boundaries and preference based on ethnic/religious grounds. Thus, projecting realities of one period onto another, which was the basis of some earlier scholarship, is hazardous, at best.

## Bibliography

*RPC* 1    A. Burnett, M. Amandry and P. Ripollès, 1992. *Roman Provincial Coinage 1: From the Death of Caesar to the Death of Vitellius* (London: British Museum).

*RPC* 2    A. Burnett, M. Amandry and I. Carradice, 1999. *Roman Provincial Coinage 2: from Vespasian to Domitian (AD 69–96)"* (London: British Museum / Paris: Bibliothèque Nationale).

*TJC*      Y. Meshorer, 2001. *'A Treasury of Jewish Coins'* (Jerusalem / Nyack, NY: Amphora).

---

[40] Kushnir-Stein 2002. The 'Year 15' coin (*RPC* 2, no. 2242, no date suggested), was likely issued by the era of 49, dating it to 63/4 CE, if only because of its similarity to the issues of Antipas. The Flavian period coins are very homogeneous and this coin does not fit in if dated by the era of 60 CE to 74/5 CE.

[41] Meshorer 1979, 163–165; Kushnir-Stein 2008.

[42] In sheer numbers, it is the coins of Tyre that dominate Galilee, the territory of 'Akko and that of Paneas in this period, as I shall demonstrate in a forthcoming study.

Adan-Bayewitz, D., 1993. *Common Pottery in Roman Galilee: A Study of Local Trade* (Bar-Ilan Studies in Near Eastern Languages and Culture 9) (Ramat Gan: Bar Ilan University Press).

Adan-Bayewitz, D., 2003. 'On the Chronology of the Common Pottery of Northern Roman Judaea/Palestine', in G .C. Bottini, L. Di Segni and L. D. Chrupcała (eds.), *One Land, Many Cultures* (Jerusalem: Franciscan Printing Press), 5–32.

Arbel, Y., Forthcoming. "The Coins Minted at Gamla— A New Perspective". In D. Syon, *Gamla III: Finds and Studies. The Shmarya Gutmann Excavations, 1976–1989* (IAA Reports) (Jerusalem: Israel Antiquities Authority).

Barag, D., 1992–1993. 'New Evidence on the Foreign Policy of John Hyrcanus I', *INJ* 12, 1–12.

Barkay, R., 2003. *The Coinage of Nysa-Scythopolis (Beth-Shean)* (Corpus Nummorum Palestinensium V) (Jerusalem: Israel Numismatic Society).

Butcher, K., 1988. '*Roman Provincial Coins. An Introduction to the 'Greek Imperials'*' (London: Seaby).

Farhi, Y., 2006. 'The Bronze Coins Minted at Gamla Reconsidered', *INJ* 15, 69–76.

Freyne, S., 2000. 'Herodian Economics in Galilee', in S. Freyne, *Galilee and Gospel: Collected Essays* (Tübingen: Mohr Siebeck), 86–113.

Goodman, M., 1983. *State and Society in Roman Galilee, A.D.132–212* (New Jersey: Rowman and Allanheld).

Goodman, M., 1999. 'Galilean Judaism and Judaean Judaism', in W. Horbury, W. D. Davies and J. Sturdy (eds.) *The Cambridge History of Judaism, Vol 3: The Early Roman Period* (Cambridge: Cambridge University Press), 596–617.

Hendin, D., 2003–2006. '*A New Coin Type of Herod Antipas*', *INJ* 15, 56–61.

Horsley, R. A., 1995. 'Archaeology and the Villages of Upper Galilee: A Dialogue with Archaeologists', *BASOR* 297, 5–28.

Kadman, L., 1961. *The coins of 'Akko-Ptolemais* (Corpus Nummorum Palestinensium IV) (Jerusalem: Israel Numismatic Society).

Kushnir-Stein, A., 2002. 'The Coinage of Agrippa II', *Scripta Classica Israelica* 21, 123–131.

Kushnir-Stein, A., 2008. 'Reflection of Religious Sensitivities on Palestinian City Coinage', *INR* 3, 125–136.

Lapin, H., 2001. *Economy, Geography, and Provincial History in Later Roman Palestine* (Texts and Studies in Ancient Judaism 85) (Tübingen: Mohr Siebeck).

Meshorer, Y., 1976. 'A Hoard of Coins from Migdal', *'Atiqot* 11, 54–71.

Meshorer, Y., 1979. 'Sepphoris and Rome', in O. Mørkholm and N. Waggoner (eds.) *Greek Numismatics and Archaeology, Essays in Honor of Margaret Thompson* (Wetteren: Cultura), 159–171.

Meshorer, Y., 1985a. *City Coins of Eretz Israel and the Decapolis in the Roman Period* (Jerusalem: Israel Museum).

Meshorer, Y., 1985b. 'The Coins of Caesarea Paneas', *INJ* 8, 37–58.

Meyers, E. M., 1976. 'Galilean Regionalism as a Factor in Historical Reconstruction', *BASOR* 221, 93–101.

Meyers, E. M., 1985. 'Galilean Regionalism—a Reappraisal', in W. S. Green (ed.), *Approaches to Ancient Judaism* vol. V, *Studies in Judaism and its Greco-Roman Context* (Brown Judaic Studies 32) (Atlanta, Georgia: Scholars Press), 115–131.

Meyers, E. M., 1997. 'Jesus and His Galilean Context', in D. R. Edwards and C. T. McCollough (eds), *Archaeology and Galilee: Texts and Contexts in the Graeco-Roman and Byzantine Periods* (Atlanta, Georgia: Scholars Press), 57–66.

Safrai, Z., 1994. '*The Economy of Roman Palestine*' (London and New York: Routledge).

Smith, M., 1971. 'Zealots and Sicarii. Their Origins and Relations', *HTR* 64, 1–19.

*Spijkerman*, A., 1978. '*The Coins of the Decapolis and Provincia Arabia*', (Jerusalem: Franciscan Printing Press).

Syon, D., 2004. *Tyre and Gamla: a Study of the Monetary Influence of Southern Phoenicia on the Galilee and Golan in the Hellenistic and Roman Periods* (Unpublished Ph.D. Dissertation, the Hebrew University, Jerusalem).

Syon, D. 2007. 'Yet Again on the Bronze Coins Minted at Gamla', *INR* 2, 117–122.

Syon, D., Forthcoming. 'The Coins', in D. Syon, *Gamla III: Finds and Studies. The Shmarya Gutmann Excavations, 1976–1989* (IAA Reports) (Jerusalem: Israel Antiquities Authority).

# ON THE GRAPHICAL INTERPRETATION OF HEROD'S YEAR 3 COINS

## Robert Bracey

## 1. Introduction

The purpose of this paper is to argue that data from die studies can be interpreted visually, through the use of formally drawn diagrams (die charts). It will be argued that particular arrangements or patterns in the die charts correspond to physical realities in the original mints. In particular, it will be suggested that this inter-die analysis reveals information about the intensity of coin production. One pattern (**UG**; see n. 22) will be suggested as the distinctive pattern of a particularly intensive production. The context of this argument is the coinage of Herod the Great, one group of which exhibits this pattern. As the pattern seems to have been very rare in antiquity this has important implications for interpreting this early issue of Herod.

It will be necessary at some points to talk about the die studies examined in terms of statistics (meta-die analysis). This will be kept to a minimum but will involve some short-hand. Lower case letters are used to represent numbers that are known, so 'n' for the number of coins in a study, '$d_o$' and '$d_r$' for the number of obverse and reverse dies. Capital letters are used when a statistical estimate is made of the original sample of any figures, for example '$D_o$' for an estimate of the original number of obverse dies, as opposed to '$d_o$' for the number of dies identified in the study.

Herod's coinage is conventionally divided into two basic groups. One group has the inscription LΓ, year 3. The other group has no date. Within these groups the coinage can be further subdivided upon the basis of types, denomination and style. Ariel and Fontanille have recently completed a die study of most of these coins. They have generously shared the data they have collected with the present author, as well as their time and expertise.

A die study has the potential to reveal details of the physical production, but it cannot tell you why someone chose to engrave a particular device. The date, LΓ, isn't going to be explained by a die study because it isn't a feature of physical production. However, many interpretations of the coinage depend upon assumptions about physical production and the analysis of the die study. As an example, we can contrast two alternative views of Herod's year 3 coinage.

Meshorer argued against the notion that year three corresponded to 37 BCE, the year in which Herod captured Jerusalem. He raised two main objections.[1] The first was that 37 BCE is four years after 40 BCE, the year in which he became king of Judaea, not three years. The second argument was that it seemed implausible that Herod would not mint any coins during the three years in which he fought against Antigonus. Meshorer suggests instead that the date refers to Herod's third year as tetrarch of Galilee, 40 BCE, and remains immobilised on the coinage until 37 BCE. In connection with this, he argues that the coins were minted at Samaria until Herod captured Jerusalem, and points to both the numbers deposited there and the difference in style between the dated year 3 coins and the undated coins.

Fontanille and Ariel have proposed a different reconstruction.[2] They suggest that the coins were issued in Jerusalem in the year in which Herod captured it. As the start of years in the

---

[1] Meshorer 1982, 9-12.

[2] Fontanille and Ariel 2006, 75.

contemporary calendar does not coincide precisely with our modern calendar there is a four month period of year three (June to September 37 BCE) when Herod would have been in control of Jerusalem and able to mint the coins there. They argue: "Methodologically, without compelling evidence to the contrary, one must prefer the view that year-three on the dated coins refers to Herod's regnal era, and that the coins under discussion date to 38/7 BCE".[3]

Both positions make assumptions about production which can be tested. Most clearly is the intensity, or rate, of production. Approximately thirty obverse dies are used. Were they employed over three years with the date unchanging, or in just four months (replacing two dies a week)? Fontanille and Ariel felt a production this rapid to be a serious difficulty and mused "If the coins were minted in Jerusalem, minting could have taken place in only four months of year-three (June–September 37 BCE). The replacement frequencies for both a third of a year or even a full year is so high, as to argue for a continued minting of the coin as a *type immobilisé*."[4]

The use of die studies to establish the volume of production is well established, and so there is some comparative data. Fontanille and Ariel depend upon an analysis by Mørkholm but we also have two large collations by de Callataÿ of Hellenistic and Classical Greek studies. The calculations of the volume of dies used have several potential problems.[5]

Firstly, there is a long standing dispute over the validity of estimating production from die studies. The number of dies used for the original production is based on statistical estimates from the surviving coins. There are various approaches based on different assumptions and though there is broad agreement on the validity of these approaches the margins of error are large. However, no agreement exists on extrapolating from the number of dies to the number of coins originally produced. Buttrey has argued that the relationship is too variable and that dies could have made widely different numbers of coins.[6] If this is true, then the number of dies provides no guide to the absolute or relative number of coins that were produced. Buttrey is correct to criticize the common approach that assumes the number of coins is constant ($N = kD_o$, where $N$ is the number of coins and $D_o$ the original number of obverse dies). The number of coins produced by a single die is a function of various factors, most unknown, and not a constant.

But Buttrey overstates the case. That the factors are unknown does not make them unknowable, and he conflates not being able to measure the production from a single die with not being able to estimate the production from a group of dies. Where coinages are similar (period, types of design, metal, etc) it is reasonable to assume that the unknown factors are similar. So if one coinage employs twice as many dies as another from the same or a related series, it probably made twice as many coins. If we take the six example coinages given in Table 1 and divide the total volume of production across the time they were issued in the results vary enormously, between a die every three weeks and a die every two and half years. Though even the largest of these productions is still smaller, per year, than Herod's coinage would be if it were struck in just four months.

This brings us to the second problem. Meta-die analysis gives us total values for production, but it tells us nothing about the rate of production. A mint might stand idle for months at a time, or several obverse dies could be fixed into different anvils and hammered simultaneously. If we know, independently of each other, how many dies were used and how long they were used for rates can be calculated. But in this case we want to know the length of time over which the dies were used. To examine that issue we need to turn to inter-die analysis and particularly graphical interpretations.

---

[3] Ibid., 74.
[4] Ibid., 85.
[5] Mørkholm 1983; de Callataÿ 1997; idem 2003.
[6] Buttrey 1993; idem 1994.

Table 1: Comparison of die studies on bronze Hellenistic coinages

| Period | Do* | Workstations | Length** | Reference |
|---|---|---|---|---|
| Messina, Litrae SerieXVIII C.317-311 | 9.4 | 1 | 7 | Caltabiano, 1993 |
| Skostokos of Thrace, c.260-245, type 2 | 5.7 | 2 | 6 | Draganov, 1993 |
| Epirus, Group VII, 234-168 | 204.5 | 1/2 | 6 | Franke, 1961 |
| Valentia, Semis, c.192-89 | 55.8 | 1/2 | 7 | Mensitieri, 1989 |
| Morgantina, Group V HISPANORVM type, c.150-190 | 18.2 | 2 | 5 | Buttrey et al. 1989 |
| Aphrodisias, Julia Salonina, c.253-268 | 25.1 | 2 | 11 | MacDonald, 1992 |
| **Herod's Type 1** | 25 | 3 | 12 | |

\* $D_o$ is an extrapolation (using the method of Carter) of the number of obverse dies originally employed to make the coinage, based on the number of known dies and known coins.

\*\* Length is the smallest number of links necessary to connect any two dies in the chart. It is an indication of how much consecutive (rather than parallel) activity the die chart represents.

## 2. Inter-die Analysis and Graphical Interpretation

The use of charts to represent the relationship between dies is as old as die studies themselves. Although Imhoof-Bloomer did not employ them his contemporary Sylvester Sage Crosby did so and his diagrams are instantly recognisable. As die studies have become larger so the charts have become more complex. Many have descended into obscure masses of crossing lines. This is partly because die charts are seen as representational rather than analytic tools. It has not been fully recognized that confusion in charts reflects confusion in the analysis. So it has become common to arrange dies on criteria unrelated to the die study (such as style, typology, etc) which frequently renders quite simple minting procedures in unintelligible ways.

Malmer first drew attention to the interpretation of dies studies through charts when she distinguished 'compacted' and 'divided' chains'.[12] She went on to demonstrate how a

---

[7] This is one of two copper types, both similar in size but the type 1 appear to represent a single work-station arrangement. If both types were considered together it would be closer to twelve dies and an alternation between 1 and 2 workstations.

[8] There is some indication in the die groups around obverse dies 322 and 330 that two work-stations may have been used but the die groups are too small to give any reason to distinguish redundant dies from multiple work-stations.

[9] The majority of the Semis form chains, the most complex has two obverses, O2 and O3, sharing two reverse dies. This could be plausibly explained either as a redundant die or as two work-stations.

[10] Though the die groups are small O2 and O3 share three reverse dies in common, and an implausibly large number for successive production.

[11] De Callataÿ (1997) presents only a small number of types. Here we focus on the Julia Salonina types, O273 to O299 issued over no more than 15 years, $d_o$=27, $d_r$=45, n =164, Do= 25.1 (by the Carter method used for other coinages in de Callatay, 1997).

[12] Malmer 1993, 45

study of die charts can reveal important information. Esty has also examined the problem of die charts and has tried to develop methods for distinguishing different procedures, such as the die-box.[13]

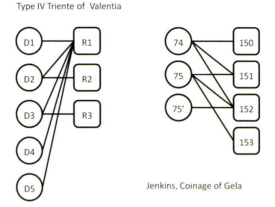

**Fig. 1:** Examples of charts

However, for this approach to work a certain formality is necessary, so I will begin by defining terms. A die chart is a representation of part or all of a die corpus in which each die appears as a node and every die combination as a line connecting exactly two nodes. Nodes can be any shape but are usually depicted as circles or squares. The most important feature is the one-to-one nature of the chart. Every node represents exactly one die in the corpus, every line exactly one die combination, and vice-versa. So chart 1 in **Fig. 1** is a die chart representing the triente of type IV minted in Valentia following the order presented by Mensitieri (1989).[14] Mensitieri's is one of about half a dozen Hellenistic copper die studies available for comparison.

While chart 2 in **Fig. 1**, based on Jenkins (1970) for a small part of the Gelan coinage,[15] is a perfectly reasonable depiction of the corpus **it is not** a die chart. For the reason that 75 and 75´ are in fact the same die slightly recut by the engravers. The importance of this formal distinction is that it ensures a fixed relationship between the die chart and the die corpus, which I will argue is important for analysis of the die charts.

---

[13] Esty 1990. Esty's article is essential reading on inter-die analysis, but was written at a time when computer tools were still too limited to deploy the theory. The theoretical outline is very similar to that shown here but as this was developed from Indian coinage (Bracey, 2009) there are differences in terminology. Esty's 'no lines crossing' is not the same as the 'planar/non-planar' distinction here. He uses 'discontinuous' for the term 'redundant' employed in this article. Here, 'discontinuous' here refers to a less intense mode of production than continuous. The most serious issue he raises is the impact that errors in the die charts might create, and he concludes "Chronological inferences from linkage alone require strong and often unverifiable hypothesis about mint operations. Additional information from sequence marks and observations of the die-states is important. In the absence of such information, the links themselves can provide only limited information about the mint operation" (Esty 1990, 221). This is a valid criticism, and it should be borne in mind how robust any results are to incorrect linkages. However, in many cases additional information is unavailable or not recorded and part of the case being developed here is that inter-die analysis does reveal valuable information about the organisation of mints.

[14] Mensitieri 1989.

[15] Jenkins 1970.

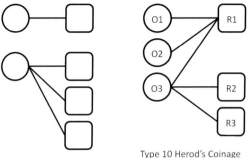

Fig. 2: Types of die charts

In all normal circumstances die charts will be two-colour; that means it is possible to colour each node using just two colours in such a way as to ensure that no die combination connects two nodes of the same colour. This is obvious in a sense, as die combinations are made between obverses and reverses, not between two obverses or two reverses, so the two 'colours' in this case are obverses and reverses.[16]

The dies in a chart need not be connected (see **Fig. 5** for an example) but often only one connected component of a chart is shown. There are only three different types of component that make up all die charts. The simplest component consists of just a single die combination and obverse and reverse, which are only known, paired. These singletons are not unusual in die studies but more common are cases where a single die is involved in several die combinations. When those dies it is connected to (the opposed dies) have no other die combinations the die is isolated, and both isolated obverses and isolated reverses are possible.

Isolated obverses are usually more common than isolated reverses because the obverse die is protected to a greater degree from the physical force of the blow that forms the coin. It is more likely to survive long enough to be paired with another reverse. Singletons and isolated dies tell us relatively little about production. More interesting are cases where many obverse and reverse dies are linked together, **a die group**. Die groups are sometimes referred to as die chains but I will reserve that term for a particular type of die group.

**Fig. 2** shows examples of a die combination, an isolated obverse, and a die group. The die group is taken from a later undated group of Herod's coinage (Ariel and Fontanille, 2012, Pl. 58). It will serve to illustrate an important point. In the figure above the sequence of the dies can be implied to run from top to bottom, the obverses and reverses breaking and being replaced (O1-O2-O3 and R1-R2-R3). However the same diagram could have been presented in a variety of ways, two of which are illustrated in **Fig. 3**. It shows how we can read left to right or obverses on the right.

---

[16] How to represent this distinction, to 'colour' obverses and reverses is an obvious issue. Colour can be used when it is available, but failing actual colour it has become normal practice to use different naming conventions for the obverse and reverse dies (for example letters and numbers, or as here prefix the dies O or R) and to give different shapes, in this case circles for obverses and squares for reverses.

Type 10 Alternative arrangements

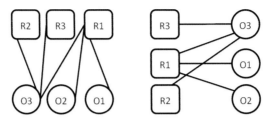

**Fig 3:** Alternative arrangements of charts

They also imply different orders of the dies. The second diagram in **Fig. 3** implies a slightly odd order. Obverse die O3 is employed first, then die O1. But O1 cannot have been introduced to replace O3 as according to the diagram O3 is employed again with R2 after O1 is used with R1. This seems rather unlikely when compared with the chain style diagram on the left or in diagram 2. It is a very simple illustration of how a diagram can give a sense of order and how some arrangements (the chain in this case) are visually more appealing and that visual appeal coincides with a more plausible interpretations.

In the limited theory on die studies it is generally assumed that die groups arranged in a chain resembling those in **Figs. 2** and **3** are the norm.[17] An obverse die is fixed into the mint's anvil, and a reverse die is employed with it. When the reverse die breaks it is replaced. When the obverse die breaks it is replaced. As long as a complete record of the original minting is preserved in extant coins a long continuous chain will be seen. Singletons and Isolated dies will occur only when the sample is incomplete or when by sheer chance both the obverse and reverses break simultaneously.

This is a simple notion but it is not what is actually found in die studies. Ancient mints seem to exhibit a much wider pattern. Chains are usually quite short; shorter than simultaneous cracking of two dies might imply, and frequently die charts cannot be arranged in a chain. So what does it mean when a die group cannot be arranged in such a way?

**Fig. 4** shows on the left a die group (the large bronzes of the Bar Kokhba revolt), arranged in the number order assigned to the dies by Mildenberg.[18] The order can be thought of in the same terms as the chains discussed above. However, this clearly isn't a chain, as chains do not have crossing lines. The mass of crossing lines are not just visually confusing they are a visual signal that there is something wrong in the reconstruction

In this case obverses O1 and O2 share in common three reverse dies (R2, R3, R4). It is therefore difficult to arrange them in rows or columns without at least some lines crossing. I won't try to demonstrate that, but it is easy to demonstrate that the diagram can be drawn in such a way the lines do not cross. One such arrangement is shown on the right in **Fig. 4**.

The reader will recall the insistence earlier on a very formal definition of the relationship between the die corpus and the die chart. This second diagram in **Fig. 4** has exactly the same dies and exactly the same die combinations represented as the first, which means it is essentially the same diagram. So any property possessed by this new diagram is possessed by all diagrams. One of these properties is planarity, the capacity to be drawn without crossing lines. So the first diagram, even though its lines crossed always had the potential to be drawn without crossing lines.

---

[17] Mørkholm 1991, ch. 2.   [18] Mildenberg 1984.

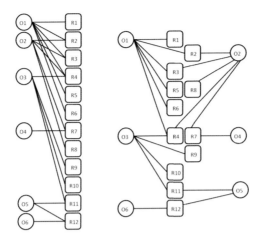

**Fig. 4:** Two versions of the same die chart

There is also our interpretation of the second diagram. The first diagram is difficult to interpret. The second is much simpler. Each column can be assumed to represent the consecutive replacements of one die by another. So O1 is replaced by O3, while O2 is replaced by O4. These obverse dies are used in parallel, each fixed in different anvils (or work-stations) while the workmen used a common set of reverse dies. As the central die pool consists of two reverse dies at any one time sometimes one die might be used with one obverse and sometimes another.

Re-arranging the chart began as an expedient, to avoid the crossing lines which made it difficult to interpret. But from the re-organisation we can draw an interpretation, that the mint employed two work-stations with a common die pool. Because the formal definition of the die chart insisted on what is true for this diagram is also true for the first diagram and true for the die corpus itself. So if this is a valid interpretation of this diagram it is a valid interpretation of both diagrams and of the corpus.

Such an interpretation has implications for the intensity of production. If the mint is employing two obverse dies simultaneously then it will exhaust them twice as fast. The suggestion that a die would have to be used every two weeks rested on the assumption that only one die were employed at a time. If two workstations were used each would need to be replaced every four weeks. This is still a rapid rate but it is now compatible with the most intense of the comparison productions in Table 1.

However, it is more complex than simply one of two workstations. **Fig. 5** shows the Vine Leaf/Palm Tree type coins of the Bar Kokhba regular Medium Bronze coinage as presented in Mildenburg.[19] This example was chosen because it makes a sharp contrast between the single die group involving obverses O1 to O3 (issued in years one and two) and the other dies O4 to O10 (issued in years two and three). Ten dies in three years is one every three and half months. However, the die chart is not composed of a chain. The first three dies form a chain. R7 and R9 are employed with both O1 and O2 which means both reverse dies were used together. This implies more than one work-station but could be explained if a 'redundant'

---

[19] The charts presented in Mildenberg do not qualify for the formal definition given above, so have been slightly modified and the order of dies 7 and 8 altered to reflect more reasonable positions. This is a copper coinage, from the same period and the same part of the world. However, as Mildenburg (1984, 60) points out, this is an ad-hoc mint during a war and so not a good comparison for the regular mint(s) of Herod.

die were employed, and at any one time only one of the two available reverse was used. The other seven dies have no linkages at all. One explanation is that the corpus is less complete for dies O4 to O10, if we had more examples of the coins then a chain would appear. In this particular case that looks implausible, as Mildenburg's study has a better sample (higher n/d) for the later dies than for the earlier ones.[20]

We are obliged to consider that there are no linkages between obverse dies in the corpus because there never were any die links. This is a pattern of production that is not uncommonly seen in die studies from the ancient world, and often with sufficiently large samples to indicate it is a reality, not just a feature of the surviving material. I will term this pattern discontinuous. A discontinuous chart implies that production was interrupted. Not just short breaks but longer more deliberate halts in production. Obviously this doesn't apply to Herod's year 3 coinage but it does have implications for the comparison with other coinages. If coinages are made in a discontinuous manner normally, a mint could greatly increase its production (and thus its use of obverse dies) simply by striking continuously. In other words the sample on which the notion of three to five months per die is based probably includes a number of mints which spent long periods of time not making coins.

I have tried to establish two general points. The first is that through die charts we can detect elements of the physical organisation of the mint, the order in which dies are struck, the number of work-stations at which obverses were used simultaneously, and how many reverses were available for use at any one time. The second, based on two roughly contemporary examples, is that the rate of production at ancient mints varied. Before looking specifically at the interpretation of Herod's coins I want to examine, theoretically, one more case – what if a mint used three work stations to produce its coinage?

As we have seen there are distinctions to be made, in ascending order of intensity, between discontinuous, single work-station, and two work station systems of production, and that these different systems are visually distinct patterns in a die chart. Dies could last many months or be used in a few weeks and this variation depended on procedures not on the volume struck.[21]

The question arises, what pattern would be distinctive of a mint that had three work-stations. An imaginary mint has three obverse dies, A B and C, fixed in separate anvils. This imaginary mint has three reverse dies (1, 2 and 3) in a common die pool. At the start of each work period the reverses are randomly assigned to a work-station. If this process is repeated indefinitely eventually all three reverses will have been paired with each of the obverse dies, and the resulting die combinations are shown in **Fig. 6**.

Diagram 6 has a special feature, it is non-planar. As explained earlier all the diagrams up to two work stations are planar, they can be drawn in such a way that no lines cross. The diagram in **Fig. 6** is special because it cannot be drawn without the lines crossing, and it has a special name, UG. UG is important because it is one of the fundamental building blocks from which all non-planar charts are built, and is known conventionally as UG[22]

---

[20] It is important that the sample has a higher ratio of known examples to dies, rather than simply being larger.
[21] The distinction between volume and rate is important. It is very unlikely that mints produced coins non-stop. They could have been idle for months or years and so the volume of production does not need to be related to the intensity when production was actually taking place.
[22] UG stands for 'Utility Graph' and draws its name from an old logic puzzle about connecting water, gas, and electricity to a row of houses. All non-planar graphs are extensions and super-graphs of UG or $K_5$ (the graph of five nodes all connected), every one. $K_5$ is a mono-coloured graph and, as discussed above, die charts are two-coloured so there is no obvious physical reality to $K_5$. For this reason only UG interests us here. The manner in which the material is presented here is intuitive but those interested will find formal accounts in any basic text on Graph Theory.

# ON THE GRAPHICAL INTERPRETATION OF HEROD'S YEAR 3 COINS 73

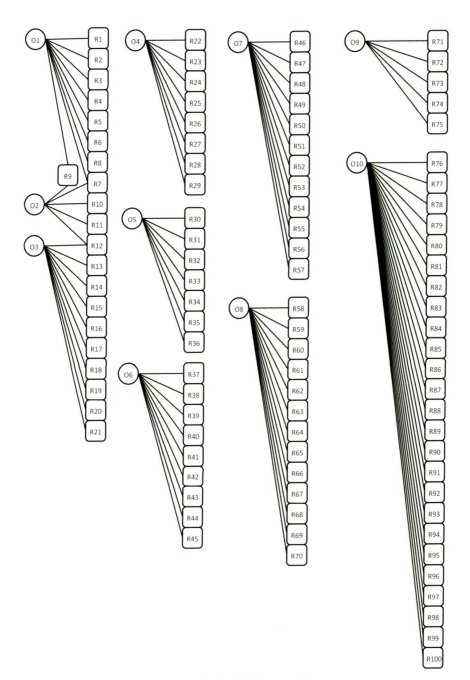

**Fig. 5:** Vine leaf / Palm tree dies

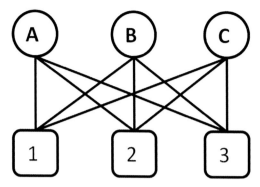

**Fig. 6:** The Utility Graph (UG)

This gives an important distinction between three or more work stations and all simpler arrangements. Assuming that our sample is close to complete, and that reverse dies survived long enough to be paired with all or most of the mint's obverse dies then the die chart will contain within it UG. This gives a test for complex minting. If a chart is non-planar (if it cannot be drawn without lines crossing) then it must contain UG, and therefore the original mint must have employed at least three work-stations.

## 3. Herod's Type 1 Coins

We can now return to Herod's coinage. In 2009 Ariel lectured on problems surrounding the interpretation of the dated coins featuring a helmet or *pileus* on a couch (see *RPC* I, p. 678) and a tripod, his type 1; see **Fig. 7**.[23] These coins showed a very complex series of die connections for which there was no obvious explanation. Non-planar charts are very unusual and this seemed a likely candidate. Ariel offered to share the data on this chart to examine the possibility.

**Fig. 7:** A composite image of one die combination of Herod's largest coin (RPC I, no. 4901)

After making several attempts to re-arrange the chart as single or two work-station arrangements.[24] It became necessary to demonstrate that the die chart contained UG and was non-planar, which would confirm the suspicion that Herod's used three work-stations.

---

23 Ariel, forthcoming.
24 This is always the first step in any interpretation of a die chart, beginning from the simplest possible arrangement and attempting to fit the chart to that, only increasing the complexity as necessary. The principle, known as parsimony or Occam's razor, underpins inter-die analysis.

**Fig. 8** shows only a part of the chart. It is this section, around O7 and O12 which is of interest, which it proved impossible to arrange the chart without crossing lines. So it was here that it made sense to search for UG.

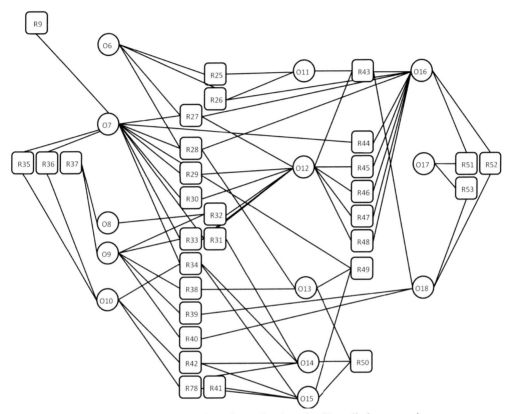

**Fig. 8:** The central section of the die chart for Herod's largest coin

It helps to simplify the chart in order to see more clearly the possible connections. There are two sorts of simplifications that can be made. The first is to remove dies which are not relevant. Any die with only a single connection, such as R9 in the top left can be eliminated and where dies connect exactly to the same complementary dies (such as R35 and R36) one can be removed. The second simplification is to eliminate dies that act only to connect two dies while retaining the connection (remember every die in UG has three connections so dies with only two connections are not part of our solution). R36 is such a die. In **Fig. 9** you can see these simple changes – elimination of R9 and R35 (with their accompanying connections) and the removal of R36 to leave a simple connection between O7 and O10.

**Fig. 10** shows these processes repeated throughout the chart. The result is much simpler and, though it is not the same chart as that in **Fig. 8**, the important point is that if we find UG in this simplified chart it must also be present in the original chart.

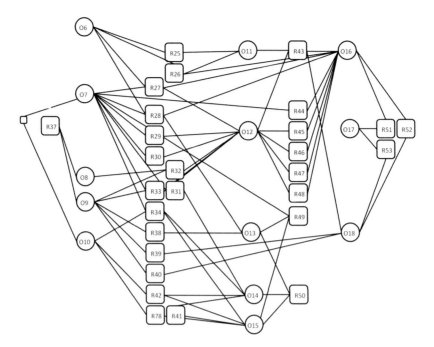

**Fig. 9:** The chart in **Fig. 8** after the first stage of simplification

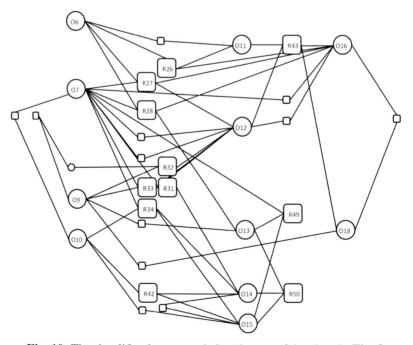

**Fig. 10:** The simplifications extended to the rest of the chart in **Fig. 8**

The simplest way to check if this simplified version is non-planar is now simply to look for examples. Let us first look to see if there are two obverses with at least three reverses in common. In fact there is more than one such pair. For example O7 and O12 share three reverses in common (R27, 31 and 33) and a lot of pairs have two reverses in common. I chose to start with O6 and O16. The connections between these two obverse dies are indicated in **Fig. 11**.

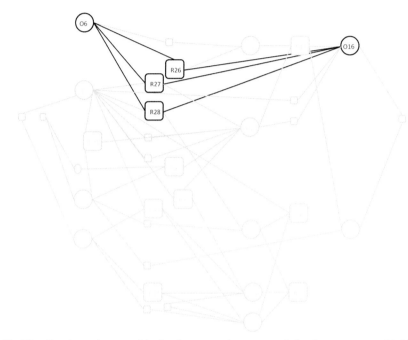

**Fig. 11:** The die chart shown with the first two obverses and the three reverses highlighted

There is no third obverse die which shares a die combination with all of R26, 27 and 28. However, the connection need not be direct. O7 is a likely candidate as it has a die combination with two of the reverses we are interested in. It also has an indirect connection through O12, R43, and O11 to the third reverse. This arrangement is shown in **Fig. 12**. If we imagine repeating the processes of simplification used to reach our present chart it can be seen that this group contains UG. All of the dies and die combinations not involved can simply be eliminated. Then the three connecting dies removed while the link is retained, connecting O7 and R26. It does not matter how long or complex this route is because it can always be simplified until we have demonstrated that the chart contains within it UG.

A partially simplified chart is shown in **Fig. 13** from which the presence of UG should be obvious. One problem, raised by Esty is that an error in the chart might create a false impression.[25] If, for example, the die combination of O16 and R27 were a mistake (a mistake in the die identification, or in the corpus, or in the drawing of the chart) and did not actually exist, this would render the conclusion invalid.

---

[25] Esty 1990.

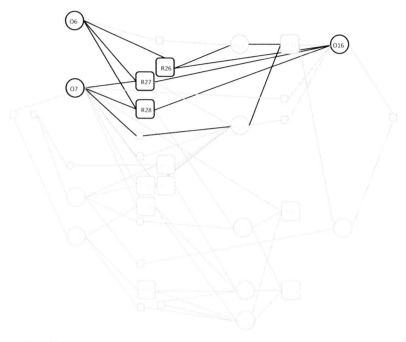

**Fig. 12:** The die chart shown with a section exhibiting UG highlighted

Before the use of computers drawing and redrawing diagrams by hand was almost certain to result in errors for complex charts. And though the charts themselves are manipulated by computer there is still a risk of errors. Several such errors were identified while this paper was being written and necessitated the redrawing of the diagrams in **Figs 8-13**. However, the chart is quite robust: examples of UG can be found in multiple ways and multiple errors would be necessary to invalidate the conclusion drawn above.

Only one aspect of the inter-die analysis has been explored here. Once it is established that three work-stations operated at the same time it is possible to establish the relationship between other dies using the same forms of analysis. For example O12 and O16 which share five reverse dies in common are arranged in the chart above (see figure 8) as if they were employed simultaneously at two different work stations. This is dictated by the connections between the two. The mint has no need to employ more than three reverse dies at a time (though it clearly employs does) and the odds of five dies surviving long enough to be used with consecutive obverses are slim. A series of such formal and intuitive leaps aided the reconstruction of the whole chart. Though only the remarkable intensity of production in the use of three work-stations really is of current interest.

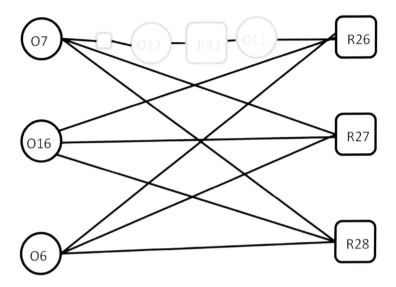

**Fig. 13:** The pattern of UG within the die chart

## 4. Implications

This production has clear implications. However, the die analysis cannot be followed blindly. It is worth stating that the pattern which emerges from the dies provides sensible fits with the pattern that emerges from variations in styles and types. If the inter-die analysis were to disagree or produce an incoherent pattern we would have to ask which one to trust.

Herod's type 1 coins begin at two distinct work-stations with a common pool of reverse dies. This initial production transforms into three work-stations. The majority of the dies are employed during this period of three work-stations before the third work-station falls out of use. This means that, though 25 (known) obverse dies are employed, work-stations A and B only employ 11 dies each over the course of production. This deduction follows from the present construction, which is inevitably provisional; the exact number of dies on A or B could be shifted up or down slightly without any violence to the reconstruction as the die linkage provides only a guide not an absolute reconstruction.

The size of the die-chart can be expressed more formally than simply counting the number of dies subjectively allocated to each work-station. The 'length' of a die chart can be expressed as the smallest number of links necessary to connect any two dies in the chart. So, on the chart shown in **Fig. 8** dies O6 and O15 are four connections apart, through R28, O15, and R50. However, **Fig. 8** is only part of a larger chart. The initial stages and the final stages of production, which can be explained by a simple two work-station model, are not shown. If those are included then it takes at least twelve steps to connect the furthest points in the diagram. So the length of whole chart is 12. In a conventional single work-station example this would equate to just seven dies.

When Fontanille and Ariel first examined the coinage they felt that explaining thirty dies in a short period of time required the dies to be used too quickly. However, this was based on an assumption that the dies were used one at a time. The previous analysis shows this was not the case. As many as three dies were used in parallel and would have taken no longer to exhaust than between 7 and 12 dies employed consecutively. If, as Fontanille and Ariel suggested, there were four months available between Herod's capture of Jerusalem and the end of year 3 each die would have lasted more than a week but not quite as long as two.[26]

This is still a more rapid use of dies than any of the examples in Appendix 1 but it is no longer an implausible rate. A minting across a long period of time, such as several years with an unchanging date would require dies to remain in use for months at a time. This is not impossible but it would seem implausible. Such lengths are achieved by not using the dies for part of the period, and if that were the case why not simply use a single work-station.

As far as the author is aware, three work-stations for copper coinage is unique for a Hellenistic coinage.[27] It would be surprising if such an arrangement did not reflect an exceptional intensity of production.[28]

## 5. Conclusion

The purpose of this paper was to outline a particular approach to the problem of interpreting the relationships between dies in a die-study, the inter-die analysis. It was argued from this that a particular pattern should be identified with the use of three work-stations and with periods of intense production at a mint. This is particularly relevant to the coinage of Herod the Great. Herod's coinage dated in the year 3 is the first issued in his reign and it has been disputed when and where it was issued. Herod's year 3 coinage shows the distinctive pattern of three work-stations. If this is unusual is hard to assess but the present author has not previously seen a bronze example of three work-stations. In any case it was unusual at Herod's mint, indicating a need for intense production with the "year 3" coins.

That intense production indicates that the coins were produced over a short space of time, and with an awareness from the start that rapid production was required. That cannot tell us where the coins were minted but it is compatible with the notion of a rapid issue following the capture of Jerusalem in 37 BC and contrary to expectations for a long period of immobilized designs.

## Appendix 1: How rare is three work-stations?

Herod's mint employed at least three distinct work-stations to produce its own coinage. 'At least' because several denominations are made and the inter-die date cannot tell us if they were produced consecutively or simultaneously. The implications of that for the dating of Herod's coinage have already been discussed. Related to that and a natural question to ask in its own right is just how rare was it for a mint to employ such an intense production.

---

[26] It might reasonably be asked why I am depending upon the obverse count rather than the reverse count. Given the enormous variation in $D_r/D_o$ ratios in ancient coinage it is clear that both cannot be reliable guides (it is possible neither is a reliable guide) to the level of production. I am inclined to think the obverse die, $D_o$ is a better guide, though without any research on the subject this is only a personal inclination.

[27] In fact this is only the second case of three work-stations the author is aware of in any metal. Single or two work-station models are the norm for almost all ancient coinages which have been subject to dies studies. The one possible exception is the argument by Carter (1981) that the enormous production of the Roman mint under the moneyer Crepusius employed 15 work-stations (anvils in his terminology). However, the method of calculation is different there and the data is still unpublished so cannot be tested by inter-die analysis. This might as suggested in the Appendix be the result of a selection bias in studies towards simpler, less complex coinage, but given the number of die studies undertaken on ancient coinages running close to or above 100 it is not a completely convincing explanation.

[28] The author was made aware of another copper die study (Faucher and Shahin 2006), on dated coins, which supports the possibility of a rapid turn-over in copper dies too late to incorporate in the article.

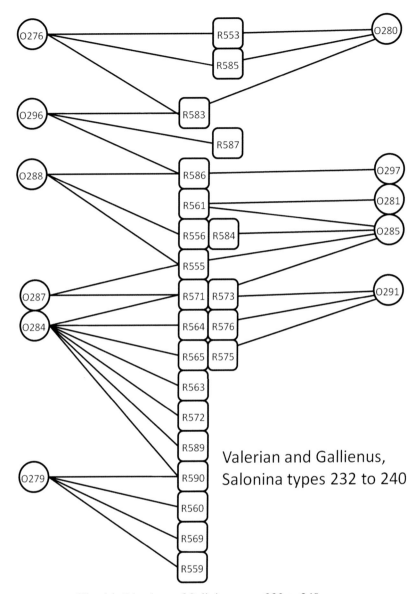

**Fig. 14:** Die chart of Salinina types 232 to 240

This question can be partly answered in regard to Herod's own reign. Only one of the types of Herod's coinage has not been the subject of a die study. Of those other types none show any signs that they were produced at three works stations, though several were made at two. One group remains unstudied, and this type is the most numerous of the coins found in archaeological contexts. It is impossible to say if that group used three work-stations or not.

Copper and bronze coinages are less likely to be the subject of die studies as the samples are usually poor due to lack of publication and the coins are often in bad condition. One comparison is with the copper coinage of the Bar Kochba revolt, already noted, and it frequently employs a pattern indicating a lack of intensity of production with its most intense periods representing only two work-stations. However, there is a difference between the official mint of a Roman client king and the temporary mint of a rebel army.

The other obvious comparisons are with Hellenistic mints, the minting tradition within which Herod operated. There are a number of these listed in de Callataÿ, which also summarises n/d (number of known coins divided by the number of know dies) values for coins. Studies with low n/d values are of no use as the full range of links will not be represented. In addition the die study has to be complete, for example Holloway does not include reverse die identifications for the bronze and so die charts cannot be reconstructed.[29] In some cases there simply weren't enough dies employed originally. For example at Morgantina one type of the HISPANORVM coins has been studied from 244 specimens, but every example is from the same obverse die.[30]

Once our various criteria, good sample numbers, large production, complete study, are considered together, only a handful of studies are left (some key statistics being given in Table 1). In fact these are generally particularly well represented coinages within larger studies.

Of these none show any signs of three work-stations. Most can be explained by a single work-station throughout, with occasional glimpses of two work-station or redundant die systems at some mints. The most complex is the coinage of Aphrodisias issued in the name of Julia Salonina, but even this can be explained easily by two work-stations with a common die-pool. **Fig. 14** shows the most complex die group in that coinage, which is also the largest die group in any of the studies. Its relative simplicity compared to the Herod type 1 coinage is obvious.

Just six coinages are hardly much on which to base a judgement. Due to the difficulty of undertaking die studies in general, and those on base metal coinages in particular, it is likely that most studies focus on the smallest, least intense productions. Perhaps three (or even more) work-stations are normal at large mints or those operating under time constraints. It was not normal at the mints mentioned, and little more than that can be said.

## Bibliography

Ariel, D. T., forthcoming. 'Lessons from a (Bronze) Die Study', *Proceedings of XIV International Numismatic Congress*, Glasgow, 2009.

Ariel, D. T., and Fontanille, J. P., 2012. *The Coins of Herod: a Modern Analysis and Die Classification* (Leiden / Boston: Brill).

Buttrey, T. V., 1993. 'Calculating Ancient Coin Production: Facts and Fantasies', *NC* 153, 335-352.

Buttrey, T. V,. 1994. 'Calculating Ancient Coin Production: Why it Cannot be Done', *NC* 154, 341-352.

Buttrey, T. V., Erim, K. T., Groves, T. D. and Holloway, R. R., 1989. *Morgantina Studies, Vol. II: The Coins* (Princeton: Princeton University Press).

de Callataÿ, F., 1997. *Recueil quantitatif des émissions monétaires hellénistiques* (Wetteren: Editions Numismatique romaine).

de Callataÿ, F., 2003. *Recueil quantitatif des émissions monétaires archaïques et classiques* (Wetteren: Editions Numismatique romaine).

Carter, G. F., 1981. 'Die-Link Statistics for Crepusius Denarii', in C. Carcassonne. and T. Hackens (eds.) *PACT 5: Statistics and Numismatics* (Strasbourg: Council of Europe).

---

29  Holloway 1969.   30  Buttrey, 1989, 57.

Caltabiano, M. C., 1993. 'La Monetazione di Messana' (Berlin: Walter de Gruyter).

Draganov, D., 1993. *The Coinage of Cabyle* (Sophia: Dios).

Esty, W. W., 1990. 'The Theory of Linkage', *NC* 150, 205-223.

Faucher, T., and Shahin, M., *2006*. 'Le Trésor de Gézéïr (Lac Mariout, Alexandrie)', *RN* 162, 135–157.

Fontanille, J. P., and Ariel, D. T., 2006. 'The Large Dated Coin of Herod the Great: The First Die Series', *INR* 1, 73-86.

Franke, P. R., 1961. *Die Antiken Münzen von Epirus* (Wiesbaden: Franz Steiner).

Holloway, R. R., 1963. *The Thirteen-Months Coinage of Hieronymos of Syracuse* (Berlin: Walter de Gruyter).

Jenkins, G. K., 1970. *The Coinage of Gela* (Berlin: Walter de Gruyter).

MacDonald, D., 1992. *The Coinage of Aphrodisias*, RNS Special Publication No.23 (London: Royal Numismatic Society).

Malmer, B., 1997. *The Anglo-Scandinavian Coinage c.995-1020* (Stockholm: Royal Swedish Academy of Letters).

Mensitieri, M. T., 1989. *La Monetazione di Valentia* (Rome: Istituto Italiano di Numismatica).

Meshorer, Y., 1982. *Ancient Jewish Coinage. Vol 2: Herod the Great through Bar-Cochba* (New York: Amphora).

Mildenburg, L., 1984. *The Coinage of the Bar Kochba War* (Typos 6), (Aarau: Verlag Sauerländer).

Mørkholm, O., 1991. *Early Hellenistic Coinage from the Accession of Alexander to the Peace of Apamea (336-186 BC)* (Cambridge: Cambridge University Press).

Mørkholm, O., 1983. 'The Life of Obverse Dies in the Hellenistic Period', in C. N. L. Brooke, B. H. I. H. Steward, J. G. Pollard and R. Volk, *Studies in Numismatic Method Presented to Philip Grierson* (Cambridge: Cambridge University Press)

# THE PREFECTS OF JUDAEA 6-48 CE AND THE COINS FROM THE MISTY PERIOD 6-36 CE

## Nikos Kokkinos

### Introduction

From the conquest of Jerusalem by Pompey in 63 BCE to that by Titus in 70 CE, Judaea, even though not directly annexed to the Roman province of Syria, was nevertheless subject to the supervision of the Syrian governor.[1] Under the Hasmonaean Hyrcanus II (63-40 BCE), who was reinstalled by Pompey to the position of the high priest and was permitted to lead the nation but without royal title (Jos., *Ant*. 20.244: πάλιν τὴν ἀρχιερωσύνην ἀποδοὺς τὴν μὲν τοῦ ἔθνους προστασίαν ἐπέτρεψεν, διάδημα δὲ φορεῖν ἐκώλυσεν), Judaea became tributary to Rome (Jos., *War* 1.154; *Ant*. 14.74). The reforms of Aulus Gabinius in ca. 57 BCE led to the complete abolition of the monarchy (Jos., *War* 1.170; *Ant*. 14.91). At this point Hyrcanus II was restricted to the care of the Temple (Jos., *War* 1.169: τὴν τοῦ ἱεροῦ παραδοὺς κηδεμονίαν αὐτῷ; *Ant*. 14.90: σχήσοντα τὴν τοῦ ἱεροῦ ἐπιμέλειαν), while an aristocracy, spread between five councils, but no doubt headed by the Herodian Antipater based in Jerusalem, managed the running of the state (Jos., *War* 1.169: καθίστατο τὴν ἄλλην πολιτείαν ἐπὶ προστασίᾳ τῶν ἀρίστων; *Ant*. 14.91: ἐν ἀριστοκρατίᾳ διῆγον). Nevertheless, under Herod the Great (40/37-4 [or 5] BCE) Judaea reverted to monarchical rule, now as an enlarged kingdom and client to Rome, and by 30 BCE it seems that it also went tax free.[2]

The death of Herod saw the partition of his kingdom among his sons, with Archelaus becoming an 'ethnarch' of Judaea, Idumaea and Samaria. It was on his banishment in 6 CE, that his realm for the first time came under direct Roman control, governed from then to the First Jewish Revolt (with the exception of the short period 41-44 CE when Herod's grandson Agrippa I became king) by officers of equestrian rank, who were subordinate to the senatorial *legati Augusti pro praetore* of Syria.[3] These officers ran the state with the help of a local aristocracy, headed by remnant members of the Herodian dynasty, while the protection of the Jewish culture and religion was put in the hands of high priests (Jos., *Ant*. 20.251: ἀριστοκρατία μὲν ἦν ἡ πολιτεία, τὴν δὲ προστασίαν τοῦ ἔθνους οἱ ἀρχιερεῖς).[4] The equestrian governors before and shortly after Agrippa I, were called officially *praefecti* (a title stressing the military character of the post, equivalent to the Greek *eparchos*, that is one in charge of an eparchy or province), whereas those from then to the First Jewish Revolt, were called *procuratores* (a title stressing the financial character of the post, equivalent to the Greek *epitropos*, that is one in charge of the administration).[5] It should also be mentioned that after

---

[1] The same may be said to have been the case since Scaurus arrived at Syria in 65 BCE, during the time of the war between the two Hasmonaean brothers, Aristobulus II and Hyrcanus II (*SVM*, 243; *KHD*, 97-98).

[2] As to whether Herod paid taxes, scholarly opinion is divided (see discussion in Kokkinos 1998, 127, n. 21). From the evidence at our disposal it seems that he did pay at least for Idumaea and Samaria, and at least until the fall of Marcus Antonius (App., *BC* 5.75/319).

[3] This may also be gathered from Josephus' reference to Coponius as of τάγματος τῶν ἱππέων (*Ant*. 18.2),

and to Marullus as ἱππάρχης (*Ant*. 18.237) – for both see Appendix 1. Cotton (1999) questions the general understanding of the status of Judaea, believing that it became an independent province only in 44 CE, but her arguments are not decisive, besides running against the fact of the issuing of coinage (and her paper unfortunately suffers from several inaccuracies which have been missed in the editing process); cf. Eck 2007, 23-51.

[4] It is a myth that Judaea during this time was led solely by a priestly class, see *KHD*, 193-96.

[5] Jones 1960; *SVM*, 1973, 358; see Appendix 1.

70 CE Judaea was promoted to a public province, governed by the commander of a legion (*legatus legionis X Fretensis*), who was of praetorian rank. Syrian supervision thus became redundant. But it was only in the 120s CE, when a second legion (*legio VI Ferrata*) was added to the province, renamed Syria Palaestina, that the governor became one of consular rank equalling the one in Syria.[6]

It is not clear whether the change of title for equestrian governors under Claudius (in the case of Judaea arguably after 48 CE, when the appointment as 'prefect' of Ti. Iulius Alexander was terminated, and before or by 52 CE, when the appointment of Ti. Claudius Felix as 'procurator' began),[7] meant more than an administrative adjustment, since provincial procurators continued to be equestrian officers, combining military, juridical and financial powers.[8] The new title may or may not imply a greater focus on the economy of the equestrian provinces under Claudius, perhaps reflected in the enhancement of power for freedmen in charge of imperial properties, as we know from Tacitus (*Ann.* 12.60: *cum Claudius libertos quos rei familiari praefecerat sibique et legibus adaequaverit*).[9] Felix was an imperial freedman who conceivably had entered the equestrian *cursus* (cf. Tac. *Hist.* 5.9), before he was promoted to govern a province.[10]

Suetonius (*Claud.* 28) says that 'he had been given the command of infantry and cavalry regiments and of the province of Judaea' (*cohortibus et alis provinciaeque Iudaeae praeposuit*).[11] It would then make sense if Felix – originally in the staff of the Emperor, possibly as *a rationibus* (*CIL* 6.8413) – advanced to an equestrian position of *praefectus cohortis peditata*, followed by that of *praefectus alae*, ultimately becoming *procurator provinciae Iudaeae*. The military positions (which would represent an early version of the equestrian *tres militiae*, minus the position of *tribunus militum*), would have been taken by Felix among the Samaritan troops partly under Ventidius Cumanus – thus the confusion of Tacitus, *Ann.* 12.54. This will explain not only how Felix was known in Judaea 'for many years' (Acts 24.10), but also why Jonathan the high priest requested Claudius to dispatch Felix as procurator of Judaea (Jos., *Ant.* 20.162). It is understood that the ex-royal Samaritan troops, the main body of the Roman army in Judaea under the prefects and procurators, were divided into one cavalry and five infantry regiments of 500 men each (Jos., *War* 2.52 = *Ant.* 17.266; cf. *Ant.* 19.365; *War* 2.236 = *Ant.* 20.122; *War* 3.66).[12] Between his military appointments and his senior procuratorship, Felix would have returned to Rome (from where he was dispatched

---

[6] Millar 1993, 107-08; 374-386.

[7] See Kokkinos 1990, based on the Bir el Malik inscription, from which it is argued that the correct *gentilicium* of Felix should be 'Claudius', and which now seems increasingly accepted (e.g. Bruun 1990, 281; Rajak 1996; Bennett 2003, 316, n. 4; Weaver 2004, 202; *idem* 2005, 244, n. 16; 248, n. 47). For an article attempting to throw doubt for the doubt's sake, and the purpose of which is difficult to comprehend, see Brenk and Canali De Rossi 2001 – the reason it is cited here is that it says to have received advice from Werner Eck and Joseph Sievers. For the date Felix was appointed governor, see *KHD*, 319, n. 186; 385-86; for his background, also see Kokkinos 2002, 31-32.

[8] Josephus (*Ant.* 2.117 – see Appendix 1 under Coponius) testifies that governors received authority of life and death. According to Brunt (1983, 55-58), their capital jurisdiction (i.e. by possessing the *ius gladii*) would have been over *peregrini*, not Roman citizens. But according to Jones (1972, 103-104), execution of *peregrini* would hardly have needed special power, and the reference may be to Roman troops under their command in Judaea; for example, see Cumanus beheading a soldier (Jos., *Ant.* 20.117).

[9] Cf. the discussion of Millar 1964; *idem* 1965.

[10] Weaver 1965, 466; Kokkinos 1990, 137, n. 74; *contra* Demougin 1988, 652. Bruun (1990, 282) states that the promotion of an imperial freedman to equestrian status, "presupposes the gift by the Emperor of the *ius aureorum anulorum* (which was an indication of fictive free birth by *restitutio natalium*)".

[11] Saddington (1980, 24) took this as a single appointment, believing that Felix would have gained a *praefectura leuis armaturae*, a "command of all military forces in a region where no legion was stationed, usually as part of the functions of a 'governor'." But Felix seems to have progressed from Samaria to Judaea as explained below (and reconsidered since by Saddington 1992).

[12] Speidel 1982/3; see Kokkinos 1990, 129-30 for discussion and earlier bibliography.

to become provincial governor) likely to hold a junior procuratorship (as in later practice), and possibly that of *procurator aquarum*.[13]

## The Prefects in Josephus

The prefectural (as against the procuratorial) period of Judaea, which lasted from 6 CE to arguably at least 48 CE, saw the official appointment of nine individuals, of whom one was a temporary placement. The Jewish historian Josephus provides us with parts of their *tria nomina*:

1. [X] Coponius [X],
2. Marcus Ambivius [X],[14]
3. [X] Annius Rufus,
4. [X] Valerius Gratus,
5. [X] Pontius Pilatus,
6. [X] [X] Marcellus,
7. [X] [X] Marullus,[15]
8. [X] Cuspius Fadus
9. Tiberius [Iulius] Alexander

With the exception of the latter, a renegade Jew belonging to a famous Alexandrian family (son of Alexander the alabarch and nephew of Philo the philosopher),[16] little or nothing is known about the background of these people. Whatever can be put together, or be guessed at, for the first eight prefects, is given briefly in Appendix 2. What is more important for our purpose here, in view of the surviving coinage, is to recognise that Josephus also provides us with scraps of evidence for working out approximately their chronology while paying attention to Roman history.[17] Archelaus the son of Herod the Great was banished in 6 CE, "in the consulship of Aemilius Lepidus and Lucius Arruntius" according to Dio (55.27.6; cf. 55.25.1). Josephus (*Ant.* 18.26) says that the census undertaken by the legate of Syria, P. Sulpicius Quirinius, which followed the annexation of Archelaus' kingdom (Judaea, Idumaea and Samaria), took place in "Year 37" of the Actian Era – or in other words sometime between September 6 CE and September 7 CE. It is thus clear that the first year of Coponius, who came to Judaea together with Quirinius (Jos., *Ant.* 18.2), must be 6/7 CE.[18] If we allocate a three year tenure to his governorship, which seems to have been normal under Augustus, Coponius would have spent in Judaea 6/7, 7/8, and 8/9 CE, while the next prefect Marcus Ambivius 9/10, 10/11 and 11/12 CE. Josephus (*Ant.* 18.31) tells us that under Ambivius, Salome I the sister of Herod the Great died, and so we may guess that this happened around

---

[13] For potential evidence, see Kokkinos 1990, 138.
[14] The MSS have 'Ambibouchus' ('Αμβιβούχος), commonly corrected to Ambibulus (as the *cognomen*), but according to Syme (1986, 275-76) it should be taken as the *nomen* Ambivius – see Appendix 2.
[15] The name is read as 'Μάριλλος' in the Codex Marcianus (13th century), possibly due to Greek pronounciation of Latin 'u' as 'y' (sounding 'i' when not in a diphthong), and so Maryllus or Marillos instead of Marullus.
[16] *PIR*² I 139; *KHD*, 198-99; 393-94.
[17] Josephus' knowledge of the prefectural period is meagre. For example, for the longest governorship of Valerius Gratus (15-26 CE), he knows only about the succession of four high priests – bare information obtained probably from a priestly list. Josephus' scanty sources post-Nicolaus of Damascus is a problem (see discussion in *KHD*, 193-96; Kokkinos 2008, 243-44).
[18] The last year of Archelaus would be Tishri 5 CE to Tishri 6 CE (*KHD*, 228, n. 83; but the suggestion there that the prefectural coins are reckoned by the Actian Era needs now to be revised – see below).

10 CE. Following on, Annius Rufus would have to be allocated years 12/13, 13/14, 14/15 CE, and this does prove accurate since Josephus (*Ant.* 18.32) informs us that during Rufus' governorship Augustus died (14 CE).

So far so good. Now, according to Josephus (*Ant.* 18.177), during the "22 years" of the reign of Tiberius (19 August 14 CE to 16 March 37 CE),[19] only "two governors" were appointed: Valerius Gratus and Pontius Pilatus. More specifically, it is said that the first ruled for "11 years" (*Ant.* 18.35) and the second for "10 years" (*Ant.* 18.89). In such a tight framework, there is hardly any scope for argument.[20] After Rufus, Gratus must therefore be allocated every year from 15/16 to 25/26 CE and Pilatus from 26/27 to 35/36 CE. As Josephus (*Ant.* 18.170, 172-6) explains, the lengthy governorships under Tiberius were part of the Emperor's policy, and this correspond perfectly well with what Tacitus (*Ann.* 1.80; 4.6) says about the Emperor's philosophy of leaving governors to their positions for the good of the provinces concerned (cf. Suet., *Tib.* 32). The next appointment, that of Marcellus, a friend (φίλος) in the staff of the then legate of Syria L. Vitellius (*cos.* 34 CE), was an *ad hoc* replacement by Vitellius when Pilatus was sent back to Rome to be tried by the Emperor (Jos., *Ant.* 18.89). Thus Marcellus may only count as an 'acting governor' during the year 36/37 CE. One Marullus was officially appointed by Caius soon after the death of Tiberius (*Ant.* 18.237).[21] He must have kept his position until the time when Agrippa I became King of Judaea (41 CE), even if he is not mentioned in connection with the dramatic events in the last year of Caius' life.[22] But let us not forget that the order of Caius to set up his image in the Jerusalem Temple, was given to the new legate of Syria, P. Petronius (Philo, *Leg.* 207; Jos., *Ant.* 18.261), and as the latter dealt directly with the Jews it is not necessary for Marullus to have appeared in the narratives.

On the death of Agrippa I (44 CE), Claudius dispatched Cuspius Fadus as the prefect of an enlarged now Roman province (Judaea, Idumaea and Samaria, as well as Galilee and Peraea, since the tetrarchy of Antipas had meanwhile passed to Agrippa I).[23] Josephus (*Ant.* 20.101; cf. 3.320) seems to be saying that near the end of the governorship of Fadus, and continuing into that of Ti. Iulius Alexander (ἐπὶ τούτοις – all MSS; cf. Euseb., *EH.* 2.12.1), a great famine afflicted the country. This famine, which is also mentioned by the Acts (11:27-30), and for which help was provided by Helena the Queen of Adiabene (Jos., *Ant.* 20.51), would have been all the more severe for the year 47/48 CE almost certainly happened to be

---

[19] Philo (*Leg.* 298) says that Tiberius ruled for "23 years", but more accurately Dio (58.28.5) gives "22 years, seven months and seven days", which is close to reality as Tiberius was short to complete his last seven months by three days.

[20] Following Eisler (cf. Kokkinos 1986b), Schwartz (1992, 184) finds these numbers suspicious, but Josephus does occasionally do his own literary calculations without following official documentation or coin eras, as for example when he gives the 'seventeenth' year from the beginning of Agrippa II's kingship as the time of the beginning of First Jewish Revolt (*War* 2.284; see Kokkinos 2003, 177). The order of events under Gratus and Pilatus, and the way Josephus is using his sources (including the possibility of tampering in the MSS tradition due to the presence of the notorious Testimonium Flavianum), have to be discussed elsewhere.

[21] It has been suggested that 'Marullus' and 'Marcellus' might be the same individual (Laet 1939, 418-19), but this disregards the unanimous authority of the MSS and the verb ἐκπέμπω ('to send') from Rome (cf. *KHD*, 283-84). The verb may be said to have been used in a non-literary sense of 'appointed', but then the same could be said for every governor who 'was sent' from Rome.

[22] For a brief reconstruction of the events in the period 38-41 CE, see *KHD*, 285, n. 74.

[23] We are not told about the arrangement of the northern territories of Agrippa I's kingdom (previously belonging to Philip the Tetrarch). But since after the death of Philip (33 CE) his tetrarchy was temporarily attached to the province of Syria, before it arguably passed controversially to Antipas (34-37 CE) and then to Agrippa I (37 CE), it makes sense that after 44 CE it would have been attached again to Syria until the time of Agrippa II (53 CE) – see *KHD*, 268-69; Kokkinos 2003, 172; cf. Millar 1993, 51-52. Note the Latin coins of Panias from this period supporting this view (*RPC* 1 4842-4).

a Sabbatical Year, as it can be calculated from the known cycle.[24] It is further possible that the following year, 48/49 CE, was time for updating the Roman census in the province (cf. *P.Oxy.* 2:255 of that year in Egypt), an event which would have created extra tensions.[25] This is precisely what we find in the narrative of Josephus (*Ant.* 20.102) under Alexander, probably during Passover 48 CE. A rebellion had to be crushed by the prefect who crucified the sons of Judas of Gamala – that is the man responsible for the resistance during the first census in 6 CE. Since the next governor, Ventidius Cumanus arrived at Judaea late in 48 CE,[26] we can safely share the years from 44 to 48 CE between Cuspius Fadus and Ti. Iulius Alexander. Accordingly, based on the literary evidence, we can hardly be wrong if we tabulate the prefects and their dates as follows:

1. Coponius: 6/7-8/9 CE (three years)
2. Marcus Ambivius: 9/10-11/12 CE (three years)
3. Annius Rufus: 12/13-14/15 CE (three years)
4. Valerius Gratus: 15/16-25/26 CE (eleven years)
5. Pontius Pilatus: 26/27-35/36 CE (ten years)
6. *Marcellus: 36/37 CE* (several months)
7. Marullus: 37/38-40/41 CE (three-and-a-half years)
8. Cuspius Fadus: 44/45-45/46 CE (two years)
9. Tiberius Iulius Alexander: 46/47-47/48 CE (two years)

**The Prefectural Coins of Judaea**

Concerning the above mentioned prefects, we have coins which must have been issued during the governorship of the first five of them, although current thought, as we shall see, allows only four. Even so this material provides welcome evidence from a thoroughly misty period in Judaean history (6-36 CE).[27] The coins refer only to individual emperors and their years of reign, and therefore attribution to different prefects depends entirely on their names and chronology as worked out from Josephus. Regarding the dates appearing on the coins under Augustus, the current assumption is that they follow the 'Actian Era', the first year of which should be 2 September 31 BCE–1 September 30 BCE (following the day of the battle – Dio 51.1).[28] This assumption goes back to F. De Saulcy in the mid-19th century and although it had been strongly challenged, it still prevails. In its defence would be the fact that Antioch on its

---

[24] For the Sabbatical Cycle, see Finegan 1998, 116-26; note that another great famine occurred under Herod the Great in ca. 25 BCE, which turned critical as it extended into the Sabbatical Year 24/23 BCE (Jos., *Ant.* 15.299-316).

[25] For a coincidence of the Sabbatical Cycle with a possible Roman Census Cycle, see Kokkinos 1989, 138-42.

[26] For the evidence, see *KHD*, 319, n. 186.

[27] From Jerusalem alone (major controlled excavations), Gitler (1996, 331) reports 462 prefectural coins (called 'Early Procurators' or 'Procurators A'), compared to 298 from Masada. Although there seems to be some misprints in the figures (should it be 476 instead of 462 by adding up individual numbers?), the total represents some 5.5% of the coins from all periods found in Jerusalem. By far the largest concentration is in the Southern Wall, given as 274 (p. 326), but should be 276 (p. 330), whatever this may mean in historical terms for the location or prefectural circumstances.

[28] It should be noted that since the day of the battle fell in the Macedonian year 32/31 BCE, some cities in Asia Minor followed this earlier reckoning (Tod 1918/19, 208, 212-13). But as far as Syria is concerned, the starting point was 31/30 BCE as can be shown, for example, from the coin of Year 29 of Actium = 3/2 BCE which is equated with Augustus' thirteenth consulship, beginning in January 2 BCE (*RPC* 1, 4155).

coins under Augustus, switched temporarily from the Caesarian Era of 49 BCE to the Actian Era of 31 BCE. But the switch must have taken place soon after the victory of Augustus, even if the earliest coins known to us from Antioch using the Actian Era date to 7/6 BCE (*BMC Syria*, 158, no. 57). There is no guarantee that after 27 BCE, when the Augustan Era (the so-called Anni Augusti) came into being, it should not have been preferred as a dating system by a new province striking coins. De Saulcy's assumption would also be defended by the fact that when Josephus refers to the census after the annexation of Judaea, as we saw, he dates it by the Actian Era. But Josephus (*Ant*. 18.26), being unaware of numismatic reckoning, only makes a literary calculation (τριακοστῷ καὶ ἑβδόμῳ ἔτει μετὰ τὴν Ἀντωνίου ἐν Ἀκτίῳ ἧτταν ὑπὸ Καίσαρος), and he never uses this era again for any event in his entire corpus.[29]

Moreover, there are problems in applying the Actian Era to the coins of the Judaean prefects. First, Josephus correctly dates the census to 'Year 37' (6/7 CE), and so the Actian Era can hardly allow any coin to date earlier than this year. But earlier coins seem to exist! The earliest figure generally accepted may only be 'Year 36', which translates into 5/6 CE, but even this is uncomfortable, for Archelaus was banished sometime in 6 CE (as we saw from Dio), and time must be provided for the arrival of the first prefect (Coponius), the liquidation of Archelaus' estate and the preparation for the census, before coins could logically be struck. Worse, it appears that the figure of 'Year 33' is found on several specimens of various quality, which are consistently rejected as misreadings. Second, since the highest figure we know is 'Year 41', translated into 10/11 CE in the Actian Era, the coin record available jumps from Marcus Ambivius to Valerius Gratus, leaving no evidence for Annius Rufus.

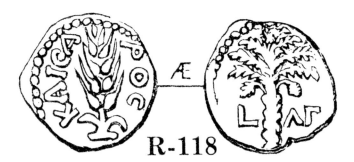

**Fig. 1:** Woodcut of a specimen dated to 'Year 33', said to be at the time in the collection of E. Wigan according to Madden (1864, 136, no. 1).

It is interesting to go back to De Saulcy and read how in 1853, based on his understanding of Josephus and the Actian Era, he could not explain the coins dated to 'Year 33' (ΛΓ), mentioned previously by Eckhel, as he had to admit that a specimen was to be found even in the then Cabinet des Médailles de la Bibliothèque Impérial.[30] In 1854, after obtaining in Jerusalem two examples of 'Year 36' (Λϛ), De Saulcy formed the opinion that coins with ΛΓ must all be misreadings of Λϛ.[31] The authoritative voice of Mommsen in 1860 had to point out that insistence on the Actian Era ignores the fact that the Augustan Era (as explained in

---

[29] He also refers only once to what would be a date reckoning by the Era of the Actian Games (*War* 1.398: Μετὰ δὲ τὴν πρώτην Ἀκτιάδα), the beginning year of which is debated between 29 (*AE* 1994, 1599), 28 (Gagé 1936, 92-100) and 27 BCE (Tidman 1950); cf. now Gurval 1995, 74-85.

[30] Saulcy 1853, 193 and n. 1; pl. XI.3; Eckhel 1794, 497.

[31] Saulcy 1854, 138-39.

Censorinus, *De Die Natali* 21.8) can legitimately be in operation here.[32] Opposition to De Saulcy then came from Reichardt in 1862, who said to have obtained in Jerusalem another coin of 'Year 33', and who wrote: "The Γ ... cannot be mistaken. It is quite different from the ς ... there is likewise sufficient space to see that it is not the half of a ς".[33] Madden in 1864, criticising De Saulcy, published yet another example of 'Year 33' (from the collection of E. Wigan – see **Fig. 1**), and mentioned that three more such copies had also been reported in Vienna.[34] By 1874, De Saulcy was forced to reconsider his case in the light of Mommsen *et al.*, and confirmation came from Madden in 1881 – at which time the Actian Era seemed to have finally been rejected.[35] Yet, quite unexpectedly, in 1887 Pick came back in support of the Actian Era, declaring that coins of 'Year 33' are misreadings, followed in 1914 by Hill in his impressive catalogue of Palestinian coins in the British Museum.[36]

**Fig. 2:** Only the reverse of what clearly seems to be a specimen of 'Year 33', belonging to a private collector in Tel Aviv, has been published by Kindler 1981, pl. 5:7 (reproduced here by courtesy of the *INJ*).

**Fig. 3:** A specimen which may or may not date to 'Year 33', from the collection of A. Reifenberg (now in the Israel Museum 98.96.15233), as published by Meshorer 1967, 105, pl. 29, no. 216 (reproduced here by courtesy of the IM).

This was a turning point, since such a textbook could not easily be argued against, and subsequent numismatists felt safe not to question the Actian Era until 1981, when Kindler published what seems to be a good specimen of 'Year 33' (**Fig. 2**).[37] Surprisingly, the major

[32] Mommsen 1860, 719, n. 190.
[33] Reichardt 1862, 274.
[34] Madden 1864, 138, n. 6; the Vienna copies are mentioned only in the German translation of Cavedoni (1856, 40, n. 22a), not in his original *Appendice alla Numismatica Biblica* (1855).
[35] Saulcy 1874, 70-72; Madden 1881, 174.
[36] Pick 1887, 306-8; *BMC* Palestine, ci.
[37] Kindler 1981.

works of Meshorer of 1982 and 2001 flatly dismissed the case, since already in 1967 (while illustrating a specimen which may or may not be reading 'Year 33' – see **Fig. 3**) he had set his preference to the Actian Era. But this was done uncritically as it is evident from the circular argument in the following statement:

> Because the Greek letter ς (= 6) appears at times on the coins of the procurator Coponius in a form somewhat similar to Γ, one obtains the date ΛΓ, that is Year 33 under Augustus. But this date conflicts [*sic*] with the unequivocal testimony of Josephus that Coponius was sent to Judaea in 6 C.E. and not, according to the 'new' date, in 3 C.E. [*sic*]. This is a further example that shows the extent to which care has to be exercised in arriving at 'imaginary' dates [*sic*].[38]

**Fig. 4:** Another specimen which may date to 'Year 33',
belonging to a dealer, as published by Meshorer in *AJC*, pl. 30, no. 2 = *TJC*, no. 312
(reproduced here by courtesy of Amphora).

Despite displaying in 1982 (*AJC*) another example which he describes as carrying a date that "looks like Γ" (see **Fig. 4**),[39] and despite ignoring Kindler's previous publication, Meshorer in 2001 (*TJC*) had only this to say:

> Some scholars have attempted to read other dates on the coins, such as 'Year 33', but this is unfounded, being due either to the poor state of preservation of the coin or its crude execution [*sic*].[40]

The fact of the matter is that regardless of the reading of 'Year 33' (the best example of which is presently that published by Kindler), what is really 'unfounded' is the insistence that prefectural coins under Augustus must be reckoned by the Actian Era. Even if 'Year 33' did not exist, the rest of the dates can still be reckoned by the Augustan Era. This is most appropriate in that Samaria, from where the main army under the prefects originated, was founded as 'Sebaste' (Augusta) in 27 BCE, as is now understood from coins and inscriptions.[41] On 16 January of that year, Imperator Caesar Divi Filius was named 'Augustus' (Sebastos), and the new Era created was backdated to 1 January. It makes good sense that this era would be adopted by the Roman administration after the exile of Archelaus. This was the only non-royal era available within the new province of Judaea/Idumaea/Samaria at the time, directly

---

[38] Meshorer 1967, 105.
[39] *AJC*, 281.
[40] *TJC*, 168.

[41] See Barag 1993, 16, n. 6; cf. *SVM*, 290, n. 9; Meimaris, Kritikakou and Bougia 1992, 140; *KHD*, 66, n. 61; 136, n. 192; 222; 225; 369; cf. Kokkinos 1985.

connected with the military colony of Sebaste. Thus by applying the Augustan Era to the prefectural coins under Augustus, we need to clearly recognise that the debated earliest date of 'Year 33' translates into 6 CE, and that the latest date of 'Year 41' into 14 CE. It can hardly be a coincidence that the first happens to mark the year Coponius arrived at Judaea, and the second the year Augustus died, as is determined from other sources. So bringing together the evidence from Josephus we have discussed above, an appropriate table incorporating the numismatic evidence (all known dates) will be as follows:

**Coponius** (*Prefectus Iudaeae* **6-9 CE**)

**Year 33** = 6 CE (perhaps *TJC*, nos. 311 & 312)
    = Ear of Corn: KAICAPOC || Palm Tree: L ΛΓ

**Fig. 5:** Yet another specimen that looks as if it reads 'Year 33', perhaps the one mentioned by Kindler (1981, 19) as belonging to the Kadman collection, published in Maltiel-Gerstenfeld 1982, 178, no. 203.

**Marcus Ambivius** (*Prefectus Iudaeae* **9-12 CE**)

**Year 36** = 9 CE (*TJC*, no. 311a)
    = Ear of Corn: KAICAPOC || Palm Tree: L Λς

**Fig. 6:** A specimen of 'Year 36' from the British Museum collection – *BMC* Palestine, 248, no. 1 (by courtesy of the BM).

### Annius Rufus (*Prefectus Iudaeae* **12-15 CE**)

**Year 39** = 12 CE (*TJC*, no. 313)
= Ear of Corn: KAICAPOC || Palm Tree: L ΛΘ

**Fig. 7:** A specimen of 'Year 39' from the British Museum collection – *BMC* Palestine, 249, no. 15 (by courtesy of the BM).

**Year 40** = 13 CE (*TJC*, no. 314)
= Ear of Corn: KAICAPOC || Palm Tree: L ΛM

**Fig. 8:** A specimen of 'Year 40' from the British Museum collection – *BMC* Palestine, 249, no. 18 (by courtesy of the BM).

**Year 41** = 14 CE (*TJC*, no. 315)
= Ear of Corn: KAICAPOC || Palm Tree: L ΛMA

**Fig. 9:** A specimen of 'Year 41' from the British Museum collection – *BMC* Palestine, 250, no. 27 (by courtesy of the BM).

Evidently the same designs continue throughout the governorships of the first three prefects until the death of Augustus. The symbols chosen by the new administration is clearly what the Romans thought to be most important products of the newly annexed land: the grain (such as corn) and the palm tree (with dates). The image of neither offended the religious preconceptions of the Jews, as we know that images of palm trees are said already to have decorated the Temple of Solomon (1 Kgs 6:29, 32; 7:36). The decision to depict this symbol for the first time on the coinage of Judaea, must have had a connection to Roman fondness of the local tree and its dates. Horace (*Ep.* 2.2.184) under Augustus had immortalised Herod's rich palm groves (*Herodis palmetis pinguibus*), and Rome very much liked the fruit, as it had become famous from the so-called 'Dates of Nicolaus' (*Sicciores ex hoc genere Nicolai*) imported by Augustus (Pliny, *N.H.* 13.45; Athen., 14.66). From the Roman point of view, the palm tree remained always the symbol of Judaea, as is shown by the captured personification of the province under this particular tree in the famous Judaea Capta coins some 65 years later (*CRE* 2, pl. 20, 4-10).

With the succession of Tiberius in 14 CE (19 August), the speed of imperial appointments, as we saw, turned slow in motion. Valerius Gratus was the first prefect to stay in office for eleven years. This seems to be reflected on the numismatic record, since coins dated from Year 2 to Year 11, are in many ways uniform:

### Valerius Gratus (*Prefectus Iudaeae* 15-26 CE)

**Year 2** = 15/16 CE (*TJC*, no. 316)
= Wreath: KAICAP ‖ Double Cornucopiae: TIB/LB

**Fig. 10:** A Tiberius specimen of 'Year 2' with cornucopiae from the British Museum collection – *BMC* Palestine, 251, no. 2 (by courtesy of the BM).

**Year 2** = 15/16 CE (*TJC*, no. 318)
= Wreath: ΙΟΥΛΙΑ ‖ Double Cornucopiae: TIB/LB

**Fig. 11:** A Julia specimen of 'Year 2' with cornucopiae from the Hendin collection – Hendin 2010, pl. 31, no. 1332b (by courtesy of D. Hendin).

**Year 2** = 15/16 CE (*TJC*, no. 319)
 = Wreath: KAICAP || Laurel Branch: LB

**Fig. 12:** A Tiberius specimen of 'Year 2' with laurel branch from the Israel Museum collection – *TJC*, pl. 73, no. 319 (reproduced here by courtesy of Amphora).

**Year 2** = 15/16 CE (*TJC*, no. 317)
 = Wreath: IOYΛIA || Laurel Branch: LB

**Fig. 13:** A Julia specimen of 'Year 2' with laurel branch from the Hendin collection – Hendin 2010, pl. 31, no. 1333 (by courtesy of D. Hendin).

**Year 3** = 16/17 CE (*TJC*, no. 320)
 = Wreath: KAI/CAP || Crossed Cornucopiae with Caduceus: TIBEPIOY/LΓ

**Fig. 14:** A Tiberius specimen of 'Year 3' with caduceus from the British Museum collection – *BMC* Palestine, 252, no. 10 (by courtesy of the BM).

**Year 3** = 16/17 CE (*TJC*, no. 321)
 = Wreath: ΙΟΥΛΙΑ ‖ Three lilies from two leaves: LΓ

Fig. 15: A Julia specimen of 'Year 3' with lilies from the British Museum collection – *BMC* Palestine, 253, no. 20 (by courtesy of the BM).

**Year 4** = 17/18 CE (*TJC*, no. 325)
 = Vine Branch with Leaf and Grapes: ΤΙΒΕΡΙΟΥ ‖ Kantharos: ΚΑΙΣΑΡΟΣ/LΔ

Fig. 16: A Tiberius specimen of 'Year 4' with *kantharos*
(by courtesy of the www.MenorahCoinProject.org)

**Year 4** = 17/18 CE (*TJC*, no. 326)
 = Vine Branch with Leaf, Tendril and Grapes: ΙΟΥΛΙΑ ‖ Amphora: LΔ

Fig. 17: A Julia specimen of 'Year 4' with amphora
(by courtesy of www.MenorahCoinProject.org)

**Year 4** = 17/18 CE (*TJC*, no. 327)
    = Wreath: TIB/KAI/CAP || Palm branch: IOYΛIA/LΔ

**Fig. 18:** A Tiberius/Julia specimen of 'Year 4' with palm branch from the British Museum collection – *BMC* Palestine, 254, no. 31 (by courtesy of the BM).

**Year 5** = 18/19 CE (*TJC*, no. 328)
    = Wreath: TIB/KAI/CAP || Palm branch: IOYΛIA/LE

**Fig. 19:** A Tiberius/Julia specimen of 'Year 5' with palm branch from the British Museum collection – *BMC* Palestine, 255, no. 38 (by courtesy of the BM).

**Year 11** = 24/25 CE (*TJC*, no. 329)
    = Wreath: TIB/KAI/CAP || Palm branch: IOYΛIA/LIA

**Fig. 20:** A Tiberius/Julia specimen of 'Year 11' with palm branch from the British Museum collection – *BMC* Palestine, 256, no. 49 (by courtesy of the BM).

Evidently the first three dates (Years 2 to 4) were struck in pairs – that is to say one coin for Tiberius and one for his mother Livia (now named Julia after adoption into the Julian gens), mostly in identical designs. The name of Tiberius as 'Caesar', or of Livia as 'Julia', was crowned by being placed within a wreath on the obverse, while the date of the mint was set within a double cornucopia, or by the sides of laurel branches, on the reverse. The wreaths underlined the fact of the recent imperial accession and the cornucopias and branches the joyful events then current: while Livia had also become the Priestess of the Divine Augustus (Dio 56.46.1), Tiberius on 10 March 15 CE had been named Pontifex Maximus (*ILS* 154). Wreaths and horns of plenty, although symbols with pagan background (attributes of Livia through her personification of Goddess Demeter/Ceres), were familiar in Jewish coinage of the past, and so no offence was posed by the new prefectural currency. In Year 3 of the coin issued in the name of Tiberius, the reverse includes a caduceus within the double cornucopia, whereas that issued in the name of Livia drops the cornucopia and displays instead a bunch of three lilies. The pagan caduceus represents a herald's wand, and as such it 'announces' a period of happiness in the context of the cornucopia (see the accompanying paper by David Jacobson). The white lilies represent virtue and hope of life (attributes of Livia through her personification of the Goddess Hera/Juno), but they would be perfectly acceptable to the Jews if we remember that 'lily-work' is mentioned in connection to the decoration of the Temple of Solomon (1 Kgs 7:19), and that the Song of Songs (2:1) reads: 'I am the rose of Sharon, the lily of the valleys'. In Year 4 there is a temporary change of motifs, before the designs quickly return (within the same year and continuing to Years 5 and 11), to the original wreath and palm branch (instead of laurel branch) type. At this point the coins issued by Gratus cease to be in pairs, and from then on are shared between Tiberius and his mother.

The temporary change of motifs in Year 4, concern the most beautiful of all prefectural examples (as well as of procuratorial later).[42] The obverse of both Tiberius and Livia's coins depicts a vine branch with leaf and grapes, whereas the reverse of Tiberius has a *kantharos* and of Julia an amphora. It is unlikely that the new designs were meant to follow the trend began by the early prefects of displaying local products. The wine of Judaea in the first century could not have been of the quality or quantity for export,[43] nor could it have been famous (like the dates) in the Roman world. Its use was largely dependent on the rituals performed by the priests. What comes to mind instead is the huge golden vine with hanging grape-clusters that stood above the portal of the sanctuary in the new building of Herod the Great (Jos., *War* 5.210; *Ant.* 15.395). Tacitus (*Hist.* 5.5) is appropriately aware of the *vitis aurea in templo reperta*. Thus the likeliest explanation for the new designs has to do with the Temple in Jerusalem and the imperial offerings, which are now (17/18 CE) being advertised for the first time. We cannot fail to remember the ἀκρατοφόροι once sent by Augustus and his wife Livia (*War* 5.562), besides the latter adorning the temple with χρυσαῖς φιάλαις καὶ σπονδείοις καὶ ἄλλων ἀναθημάτων πολυτελεστάτων (Philo, *Leg.* 319; cf. 157, 309-19). Gratus may have wanted to remind the Jews of imperial liberality, particularly since he seems to have been in trouble with the local priesthood, after appointing and deposing four high priests in the space of three years. It was about this time that the Jews put pressure on Rome for a diminution of the tribute (Tac., *Ann.* 2.42), no doubt by complaining initially to the prefect. We need to remember the timing of this mint, since on 1 January 18 CE Germanicus entered the consulship in Nicopolis, at the outset of his grand

---

[42] See further description in Kokkinos 1986b, where a possible retouched specimen of Year 4 as Year 7 was pointed out.

[43] Cf. Safrai 1994, 75-77.

(and fatal) tour of the East, which would have taken him through Judaea.[44] This tour marked the 'half-centenary' anniversary of the victory of Augustus (or the defeat of Antonius from the perspective of Germanicus' family background) at Actium in 31 BCE.

The last coin, Year 11, attributed to Gratus, which persists with his original wreath and palm (instead of laurel) branch designs for Tiberius and Livia, coincides with the end of a turbulent period in the imperial house and comes almost as a relief to the trouble: Livia's serious illness of 22 CE (Tac., *Ann.* 3.64, 71), followed by a difficult year for Tiberius when he lost his son Drusus, one of his grandsons, and a good friend in 23 CE (Tac., *Ann.* 4.3, 8, 11, 15; Dio 57.22). The same coin reported as of Year 14 (*TJC*, no. 329c) is a misreading of a poor specimen as explained by Meshorer.[45] There will not be another issue for the next five years, making it almost certain that a new prefect had arrived.

The policy of Tiberius of extending the appointments of provincial governors is further in evidence with Pontius Pilatus who stayed in Judaea for ten years. Nevertheless, the coins attributed to him (Years 16-18) cover only the period 29/30-31/32 CE, another turbulent period in Rome, which began with the death of Livia and ended with the execution of L. Aelius Sejanus. Significantly, this was the very period which must have been covered by the missing Book 5 of Tacitus' *Annals*. The following table puts the numismatic evidence in context:

**Pontius Pilatus** (*Prefectus Iudaeae* **26-36 CE**)

  **Year 16** = 29/30 CE (*TJC*, no. 331)
  = Simpulum: ΤΙΒΕΡΙΟΥ ΚΑΙCΑΡΟC LIϛ || Three ears of grain tied to a metal tripod: ΙΟΥΛΙΑ ΚΑΙCΑΡΟC

Fig. 21: A Tiberius/Julia specimen of 'Year 16' with *simpulum* from the collection of Fontanille (by courtesy of J. P. Fontanille).

---

[44] See Kokkinos 2002, 17-24; 246-47.

[45] A lead weight in the Israel Museum said to have come from Galilee, but which Meshorer (1986) correctly thinks that it should be Judaean or Samarian, is dated according to him to 'Year 15' (ΕΤΟΥ ΕΙ) and thus would belong to Pilatus' administration in 28/29 CE. However, the photograph is not clear and the date (with unabbreviated the Greek word for year) may better read 'Year 10' (ΕΤΟΥC Ι). In such a case, it belongs to Gratus, dating to 23/24 CE.

**Year 17** = 30/31 CE (*TJC*, no. 333)
 = Lituus: TIBEPIOY KAICAPOC || Wreath: LIZ

**Fig. 22:** A Tiberius specimen of 'Year 17' with *lituus*
(by courtesy of www.MenorahCoinProject.org)

**Year 18** = 31/32 CE (*TJC*, no. 334)
 = Lituus: TIBEPIOY KAICAPOC || Wreath: LIH

**Fig. 23:** A Tiberius specimen of 'Year 18' with *lituus*
(by courtesy of www.MenorahCoinProject.org)

Regardless of whether his acts were incidental or purposeful, Pilatus was clearly insensitive to the Jews in matters of religion, as we know from Josephus (*Ant.* 18.55-59) and Philo (*Leg.* 299-305). It is thus not surprising to find that the symbols displayed on the coins attributed to him, are strikingly foreign to Jewish culture and must have left a bad taste, if not directly offended by promoting the imperial religion of Rome in a religiously exclusive Judaea.[46] To be sure, the symbols of Year 16 need not be taken as designed to provoke, because they appear on a joined issue of Tiberius and Livia, minted at a time that can only be connected to Livia's death at the beginning of 29 CE (Tac., *Ann.* 5.1; Dio 58.2.1). The small ladle for libation on the obverse, the *simpulum*, would signify religious ritual to her spirit, in the presence of a metal tripod on the reverse often used by pagan priests, on which three ears of grain are bound, drooping soberly to the ground. But the *lituus* of Years 17 and 18, being a curved staff used by the augurs in quartering the heavens, appearing on issues of Tiberius now without Livia, could not have had any excuse to give to the Jews. Tiberius was known to be following augury and astrology with passion (Jos., *Ant.* 18.212; Suet., *Tib.* 69), and Pilatus' coins clearly

---

[46] Contra Bond 1996; cf. Taylor 2006.

support the Emperor's views. Thus Pilatus is not worried about local reaction, in a similar way he openly supported the Tiberieum, almost certainly a religious building, dedicated to the Emperor, albeit in Caesarea-on-Sea.[47]

Saddington doubts the intentions of the prefect, saying that "[h]ad Pilate really wished to offend he would have put a portrait of Tiberius on the coins".[48] But this is easier said than done. There was no reason for Pilatus to be extreme, and a portrait in the round or a statue would have been even more intolerable to the Jews (as it was proved to be under Caius), yet such an act would have needed authorisation from Rome and impossible for him to get. However, we should not forget that the portrait of Tiberius was anyway in view in Jerusalem, depicted on the Roman *denarii*, which were used for the payment of the 'census-tax' (τὸ νόμισμα τοῦ κήνσου – Mt 22:19; cf. Mk 12:13-17; Lk 20:20-26; cf. *OGIS* 629). The coin shown to Jesus may well have been carried in the pockets of the Hellenised 'Herodians' rather than those of the Pharisees present in the Gospels' story, but it makes no difference. The fact is that we are talking about currencies of some value, which once released to circulation could not easily be rejected, recalled or disappear. The coins of Pilatus of Years 17 and 18 were surely offensive, and yet many examples have been found in Masada where the Zealots should have avoided them.[49] Money is money – or to put it in a Greek saying ὁ σκοπὸς ἁγιάζει τὰ μέσα ("the end justifies the means", or literary "the aim makes the means holy").

It should also be noticed that Sejanus was executed on 18 October 31 CE,[50] and as it happens the coins attributed to Pilatus come and stop in that year. His fellow equestrian, who had reached the top of the *cursus honorum* as *praefectus praetorio*, was supposed to be an enemy of the Jews in Rome according to Philo (*Leg.* 159-160; *Flacc.* 1.1).[51] Philo (*Leg.* 161) also implies that Sejanus would have influenced anti-Jewish decisions in the provinces, if Tiberius later had to warn against such a policy by issuing instructions to the governors (called here ὕπαρχοι). Philo (*Leg.* 302) further describes the conduct of Pilatus in Judaea as being full of "briberies" (δωροδοκίας), "insults" (ὕβρεις), "snatchings" (ἁρπαγὰς), "injuries" (αἰκίας), "abuses" (ἐπηρείας), "repeated killings without trial" (ἀκρίτους καὶ ἐπαλλήλους φόνους),[52] and "supremely grievous cruelty" (ἀργαλεωτάτην ὠμότητα). There is no wonder then that the paths of the two equestrian officers were to be brought together by Eusebius (*E.H.* 2.5.6-7), even if a direct link is not made clear or could be proved. But Pilatus continued to provoke after the death of Sejanus, such as in the episode of the shields set up in Jerusalem (Philo, *Leg.* 299-305), the dedication of the Tiberieum in Caesarea (perhaps on the Emperor's 75th birthday in 33 CE),[53] the sacred treasury from which he took money for an aqueduct in Jerusalem (Jos., *War* 2.175-177; *Ant.* 18.60-62), the crucifixion of Jesus (Jos., *Ant.* 18.63-64, arguably during the Passover of 36 CE),[54] and finally the slaughter of the followers of a Samaritan prophet (Jos., *Ant.* 18.85-

---

[47] For the famous inscription, see now Lehman and Holum 1999, 67-70, no. 43, pl. 36; cf. Kokkinos 1989, 142, where the year of 33 CE was suggested as being exceptional due to the coincidence of Tiberius' seventy-fifth *natalis* (the word may be restored on the inscription), with the half-centenary of Augustus' *saeculum*, the *decennium* from the death of Drusus the Younger', the 203rd Olympic Games and probably the Games of Caesarea. Alföldy's suggestion (1999, 93-105) that the building may instead have been a tower can hardly draw evidence to its favour, and the context of the 'Drusion' in Josephus' text needs to be discussed elsewhere.

[48] Saddington 1997, 25.
[49] Meshorer 1989, 96-97.
[50] *KHD*, 275, n. 41; Kokkinos 2002, 26.
[51] See Smallwood 1970, 243-45.
[52] Contrast the fair trial that Jesus was supposed to have received in the Gospels, but as a late event this may reflect a change of attitude by Pilatus in having to follow the instructions which he would have received from Tiberius, that "punishment was not falling on all but only on the guilty" (Philo, *Leg.* 161).
[53] See *CIL* 6.2025a of 33 CE and above note 47.
[54] Kokkinos 1989; cf. Kokkinos 1986a; *KHD*, 266-70.

87).⁵⁵ This last act became the straw that broke the camel's back, as Pilatus was sent back to Rome to face the Emperor.

## Conclusion

The change of title from *praefectus* to *procurator* for equestrian governors under Claudius, took place, in the case of Judaea, arguably after 48 CE and before or by 52 CE. This is based on combining information from the Bir el-Malik inscription (as reconstructed by the present writer) with Josephus and Tacitus. So the prefectural period (as against the procuratorial) lasted from 6 CE to at least 48 CE. During this period, and following mainly Josephus, we know the official appointment of nine individuals: Coponius, Marcus Ambivius, Annius Rufus, Valerius Gratus, Pontius Pilatus, Marcellus, Marullus, Cuspius Fadus and Ti. Iulius Alexander. The nomenclature of these prefects may partly be restored, and more so if we consider the neglected question of their background (as treated lightly in Appendix 2), suggesting interesting equestrian interconnections.

Coins can be attributed to the first five of them on the basis of chronology, as their legends refer only to individual emperors dated by year of reign, which can then be set against the dates for each prefect as worked out from Josephus. Concerning the early prefects, it is shown here that available coins should be attributed to Coponius (6/7-8/9 CE), Marcus Ambivius (9/10-11/12 CE) and Annius Rufus (12/13-14/15 CE). It is currently believed that the latter issued no coins, but this is to misinterpret the era in operation. Under Augustus in Judaea it was not the Actian Era (31/30 BCE) which would have been preferred by the authorities, but the Augustan Era (27 BCE) as determined locally by the foundation of Sebaste from where the main army under the prefects originated. This may be proved by specimens reading 'Year 33'. They must not date earlier than 6 CE when the province was founded.

While the early prefects used the same designs on their coins, depicting important products of the newly annexed land (palm tree and corn), Valerius Gratus (15/16-25/26 CE) was the first to turn his view on Rome under Tiberius. His designs however could not have offended. Focussing on the Emperor and his mother Livia, now named Julia, Gratus stressed current joyful events and reminded the Jews of imperial liberality (counterbalancing bad taxing) by using symbols familiar to Judaism (wreaths, cornucopiae, laurel branches, lilies, vine branches with grapes, and imperial vessels offered to the Temple). His long prefecture, as much as that of his successor Pontius Pilatus (26/27-35/36 CE), were clearly in line with the wider policy of Tiberius. Yet Pilatus himself broke with the tradition of designing coins tactfully, as he used symbols on them quite insensitively. Particularly the depiction of the *lituus* of Years 17 and 18 must have left a bad taste among the Jews. It can hardly be a coincidence that the timing of the mint coincided with the widely anti-Jewish influence of Pilatus' equestrian superior L. Aelius Sejanus, who was executed on 18 October 31 CE.

---

⁵⁵ In Egesippus (or confusingly 'Hegesippus' like the Early Christian writer), the Latin paraphrase of Josephus' *War* in 5 books (not to be confused with the Latin translation of Pseudo-Rufinus), the crucifixion of Jesus follows the Samaritan episode (cf. Eisler 1931, 293).

## Appendix 1: The titles 'prefect' and 'procurator' in the sources

The terminology used by Josephus to describe the governors of Judaea who were appointed as 'prefects' (ἔπαρχοι) at least until 48 CE, is partly anachronistic (Coponius; Pilatus), partly inconsistent (Fadus; Alexander), and partly correct (Gratus; Marullus) – cf. now Eck 2007, 27-31. Among the earlier sources, the two inscriptions from Caesarea and Bir el-Malik accurately reflect the official title for Pilatus and Alexander respectively. Philo is also anachronistic in regard to Pilatus, which may suggest that his *Legatio* would not have been completed (or edited) before the governorship of Cumanus (48/49-51/52 CE), when the change of name would have taken place (if not under Felix) – a point which should be considered in estimating the date of writing of the *Legatio ad Gaium* and the time of Philo's death (cf. Smallwood 1970, 300; Morris 1987, 816, n. 15). While the Gospels avoid both terms, the only later source, Tacitus, is also anachronistic concerning Pilatus. By contrast, the terminology used by Josephus to describe the governors of Judaea who were appointed as 'procurators' (ἐπίτροποι) after about 48 CE, is inconsistent only once (Festus) and once wrong (Albinus)!

**Coponius** (6/7-8/9 CE) = three years
*War* 2.117: τῆς ἱππικῆς τάξεως ('of equestrian order') – εἰς ἐπαρχίαν... ἐπίτροπος... πέμπεται ('to an eparchy... as procurator... was sent out') – μέχρι τοῦ κτείνειν λαβὼν... ἐξουσίαν ('receiving authority even to the infliction of capital punishment' [i.e. the *ius gladii*]).
*Ant.* 18.2: τάγματος τῶν ἱππέων ('[had been in charge] of a cohort of cavalrymen') – συγκαταπέμπεται... ἡγησόμενος... ἐπὶ πᾶσιν ἐξουσίᾳ ('was sent along with [Quirinius]... to rule... with full authority')

**Marcus Ambivius** (9/10-11/12 CE) = three years
*Ant.* 18.31: διάδοχος δ᾽αὐτῷ [Κωπωνίῳ] τῆς ἀρχῆς παραγίνεται... ('successor of him [Coponius] in office was made...')

**Annius Rufus** (12/13-14/15 CE) = three years
*Ant.* 18.32: διαδέχεται... ('succeeding...')

**Valerius Gratus** (15/16-25/26 CE) = eleven years
*Ant.* 18.33: πέμπτὸς... ἔπαρχος διάδοχος...᾽ Ρούφῳ ('dispatched... as eparch the successor... of Rufus')
*Ant.* 18.177: διοικήσ[ω]ν... ('to administer...')

**Pontius Pilatus** (26/27-35/36 CE) = ten years
Caesarea inscription: [*praef*]*ectus Iuda*[*ea*]*e*
Philo, *Leg.* 299: τῶν ὑπάρχων ἐπίτροπος ἀποδεδειγμένος τῆς Ἰουδαίας ('one of the hyparchs who became procurator of Judaea')
Lk 3:1: ἡγεμονεύοντος Ποντίου Πιλάτου τῆς Ἰουδαίας... ('while Judaea was governed by Pontius Pilatus')
Mt 27:1: Πιλάτῳ τῷ ἡγεμόνι... ('to Pilatus the governor')
*War* 2.169: Πεμφθεὶς δὲ εἰς Ἰουδαίαν ἐπίτροπος ('Being sent to Judaea as procurator')
*Ant.* 18.35: διάδοχος ('successor')
*Ant.*18.55: ἡγεμὼν ('governor')
*Ant.* 18.177: διοικήσ[ω]ν... ('to administer...') – διεδέξατο τὴν ἡγεμονίαν ('succeeded in the governorship')
Tac., *Ann.* 15.44.3: *procurator*

**Marcellus** (*36/37 CE*) = *several months*
*Ant.* 18.89: Μάρκελλον τῶν αὐτοῦ φίλων ἐκπέμψας ἐπιμελητὴν τοῖς Ἰουδαίοις

γενησόμενον... ('he [Vitellius] sent Marcellus, one of his friends, to become the overseer of the Jews' [or superintendent – in other words an 'acting governor'])

**Marullus** (37/38-40/41 CE) = three-and-a-half years
*Ant.* 18.237: ἱππάρχην δὲ ἐπὶ τῆς Ἰουδαίας ἐκπέμπει Μάρυλλον. ('A commander of cavalry, Marullus, he [Caius] sent to take over Judaea.')

**Cuspius Fadus** (44/45-45/46 CE) = two years
*War* 2.220: ἐπαρχίαν ποιήσας ἐπίτροπον πέμπει... ('reducing it to an eparchy, he sent as procurator...')
*Ant.* 15.406: ὁ τῆς Ἰουδαίας ἐπίτροπος ('the procurator of Judaea')
*Ant.* 19.363: ἔπαρχον... τῆς Ἰουδαίας... ἀπέστειλεν ('eparch... of Judaea... he sent')
*Ant.* 20.2: ὡς εἰς τὴν Ἰουδαίαν ἐπίτροπος ἀφίκετο ('he arrived in Judaea as procurator')
*Ant.* 20.97: τῆς Ἰουδαίας ἐπιτροπεύοντος ('while procurating over Judaea')
*Ant.* 20.99: τῆς ἐπιτροπῆς χρόνους ('the years of procuratorship')

**Ti. Iulius Alexander** (46/47-47/48 CE) = two years
Bir el-Malik inscription: ἐπάρ[χου Ἰουδαίας] ('epar[ch of Judaea]'
*War* 2.220: ἐπαρχίαν ποιήσας ἐπίτροπον πέμπει... ('reducing it to an eparchy, he sent as procurator...')
*War* 2.223: ἐπαρχίας διαδέχεται τὴν ἐπιτροπήν... ('he was succeeded in the procuratorship of the eparchy...')
*Ant.* 20.100: διάδοχος ('successor')
*Ant.* 20.103: διάδοχος ('successor')
*Ant.* 20.107: ἐπιτροπεύσαντες ('[those previously] procurating')

**Ventidius Cumanus** (48/49-51/52 CE) = four years
*War* 2.223: ἐπαρχίας διαδέχεται τὴν ἐπιτροπήν... Κουμανὸς ('he was succeeded in the procuratorship of the eparchy... by Cumanus')
*Ant.* 20.103: διάδοχος ('successor')
*Ant.* 20.105: τὰ κατὰ τὴν Ἰουδαίαν πράγματα διοικοῦντος ('while administering affairs in Judaea')
*Ant.* 20.107: ἐπιτροπεύσαντες ('[those previously] procurating')
Tac., Ann. 12.54: *cui [Ventidio] pars provinciae habebatur... huic [Ventidio] Galilaeorum natio... procuratoribus*

**Tiberius Claudius Felix** (52/53-56/57 CE) = five years
Bir el-Malik inscription: ἐπιτρόπου Σε[βαστοῦ Ἰουδαίας] ('procurator of Au[gustus in Judaea]')
Acts 23:24: πρὸς Φήλικα τὸν ἡγεμόνα... ('to Felix the governor...')
Acts 23:26: τῷ κρατίστῳ ἡγεμόνι Φήλικι... ('to his excellency the governor Felix...')
Acts 23:33: τῷ ἡγεμόνι... ('to the governor')
Acts 24:3: τῷ ἡγεμόνι... ('to the governor')
Acts 24:10: τοῦ ἡγεμόνος... ('of the governor')
Acts 24:27: διάδοχον ('successor')
*War* 2.247: Ἰουδαίας μὲν ἐπίτροπον Φήλικα... ἐκπέμπει τῆς τε Σαμαρείας καὶ Γαλιλαίας καὶ Περαίας... ('he sent Felix to Judaea as procurator also of Samaria, Galilee and Peraea')
*War* 2.252: εἰς δὲ λοιπὴν Ἰουδαίαν Φήλικα κατέστησεν ἐπίτροπον ('to the rest of Judaea he appointed Felix as procurator')
*War* 2.271: τὴν ἐπιτροπήν... ('the procuratorship')
*Ant.* 20.137: Πέμπει δὲ καὶ Κλαύδιον Φήλικα... τῶν κατὰ τὴν Ἰουδαίαν προστησόμενον

πραγμάτων... ('He also sent Claudius Felix... to take care of the affairs in Judaea')
*Ant.* 20.162: τῆς Ἰουδαίας ἐπίτροπον... ('procurator of Judaea')
*Ant.* 20.182: διάδοχος ('successor')
Tac., *Ann.* 12.54: *iam [Felix] pridem Iudaeae impositus... Felici Samaritae parerent... procuratoribus...*
Suet., *Claud.* 28.1: *Felicem... provinciae Iudaeae praeposuit.*

**Porcius Festus** (57/58-58/59 CE) = two years
Acts 24:27: διάδοχον ('successor')
Acts 27:24: κράτιστε Φῆστε... ('Your excellency Festus...')
Acts 27:30: ὁ ἡγεμὼν ('the governor')
*War* 2.271: Διαδεξάμενος... τὴν ἐπιτροπὴν ὁ Φῆστος... ('succeeding... to the procuratorship, Festus...')
*Ant.* 20.182: διάδοχος ('successor')
*Ant.* 20.193: Φῆστος ὁ ἔπαρχος ('Festus the eparch')

**[Lucceius?] Albinus** (59/60-62/63 CE) = four years
*War* 6.303: οὗτος [Ἀλβῖνος] γὰρ ἔπαρχος ἦν ('because him [Albinus] was the eparch')
*Ant.* 20.197: Πέμπει δὲ... Ἀλβῖνον εἰς τὴν Ἰουδαίαν ἔπαρχον... ('He sent... Albinus to Judaea as eparch')
*Ant.* 20.215: διάδοχον ('successor')
*Ant.* 20.252: διάδοχος ('successor')

**Gessius Florus** (63/64-64/65 CE) = two years
*Ant.* 18.25: ὃς [Florus] ἡγεμὼν ἦν ('whom [Florus] was the governor')
*Ant.* 20.215: διάδοχον ('successor')
*Ant.* 20.252: διάδοχος ('successor')
*Ant.* 20.257: τῆς ἐπιτροπῆς Φλώρου ('of the procuratorship of Florus')
Tac., *Hist.* 5.10.1: *Gessium Florum procuratorem...*


## Appendix 2: The background of the prefects

The potential antecedents, origins and families of the Roman prefects of Judaea (at least up to 48 CE), will be treated lightly in this appendix. It is hoped that more will be written elsewhere.

### Coponius (*PIR²* C 1285; *LP* 34.1)

The *nomen* 'Coponius' is fairly rare, but we do know of a Titus Coponius and his grandchildren, Titus and Caius, members of a prominent family from Tibur (Cicero, *Pro Balbo* 23/54). A Caius Coponius, a republican moneyer, appears on Roman coins issued in 49 BCE (*RRC*, no. 444). Velleius (2.83.2) further refers to a dignified praetorian, who was the father-in-law of P. Silvius Nerva. In a *senatus consultum* which seems to date around 139 BCE (*ARS*, Doc. 41), but which Josephus (*Ant.* 14.145-148) misplaced under Julius Caesar, there is also a mention of a "Lucius Coponius, son of Lucius, of the Colline tribe" assisting with the drafting of the decree. It should be noted that a distant echo of the name of the prefect of Judaea may exist in the reference to the 'Gate of Kiponus', one of the Jerusalem Temple's gates (*m. Midd.* 1.3).

### Marcus Ambivius (cf. *PIR²* A 557; *LP* 34.2)

Regarding Marcus Ambivius, the MSS give his name as 'Ambibouchus' (Ἀμβιβούχος), commonly held to represent the *cognomen* 'Ambibulus' following Niese's conjecture (*SVM* 382; Smallwood 1976, 156, n. 48). However, according to Syme (1986, 275-6; cf. Birley

1994) the reading should be taken as a corruption of the *nomen* 'Ambivius'. Syme states that the style of *praenomen* + *cognomen* is not easy to match in the pages of Josephus, yet even only among the prefects, one can cite 'Tiberius Alexander' as an example (see also the consuls of 49 BCE, L. Lentulus and C. Marcellus – Jos., *Ant*. 14.228). In contrast, Syme's proposed style of *praenomen* + *nomen* is the odd one in the list of the prefects as given above. However, as this may not be a major problem, I am inclined to follow Syme, for if he is right an interesting background is found for our second prefect: he may be the son of Marcus Ambivius, an author on domestic economy known to Columella (*De Re Rustica* 12.4.2), whose *patria* may be sought in old Latium or in the Sabine country.

### Annius Rufus (*PIR*² A 686; *LP* **34.3**) and Valerius Gratus (*PIR*¹ V 58; *LP* **34.4**)

Syme (1986, 275) said that "[n]othing can be done with Annius Rufus and Valerius Gratus (typical for drab nomenclature)". But a background for them could be suggested from other contexts in Josephus. A Rufus and a Gratus are mentioned as what would seem to be royal στρατηγοί (the one of infantry and the other of cavalry) of the original troops from Samaria/Sebaste under Herod the Great (Jos., *War* 2.52; *Ant*. 17.266) – that is to say the very troops which were subsequently organised into the army of the prefects. It is possible that they were promoted later to the prefectural position, one after the other in the same order. Whether they were originally equestrians or entered the equestrian career upon completion of the city's magisterial position of στρατηγοί (cf. *duoviri*) is not important here. A detailed study in the course of examining a fragmentary inscription from Samaria (first published by Reisner 1910, 259), the first line of which could possibly be restored as [συστρα]τηγούντων Ἀννίου Ρο[ύφου καὶ Βαλερίου Γράτου], or in other words mentioning the joined service of two *stratēgoi*, the first of whom is called Annius Ru[fus], was made by Kokkinos and Vardaman in an unpublished paper of the 1980s (cf. the latter's own version in Vardaman 1998, but with reservations). This suggestion seemed to be reinforced by the present writer's new reading and restoration of the first word of the second line as [Ἡρ]ῳδεί[α]ν (though less likely it could also be Ὠδεί[ο]ν). But the problem is that the palaeography of the inscription itself would seem to point to the second century CE, and an argument has to be made for the original text to have been copied later when the 'basilica' was rebuilt. Finally, a daughter of Gratus (presumably a Valeria Grata) may have married Ti. Iulius Mellon (an imperial freedman and procurator in Jamnia before C. Herennius Capito), from whom she would have had a daughter called 'Iulia Grata' (a grand-daughter of Valerius Gratus) – thus the existence of an inscription apparently belonging to a sarcophagus and mentioning Mellon's daughter 'Iulia Grata' (first published by Avi-Yonah 1946, 83-85, no. 1, pl. 35.1).

### Pontius Pilatus (*PIR*² P 815; *LP* **34.5**)

Surprisingly, we know nothing about the antecedents, origin or family of Pontius Pilatus – despite the inscription from Caesarea, the description by Philo, the accounts in the Gospels, and the references in Josephus and Tacitus. But as Birley (1994, 126) noted, we can still point to the Samnite Pontii and to the extreme rarity of the *cognomen*. Saddington (1997, 27) sees the *cognomen* as undeniably military. The *pilum* was a javelin, the legionary's main weapon, and he reasonably asks: "Had Pilate performed a spectacular feat with a javelin? Or was he made a *primus pilus* [i.e. the most senior centurion in a legion who commanded the first century of the first cohort]…?"

### Marcellus (*PIR*² M 193; *LP* **34.6**)

Smallwood (1976, 171) says of Marcellus "otherwise unknown" – but a case can be made for his identity. Although the cognomen Marcellus is found in too many Roman families to begin thinking of sorting them out, there is one family, the Vetii, which provides a very interesting if coincidental context. M. Vettius Marcellus (*PIR*² V 333) originated in Teate Marocinurum, the very place from where another equestrian came, the famous C. Herennius Capito, the imperial procurator of Jamnia (cf. above under Gratus). The interrelations between contemporary families of equestrians have long been noted (see Demougin 1988, 660). Vettius Marcellus went on to become procurator of Thrace in 46 CE, but his story and possible identification with the 'acting governor' of Judaea will have to be discussed elsewhere.

**Marullus** (*PIR*² **M** 352; *LP* **34.7**)
The remark of Smallwood (1976, 174), that Marullus is "otherwise completely unknown", is quite true, even though the *cognomen* of this prefect was fairly rare. We know only a few Roman families carrying it, such as the Iunii, Eggii and Maecii. For the latter, note that the Emperor Gordian I was said to be the son of Maecius Marullus and Ulpia Gordiana (*Vita Gordiani Senioris* 2.2). On balance, and judging from the frequency of the *nomen*, it might be that the Judaean prefect should be sought among the Eggii.

**Cuspius Fadus** (*PIR*² **C** 1635; *LP* **34.8**)
Although many Cuspii, carrying the *praenomina* Caius, Lucius and Titus, are known from the epigraphical record, the family which must be pointed out is the prominent one of Pompeii. C. Cuspius Pansa, whose house has been located there (*Regio* IX, 1, 2), was an important local politician (see Mouritsen 1988, 133). A possible connection of Cuspius Fadus, prefect of Judaea, with Pompeii has been noted long time ago. Gordon (1927, 169) wrote:

> A curious graffito in the house of the Cuspii celebrates certain *iudicia Augusti Augustae* in their favour. If the Cuspius Fadus... belonged to the same family, we have an illustration of the special service which these Campanian nobles could render to the imperial government; their trade relations with the east and their familiarity with Greek made them peculiarly well adapted to the administration of the eastern provinces.

**Bibliography**

The following abbreviations (other than journal) are used in this paper:

*AE* = *L'Année Epigraphique*; *AJC* = Y. Meshorer, *Ancient Jewish Coinage*, vol. 2 (New York: Amphora Books, 1982); *ARS* = *Ancient Roman Statutes*, ed. by A.C. Johnson *et al.* (Clark, NJ: The Lawbook Exchange Ltd., 2003); *BMC* Palestine = *Catalogue of the Greek Coins in the British Museum: Vol. 27 Palestine*, ed. by G. F. Hill (London: British Museum, 1914); *BMC* Syria = *Catalogue of the Greek Coins in the British Museum: Vol. 20 Galatia, Cappadocia and Syria*, ed. by W. Wroth (London: British Museum, 1899); *CIL* = *Corpus Inscriptionum Latinarum*; *CRE* = *Coins of the Roman Empire in the British Museum*, vol. 2, ed. by H. Mattingly (London: The British Museum Press, 1930); *KHD* = N. Kokkinos, *The Herodian Dynasty: Origins, Role in Society and Eclipse* (Sheffield: Sheffield Academic Press, 1998); *LP* = B. E. Thomasson, *Laterculi Praesidum I* (Gothenburg: Radius, 1984); *OGIS* = *Orientis Graeci Inscriptiones Selectae*, vols. 1-2, ed. by W. Dittenberger (Leipzig: S. Hirzel, 1903-1905); *P.Oxy.* = *The Oxyrhynchus Papyri*; *PIR*² = *Prosopographia Imperii Romani: saec. I, II, III*, ed. by E. Groag *et al.*, 2nd ed. (Berlin: W. de Gruyter, 1933– ); *RPC* = *Roman Provincial Coinage: From the Death of Caesar to the Death of Vitellius, 44 BC-AD 69*, vol. 1, ed. by A. Burnett, M. Amandry and P. Pau Ripollès (London/Paris: The British Museum Press/Bibliothéque Nationale de France, 1992); *RRC* = M. H. Crawford, *Roman Republican Coinage* (London: Cambridge University Press, 1974); *SVM* = E. Schürer, rev. and ed. by G. Vermes, F. Millar and M. Black, *The History of the Jewish People in the Age of Jesus Christ*, vol. 1 (Edinburgh: T. & T. Clark, 1973); *TJC* = Y. Meshorer, *A Treasury of Jewish Coins* (Jerusalem: Ben-Zvi Press; Nyack, NY: Amphora Books, 2001).

Alföldy, G., 1999. 'Pontius Pilatus und das Tiberieum von Caesarea Maritima', *SCI* 18, 85-108.
Avi-Yonah, M., 1946. 'Newly Discovered Latin and Greek Inscriptions', *QDAP* 12, 84-102.
Barag, D., 1993. 'King Herod's Royal Castle at Samaria-Sebaste', *PEQ* 125, 3-18.
Bennett, Ch., 2003. 'Drusilla Regina', *CQ* 53, 315-319.
Birley, A. R., 1994. 'A Prosopography of Julio-Claudian Equites', *CR* 44, 126-127.
Bond, H. K., 1996. 'The Coins of Pontius Pilate: Part of an Attempt to Provoke the People or to Integrate them into the Empire?', *JSJ* 27, 241-262.
Brenk, F. E. and Canali De Rossi, F., 2001. 'The 'Notorious' Felix, Procurator of Judaea, and his Many Wives', *Biblica* 82, 410-417.
Brunt, P. A., 1983. 'Princeps and Equites', *JRS* 73, 42-75.
Bruun, Ch., 1990. 'Some Comments on the Status of Imperial Freedmen', *ZPE* 82, 271-285.
Cavedoni, D. C., 1856. *Biblische Numismatik*, German trans. A. von Werlhof (Hannover: Hahn'sche Hofbuchhandlung).
Cotton, H., 1999. 'Some Aspects of the Roman Administration of Judaea/Syria-Palaestina', in W. Eck (ed.), *Lokale Autonomie und römische Ordnungsmacht in den Kaiserzeitlichen Provinzen vom 1. bis 3. Jahrhundert* (München: Oldenbourg), 75-91.
Demougin, S., 1988. *L'ordre équestre sous les Julio-Claudiens* (Rome).
Eck, W., 2007. *Rom und Judaea* (Tübingen: Mohr Siebeck).
Eckhel, J., 1794. *Doctrina Numorum Veterum*, Pars I. Vol. III (Vienna: Sumptibus J. V. Degen).
Eisler, R., 1931. *The Messiah Jesus and John the Baptist* (London: Methuen & Co. Ltd).
Finegan, J., 1998. *Handbook of Biblical Chronology*, rev. edn. (Peabody, MA: Hendrickson).
Gagé, J., 1936. 'Actiaca', *MEFR* 53, 37-100.
Gitler, H., 1996. 'A Comparative Study of Numismatic Evidence from Excavations in Jerusalem', *LA* 46, 317-362.
Gordon, M. L., 1927. 'The *Ordo* of Pompeii', *JRS* 17, 165-183.
Gurval, R. A., 1995. *Actium and Augustus: The Politics and Emotions of Civil War* (Ann Arbor, MI: The University of Michigan Press).
Hendin, D., 2010. *Guide to Biblical Coins*, 5th edition (New York: Amphora).
Jones, A. H. M., 1960. 'Procurators and Prefects', *Studies in Roman Government and Law* (Oxford), 115-125.
Jones, A. H. M., 1972. *The Criminal Courts of the Roman Republic and Principate* (Oxford: Blackwell).
Kindler, A., 1981. 'A Re-Assessment of the Dates of Some Coins of the Roman Procurators of Judaea', *INJ* 5, 19-21.
Kokkinos, N., 1985. 'A Coin of Herod the Great Commemorating the City of Sebaste', *LA* 35, 303-306.
Kokkinos, N., 1986a. 'Which Salome Did Aristobulus Marry?', *PEQ* 118, 33-50.
Kokkinos, N., 1986b. 'A Retouched New Date on a Coin of Valerius Gratus', *LA* 36, 241-246.
Kokkinos, N., 1989. 'Crucifixion in AD 36: The Keystone for Dating the Birth of Jesus', in E. J. Vardaman & E. M. Yamauchi (eds), *Chronos, Kairos, Christos: Nativity and Chronological Studies Presented to Jack Finegan* (Winona Lake, IN: Eisenbrauns, 1989), 133-163.
Kokkinos, N., 1990. 'A Fresh Look at the *gentilicium* of Felix Procurator of Judaea', *Latomus* 49, 126-141.
Kokkinos, N. 1998. 'The Relative Chronology of the Nativity in Tertullian', in E. J. Vardaman (ed.), *Chronos, Kairos, Christos II: Chronological, Nativity, and Religious Studies in Memory of Ray Summers* (Macon, GA: Mercer University Press), 119-131.
Kokkinos, N. 2002. *Antonia Augusta: Portrait of a Great Roman Lady*, expanded version (London: Libri).

Kokkinos, N. 2003. 'Justus, Josephus, Agrippa II and his Coins', *SCI* 22, 163-180.
Kokkinos, N., 2008. 'The Foundation of Bethsaida-Julias by Philip the Tetrarch', *JJS* 59, 236-51.
Laet, S. J. De, 1939. 'Le successeur de Ponce Pilate', *L'antiquité Classique* 8, 413-419.
Lehman, C. M. and Holum, K. G., 2000. *The Greek and Latin Inscriptions of Caesarea Maritima* (Boston, MA: The American Schools of Oriental Research).
Madden, F. W., 1864. *History of Jewish Coinage* (London: Bernard Quaritch).
Madden, F. W., 1881. *Coins of the Jews* (London: Trübner & Co.).
Maltiel-Gerstenfeld, J., 1982. *260 Years of Ancient Jewish Coins: A Catalogue* (Tel Aviv: Kol Printing Service Ltd).
Meimaris, Y. E., Kritikakou K. and Bougia, P., 1992. *Chronological Systems in Roman-Byzantine Palestine and Arabia: The Evidence of the Dated Greek Inscriptions* (Athens: The National Hellenic Research Foundation).
Meshorer, Y., 1967. *Jewish Coins of the Second Temple Period*, English trans. I. H. Levine (Tel Aviv: Am Hassefer and Massada).
Meshorer, Y., 1986. 'A New Lead Weight', *The Israel Museum Journal* 5, 106.
Meshorer, Y., 1989. 'The Coins of Masada', in Y. Yadin and J. Naveh (eds.), *Masada I: The Yigael Yadin Excavations 1963-1965* (Jerusalem: Israel Exploration Society), 71-132.
Millar, F., 1964. 'Some Evidence on the Meaning of Tacitus *Annals* XII.60', *Historia* 13, 180-187.
Millar, F., 1965. 'The Development of Jurisdiction by Imperial Procurators: Further Evidence', *Historia* 14, 362-367.
Millar, F., 1993. *The Roman Near East 31 BC-AD 337* (Cambridge, MA: Harvard University Press).
Mommsen, Th., 1860. *Geschichte des Römischen Münzwesens* (Berlin: Weidmannsche Buchhandlung).
Morris, J., 1987. 'The Jewish Philosopher Philo' in E. Schürer, rev. and ed. by G. Vermes, F. Millar and Martin Goodman, *The History of the Jewish People in the Age of Jesus Christ*, vol. 3.2 (Edinburgh: T. & T. Clark), 809-889.
Mouritsen, H., 1988. *Elections, Magistrates and Municipal Élite. Studies in Pompeian Epigraphy* (Rome).
Pick, B., 1887. 'Zur Titulatur der Flavier', *ZN* 14, 294-374.
Rajak, T., 1996. 'Felix' in S. Hornblower and A. Spawforth (eds.), *Oxford Classical Dictionary*, 3rd edition (Oxford: Oxford University Press), 592.
Reichardt, H. C., 1862. 'Inedited Coins of Judaea', *NC*, n.s. 2, 268-277.
Reisner, G., 1910. 'Harvard Expedition to Samaria', *HTR* 3, 248-263.
Saddington, D. B., 1980. 'Prefects and Lesser Officers in the Auxilia at the Beginning of the Roman Empire', *The Proceedings of the African Classical Associations* 15, 20-58.
Saddington, D. B., 1992. 'Felix in Samaria – A Note on Tac. *Ann.* 12.54.1 and Suet. *Claud.* 28.1', *Acta Classica* 35, 161-164.
Saddington, D. B. and Vogel, U. R. D., 1997. 'An Unpublished Coin of Pontius Pilate – And Some Speculations about his Career', *Akroterion* 42, 23-29.
Safrai, Z., 1994. *The Economy of Roman Palestine* (London and New York: Routledge).
Saulcy, F. De, 1853. 'Lettre a M. de la Saussaye sur les monnaies de cuivre frappes a Jérusalem, par l'ordre des gouverneurs romains de la Judée, depuis le règne d'Auguste jusqu'a celui de Néron', *RN* 1853, 186-201.
Saulcy, F. De, 1854. *Recherches sur la Numismatique Judaïque* (Paris: Typographie de Firmin Didot Frères).
Saulcy, F. De, 1874. *Numismatique de la Terre Sainte* (Paris: J. Rothschild).

Schwartz, D. R., 1992. 'Pontius Pilate's Appointment to Office and the Chronology of Josephus' *Antiquities*, Books 18-20', in D. R. Schwartz, *Studies in the Jewish Background of Christianity* (Tübingen: J. C. B. Mohr), 182-201.

Smallwood, E. M., 1970. *Philonis Alexandrini Legatio ad Gaium* (Leiden: E. J. Brill).

Smallwood, E. M., 1976. *The Jews Under Roman Rule* (Leiden: E. J. Brill)

Speidel, M. P., 1982/3. 'The Roman Army in Judaea under the Procurators', *Ancient Society* 13/14, 233-240.

Syme, R., 1986. 'Three Ambivii', *The Classical Quarterly* 36, 271-276.

Taylor, J. E., 2006. 'Pontius Pilate and the Imperial Cult in Roman Judaea', *NTS* 52, 555-582.

Thomasson, B. E., 1984. *Laterculi Praesidum I* (Gothenburg: Radius).

Tidman, B. M., 1950. 'On the Foundation of the Actian Games', *CQ* 44, 123-125.

Tod, M. N., 1918/9. 'The Macedonian Era', *BSA* 23, 206-217.

Vardaman, E. J., 1998. 'Were the Samaritan Military Leaders, Rufus and Gratus, at the Time of Herod's Death, the Later Roman Judean Governors Who Preceded Pontius Pilate?', in E. J. Vardaman (ed.), *Chronos, Kairos, Christos II: Chronological, Nativity, and Religious Studies in Memory of Ray Summers* (Macon, GA: Mercer University Press), 191-202.

Weaver, P. R. C., 1965. 'Freedmen Procurators in the Imperial Administration', *Historia* 14, 460-469.

Weaver, P. R. C., 2004. '*P. Oxy. 3312* and Joining the Household of Caesar', *ZPE* 149, 196-204.

Weaver, P. R. C., 2005. 'Phaon, Freedman of Nero', *ZPE* 151, 243-252.

# THE COINAGE OF THE GREAT JEWISH REVOLT AGAINST ROME: SCRIPT, LANGUAGE AND INSCRIPTIONS

Robert Deutsch

## 1. Introduction

The predominantly-used languages and scripts at the time of the First Jewish Revolt were Greek, Latin and Aramaic. Numismatic finds from the Revolt period, the coinage of Agrippa II, and local city coins of the time all testify to the fact that the primary language in use at the time in Judaea was Greek.[1] Epigraphic material also testifies to the extensive use of Greek and Aramaic, as seen on contemporary ossuaries, on the Masada ostraca, and elsewhere.[2] Nevertheless, the inscriptions of the Great Revolt coins are written in paleo-Hebrew script, in Hebrew, similar to the Hasmonaean coins which were minted until the year 37 BCE.[3] While the Hebrew and Aramaic languages bear great similarities, the scripts in which they are written differ significantly. As a result one has to assume that the general populace would not have been able to decipher the script on the coins of the revolt, nor understand what was written on them, despite the fact that these are short two-word slogans intended to express a declaratory message or aspiration.[4] Those who would have been well-versed in the reading of ancient Hebrew were the scribes and the Temple priests. This we know from the epigraphic evidence of the Judean Desert caves, commonly known as the "Dead Sea Scrolls".[5] According to one view, these scrolls may have originated in the Temple and were deposited in the desert caves to prevent them falling into Roman hands.[6] The scrolls were generally written in the square Aramaic script, but some of them are also written in the paleo-Hebrew script and a few in Greek.[7]

## 2. Deciphering the Slogans and their Meaning

The deciphering of the inscriptions on the Great Revolt coins is critical, as the coins are a primary form of evidence for the revolt and they cast light on the events of the period. In ancient times, coins were a primary means for spreading propaganda. The same is the case during the revolt period in which the Zealot leaders spread their political and religious beliefs through the means of the slogans on the coins they minted. For this reason, the inscriptions allow us to understand the rebels' motivation, intentions and beliefs. This information can be compared with the historical material furnished by Josephus in order to determine whether they can be correlated with one another, or whether the two sources contradict each other.

Scholarly opinion is divided as to the meaning of the inscriptions, and even about the intellectual concepts employed by the Zealots. Opinions vary widely and cover a whole spectrum of assumptions relating to different intentions and causes, be they religious, messianic or belligerent ones.[8]

The inscriptions appearing on the revolt coins can be divided into three different categories; see **Figs 1-8**:

---

[1] Meshorer 2001, 233-240.
[2] Rachmani 1994, 12-13; Yadin and Naveh 1989, 8.
[3] Meshorer 2001, 201-220.
[4] Mildenberg 1984, 69-70; Goodman 2005, 164; *idem* 2007, 14.
[5] Skehan et al. 1992.
[6] Golb 1985.
[7] Skehan et al. 1992, 17-160, Pls 2-37; Howard 1978.
[8] Kanael 1953; *idem* 1974; Hengel 1989; Price 1992; Meshorer 2001; Rappaport 2007; Goodman 2007.

**Fig. 1:** *Ob*v. (Silver) Shekel of Israel, (Year) One; *R*ev. Jerusalem (the) Holy.
Photographs of the Author.

**Fig. 2:** *Ob*v. Half of a (Silver) Shekel, Y(ear) Two; *R*ev. Jerusalem the Holy.
Photographs courtesy of Chaim Kaufman.

**Fig. 3:** *Ob*v. Quarter of a (Silver) Shekel, (Year) One; *R*ev. Jerusalem (the) Holy.
Photographs courtesy of the late Abraham Bromberg.

**Fig. 4:** *Ob*v. Quarter of a (Silver) Shekel; *R*ev. (Year) Four.
Photographs courtesy of Lisa Knothe.

# THE COINAGE OF THE GREAT JEWISH REVOLT AGAINST ROME: SCRIPT, LANGUAGE AND INSCRIPTIONS

**Fig. 5:** Bronze Prutah from the First Year. *Obv.* (... Is)rael; *Rev.* Jerusalem (the) Holy. Photographs of the Author.

**Fig. 6:** Bronze Prutah, *Obv.* Freedom of Zion; *Rev.* Year Two. Photographs of the Author.

**Fig. 7:** Bronze Prutah, *Obv.* Freedom of Zion; *Rev.* Year Three. Photographs of the Author.

**Fig. 8:** 1/8 Bronze, *Obv.* For the Redemption of Zion; *Rev.* Year Four. Photographs courtesy of Abe Sofaer.

The first group includes the religious messages and ideological slogans: ירושלים הקדושה (Jerusalem the Holy), חרות ציון (Freedom of Zion), and גאלת ציון (Redemption of Zion); the second group expresses a revival of ideas from the Biblical period, with the renewed usage of the terms *Shekel* and *Israel* in the inscriptions שקל ישראל (Shekel of Israel) חצי השקל (Half of the Shekel) and רבע השקל (Quarter of the Shekel). The third group symbolizes the opening of a new era, with the years counted from the start of the revolt. This group includes the dating of the coins from Years 1 to 5 (66-70 CE). All of these inscriptions chosen by the rebels for use on the coins express different messages, but all have the same purpose: to herald the Zealot vision.

## 3. Jerusalem the Holy

ירושלים הקדושה – (Jerusalem the Holy) is a phrase which appears on all of the silver Jewish revolt coins: shekel, half-shekel and quarter-shekel, and also on the unique Year 1 bronze prutah (**Figs 1b-3b, 5b**). This inscription appears right from the onset of the revolt in order to create an affinity between the holiness of Jerusalem and its Temple with the revolt, which broke out in Jerusalem. This affinity provided the moral justification for the violent actions of the Zealot leaders and succeeded in large measure to unite the people in their support.

The version of this inscription presented on the coins of Year 1 is written with defective spelling: ירושלם קדשה, but from Year 2 through 5 it is written in full and with the noun-form ירושלים הקדושה. Most scholars have not paid any particular attention to these two different spellings as the name of the Judaean capital appears in both forms in the Hebrew Bible, both with the י after the ל and without (Josh 10:13; Judg 1:7; Jer 26:18; Esth 2:6, etc.). Jerusalem as a holy city appears twice in the Bible (Isa 52:1; Neh 11:1); the sacred nature of the city stems from the location of the Temple there, since its establishment, according to biblical tradition, by King Solomon in the 10th century BCE.[9] The definition of Jerusalem as sacred on the revolt coins expressed the rebels' powerful feeling for the holiness of Jerusalem and its Temple. This inscription is particularly relevant to the symbol appearing on the centre of the coin, identified as the priestly staff, which is also clearly linked to the Temple. It is unclear why the defining ה is omitted here, as this is in contradiction of the grammatical rules. An examination of the inscription as it appears written on the Year 1 coins: ירושלמקדשה, reveals that it includes the words של מקדש (belonging to the Temple); this is only possible when written without the defining ה and the characters י and ו. Therefore it is possible that these letters were purposefully omitted. Scholarly opinion is divided as to the significance of this inscription, and numerous explanations as to its meaning have been offered: Kindler held that the inscription ירושלים הקדושה denoted the minting authority, and that the coins were issued in the name of Jerusalem the Holy, while refraining from mentioning the leaders of the revolt.[10]

Meshorer saw in these coins a "political statement" similar to that on the Tyrian shekels, which in his opinion the silver shekels replaced. He held that the inscription "Jerusalem the Holy" was intended to declare that "from now on, Tyre is no longer the holy city, and Jerusalem is its replacement".[11] His suggestion has been rejected by other scholars.

Hengel stresses that the freedom of the whole of Israel was dependent on the independence of the Jerusalem Temple, and that the expressions "Jerusalem the Holy", "Zion" and "Freedom" were all parallel ideas of paramount importance for the rebels, expressing the prophecies of Isaiah (52:1-2) and Ezekiel (44:9) regarding the freedom and the purity of Jerusalem. According to Hengel, the inscriptions on the coins attest to a dual belief among

---

[9] Hengel 1989, 118.
[10] Kindler 1974, 52.
[11] Meshorer 2001, 116.

the rebels: one of the holiness of the Messianic visions of the Hebrew prophets, and the other of the freedom of Jerusalem and its Temple.[12] Hengel is essentially repeating Josephus' claim that the reason for the Jewish revolt was the Jews' yearning for freedom and liberty,[13] and as a result he deciphers the coins' inscriptions in the same manner.

## 4. "Jerusalem the Holy" Written on Gamala Bronze Shekels?

On the Gamala bronze coins, which are barbarous imitations of the silver coins, an abbreviated inscription in defective spelling appears: (ירשלם הק(דושה)) (after Meshorer) or (יורשלם הק(דושה)) (after Syon).[14] Assuming that Naveh's suggestion as to the deciphering of this inscription is correct,[15] then it is possible to connect the inscriptions on both sides of the coin to read:
לגאלת ירושלם הק(דשה) - *for the redemption of Jerusalem the Holy.*[16]

If this reading is correct, it is clear that the statement made here is quite different from that on the Jerusalem shekels. While there the declaration is that Jerusalem is a holy city, here the statement is a sort of prayer, or an expression of hope for redemption (apparently during a period of significant distress).

The reading of the legend around the chalice in paleo-Hebrew, as לגאלת, makes sense, but it is not the most logical option; a preferable suggestion is to read this as written in Aramaic script בגמלא - *in Gamala*.[17] In any case, the accuracy of the readings of these crude inscriptions is doubtful.

## 5. Shekel of Israel

The inscription *Shekel of Israel*, *Half-Shekel* and *Quarter-Shekel* which appear on the silver coins denote their value in relation to the actual weight of the material from which the coin is manufactured, that is the amount of silver equivalent either to a whole shekel, half of a shekel, or quarter of a shekel (**Figs 1a-4a**).

The shekel was a common unit of weight, attested in the Bible and used for different metals: "600 shekels of iron" (1 Sam 17:7), "a single gold ingot, 50 shekels in weight" (Jos. 7.21), "give the king of Assyria 50 shekels of silver" (2 Kgs 16:20) etc. As well as the shekel, which is the whole unit, scripture also often refers to its parts: "a half-shekel of the holy shekel" (Num 38:13), "a quarter-shekel of silver" (1 Sam 9:8), "donate for us a third of a shekel a year to the Temple corvée" (Neh 10:33), etc.

On the shekels of the revolt, the whole unit "shekel" is accompanied by the word "Israel" (signifying *of Israel*). From this we can assume that use of the prefix: *he* (the) in the legend on the other coins: "half of *the* shekel" and "quarter of *the* shekel" also signifies this "Hebrew" weight.

Another inscription mentioning Israel appears on the unique Year 1 bronze prutah: (יש)ראל (**Fig. 5a**). The inscription is not completely stamped, and the two logical options for its completion are (לגאולת) (יש)ראל or (לחרות) (יש)ראל. In any case, there is little point in deliberating over the significance of these inscriptions, as there are other options of completing them, and it is more reasonable to wait for the discovery of another such prutah with a complete inscription.[18]

The use of the term *Israel* on the coins is an innovation, and its appearance requires an attempt at explanation. Kadman did not discuss the appearance of the inscription *Shekel of Israel* in his chapter on inscriptions.[19] Meshorer also ignored the question, and made

---

[12] Hengel 1989, 118.
[13] *Ibid*. 110-112.
[14] Meshorer 2001, 131; Syon 2004, 56.
[15] Syon 2004, 57, n. 23.
[16] Meshorer 2001, 131.
[17] Farhi 2006, 74.
[18] Deutsch 1994.
[19] Kadman 1960, 96-98.

no comment on the use of the term *Israel* in connection with the new shekels. Goodman, however, notes that the name of the new province is *Israel* as opposed to *Judaea.* Goodman suggests that the rebels were inclined to avoid defining themselves as "Judaeans", and that this is evident on their coins as well. This may have been a result of the fact that the Roman name for the area was *Judaea,* and consequently, they avoided its use.[20]

There are a number of possible explanations for the use of the word *Israel* in connection with the shekel unit. It may be a reference to the geographical entity, the Land of Israel, or to the historical kingdom of Israel. Similarly, it may refer to the Jews, as the people of Israel, or to Judaism as the religion of Israel; also possibly to the shekel as a Hebrew unit of weight.

According to the Scriptural story Jacob was re-named "Israel" after wrestling with the Angel of God (Gen 32:29; Hos 12:4-5).

In the Hebrew Bible, the names *Israel* and *Children of Israel* came to represent the Jewish people, while in extra-Biblical sources, the earliest mention is on the celebrated Victory Stele of Merneptah, dated to c. 1220 BCE. Here the name *Israel* is prefixed by the word "people" or "nation".[21] Following the split of the United Monarchy of David and Solomon in around 920 BCE, according to the biblical narrative, "Israel" came to be used as the name of the Northern Kingdom alongside Judaea to its south. On the Mesha stele, dated to c. 825 BCE, the term "King of Israel" appears a number of times in reference to Israel as a kingdom, also, "Israelite prisoners of war".[22] On another royal inscription, from the last quarter of the 9th BCE found at Dan, the name "Israel" appears once again in reference to the kingdom: "King of Israel".[23] In the Shalmaneser III stele, Ahab, King of Israel, is referred to as "the Israelite".[24] In 721 BCE, Sargon II of Assyria conquered Samaria, the capital, taking over 27,000 of its inhabitants into exile, and the Kingdom of Israel effectively ceased to exist.[25]

Nevertheless, the use of the term "Israel" never ceased, and it appears commonly in the New Testament (Matt 2:6; Luke 2:32; John 1:31, 49, etc.). But the term *Israel* is completely absent from the epigraphic record and re-appears only in 66 CE on the revolt coins. In the *Bellum Judaicum*, Josephus does not use the term even once, despite the fact that he uses it frequently in the *Antiquitates Judaicae,* which was a later work in which Josephus reworked the Biblical accounts.[26] His avoidance in referring to Israel even a single time in the *Bellum Judaicum* was apparently not by chance, but the reason for this is unclear. It may be connected in some way with the use the rebels made of the term in dating their revolt.

The appearance of the term *Israel* in the New Testament is particularly worthy of mention, as its composition was roughly contemporary to the Jewish revolt, and it was written from Millennarian motives similar to those which sparked the rebellion. The term *Israel* in the New Testament sometimes refers to the people: "a ruler will come out who will shepherd my people Israel" (Matt 2:6) "a light to enlighten the eyes of the nations and the glory of your people Israel" (Luke 2:32) "and Israel pursuing the law of Righteousness" (Rom 9:31). In other passages, *Israel* refers to the land: "and return to Israel" (Matt 2:20), "and he arose and took the child and returned to Israel" (Matt 2:21) "you shall not succeed in passing the cities of Israel" (Matt 10:23) etc. If so, the term Israel is defined by its context, sometimes as the country and sometimes as the people.

The second Jewish rebellion against the Romans, known as the Bar-Kokhba revolt, took place during the reign of Hadrian (132-135 CE) and, like the Great revolt, broke out as the result of religious and millenarian reasons. Independent coins were also minted in this period, declaring

---

[20] Goodman 2005, 164-166; *idem* 2007, 14-15.
[21] *ANET* 378, and n. 18; Kitchen 2003, 451.
[22] *ANET* 320.
[23] Biran and Naveh 1995, 12, line 8.
[24] *ANET* 279.
[25] *Ibid.* 284-285.
[26] See the index of the Loeb edition of Josephus, under 'Israel' and 'Israelites'.

the freedom of the Jewish people in the Land of Israel, and were dated like the Great Revolt coins from the revolt's first year onwards. All the symbols which appear on the bronze coins of the Great Revolt, the palm tree, *lulav*, *etrog*, vine leaf and amphora, appear also on the Bar-Kokhba coins. Similarly, paleo-Hebrew script and the Hebrew language were employed on the Bar-Kokhba coins. As a result, it seems reasonable to compare the inscriptions appearing on the coins of the two revolts. Simon Bar-Kokhba adopted the title "Prince of Israel" alongside another leader referred to as "Eleazar the Priest". On the Year 1 Bar-Kokhba coins the following legend appears: "Year One of the Redemption of Israel", and on the Year 2 coins "Year 2 of the Freedom of Israel".[27] Similarly, in the Bar-Kokhba letters, dated to relatively early in the rebellion: "during the month of Kislev in the year three of Simon Bar-Kokhba, prince of Israel", or in relation to the redemption of Israel: "20th Shevat, Year 2 of the redemption of Israel, from Simon Ben-Kosiba, prince of Israel, dwelling at Herodion", while in a further Aramaic document the following phrase appears: "1st of Iyar, Year 1 of the redemption of Israel", also in other documents.[28]

From the use that Bar-Kokhba made of the term "Israel" when he adopted the title of "Nasi Israel" and the fact that he dated his letters according to the redemption of Israel, it is clear that he was referring to "the people of Israel".

If so, one may then conclude that the term "Shekel of Israel" can have two different meanings:

1) Shekel of (the Land) of Israel; 2) Shekel of (the People) of Israel.

Seeing as these coins were used to pay the half-shekel contribution to the upkeep of the Jerusalem Temple, and paid only by adult male Jews (Exod 30:12-16), we can assume that the meaning was "Shekel of (the people) of Israel". Despite this fact, the two ideas do not contradict one another, and we cannot deny the possibility that the term "Shekel of Israel" may include both meanings: "Shekel of the Land and People of Israel".

## 6. Freedom of Zion, Redemption of Zion

On the bronze coins issued during Years 2 and 3 of the revolt the phrase "Freedom of Zion" (חרות ציון, sometimes written defectively חרת ציון) (**Figs 6a-7a**), while on the Year 4 bronze coins the phrase "For the Redemption of Zion" (לגאלת ציון) appears (**Fig. 8a**). This is the first time that the term "Zion" appears on Jewish coins. "Zion" is a common synonymous term for Jerusalem, in connection to the city's religious function with particularly spiritual connotations. Josephus makes no use of this term in *Bellum Judaicum*, but it does appear in the New Testament ("Daughter of Zion": Matt 21:5; John 12:15).

Kadman made no reference to the use of the term while Meshorer suggested that it referred to the whole of the Land of Israel, as in the common phrase "Land of Zion".[29]

Other scholars have related to the idea of "Zion" as a synonym for Jerusalem which is based on the Hebrew Bible, "the City of David and the Fortress of Zion" (2 Sam 5:7-9), with particular reference to Jerusalem as the location of the temple, and the spiritual centre of the Jewish people.[30]

Kanael suggested interpreting the inscription "the redemption of Zion" as an expression of the Messianic claims and the vision of the End of Days expressed by Simon Bar-Kokhba, as opposed to John of Gischala, who used the more moderate term "freedom" in emphasizing political liberty.[31]

---

[27] Mildenberg 1984, 29-31.
[28] Yadin *et al*. 2002, 44, 58, 66, 144.
[29] Kadman 1960, 97; Meshorer 2001, 122.
[30] Levenson 1992.
[31] Kanael 1953, 20.

Hengel does not support Kanael's suggestion, and holds that John of Gischala also made Messianic claims, and may well have seen himself as a saviour who would bring about Israel's salvation.[32] Hengel concludes that the terms "Zion" and "Freedom" are parallel ideas to that of "Jerusalem the Holy", used by the rebels to express the achievement of the purity and freedom of Jerusalem.[33] Hengel believes that these inscriptions appearing on the coins actually express the rebels' millennarian vision and their determination to fight the Romans to the bitter end.[34]

According to Goodman, the slogans chosen by the mint authority constitute the declaration of a new political entity which identifies itself as Jerusalem, and the key-words accompanying it are freedom and holiness.[35] By contrast, Price describes the slogans appearing on the revolt coins as propagandist and warlike rhetoric.[36] Similarly, Kindler sees the inscriptions as slogans of war.[37]

If so, there are three primary approaches to deciphering the phrases "Freedom of Zion" and "Redemption of Zion":

1) Messianic claims and millennarian visions (Kanael and Hengel).
2) The declaration of the establishment of an independent political entity (Kanael and Goodman).
3) Propaganda and war rhetoric (Kindler and Price).

In conclusion as to the nature of the two phrases, we can state that there is no contradiction between the different scholarly opinions, but that they may be regarded as essentially different aspects of the same idea. These three approaches all combine neatly with the rebels' intention of declaring an independent political entity based on a Messianic vision, and this is indeed an expression of propaganda and warlike rhetoric to encourage the rebels to achieve this freedom and salvation.

## 7. The Dates

Alongside the slogans, inscriptions on each of the coins mark the dates of the Great Revolt according to the years of the Jewish war against the Romans. On the silver coins (**Figs 1a-3a, 4b**), the dates always appear as letters or abbreviations:

א, ש״ב, ש״ג, ש״ד, ש״ה

While on the bronze coins (**Figs 6b-8b**), the dates are always expressed in complete words:

שנת שתים, שנת שלוש, שנת ארבע

There is no convincing explanation for the reason of the addition of the letter ש to represent the word שנה (year) on the silver coins following the first year, when that year was simply denoted by an א.[38]

There is no doubt that the denoting of the dates in this manner comes to herald the beginning of a new era, an era counted from the beginning of "Zion's freedom". Similarly the dating

---

[32] Hengel 1989, 117, 297.
[33] *Ibid.*, 118-122.
[34] *Ibid.*, 403.
[35] Goodman 2007, 14.
[36] Price 1992, 197.
[37] Kindler 1974, 52.
[38] See also the irregular quarter-shekel coins of Year 4 (Fig. 4), on which the year was also denoted only by the letter ד (dalet) (Meshorer 2001, no. 210).

# THE COINAGE OF THE GREAT JEWISH REVOLT AGAINST ROME:
## SCRIPT, LANGUAGE AND INSCRIPTIONS

expresses the power of the rebellion and its longevity, in order to bolster popular morale. A similar phenomenon is seen at the beginning of the Bar-Kokhba revolt, whose coins are also dated according to the years of the revolt for the first two years (this ceases in the third year).

With reference to the bronze coins of Year 4 of the Great Revolt, it may be the case that the inscriptions from both sides of the coin should be read as a single phrase:

שנת ארבע לגאולת ציון - *Year 4 of the Redemption of Zion*

This is backed up by the prefix ל (For the), which appears before the word גאולת (redemption). By contrast, however, the inscriptions on the Year 2 and 3 coins cannot be combined in this manner, as the resulting שנת שלוש חרות ציון or שנת שתים חרות ציון lacks the prefix ל needed to connect the two phrases grammatically. Nevertheless, it seems reasonable to assume that the intention of those minting the coins was to say "this is the second/third year of the freedom of Zion". It may well be the case that the differences between the bronze coins of Years 2-3 and those of Year 4 is the result of the fact that they were minted by different minting authorities.

## 8. Conclusion

An examination of the slogans used on the coins of the Great Revolt reveals the following messages: "Jerusalem the Holy" - Jerusalem which was the capital city of Judaea, and was indeed considered holy to the Jews by virtue of the Temple which stood on the Temple Mount and the rituals which were practiced in it.

The other two slogans: "Freedom of Zion" and "Redemption of Zion" both relate to the freedom from Roman domination. And indeed this freedom, though brief, less than a full five years, was real, and is expressed in the minting of the coins which was an overt act of political independence.

The use of the ancient paleo-Hebrew script on the coins was intended to link the contemporary Jewish leaders of the Second Temple period with the earlier era of the First Temple and the Jewish Kingdom, as expressed in the biblical accounts.[39] In the same manner, the use of terms such as "Zion" and "Israel" was intended to emphasize the connection between the earlier period of the First Temple and the time of the Second Temple and the current Jewish rebellion.

If so, then the slogans used on the coins clearly express the aspirations of the Jewish rebels, firstly their aspiration to religious freedom, expressed by "Jerusalem the Holy" (and the ritual symbols), and secondly, the hope for political independence, expressed by "Freedom of Zion" and the dating of the coins, also in the expression of divine salvation with the yearning for "the Redemption of Zion" towards the end of the rebellion. These slogans actually express religious and even Messianic sentiments, which are repeated with only minor variations 62 years later, during the Bar-Kokhba revolt.[40]

---

[39] Meshorer 2001, 40-41.

[40] Mildenberg 1984, 29-31.

## Bibliography

*ANET* – *Ancient Near Eastern Texts Relating to the Old Testament*, ed. J. B. Pritchard, 3rd edn. (Princeton, NJ: Princeton University Press, 1969).

Biran, A., and Naveh, J., 1995. 'The Tel Dan Inscription: A New Fragment', *Israel Exploration Journal* 45, 1-18.

Deutsch, R., 1994. 'A Unique Prutah from the First Year of the Jewish War against Rome', *Israel Exploration Journal* 12, 71-72.

Golb, N., 1985. 'Who Hid the Dead Sea Scrolls ?', *Biblical Archaeologist* 48, 68-82.

Goodman, M., 2005. 'Coinage and Identity: The Jewish Evidence', in C. Howgego, V. Heuchert and A. Burnett (eds.), *Coinage and Identity in the Roman Provinces* (Oxford: Oxford University Press), 163-166.

Goodman, M., 2007. *Rome and Jerusalem; The Clash of Ancient Civilizations.* (New York: Vintage Books).

Farhi, Y., 2006. 'The Bronze Coins Minted at Gamala Reconsidered', *Israel Exploration Journal* 15, 69-76.

Hengel, M., 1989. *The Zealots, Investigation into the Jewish Freedom Movement in the Period from Herod I Until 70 A.D.* (2nd edn, translated by D. Smith) (Edinburgh: T. and T. Clark).

Howard, G., 1978. 'The Name of God in the New Testament', *Biblical Archaeology Review* 4.1, 12-14, 52.

Kadman, L., 1960. *The Coins of the Jewish War of 66 – 73 C.E.* (Tel-Aviv: Schocken).

Kanael, B., 1953. 'The Historical Background of the Coins Year Four of the Redemption of Zion', *Bulletin of the American Schools of Oriental Research* 129, 18-20.

Kindler, A., 1974. *Coins of the Land of Israel; Collection of the Bank of Israel* (Jerusalem: Keter).

Kitchen, K. A., 2003. *On the Reliability of the Old Testament* (Grand Rapids, MI: Eerdmans).

Levenson, J. D., 1992. 'Zion Tradition', *The Anchor Bible Dictionary* 6 (New York: Doubleday), 1098-1102.

Meshorer, Y., 2001. *A Treasury of Jewish Coins* (Nyack, NY: Amphora).

Mildenberg, L., 1984. *The Coinage of the Bar Kokhba War* (Aarau / Frankfurt am Main / Salzburg: Sauerländer).

Price, J. J., 1992. *Jerusalem Under Siege, The Collapse of the Jewish State 66-70 C.E.* (Leiden: Brill).

Rachmani, L.Y., 1994. *A Catalogue of Jewish Ossuaries in the Collection of the State of Israel* (Jerusalem: Israel Antiquities Authority / Israel Academy of Sciences and Humanities).

Rappaport, U., 2007. 'Who Minted the Jewish War's Coins', *Israel Numismatic Research* 2, 103-116.

Skehan, P. W. *et al.*, 1992. 'Qumran Cave 4; IV: Paleo-Hebrew and Greek Biblical Manuscripts', *Discoveries in the Judaean Desert* IX (Oxford: Clarendon).

Syon, D., 2004. *Tyre and Gamla,* unpublished PhD dissertation (Hebrew University, Jerusalem).

Yadin, Y., *et al.*, 2002. *The Documents from the Bar Kokhba Period in the Cave of the Letters* (Jerusalem: Israel Exploration Society).

Yadin, Y., and Naveh, J., 1989. 'The Aramaic and Hebrew Ostraca and Jar Inscriptions', *Masada* I (Jerusalem: Israel Exploration Society), 1-68.

# JEWISH COINAGE OF THE TWO WARS, AIMS AND MEANING

David Hendin

## 1. Introduction

The coins of the Jewish War (66-73 CE) and the Bar Kokhba Revolt (132-135 CE) have been widely discussed for more than 150 years.[1] Just as the wars, their coins share similarities and important differences. Equally noteworthy, the coins of the two Jewish wars against Rome contrast dramatically to all three series of ancient Judaean coins that preceded them.

Fig. 1  Fig. 2

**Fig. 1:** Yehud, Persian Period. Hendin 2010, no. 1059; Meshorer 2001, no. 15 (2:1).
**Fig. 2:** Yehud, Ptolemaic Period. Hendin 2010, no. 1087; Meshorer 2001, no. 32 (2:1).

Based on these dissimilarities one might be tempted to observe that the coinage of the two wars was the only fully realized independent Jewish coinage in ancient times. The Yehud coins of the Persian (**Fig. 1**) to the Macedonian periods are probably satrapal issues, and those of the Ptolemaic period (**Fig. 2**) are local mint Ptolemaic issues.[2] All of the coins of the Yehud series are fractional units, mostly lighter than one gram, and there is not a single full unit coin (shekel or stater) known to exist.

Fig. 3  Fig. 4  Fig. 5

**Fig. 3:** Early Jerusalem bronze of Hyrcanus I paying homage to Antiochus VII. Hendin 2010, no. 1131; Meshorer 2001, p. 30.
**Fig. 4:** Hyrcanus I bronze with name Yehohanan. Hendin 2010, no. 1137; Meshorer 2001, type I.
**Fig. 5:** Mattatayah Antigonus bronze. Hendin 2010, no. 1168; Meshorer 2001, no. 41.

The Hasmonaean coinage was issued by Jewish high priests and kings, but the series began with coins that paid homage to Seleucid overlords (**Fig. 3**), who controlled the right of the Jews to issue coins.[3] This resulted in Jewish royal issues of exclusively small denomination bronze coins (**Fig. 4**) until the unusual coins of Mattatayah Antigonus, minted concurrently with Herod being declared king. The coin types of Mattatayah are derivative of the previous Hasmonaean issues except for the small bronze coin depicting the showbread table and the menorah (**Fig. 5**). Legends on Hasmonaean coins are predominantly paleo-Hebrew, but also

---

[1] The author gratefully acknowledges Peter Van Alfen, Isadore Goldstein, David Vagi, and Donald Simon for their important suggestions and comments.

[2] Barag 1994-1999.

[3] Hendin 2010, 157-163 for examples and discussion.

include Greek and Aramaic.

Herod I built the magnificent Second Temple, but he was fully subservient to Rome. Herod was named king of the Jews in 40 BCE by the Roman Senate and approval of the triumvirate. Like the Hasmonaeans, he had no right to mint silver coins.[4] All the coins of Herod and his descendants were inscribed in Greek (**Fig. 6**), and they are considered to be Roman provincial coins rather than sovereign Judaean issues.[5]

**Fig. 6:** Herod I bronze. Hendin 2010, no. 1169; Meshorer 2001, no. 44.

The coins of the two Jewish wars against Rome, however, were painted with a different palette than the earlier Judaean coins. First, they include full denomination silver shekels or sela'im (in the case of Bar Kokhba) that were denied to the previous Jewish administrations, as well as multiple bronze denominations. Second, their exclusive language is paleo-Hebrew.[6] Third, all of the motifs on the coins are specifically Jewish in nature. The early small silver of the Persian through the Ptolemaic periods mainly imitated Greek issues. Hasmonaean and early Herodian coins had mostly agrarian motifs and abstract pagan symbols. They were not overtly Jewish, but simply were not offensive to the Jewish populations among which they circulated.[7] Finally one cannot overlook the large output of good quality coins during difficult circumstances during both wars.

## 2. The Reason to Mint

The earliest Greek coins were struck from the purest available metal. They had specific value only within their issuing state, and if one wanted to undertake transactions outside the immediate area, coins needed to be weighed. Eventually trading metals ceased to be a commodity transaction and, via circulating coins, became a purchase; also at this time coins began to be counted, instead of weighed, and the concept of fiduciary coinage began.[8]

Reasons to mint coins in antiquity were varied and are generally not fully understandable from a modern perspective.[9] In spite of this, two primary motivations for the production of coinage that we can detect in antiquity are military payments and generating a profit.[10] While

---

[4] Meshorer (2001, 72-78) theorized that the late Tyre *shekels* marked KP were Herod's silver coins. This is convincingly contested by Levy 2005, 885; *idem* 1993, 267-274.

[5] All of them are listed in *Roman Provincial Coinage* I and II.

[6] Mildenberg (1984, 66) describes the script on Jewish War coins as "formal paleo-Hebrew" and that on the Bar Kokhba Revolt coins as "cursive paleo-Hebrew." However, similarities far outweigh differences.

[7] This ceased with coins of Herod Philip and thereafter most Herodian dynastic coins carry local or imperial portraits.

[8] Seaford (2004, 145) notes "The result is the paradox that even coinage of unadulterated silver (let alone bronze) may tend to become in effect fiduciary coinage: although the silver contributes to confidence, it is not envisaged as a commodity. And so whereas we frequently hear of metal artefacts being melted down to make coins, we do not hear of Greek coins being smelted down by Greeks to create bullion or artefacts."

[9] Howgego, 1990.

[10] Le Rider 2001; *idem* 1989, 1-25.

almost all manufactured coins were fiduciary, production of the greatly overvalued "fiduciary" bronzes was far more profitable than that of precious metal coins.[11] During the Hellenistic period in Judaea it was a royal prerogative to issue coins, and this grant was made to the Jews by Antiochus VII (I Macc. 15:6).

The evolution from exchange of metal pieces to coinage went beyond a strict economic enterprise. As Peter Van Alfen notes, once coins became struck objects rather than chopped fragments, "the monetary instrument could now advance upon levels of political symbolism that were unattainable with anonymous bits."[12] This concept is applicable to Judaean coinage, since there were both political and religious issues to be considered.[13] Leo Mildenberg describes coins as "the best mass media of the time."[14] This discussion focuses primarily on use of coinage as a mode of disseminating political information during the two wars.

Neither military payments, nor profits were likely motivating factors in the production of the Jewish precious metal coinages. It is likely that the Jewish War silver coins were used to pay Temple dues,[15] probably not replacing the standard Tyre shekels and half-shekels, but supplementing them as the "shekels of Israel" became increasingly available. This explains why the shekels were made from such pure silver (see the discussion below). Already by this time the debased silver tetradrachms of Nero had entered the local markets, but it would have been untenable for a Jewish authority to strike coins that would not be accepted at the Temple.

During the Jewish War, the ability to manufacture coins not only enriched the group that issued them, but highlighted political independence and conveyed important messages to the Jewish populations. During the Bar Kokhba Revolt, no minting was profitable (see discussion below).

At the time of the Jewish War there were many silver coins of Tyre as well as Seleucid, Ptolemaic, and Roman coins in wide circulation in the area,[16] not to mention many small bronze coins from Hasmonaean and Herodian times, and from the Roman governors of Judaea (prefects and procurators).[17] Robert Deutsch, most recently, suggests that the Jewish War silver coins were made from melted and further purified Tyre shekels that came from the Temple treasury.[18] Thus the Jewish War silver did not offer the manufacturers as much profit as might have been realized.

One may cogently argue that the only ancient coins minted that did not carry any fiduciary value were those from the Bar Kokhba Revolt. Re-making the coins already in circulation by the Bar Kokhba administration was a cost centre "the investment of much labour without any financial gain," notes Meshorer.[19] Thus any "fiduciary profit" had already been extracted during the original manufacture of these coins from raw material, since the flans for every Bar Kokhba coin came from coins already in circulation. Thus the Bar Kokhba government

---

[11] Mørkholm *et. al.* 1991, 6.

[12] Van Alfen 2009.

[13] See Hendin 2007-2008 for a discussion of these matters regarding Hasmonaean coinage.

[14] Mildenberg 1984, 72.

[15] Eventually the reason for the relative rarity of both Tyrian and Jewish half-shekels needs to be examined. The Temple dues were a half-shekel a year. It had to be inconvenient to have few half-shekels, since if the full shekel was used to pay at the Temple a "kolbon" or fee of either around 2.1% or 4.2% had to be added (and it is generally believed that a money changer would charge approximately the same fee to break a single Tyre *shekel* into two half-shekels). Even if a full shekel was used for two persons, a "kolbon" still needed to be paid since otherwise the two would have had to use a money changer to obtain two half-shekels; the transaction thus reflects on the early rabbinic principal of "Yafeh koach hekdesh," in which the Temple had to be the greater beneficiary in any transaction.

[16] Jos., *War* 5.421 and 550-552 observes that Jewish War rebels had and held gold and silver Roman coins.

[17] It is widely assumed that Tyre ceased minting its shekels in or around 66 CE because by that time their principal use was for Jews, who required them to pay the Temple tax, and there was no reason for Tyre to continue minting them since other nearby Roman provincial mints, principally Antioch, had started minting debased silver Roman imperial tetradrachms.

[18] Deutsch 2009a and personal communications.

[19] Meshorer 2001, 142.

sacrificed the ability to profit from coinage in favour of the clearly more significant need to distribute a political message from hand to hand on an ongoing basis. During the Bar Kokhba Revolt the Jerusalem Temple no longer existed, so any perceived economic rationale for creating large silver coins was simply a wistful desire for a return to using large silver coins as Temple dues. It was not a reality since the large Bar Kokhba silver coins were not very pure: they were invariably struck upon debased silver coins of Antioch or Tyre from the time of Nero through Hadrian.

Because neither Seleucids nor Romans had previously allowed the Jews to issue silver coins, the autonomous series of silver coins of the Jewish War made a major political statement—"an ostentatious demonstration of the recovery of independence,"[20] writes Roth, who suggests that coin minting by an autonomous Jewish government "was a religious as well as a patriotic necessity."[21]

Rappaport believes that the silver coinage of the Jewish War was "first and foremost minted to provide for the Temple's expenditure for provisions and maintenance."[22] He believes that the high priests and rich nobles were acting as if they supported the revolt in order to attempt to avoid what they believed would be a hopeless confrontation with Rome.[23]

Religious necessity for the Jewish War silver, however, is not clear. There was ample coinage in circulation and available in the Temple treasury, including the shekels and half-shekels of Tyre that had been collected for decades. This suggests that the creation of the Jewish War silver coins was intended to send the dramatic message of independence not only to Rome but to the local Jewish population. Paying for commodities (sacrificial animals, wine, incense, olive oil, wheat, and related products) and services (craftsmen and other workers) required by the Temple was an excellent method of moving the coins into circulation.

Fig. 7: Alexander Jannaeus bronze with paleo-Hebrew and Greek. Hendin 2010, no. 1148; Meshorer 2001, type N.

All the Hasmonaean coins and most of those of the Herodian princes carried descriptive legends. The Hasmonaean formula generally repeated such as "Yehonatan the high priest and the Community of the Jews" in Hebrew and "(of) King Yehonatan" in Greek (**Fig. 7**).

Herod I, Archelaus, and Antipas each issued coins with Greek legends stating "(of) King Herod" "ethnarch" or "tetrarch." Philip's coins were similar but carried obverse portraits and legends pertaining to Augustus and Tiberius (as well as Philip's own portrait). Herod I's grandson Agrippa I issued coins describing himself as "The Great King" and "Friend of Caesar,"[24] as well as a remarkable coin proclaiming "A vow and treaty of friendship and alliance between the great King Agrippa and Augustus Caesar, the Senate and the People of Rome."[25]

On the other hand, the coins struck during Jewish War and the Bar Kokhba Revolt employed carefully worded patriotic slogans.

---

[20] Roth 1962, 34.
[21] *Ibid.*, 33.
[22] Rappaport 2007, 104.
[23] *Ibid.*
[24] Hendin 2010, nos. 1245-1246, 1248-1250; Meshorer 2001, nos. 121-122, 124-126.
[25] *Ibid.*, no. 1248; Meshorer 2001, no. 124.

## 3. The Minting Authorities

No minting authority is named on the coins of the Jewish War. It has been suggested that "Jerusalem" refers to the minting authority, but it seems more likely that Jerusalem was designated as the place of minting rather than the minting authority.[26]

Since the Jewish War was chaotic and factious from its outset; it is all the more remarkable that the Jews were able to create consistently high quality coins. The anonymity of a minting authority suggested a Jewish national unity that did not exist on the ground since there were several factions of Jews, some diametrically opposed to each other.

Fig. 8                               Fig. 9

**Fig. 8:** Bar Kokhba bronze naming "Simon, prince of Israel" in paleo-Hebrew. Hendin 2010, no. 1378; Meshorer 2001, no. 222.

**Fig. 9:** Bar Kokhba silver zuz naming "Eleazar the Priest" in paleo-Hebrew. Hendin 2010, no. 1374; Meshorer 2001, no. 218.

**Fig. 10:** Bar Kokhba bronze coin naming "Jerusalem" in paleo-Hebrew. Hendin 2010, no. 1404 Meshorer 2001, no. 255.

Coins of the Bar Kokhba Revolt, on the other hand, were commonly struck with the name "Simon" referring to Bar Kokhba (Ben Kosiba),[27] who styled himself "*Nasi Y'srael*" or "Prince of Israel" (in modern Hebrew the word *Nasi* translates as "president") (**Fig. 8**). Another individual, Eleazar the Priest (**Fig. 9**), is mentioned on coins from of the first year of the Bar Kokhba Revolt, but not later.[28] Mildenberg posits that Simon was not the minting authority for coins of the Bar Kokhba Revolt, but was the leader and figurehead of a government.[29] Jerusalem was also named on the Bar Kokhba (**Fig. 10**) coins and seems to carry the same weight as Simon's name on both silver and bronze denominations.

---

[26] Mildenberg 1984, 61-62.
[27] Yadin 1971,17-27 for a discussion regarding Simon's full name.
[28] *Ibid.*, 27.

## 4. Israel versus Judaea

Fig. 11                               Fig. 12

**Fig. 11:** Herod Antipas bronze naming "Tiberias" in Greek. Hendin 2010, no. 1212; Meshorer 2001, no. 88.
**Fig. 12:** Bar Kokhba silver zuz with paleo-Hebrew legend "Year two, freedom of Israel." Hendin 2010, no. 1390; Meshorer 2001, no. 24

Another significant difference between the coins of the two Jewish wars and the earlier Jewish coins with paleo-Hebrew or Aramaic legends is the naming of the land in which these coins were struck.

Coins of the Persian through the Ptolemaic period refer to the area as "Yehud" or "Yehudah," the name of the Persian satrapy referring back to the Iron Age name Yehudah. Hasmonaean coins refer to the "High Priest and the Council of the Jews (or Judaeans)." Herod I's coins never mention a territorial or mint name, but coins of his son Antipas refer to the city of Tiberias (**Fig. 11**), and some coins of his grandson Agrippa I mention Caesarea.

Why, then, do the coins of the Jewish War, and later the Bar Kokhba Revolt, cite the native land of the Jews as "Israel" instead of "Judaea"? (**Fig. 12**)

A number of reasons for this may exist. The term Israelites (also known as the Twelve Tribes or Children of Israel) refers to the descendants of Jacob (Israel). More generally it also refers to the worshippers of the god of Israel, irrespective of their ethnic origin. On the other hand, Judaeans are a specific regional group who lived in Judaea. From this period there are references to other Jewish geographic groups, such as the Galileans.

One may also surmise that at this time there was an effort to be inclusive for all Jews, some of whom may have identified with the ten lost tribes which disappeared from biblical accounts after the return of the tribes of Judah and Benjamin from Babylon.

Goodblatt discusses uses of "Judaea" and "Israel" in detail, and relates the coins to literature of the first and second centuries. He wonders if the later preference of Israel over Judaea could "reflect an attempt to differentiate the rebel regime(s) from the Hasmonaean-Herodian state 'of the Judeans,' or from the Roman province of Iudaea? Certainly the rebels would want to emphasize the discontinuity with the Imperial provincial structures."[30] He further observes that "Rabbinic materials emerge as a literature beginning in the late first century. The earlier strata of rabbinic literature thus reinforce the preference for an Israel nationalism evidenced among the rebels of 66 and 132."[31]

Goodman suggests that perhaps the Jews eschewed the name "Judaea" simply because it was the name used by Rome to refer to their province.[32] One also notes that by the time of the two Jewish Wars, significant communities of Jews had been established in foreign capitals such as Alexandria (Jos., *Ant*. 15.113) Antioch (*Ibid.*,12.119-120), Sidon (*Ibid.*, 14.323), and Tyre (*Ibid.*, 14. 314). It is therefore possible that the use of the broader term of "Israel" for the physical state being sought by the rebels was intended to differentiate from "Jews" or "Judaeans" who no longer lived in the area, but belonged to the rapidly growing Jewish Diaspora that increasingly supported Jewish activity in and around Jerusalem

---

[29] Mildenberg 1984, 62-65.
[30] Goodblatt 2006, 137.
[31] *Ibid.*, 139.
[32] Goodman 166.

## 5. Early Zionistic Slogans

Fig. 13              Fig. 14

**Fig. 13:** Jewish War with paleo-Hebrew legends "Shekel of Israel" and "Jerusalem the Holy," dated 'year 3'. Hendin 2010, no. 1361; Meshorer 2001, no. 202.

**Fig. 14:** Tyre, Phoenicia, silver shekel, Greek translates as "of Tyre, the Holy and Inviolable" dated year 168 = 42/43 C.E. Hendin 2010, no. 1620b.

Precise wording in the legends and selection of the images on the coins of the Jewish wars suggests that the leaders had a clear understanding of using coins for political communication.

The first coins minted in the 66 CE were silver shekels and half-shekels with the legends "Shekel of Israel" or "half [of] the shekel," and "Jerusalem [the] holy." (**Fig. 13**) In this last legend we see a parallel to the legend on the contemporary Tyrian silver coins which carry the legend ΤΥΡΟΥ ΙΕΡΑΣ ΚΑΙ ΑΣΥΛΟΥ (of Tyre, the Holy and Inviolable). (**Fig. 14**) The coins suggest that ΤΥΡΟΥ ΙΕΡΑΣ was being replaced by the "[the] holy Jerusalem."

Even though the striking of the Jewish silver shekels was revolutionary, their legends were rather generic. Without reference to any specific issuing authority, they could be embraced by all of the Jews, whether they were pro-peace, zealots, or middle-of-the-road.

Fig. 15              Fig. 16

**Fig. 15:** Jewish War bronze dated "year 2." Hendin 2010, no. 1360; Meshorer 2001, no. 195.
**Fig. 16:** Jewish War bronze dated "year 3." Hendin 2010, no. 1363; Meshorer 2001, no. 204.

The slogans on the lower value coins, used daily in the markets, differed in tone. Huge numbers of bronze prutot were dated to the second (**Fig. 15**) and third (**Fig. 16**) years of the war, and each carried the words, "[for the] freedom of Zion." The larger denomination bronze siege issues, discussed further below, are inscribed "for the redemption of Zion." These are perhaps the earliest recorded Zionistic slogans.[33]

Each "phrase akin to a slogan"[34] represented a rallying cry for the Jews. For years, the Romans had effectively used their coins to carry political messages; now the Jews did likewise for the first time to communicate their message of hope for a free Jerusalem and a free people. After the initial Jewish victories against Gallus, things began to go badly. By the middle of the year 68, Vespasian and his troops had crushed the revolt throughout the land; only Jerusalem and the zealot fortresses of Machaerus, Herodium, and Masada remained in Jewish hands.

---

[33] The modern word Zionism, according to the *Encyclopedia Judaica*, "first appeared at the end of the 19th century, denoting the movement whose goal was the return of the Jewish people to *Eretz Israel*." But the word Zion itself is ancient, referring most often to the city of Jerusalem or the people of Judaea.

[34] Meshorer 1982, 110.

**Fig. 17**  **Fig. 18**

**Fig. 17:** Jewish War bronze "half." Hendin 2010, no. 1367; Meshorer 2001, no. 211.
**Fig. 18:** Jewish War bronze "quarter." Hendin 2010, no. 1368; Meshorer 2001, no. 213.

By the fourth year of the war, Jerusalem was under siege by Titus. Vespasian had ascended to the throne in Rome and the tide had turned dramatically against the Jews. At this time, the legends and the nature of the Jewish bronze coins had changed. There are larger denominations, with the words "half" (**Fig. 17**) and "quarter" (**Fig. 18**) which seem to be fiduciary fractions of silver *shekels*. The slogan, "freedom of Zion" is replaced by, "redemption of Zion."

Roth points out that the slogan change in the fourth year was "certainly not accidental [and] may well reflect the fresh political circumstances of this time, for Simon bar Giora had by now entered Jerusalem and established his supremacy there."[35] It is also possible that the change in language reflects the Jewish insurgents' realization that they would soon be defeated by the Roman war machine. Hence, the change in tone from the call for physical "freedom" from oppression versus "redemption" or "salvation," which has a more spiritual tone.

Goldstein and Fontanille observe that "freedom does not necessarily imply confrontation and can conceivably be obtained by mutual consent, possibly as a result of negotiation, whereas redemption denotes salvation or a forced release from a status of war and oppression."[36]

Jerusalem was destroyed early in the war's fifth year. The Jewish Diaspora around the world was expanded by Jewish captives taken to Rome, or those who made their way to other Jewish communities outside the Land of Israel. Emotionally as well as practically, many Diaspora Jews of the first century CE looked toward a day that their Temple might be rebuilt and they would return to their holy Jerusalem. In the meantime, Rabbi Yohanan ben Zakkai received Vespasian's permission to establish a school of Jewish learning in Yavne (Jamnia): this represents the end of Judaism as a cultic religion of sacrifices at the Temple in Jerusalem, and the transition to Rabbinic Judaism where prayer replaces sacrifice and the heavenly Jerusalem replaces the earthly Jerusalem.[37]

Goodblatt discusses the use of the word Zion on the coins and in the literature of the first century, as well as the fact that the word Zion, possibly referring to the biblical name of the Temple as "Mt. Zion," is missing completely from the coins of the Bar Kokhba Revolt. He suggests that "perhaps the post-70 masters deliberately dropped the name as part of an effort to avoid the emotional response evoked by the name 'Zion.'"[38] Goodblatt notes that Josephus does not use the word "Zion," nor do early rabbinic documents, that were "most likely to preserve usage from the late first and second centuries."[39] Goodblatt also mentions the possibility that modern discussion of the word Zion on the coins of the Jewish War could be anachronistic, based upon the use of the word in the nineteenth- and early twentieth-century political movements that led to the establishment of modern Israel, although he maintains a possible beginning of Zionism amongst the Jews of the first century.[40]

---

[35] Roth 1962, 43.
[36] Goldstein & Fontanille 2006, 21.
[37] Neusner, 1970; *idem* 1970a.
[38] Goodblatt, 2006, 202.
[39] *Ibid.*, 202.
[40] *Ibid.*, 203.

Rappaport proposes that the silver coins of the Jewish War were struck by the pre-Zealots and Zealots in collaboration with Temple authorities. The Zealots, he points out, "did not have a charismatic or messianic leadership, but a collective one."[41] Further supporting this idea is Josephus' report that the head of this faction, Eleazar ben Hananya, held "a great part of the public treasure" (Jos., *War* 2.564). He points to Simon bar Giora, head of another faction that gained strength in the second year, as the possible issuer of the bronze coins.[42]

Goodblatt suggests that "perhaps both the silver and the bronze coinage carried the message of the rebel leaders. If so their attempt to mobilize the masses to fight for what the Zionist anthem *Hatiqvah* calls '*Eretz Zion, Yerushalim*'…. 'the land of Zion and Jerusalem,' justifies our characterizing the ideology of the rebels as ancient Zionism—or Zion nationalism."[43]

Absence of the word Zion on the coins of Bar Kokhba, gives credence to suggestions that it related somehow to the Temple, which no longer existed. Zion is completely replaced by Israel or "Jerusalem," as in "for the redemption of Israel" and "for the freedom of Jerusalem." References to Jerusalem express desires to regain the city, but there is no evidence that Bar Kokhba succeeded at any point in the war. In controlled excavations in Jerusalem, scores of thousands of coins have been found, but among them were only four coins of Bar Kokhba.[44]

## 6. Overcoming the Language Barrier

Both series of Jewish war coins used similar forms of the paleo-Hebrew script derived from the Iron Age, by this time all but forgotten. Misunderstanding about the epigraphy on the Hasmonaean coins led, by extension, to misunderstandings of the coins of the wars.[45] The paleo-Hebrew inscriptions are remarkable for their form as well as their content. This script was essentially discontinued several hundred years earlier and "saw only very limited use in the Maccabean age."[46] During this period, Aramaic was the principal language and script of the Jewish people. According to Josef Naveh, "Texts written in the Hebrew script in the Second Temple period are rare… These texts are official in nature and seem to indicate that the use of the Hebrew script in this period had nationalistic connotations."[47] The texts Naveh refers to are seals, scrolls, and coins. The use of this archaic Hebrew script "represented the former glory of the Davidic kingdom which the Hasmonaean rulers attempted to regain and restore."[48] Among the Hasmonaean coins, most types are inscribed with the paleo-Hebrew script. Thus, even the script selection was part of the effort of the Jewish leaders to make a statement about themselves and their kingdom. It would be used, even if few could read it.

Among the Dead Sea Scrolls, the only manuscripts in paleo-Hebrew are from the Pentateuch and Job.[49] In some other scrolls written in Aramaic script, only the Tetragrammaton is written in paleo-Hebrew, "thus indicating that the scribes who preserved this script knew that it was the original Hebrew one and its archaic flavour made it suitable for writing the name of the Lord."[50]

---

[41] Rappaport 2007, 109.
[42] Rappaport 2007, 111-112.
[43] Goodblatt 2006, 203.
[44] Ariel 1982, 293.
[45] Largely due to the paleo-Hebrew script, controversies raged over these *shekels* for hundreds of years. Originally most scholars believed that the "thick Jewish *shekels*," as they were called in the late 1800s and early 1900s, were issued under Simon Maccabee. By the mid-twentieth century, however, it became clear that Simon never issued coins. Archaeological and historical evidence has proved that the silver Jewish shekels date from the Jewish War (Hendin 2010, 339-340).
[46] Kanael 1963, 44.
[47] Naveh 1987, 119.
[48] Meshorer 1982, 51.
[49] VanderKam and Flint 2002, 151.
[50] Meshorer 2001, 40.

One of the earliest known inscriptions using paleo-Hebrew was the Gezer Calendar, which is dated to the late tenth century BCE. It is closely related to Phoenician inscriptions from the same period. The paleo-Hebrew script was used on jar handles dating from the late eighth century BCE and to stone scale weights of Judah dating to eighth to sixth centuries BCE, as well as hundreds of stone and bone seals dating from the eighth to sixth centuries BCE. The earliest known fragments of a biblical text are written in paleo-Hebrew script and make up the Priestly Benediction in Numbers 6:24–26: "The Lord bless you and protect you. The Lord makes his face to shine upon you and be gracious to you. The Lord lift up his countenance to you and give you peace." It is inscribed on a small silver scroll found in a burial cave at Ketef Hinnom and dated to the late seventh century BCE.[51]

After the Babylonian capture of Judah and the exile of many Jews in 586 BCE, those who remained behind continued to use paleo-Hebrew script. Two generations later, when a number of Jews returned from exile, their language had become Aramaic and only those Jews who stayed behind continued to use paleo-Hebrew script. Soon both the Aramaic language and the "square" Hebrew script became the official means of communication in ancient Judaea.

In summary, it is impossible to undertake a meaningful epigraphic study of the paleo-Hebrew script used on the coins of the Maccabees, the Jewish War, or the Bar Kokhba Revolt, because it was an alphabet hundreds of years past regular use.

Instead of evolving as a living alphabet, variations in script forms resulted from the way individual engravers and their assistants or apprentices cut these letters into the coin dies. Since artisans were almost surely not familiar with the archaic script, one may assume that each workshop was supplied with a written version of the legends to be used. Meshorer notes that these may have been copied from "the letters from ancient manuscripts which were no doubt kept in the library of the Temple at Jerusalem."[52] More style differences were surely introduced by the die cutters who used chisels and other tools to make die cuts, often smaller than an eyelash, and also to engrave the inscriptions in confusing mirror-writing in the dies.

Equally significant to the general lack of use of paleo-Hebrew in the first and second centuries, is the consensus that "Judean society in antiquity was no more literate than the surrounding cultures. In other words, the vast majority of Judeans were illiterate."[53] Thus the majority of Jews were not likely to have read the Aramaic (square Hebrew) letters any more easily than the obsolete paleo-Hebrew.

However, lack of literacy need not reduce the efficacy of messages or their transmission via coins. Considering the strong Jewish oral traditions, it is likely that the coins provoked patriotic discussion among the rebels. One can imagine a Jewish rebel passing along a coin during a transaction: "Look, it is written in the language used by King David, do you know what it says? 'For the freedom of Zion.'" Now the coin and the verbal legend, playing on tales of the glorious, distant past, could pass from hand to hand into every corner of Judaea where the rebels carried on their lives.

Mildenberg wrote that although there has never been a hoard in which the coins of the Jewish War and the Bar Kokhba Revolt are found together, "this in no way precludes the possibility that Bar Kosiba's men knew of the rebel coins from the Bellum Judaicum or even that they had seen such coins," Mildenberg observes.[54] However, during the conference at which this paper was delivered, the author learned from the presentation of Dr Boaz Zissu

---

[51] Barkay *et. al.* 2003, 162-171. The cave at Ketef Hinnom was excavated by Gaby Barkay and the scroll was later identified by Ya'akov Meshorer, then chief curator of Archaeology at The Israel Museum, Jerusalem.

[52] Meshorer 1967, 48.

[53] Goodblatt 2006, 33, discusses this in some detail and provides a good bibliography on the limited literacy in ancient Judaea.

[54] Mildenberg 1984, 68.

that he and colleagues had discovered just such a hoard. It was found in the Te'omim Cave (Mŭghâret Umm et Tûeimîn) in the Western Jerusalem Hills, and consisted of 10 coins—six Roman and four Judaean—discovered *in situ* together with a bronze sewing needle. Two of the Judaean coins were Bar Kokhba zuzim, one was a Hasmonaean bronze, and the fourth was a Jewish War silver shekel dated year two (67/68 CE).[55] Zissu has also discovered a second hoard containing both Jewish War and Bar Kokhba Revolt silver coins.[56]

Thus it is now proven that Bar Kokhba's followers were well aware of the nature of the coins of the Jewish War. Furthermore they were also familiar with Hasmonaean bronze coins!

This fresh evidence serves to solidify Goodman's belief that the Bar Kokhba coins show a "clear desire to link their uprising with the revolt that ended in AD 70."[57]

## 7. Communicating via Symbols

Language, of course, is not the only way to communicate; symbols and images can be equally effective, such as the portraits of Roman emperors on their coins which circulated to the far reaches of the empire and made impressions upon even those who could not read. This could not occur on Judaean coins, because between the second century BCE and the first century CE, the Jews in their land, with few known exceptions, strictly obeyed the biblical admonition against graven images:

> Thou shalt not make unto thee a graven image, nor any manner of likeness, of any thing that is in heaven above, or that is in the earth beneath, or that is in the water under the earth" (Exod 20:4).

This Pentateuchal code sternly prohibits making any graven image of man or beast, and is repeated (Deut 5:8) and expanded upon:

> … lest ye deal corruptly, and make you a graven image, even the form of any figure, the likeness of male or female, the likeness of any beast that is on the earth, the likeness of any winged fowl that flieth in the heaven, the likeness of anything that creepeth on the ground, the likeness of any fish that is in the water under the earth (Deut 4:16–18).

The prohibition is presumably aimed directly at the manufacture of such images for the purpose of worship. While that reservation is hinted at (see Deut 4:19 and Exod 20:19–21), it is not spelled out in the biblical text. This ambiguity allowed Jewish culture to run the gamut from outright prohibition of figurative art of any kind to complete disregard of the prohibitions. However, on the coins of the Herodian and Hasmonaean dynasties struck for circulation in areas of mainly Jewish population, and even on the coins struck under Roman prefects and procurators, this prohibition was mostly obeyed.

On the other hand, with few exceptions neither Hasmonaean nor early Herodian coins carried overtly Jewish symbols. Cornucopias, anchors, flowers, helmets, branches, and wreaths can be ascribed a Jewish character on these coins, but originated on Greek and Roman issues.[58] Many symbols used on the coins of Herod I are likely Augustan in their origin,[59] and some, such as the winged caduceus, might have been gravely offensive to the local population if their contexts had been widely understood. In spite of the clearly pagan imagery on Herod's coins, his

---

[55] Zissu, Eshel, Langford and Frumkin, in press.
[56] Zissu, personal communication, November 2010.
[57] Goodman 2005, 166.
[58] Hendin 2007-2008, 76-91.
[59] Ariel 2009.

minters managed to avoid outright graven images with the exceptional use of the eagle shown on Herod's half-prutah.[60] In this case it is generally believed that Herod's minters intended the eagle to represent a facsimile that Herod had posted above the entrance to the Jerusalem Temple; the eagle also appears on scores of contemporary Ptolemaic and Seleucid issues.

**Fig. 19:** Bar Kokhba silver sela depicting the Jerusalem Temple and lulab and etrog. Hendin 2010, no. 1373; Meshorer 2001, no. 218.

However, virtually all of the symbols on coins struck during both Jewish wars against Rome go well beyond simply being inoffensive the local population. They are distinctly Jewish, and refer to two basic motifs: the Jerusalem Temple and the popular festival of harvest thanksgiving, Sukkot (**Fig. 19**), also known as the Feast of Tabernacles (booths).

Sukkot was a popular holiday in ancient times, and one of the three pilgrimage festivals during the days of the Second Temple.[61] It was a holiday of harvest and thanksgiving with great festivity and rejoicing. It was referred to as "the festival of the Lord"[62] or simply "the festival,"[63] and Moses directed the children of Israel to read the Law every seventh year on Sukkot (Deut 31:10-11). Moses had been commanded by God that "On the first day you shall take the product of hadar trees, branches of palm trees, boughs of leafy trees, and willows of the brook" (Lev 23:40).[64]

The ritual chalice depicted on the obverse of the *shekels*, half-*shekels* and quarter-*shekels* of the first year may be related to Sukkot. Romanoff suggests it was related to the Omer, a sacrifice of first fruits mentioned in Leviticus:

> When ye are come into the land which I give unto you, and shall reap the harvest thereof, then ye shall bring the sheaf of the first-fruits of your harvest unto the priest. And he shall wave the sheaf before the Lord, to be accepted for you ... (Lev 23:9–11).

Earlier descriptions of this cup suggested it was related to drinking wine, but Romanoff argues, "It is doubtful whether or not the vessel was a drinking cup. The dotted [beaded] border would make drinking almost impossible. The cup, '*kos*', in the Temple was used for sacrificial blood; while the drinking of wine in the Temple was forbidden, and ... the Jewish coins do not contain any symbol of blood sacrifices." Romanoff continues by explaining that "The 'chalice', or 'cup', rather signifies the golden vessel that contained the Omer and was used on the second day of Passover when a measure of barley, a tenth of an ephah, equal to one and a half pints of fine flour, was offered to the Temple as the first-fruits of the field. The waving of this vessel in different directions during the offering corresponded to the waving of the lulav."[65]

---

[60] Hendin 2010, no. 1190; Meshorer 2001, no. 66.
[61] The three were Passover, Shavout (Pentacost) and Sukkot (Feast of Tabernacles).
[62] Lev 23:39; Judg 21:19.
[63] 1 Kgs 8:2, 8:65; 12:32; 2 Chron 5:3; 7:8.
[64] Sukkot remains a popular and widely celebrated Jewish holiday in modern times, but its profile to non-Jews, and also among secular Jews outside of Israel has been eclipsed by the commercialized version of Chanukah, Passover (which Christians relate to Easter), and the High Holy Days of Rosh Hashanah and Yom Kippur.
[65] Romanoff 1944, 22-23.

On the other hand, Goldstein and Fontanille point out that an omer cup is not described in any ancient sources, and believe it is equally likely that this is a generic Temple chalice, perhaps a chalice offering salvation. In either case we note that this chalice with a beaded rim is the only design that is repeated on both the silver and the bronze coins of the Jewish War.

The grouping of three pomegranate buds on the *shekels* has often been described as hanging on a sprig or branch. Deutsch, however, asserts that this symmetrical object more likely represents a man-made staff, "such an artefact matches a sacred object, a staff used by the high priests in the Temple and explains its appearance on the silver coins.[66] Therefore the staff is likely to represent the minting authority, which is the high priesthood or the Temple as an institution."[67]

The small bronzes of the second and third years[68] carry images of an amphora and a vine leaf on tendril. Similar designs were used earlier on a coin of Valerius Gratus. But, if one compares that coin to the prutot of the Jewish War, one can see that the vessels are different. Both the procurator coins and the Jewish War coins depict a vessel on one side and a vine leaf on the other side. Romanoff[69] and Meshorer,[70] among others, conclude that this supports the supposition that the Jewish War amphora was probably used for wine libations.

Meshorer suggests that the Jewish War bronze coins represent the antithesis of the Roman motifs. The amphorae "on the Jewish issues may symbolize the sacred libations of wine made in the Temple. The vessels depicted on the coins of the revolt are not copies of the Roman amphorae; they are Jewish and of a different style than the classical Greco-Roman models represented on the coinage of Valerius Gratus."[71]

Romanoff adds that "From mishnaic sources we learn that only two liquids, water and wine, usually required covers."[72] This requirement is of interest since the amphora shown on the 'year three' coin is clearly covered and coupled with the vine leaf reverse one may assume its relationship to the "fruit of the vine" so important in Jewish liturgy until today.

> They used to fill a golden flagon holding three logs with water from Siloam. When they reached the Water Gate, they blew on the shofar a sustained, a quavering and another sustained blast. The priest whose turn of duty it was went up the Altar-Ramp and turned to the right where were two silver bowls.... They had each a hole like a narrow snout, one wide and the other narrow so that both bowls emptied themselves together.... The bowl to the west was for water and that to the east was for wine.... As was the rite on a weekday so was the rite on a Sabbath save that on the eve of the Sabbath they used to fill with water from Siloam a golden jar that had not been hallowed, and put it in a special chamber. If it was upset or uncovered, they refilled it from the laver, for wine or water which has been uncovered is invalid for the Altar (m. *Sukk*. 4, 9-10).

"Here we have our vessels," E.W. Klimowsky writes. "The big golden flagon holding three logs was that with a lid and also the one without it, which is on the coins of the First Jewish War." He adds that in describing the "natural size of the golden amphora, the Mishnah reports

---

[66] An ivory pomegranate inscribed "[Belonging] to the Temple of [Yaweh], consecrated to the priests" in paleo-Hebrew script was purchased by The Israel Museum in the 1980s. In 2005 a committee of the Israel Antiquities Authority and the Israel Museum found the pomegranate to date to the Late Bronze Age, but the inscription to be a modern addition (Goren et. al. 2005).

[67] Deutsch 2009a and personal communications.

[68] And what seems to be a prototype prutah of the first year (Deutsch 1992-93, 36-37 and Hendin 2010, 354-355).

[69] Romanoff 1944, 31-33.

[70] Meshorer 2001, 121.

[71] Meshorer 1982 II, 112.

[72] Romanoff 1944, 31.

that the contents were three logs of water taken from Siloam. This would be about one and a half pints [24 oz.]...[thus] the size of the golden amphora was not considerable."[73]

**Fig. 20:** Jewish War bronze depicting chalice.
Hendin 2010, no. 1369; Meshorer 2001, no. 214.

Bronze coins struck during the fourth year, possibly the first siege coins in history,[74] are markedly different. Among them are the only bronze coins of the Jewish War that reproduce an image that appears on the *shekels* and half-*shekels*—the chalice (**Fig. 20**). *All* of the other images on the bronze coins of the fourth year refer directly to the holiday of Sukkot, which may reflect a yearning by local and Diaspora Jews to fully restore freedom from the tightening Roman yoke.

As a simple palm branch, we have already seen the *lulav* on coins of John Hyrcanus I, Alexander Jannaeus, Herod I, and Herod Antipas. Now, with the coins of the fourth year of the Jewish War, "the four species" as symbols of Sukkot and the pilgrimage to Jerusalem take centre stage.

On the largest denomination, designated "half," we see a date palm tree with collecting baskets. According to rabbinic tradition, the "honey" listed among the seven species that bless the land of Israel was the honey from dates (Deut 8:8).[75] Its reverse depicts two *lulav* bunches flanking an *etrog* (citron). The second denomination, designated "quarter" depicts an *etrog* on its obverse and two *lulav* bunches on its reverse. The third denomination, which is not named but by size and weight assumed to be an "eighth," depicts the ritual chalice on its obverse and a lulav bunch flanked by two *etrogs* on its reverse.

We can understand the importance of these symbols since Leviticus mentions some of the special observances of Sukkot:

> ... And ye shall take you on the first day the fruit of goodly trees, branches of palm-trees and boughs of thick trees, and willows of the brook, and ye shall rejoice before the Lord your God seven days....Ye shall dwell in booths seven days; all that are home-born in Israel shall dwell in booths; that your generations may know that I made the children of Israel to dwell in booths, when I brought them out of the land of Egypt... (Lev 23:39–43).

These were "the four species." The "fruit of goodly trees" is the citron, a lemon-like citrus fruit (*etrog* in Hebrew); the "boughs of thick trees" are myrtle twigs (*hadasim*); the palm branch is called *lulav*; and willows are called *aravot*. In the ancient world, there was a great

---

[73] Klimowsky 1974, 80. Isadore Goldstein, in a personal communication, notes that the exact amount of the liquid measure "log" is not a simple calculation, but in any case three logs would not be greater than 1.8 litres (around 61 oz.).

[74] Newell (1913, 544) notes "they were struck in the city of Jerusalem itself when that city was being closely invested by Titus and his army; by the fictitious value inscribed on them they show that though of bronze, they were intended to pass as the half and quarter of a silver *shekel*..."

[75] The earliest Judaean appearance of the date palm tree (as opposed to the palm branch) occurs on a coin of Herod Antipas in 1 BCE/CE (Hendin 1198) and subsequently on coins of the Roman governors of Judaea.

deal of symbolism linked to palm branches, not only by the Jews, but by the Greeks and Romans as well. Nike often holds a palm branch.

After the Jerusalem Temple was destroyed in 70 CE, Rabbi Johanan ben Zakkai ruled that wherever Jews celebrate the holiday of Sukkot, they should take "the four species" in their hand for seven days to commemorate the Temple. They were held while reciting certain prayers and psalms.

Themes of Sukkot and of the rebuilding of the Jerusalem Temple continue on coins of the Bar Kokhba Revolt.

## 8. Temple and Other Bar Kokhba Symbols

Although issued in a period of severe economic and political stress, Bar Kokhba's coins are the most diverse series of ancient Jewish coins. At this time a bold image of the Jerusalem Temple was introduced together with sacred vessels, musical instruments, grapes, vines, and vine leaves. The theme of Sukkot is continued with images of the *etrog* and *lulav*.

Meshorer summarizes various proposals as to the identification of the tetrastyle structure, and concludes that it is "a schematic geometric shape representing the Temple to all who viewed it, but not the actual building." Given historic descriptions of the Jerusalem Temple, it may be less "schematic" than Meshorer suggests. The Temple facade is shown on Bar Kokhba coins in several variations.

Isadore Goldstein makes remarkable observations about the depiction. First, he notes, that the wavy line and the cross or star above the Temple are not fanciful, but have a literal meaning. The Mishnah says that "a golden vine was positioned over the entrance to the sanctuary and hung over the beams" (*m. Midd.* 3.8). Only the vine was hung initially. The golden leaves and grapes (singly or in bunches) were added as donations from the people.[76] Thus Goldstein suggests that the schematic view shown on the coins was a prospect of the sanctuary, a view that could be seen from the Temple courtyard.[77]

Goldstein points to another portion of Mishnah (*m. Yom.* 3:10), that says, "Helena set a golden candelabra over the door of the Sanctuary." This refers to a gift from Helena, queen of Adiabene, a converted Jew who visited Jerusalem and was buried there around 56 CE. Goldstein cites other rabbinic literature that says that this candelabrum sparkled with rays and reflected light that could be seen from many places in Jerusalem. Thus, he concludes, "there are many renditions of the star form, but they all represent the artist's interpretation of the chandelier or of its twinkling."[78]

Dan Barag suggests that the object between the central pair of columns is the showbread table.[79] Previously, Romanoff suggested it might be the Ark of the Covenant.[80] Reifenberg suggested an Ark of the Torah with scrolls.[81]

The Babylonian Talmud states that while a man could not make a house or a porch copied from the Temple or "a table after the design of the table [in the Temple] or a candelabrum after the design of the candelabrum. He could, however, make one with five, six, or eight [branches] but with seven he may not make it even though it be of other metals" (*b. A. Z.* 43 a).

Thus Meshorer suggests that the Temple is depicted, but possibly not accurately because of the prohibition.[82]

---

[76] *m. Midd.* 3.8. "A vine of gold stood over the entrance to the sanctuary. Those who wished to donate—a leaf, grape, or cluster he would bring and hang it on her (on the vine)."
[77] Goldstein 2010 and personal communications.
[78] Ibid.

[79] Barag 1986, 217-222.
[80] Romanoff 1944, 40.
[81] Reifenberg 1947, 30-32.
[82] See Jacobson 2007 for the most thorough discussion to date of the nature of the Temple shown on these coins.

Goldstein suggests that the area between the central columns of the Temple may simply depict the sanctuary entrance, with a generic or "cultic" object inside. He also observes that the horizontal ladder-like object is not a balustrade or fence as some have suggested but represent the twelve steps leading up to the Temple that were described by both Josephus and in the Mishnah. "Not one of the dies recorded by Mildenberg depicts more than twelve steps,"[83] he observes.

**Fig. 21**        **Fig. 22**        **Fig. 23**

**Fig. 21:** Bar Kokhba silver zuz depicting trumpets. Hendin 2010, no. 1417; Meshorer 2001, no. 276b.
**Fig. 22:** Bar Kokhba silver zuz depicting lyre. Hendin 2010, no. 1424; Meshorer 2001, no. 272a.
**Fig. 23:** Bar Kokhba silver zuz depicting harp. Hendin 2010, no. 1389; Meshorer 2001, no. 238.

Trumpets (**Fig. 21**) and several styles of lyres (**Fig. 22**) or harps (**Fig. 23**) are also shown on Bar Kokhba coins. The trumpets recall almost identical instruments depicted on the Arch of Titus as well as an inscription discovered on a stone from the Jerusalem Temple, now in the Israel Museum, that declares, "To the place of trumpeting…to herald."[84] The block, according to Mazar, had probably been a part of the parapet of the Temple, where, on the evening of Sabbath, "one of the Priests would ascend…and sound a trumpet to signal the advent of the holy day, and at sundown the process was repeated to announce its conclusion."[85] Silver trumpets were also used during the Sukkot ceremonies in the Temple (*m. Sukk.* 5.5).

The harp, which has a sound box shaped like a skin bag (*nevel* in Hebrew, *chelys* in Greek), and the narrower lyre, with a chest-like sound box (*kinor* in Hebrew, *kithara* in Greek), have been associated with the Jewish religion and worship since ancient times.

Praise him with lyre and harp (Ps 150:3).

The *lulav* bunch and *etrog* are shown on the tetradrachms, and the *lulav* bunch stands alone on the didrachm. Other coins depict only a branch, either palm or willow.

Grape clusters and vines already appeared on a coin of Herod I and his son Archelaus, and a vine leaf was used on Jewish War prutot. Grape bunches and vines are a common motif in Jewish art of the first and second centuries and seem to be related not only to the agricultural bounty of the land and related celebrations such as Sukkot, but also to use of "the fruit of the vine" in Jewish ritual from ancient times. Barag writes that the use of these motifs on coins "manifests the hope for the resumption of another essential part of the cult, the pilgrimage on the three festivals demonstrated by the symbols of Sukkot."[86] The grape, vine and vine leaf motifs could also relate to the golden vine that hung over the Temple sanctuary, with its donated leaves, grapes, and grape clusters hung upon it.

---

[83] Goldstein, 2010.
[94] Mazar 1975, 138-139.
[85] *Ibid.*, 138.
[86] Barag 1986, 221.

**Fig. 24:** Bar Kokhba silver zuz depicting bunch of grape and jug with willow branches. Hendin 2010, no. 1433; Meshorer 2001, no. 285.

The jug (**Fig. 24**) appearing on the Bar Kokhba zuzim is also connected to Sukkot, according to Yonatan Adler, who believes it represents "the golden flagon used in the water libation ceremony performed on the Temple altar during the Feast of Tabernacles. The branch appearing to the side of this flagon, previously identified as a palm frond, should be recognized instead as a willow-branch, symbolizing the willow-branch ceremony that took place at the Temple altar in conjunction with the water libation ceremony ... the numismatic evidence provided by the Bar Kokhba denarii is the only evidence of the willow-branch ritual outside of Rabbinic literature."[87]

In ancient times, the willow branch ritual was carried out daily in the Jerusalem Temple. According to the Talmud:

> There was a place below Jerusalem called Motsa. They went down to there, and collected young willow branches, and then came and set them upright along the sides of the altar, with their tops bent over the top of the altar. They then sounded a prolonged [trumpet] blast, a quavering note, and a prolonged blast (*m. Sukk.* 5.5-6).

**Fig. 25:** Bar Kokhba bronze with seven-branched palm. Hendin 2010, no. 1408; Meshorer 2001, no. 260a.

Somewhat surprisingly the menorah motif is completely missing from the coins of the Jewish Wars, and we have no indication why. However, the most extensive use of the palm tree on ancient Jewish coinage occurs during the Bar Kokhba Revolt, and in almost every instance, even on the irregular coins, the palm tree is shown with seven branches (**Fig. 25**). (This is also true for the palm tree on the bronze half-shekel of the Jewish War.) Possibly this form of the local date palm is a reference to the seven-branched menorah.

---

[87] Adler 2007-2008, 135. Given this discussion, one must also consider that some of the so-called palm-branch motifs on coins of Herod I, Herod Antipas, and the Bar Kokhba Revolt might, have been intended as willow branches.

## 9. Minting the Coins

While the manufacturing of the coins of the two Jewish wars were not similar to each other, both are unusual as compared to other contemporary coinages. In the case of the Jewish War the small bronzes of mostly the second and third years were manufactured in the same way as earlier coins of the governors of Judaea (prefects and procurators) and the earlier royal Jewish houses. The quality of workmanship, however, was much better overall during the Jewish War, and precise manufacturing was a hallmark of the silver coins. They were uniform in weight, purity, shape, and striking.[88] Engraving of the dies[89] was the best in the history of Judaea, and Roth notes that for the first time we can clearly see "a mint geared for large-scale production, not with the work of part-time amateur artisans."[90]

This is rather remarkable considering the ongoing civil war and changes among Jerusalem's Jews. The political situation was certainly "not consistent with the stable minting of coins by the rebels' government throughout the five years of the revolt,"[91] Rappaport notes. It is indeed remarkable that the changing situation among the Jews did not affect the striking of the silver coins, which reflected a "relatively settled condition and the confident atmosphere of the country at the time," according to Roth.[92]

Silver shekels and fractions of shekels of the Jewish war were not only unusually thick for ancient coins, but uniformly round, and struck with hammered edges which, according to experiments by Deutsch and Drei, were hammered prior to striking.[93] Compared to both the early and later style Tyre shekels and fractions, one notes that the only physical similarity between the two coin types is pureness of silver—around 96% for the Tyre coins and 98% for the Jewish War coins.[94]

Also noteworthy is the fact that the weight of the Jewish War prutah is the highest for any Jewish coin struck since the first issues of the Hasmonaean Dynasty.[95] Even though the bronzes were a fiduciary coinage, it appears as if the people behind the coins of the Jewish War wanted to make certain that they made a good impression.

Bar Kokhba coins, on the other hand, were created without the benefit of a fully-equipped mint. Probably due to limited resources, every coin of the Bar Kokhba Revolt was struck upon a coin already in circulation in the area. Meshorer believed that the overstriking was done for political reasons, "a sort of small act of vengeance and a clear political declaration."[96] I do not agree with this conclusion and as evidence I cite Greek coins, Jewish coins, and Nabataean coins[97] which were overstruck by the Bar Kokhba mint. This suggests that these minters were simply pulling coins from circulation, and the reason they overstruck more Roman and Roman provincial coins was simply that there were more in local circulation at the time. While it is simple for a modern numismatist to take the time to observe (often mere) traces of previous coins on all Bar Kokhba issues, this was not as noticeable to the

---

[88] Regarding this precision, Goldstein and Fontanille (2006, 17) show, remarkably, that even though the reverses of the Jewish *shekels* and half-*shekels* are virtually identical throughout the war, new reverses were created each year, and there are only extremely rare instances (such as between year four and year five half-*shekels*) when the same reverse die is used in more than a single year.

[89] Deutsch (2009a, 3) has recorded 1,220 Jewish War *shekels* and half-*shekels* from 515 individual dies of which 85 were obverse dies and 430 reverse dies.

[90] Roth 1962, 40.

[91] Rappaport 2007, 103.

[92] Roth 1962, 39.

[93] Deutsch 2009a, 2.

[94] Deutsch 2009, 67.

[95] Hendin 2009. The average *prutah* during the Jewish War, 2.51 grams, was the strongest *prutah* weight average since the earliest Seleucid-Hasmonaean coins of Jerusalem, which average 2.47 grams. In the interim the average of some of the small prutot during Hasmonaean and Herodian times fell as low as less than one gram.

[96] Meshorer 1982 II, 137.

people handling the coins in commerce. The Bar Kokhba slogans and images were more than sufficient to make their point.

Some Bar Kokhba coins were saved by patriotic Jews for many years and used as jewellery[98] or carefully collected even as worthless tokens and kept together with one's greatest wealth.[99]

## 10. Dating Formulas

Jewish coins of both wars were dated by eras based on the wars from the Jewish perspective. In any case the Romans considered both issues to be illegal rebel currency.

Jewish War coins are somewhat inconsistent in the dating formula of the silver coins, since those of the first year are marked with a Hebrew letter signifying "one" but coins of the second through fifth years are marked with two letters, the first abbreviating the word "year" and the second indicating the numbers two through five. One may suggest that the first coins struck were prototypes for a new era of Jewish government in Jerusalem. Since it was not known from the outset if the rebellion would last for months or years, the coins were marked with the Hebrew letter aleph, which was meant to signify "first" as in "first [money of] Holy Jerusalem" to contrast them with the coins of Holy Tyre that had long been (and continued to be) in circulation in Jerusalem and Judaea.[100]

Once the first year ended it was then a matter of political emphasis to designate each year as an additional significant period in the era of the Jewish battle against Rome, hence the designations "year two" and so on.[101]

In the case of Bar Kokhba's coins it is somewhat the opposite. There was no Jewish establishment or Temple, together with its political structure, and Bar Kokhba aspired to control Jerusalem, but never captured it. Therefore it was in the second revolt's interest to begin with a clear dating era. There was little to lose, this was a guerrilla war and the very statement that coins were struck in the "first year" had an aggressive posture. As the tide turned by the end of the second year of the Bar Kokhba Revolt, those designing the coins may have believe it would serve them better to no longer date the coins, but simply to continue issuing them with their patriotic slogans.

---

[97] *Ibid.*, 115.
[98] *Ibid.*, 162-163.
[99] Hendin 2000-2002. This group of 16 bronze, silver and gold coins contains was found in an oil lamp. Although the latest coin in the group is attributed to Antoninus Pius in 151-152 CE in Rome (more than 15 years after the end of the Bar Kokhba Revolt), the hoard contained seven Bar Kokhba coins including coins from each year of the three years of the war. The inclusion of invalidated bronze coins carefully selected from each year of the Bar Kokhba Revolt can only be explained as a "collection."
[100] Other silver coins, Tyre *shekels* for example, typically bear the date of a first year, using the symbol signifying year or number, L (or sometimes ETOY).

Since Tyre had a long prior history of issuing coins dated to specific eras, there was no reason to hesitate using "year one" if a new era was to be followed. But to the Jews, in all of their history, this was a unique event, the first ever Jewish silver coins.
[101] The only exception is the unusual and rare quarter-*shekel* of the fourth year which, for unknown reasons, avoids motifs of all previous silver coins and also carries the Hebrew letter "daled," for four (Hendin 2010, no. 1366; Meshorer 2001, no. 210). From all other technical standpoints it seems clear that this coin was minted at the same place as the other Jewish War silver coins, even though its motifs are unique.
[102] Hart 1952.

## 11. The Roman Commentary

The extensive Flavian IVDAEA CAPTA series was Rome's victorious response to the Jewish War. This was the most extensive and varied series of specific victory coins in Roman coinage to date, and H. J. St. Hart correctly describes these coins as the "Official Commentary."[102]

**Fig. 26:** Vitellius bronze as depicting the Jewish victory. Hendin 2010, no. 1463.

We will not discuss the series in detail here other than to note that the series began with coins struck by Vitellius in 69 (**Fig. 26**). Nero had earlier sent Vespasian to take charge of the war in Judaea, and Vitellius took advantage of his brief months in office to make note of positive progress. Only when Vespasian became emperor did the Roman mints ramp up the IVDAEA CAPTA series, and hundreds of thousands (or more) coins were struck under Vespasian and Titus. Domitian was not active in the Jewish War, nevertheless, he struck a series of provincial coins in Caesarea Maritima that plays upon the Flavian dynasty's Jewish victory as a theme.

Nerva's FISCI IVDAICI CALVMNIA SVBLATA may suggest that Nerva eliminated some of the insults around the collection of the Jewish Tax established during Domitian's brutal rule. More recently, however, a few historians and numismatists have rejected that explanation, since if it was true it would represent the only time in history that Rome issued something akin to an apology for any reason on its coins.[103] Manfred Lehman explains that the Jews had "continued to collect various taxes right under the noses of their Roman occupiers ... It was the Jewish tax system that was the 'insult' to Rome, not the Roman tax imposed on the Jews, that the Fiscus Judaicus coin refers to, because the Jews collected several types of taxes. It was the cessation of this insult—these Jewish Taxes—that the coin celebrates."[104] Heemstra, in this volume, suggests that the coin provides evidence "that the new emperor no longer permitted people to be accused of living [illegally by Roman law] a Jewish life."[105]

Hadrian's coins relating to his travel, in 130 AD, to Judaea with the legend ADVENTI AVG IVDAEAE were struck prior to the Bar Kokhba War, and so cannot be construed as any sort of response.

## 12. Conclusion

The coins of the two Jewish wars against Rome were rooted in the desire for an autonomous nation. Political, religious, and economic elements all played roles in the creation of these coinages. Based upon the differences between the coins of the two Jewish wars and all Jewish coinage that preceded them, and examining the slogans, imagery, and extensive manufacture of these coins during extremely difficult times, we conclude that the principal motive of the coins was political and psychological—to make bold statements of Jewish sovereignty, whether or

---

[103] Hendin 2010, 458 for this theory discussed by David Vagi.

[104] Lehman 1993.

[105] Heemstra 2012

not it actually existed, to both Jews and Romans. The impressive silver coins of the Jewish War, with their anonymous minting authority, suggested to both Jews and Romans a Jewish unity that did not exist. On a contrarian note, it seems likely that most Bar Kokhba coins were struck upon circulating Roman or provincial coins because Bar Kokhba's government did not have the resources to produce their own flans. Thus the use of these, and other coins taken from circulation, was more of a practical than a political matter.

**Bibliography**

Adler, Y., 2007-2008. 'The Temple Willow-Branch Ritual Depicted on on Bar Kokhba Denarii', *INJ* 16, 131-135.

Ariel, D.T., 2009. 'The Coins of Herod the Great in the Context of the Augustan Empire', in D. M. Jacobson and N. Kokkinos, *Herod and Augustus: Papers Presented at the IJS Conference 21st-23rd June 2005* (Leiden & Boston: Brill, 2009) 113-126.

Ariel, D.T., 1982. 'A Survey of the Coins in Jerusalem (Until the End of the Byzantine Period)', *Studium Biblicum Franciscanum Liber Annuus* 32, 273–326.

Barag, D., 1994-1999. 'The Coinage of Yehud and the Ptolemies', INJ *13, 27-38*.

Barag, D., 1986. 'New Evidence for the Identification of the Showbread Table on Coins of the Bar Kokhba War', *Proceedings of the 10th International Congress of Numismatics*, London, 217-222.

Burnett, A., Amandry, M., Ripolles, P., 1992. *Roman Provincial Coinage*, Vol. I Parts I and II (London: British Museum / Paris: Bibliothèque Nationale).

Burnett, A., Amandry, M. and Carradice, I., 1999. *Roman Provincial Coinage,* Vol. II Parts I and II (London: British Museum / Paris: Bibliothèque Nationale).

Deutsch, R. 2009. *The Jewish Coinage During the First Revolt Against Rome*, 66-73 CE (Unpublished PhD dissertation submitted to the Senate of Tel Aviv University).

Deutsch, R. 2009a. English summary of the above.

Goldstein, I., 2010. 'Bar Kokhba Sela—The Design Schemes', *The Celator* 24, 3, 42-43.

Goldstein, I. and Fontanille, J.P., 2006. 'A New Study of the Coins of the First Jewish Against Rome, 66-70 CE'. *American Numismatic Association Journal* 1, 2, 9-32.

Goodblatt, D., 2006. *Elements of Ancient Jewish Nationalism.* (Cambridge: Cambridge University Press).

Goodman, M., 2005. 'Coinage and Identity: The Jewish Evidence', in C. Howgego, V. Heuchert, V. and A. Burnett (eds.), *Coinage and Identity in the Roman Provinces*, (Oxford: Oxford University Press), 163-166.

Goren, Y., et. al., 2005. 'A Re-examination of the Inscribed Pomegranate from the Israel Museum', *IEJ* 55, 3-20.

Hart, H. St. J., 1952. 'Judaea and Rome: the Official Commentary', *Journal of Theological Studies*, 172-198.

Heemstra, M. 2012. 'The Interpretation and Wider Context of Nerva's Fiscus Judaicus Sestertius' in this volume.

Hayek, F. A. 1976. *Denationalization of Money: The Argument Refined. An Analysis of the Theory and Practice of Concurrent Currencies*. (London: The Institute of Economic Affairs), 25.

Hendin, D., 2010. *Guide to Biblical Coins, 5th Edn.* (Nyack, NY: Amphora).

Hendin, D., 2007-2008. 'Numismatic Expressions of Hasmonean Sovereignty', *INJ* 16, 76-91.

Hendin, D., 2000-2002. 'A Bar Kokhba Lamp Hoard Collection', *INJ* 14, 180-84.

Howgego, C., 1990. 'Why Did Ancient States Strike Coins?' *Numismatic Chronicle* 150, 1-25.

Jacobson, D.M., 2007. 'The Temple on the Bar Kokhba Tetradrachms', *NC*, 1-3.

Klimowsky, E.W., 1974. *On Ancient Palestinian and Other Coins, Their Symbolism and Metrology* (Tel Aviv, Israel Numismatic Society).

Lehman, M.R., 1993. 'Where the Temple Tax Was Buried', *Biblical Archaeology Review* November/December, electronic edition.

Le Rider, G., 2001. *La naissance de la monnaie : pratiques monétaires de l'Orient ancien* (Paris: Presses universitaires de France), Chapter 2.

Le Rider, G., 1989. 'A propos d'un passage des Poroi de Xénophon : la question du change et les monnaies incuses d'Italie du Sud', in Kraay-Morkholm essays: *Numismatic studies in memory of C.M. Kraay and O. Mørlkholm* by Le Rider, G.; Jenkins, K.; Waggoner, N.; Westermark, U. Louvain-la-Neuve: [159]-172.

Levy, B., 1993. 'Tyrian Shekels and the First Jewish War', in *Proceedings of the 11th International Numismatic Congress* (Brussels 1991), 267-274.

Levy, B., 2005. 'Later Tyrian Shekels: Dating the 'Crude Issues, Reading the Controls', in *XIII Congresso Internacional de Numismatica* (Madrid 2003) 1, 885-890.

Mazar, B., 1975. *The Mountain of the Lord: Excavating in Jerusalem* (New York: Doubleday).

Meshorer, Y., 2001. *A Treasury of Jewish Coins* (Nyack, NY: Amphora).

Meshorer, Y., 1982. *Ancient Jewish Coinage* I and II (Dix Hills NY: Amphora).

Meshorer, Y., 1967. *Jewish Coins of the Second Temple Period* (Tel Aviv: Am Hasefer).

Mildenberg, L., 1984. *The Coinage of the Bar Kokhba War* (Salzburg: Verlag Sauerländer).

Neusner, J., 1970. *A Life of Yohanan Ben Zakkai Ca. 1-80 CE* (Leiden: Brill).

Neusner, J. 1970a. *Development of a Legend* (Leiden: Brill).

Newell, E.T., 1913. 'The Oldest Known Siege-Pieces', *Numismatist* 26, 643.

Rappaport, U., 2007. 'Who Minted the Jewish War's Coins?' *INR* 2, 103-116.

Romanoff, P., 1944. *Jewish Symbol on Ancient Jewish Coins*, 1971 reprint (New York: American Israel Numismatic Association).

Roth, C., 1962. 'Historical Implications of the Jewish Coinage of the First Revolt', *IEJ* 12.1, 33-46.

Seaford, R., 2004. Money and the Early Greek Mind: Homer, Philosophy, Tragedy (Cambridge: Cambridge University Press).

Van Alfen, P., 2009. Personal communications regarding works in progress.

Yadin, Y., 1971. *Bar Kokhba* (New York: Random House).

Zissu, B., Eshel, H., Langford B., and Frumkin, A., in press 2012. 'Coins from the Bar-Kokhba Revolt Hidden in Me'arat Ha-Teomim (Mugharet Umm et-Tueimin), Western Jerusalem Hills', in *Studies in Honour of Arnold Spaer, INJ* 17.

# THE SIGNIFICANCE OF THE CADUCEUS BETWEEN FACING CORNUCOPIAS IN HERODIAN AND ROMAN COINAGE

David M. Jacobson

## 1. Introduction

Herod the Great's most common coin bears an emblem on its reverse comprising a caduceus set between conjoined, facing cornucopias;[1] see **Fig. 1**. The presence of the pagan symbols ought not to surprise us. Among the corpus of Jewish coins, those of the Herodians, and especially those of its first monarch are notable for their pagan motifs.[2] The Dioscuri *pilos*, tripod of Apollo, eagle of Jupiter/Zeus, winged caduceus of Hermes/Mercury, poppy-head of Demeter and the palm branch with fillet, often associated with Athena Nike, stand out in this context. Several of these symbols appear regularly on the coins issued by Hellenistic monarchies and those of Rome, as previously noted by this author.

**Fig. 1:** Judaea, Herod the Great (37-4 BCE). AE prutah (15 mm), Jerusalem mint. Anchor; inscr.: BACI HPWΔ / Caduceus between two conjoined, facing cornucopias. *TJC* 59a; *RPC* I 4910. Courtesy of Isadore Goldstein, Zuzim Judaea, Brooklyn, NY (no. cns25sh).

These pagan coin types are entirely consistent with Herod's cultural and religious outlook. While Herod the Great (who ruled Judaea from 37 to 4 BCE), is especially remembered for rebuilding the Jewish Temple in Jerusalem on an impressive scale, he was also an enthusiastic benefactor of pagan cults, erecting three temples in his own kingdom, to the Emperor Augustus and *Dea Roma*, at Samaria-Sebaste (Jos., *Ant*. 15.298; *War* 1.403), Caesarea Maritima (Jos., *War* 1.414; *Ant*. 15.339) and at Paneas (Banias) (Jos., *War* 1.404; *Ant*. 15.363–364).[3] Herod also provided resources and encouragement for the construction of pagan temples outside his kingdom (*Ant*. 15.329), for example in Rhodes (Jos., *War* 1.424; *Ant*. 16.147), Berytus (Beirut) and Tyre (Jos., *War* 1.422). From an inscribed base, we also know about an honorific statue to Herod that was set up in a temple to the Semitic deity, *Ba'al Shamin*, at Si'a near Kanatha (present-day al-Qanawat) in the Hauran, presumably in appreciation of a donation that he had made to it.[4] G. Fuks has documented the evidence for Herod's strong preference for Greco-Roman rituals and customs and his participation in sacrifices in Rome in the Capitoline temple (Jos., *War* 1.285; *Ant*. 14.388).[5] Also relevant in this context are Herod's institution of athletic and gladiatorial games in Jerusalem (Jos., *Ant*. 15.267–276) and setting up a golden eagle, the principal attribute of Zeus/Jupiter, over the principal gate of the Temple (Jos., *War* 1.650; *Ant*. 17.151). Josephus noted that Herod hankered after temples, statues and other

---

[1] *TJC* 59; *RPC* I 4910.
[2] *AJC* 2, pp. 18-30; *TJC*, pp. 61-78; Jacobson 1986, 159–165; Jacobson 2007
[3] For the archaeological evidence of these temples, see, e.g., Netzer 2006, 85–89 (Samaria); 103–106 (Caesarea); 218–222 (Paneas).
[4] *OGIS* 415 = *IGRR* III 1243.
[5] Fuks 2002.

dedications to himself from his subjects, in much the way that he had honoured his Roman masters, Augustus and Marcus Agrippa (Jos., *Ant.* 16.157-158),[6] and had himself received honours from gentile communities abroad.[7]

The Hasmonaeans, beginning with John *Hyrcanus* I (135-104 BCE), employed a pomegranate on a stalk between facing cornucopias as their principal dynastic emblem;[8] see **Fig. 2**. It is not entirely clear what symbolic meaning they pinned to this device, if any, beyond the obvious one of wishing to promote an image of the fecundity of their rule.[9]

**Fig. 2:** Judaea, John Hyrcanus (135-104 BCE). Æ Prutah (13 mm), Jerusalem mint; after 125 BCE. Paleo-Hebrew inscription, "Yehokhanan / hakohen hagad/ol vekhever haye/hudim" = John the High Priest and the assembly of the Jews' with Greek letter 'A' above, within wreath / Pomegranate on a stalk between facing cornucopias. *TJC* A3. The 'A' may refer to Alexander II *Zabinas*.

The twin cornucopia device seems to have derived from the Ptolemies. Conjoined cornucopias first appear as regular symbols on high denomination Ptolemaic coins struck by Ptolemy II Philadelphus (283-246 BCE) to commemorate his sister and consort, Arsinoë II, after her death in about 268 BCE; see **Fig. 3**. This motif is believed to symbolise the beneficent rule of this sibling pair, a correspondence strengthened by each cornucopia being tied by a fillet band of cloth, indicative of a royal diadem (Rice 1983, 202-208). The horn of plenty, that of Amaltheia the she-goat wet nurse of Zeus in Greek mythology, was chosen as the suitable icon for the Ptolemies.[10]

---

[6] Herod is quoted as "saying that he was less intent upon observing the customs of his own nation than upon honoring them [his patrons, Augustus and the Romans]" (Jos., *Ant.* 15.330)

[7] Besides the inscribed base of the statue of Herod in the temple of Ba'al Shamin at Si'a, four other honorific inscriptions to Herod are known outside Judaea (Jacobson 1993/4; Kokkinos 1998, 137, n. 195; 352). Three belong to statues erected by Greek cities to him in appreciation for benefactions, two in Athens and one in Kos. There is also a building inscription mentioning Herod, probably from a structure belonging to the Panhellenic sanctuary on the island of Delos, to which he had evidently made a donation.

[8] There has been a longstanding debate about the nature of the item between the facing cornucopias on this series of Hasmonaean pieces, which drew in the pioneering scholars of ancient Jewish coins. C. Cavedoni (1850, 22), supported by F.W. Madden (1864, 54 and n. 3) and G.F. Hill (*BMC Palestine*, p. 188), identified it as a poppy-head. This attribution was contested by F. de Saulcy (1854, 97 and n. 1), who considered it to be a pomegranate. In more recent times, the examination of better preserved representations has resulted in the balance of scholarly opinion tilting towards the view of de Saulcy (*TJC*, pp. 33-34, 64; cf. Romanoff 1944, 44). The emphatic Jewish character of the inscription on the obverse of these coins is consistent with the portrayal of a subject on the reverse that had biblical associations.

[9] Barag and Qedar (1980, 17) have suggested that the cornucopias in this motif were possibly intended to refer to 'the fertility of the Land of Israel'.

[10] On Amaltheia and her representations in classical literature and art, see Henig 1981.

# THE SIGNIFICANCE OF THE CADUCEUS BETWEEN FACING CORNUCOPIAS IN HERODIAN AND ROMAN COINAGE

**Fig. 3:** Ptolemaic Kings, Ptolemy II (253/2-246 BCE). AV Oktadrachm (26 mm). Veiled and diademed bust of Arsinoë II wearing stephane, r., l to l. / double cornucopia bound with fillet; inscr. ΑΡΣΙΝΟΗΣ ΦΙΛΑΔΕΛΦΟΥ. *Svoronos (Ptolemaion)* 1498. Spink Auction 5014 (28.09.2005), Lot 152. Courtesy of Spink & Son Ltd., London.

The following historical background may account for the choice of the conjoined cornucopias by John *Hyrcanus* I. This Hasmonaean ruler had been a tightly controlled client of the Seleucid king, Antiochus VII *Sidetes* (138-129 BCE), who obliged him to join his campaign against Parthia in 130/29 BCE. However, he managed to escape the disaster that overtook Antiochus (Jos., *Ant.* 13.250-53). The death of Antiochus in 129 BCE led to the succession of the weak Demetrius II, who immediately became embroiled in internal struggles, which afforded *Hyrcanus* the opportunity to expand Judaean territory. Demetrius almost immediately went to war against Ptolemy VIII *Physcon* of Egypt (170-116 BCE). *Physcon* responded by setting up a rival pretender to Demetrius, Alexander II *Zabinas*,[11] who he presented as an adopted son of an earlier pretender raised to the Seleucid throne by the Ptolemies, Alexander I *Balas* (150-145 BCE). Ptolemaic influence on the regime of *Zabinas* (128-123/2 BCE) would logically account for the appearance of Ptolemaic-style cornucopias on some of his coins;[12] see **Figs 4(a)-(b)**.

**(a)** **(b)**

**Fig. 4:** Seleucid Kings, Alexander II *Zabinas* (128-123/2 BCE). Æ 21 mm, Antioch mint; struck c. 125-122 BCE. Radiate and diademed bust of Alexander II, r. / **(a)** Filleted double cornucopias, Α above wreath to inner l., Π to inner r.; inscr. ΒΑΣΙΛΕΩΣ ΑΛΕΞΑΝΔΡΟΥ. *SC* (II) 2237h; **(b)** Two intertwined cornucopias, Σ above grain ear to l., Α to r.; same inscr. *SC* (II) 2235.1. Classical Numismatic Group, Electronic Auction 200 (03.12.2008), Lot 151. Courtesy of Classical Numismatic Group, Inc.

---

[11] The different spelling of Alexander II's nickname found in the modern literature is due to the varied orthography used in the ancient sources. Zabinas is one of the Greek versions that is encountered, e.g., in Diodorus Siculus (34/5.22.1) and in Porphyry (*apud* Euseb. *Chron.* Ed. Schoene I, p. 258). Josephus (*Ant.* 13.268) renders it Zebinas, while Justinus, in the Prologus to Book 39 of his Epitome of Pompeius Trogus' Philippic Histories refers to this Seleucid monarch in Latin as Alexander Zabinaeus. This name stems from the Aramaic, Zebina (which also appears thus in Ezr 10:43), and means "the bought one", as correctly interpreted by Porphyry (*loc. cit.*).

[12] Barag and Qedar 1980, 16. Following Ptolemaic custom, the twin cornucopias motifs on Zabinas' coins may refer to his marriage with a Ptolemaic princess, following the practice of his Seleucid predecessors and in view of his close dependence on Ptolemy VIII *Physcon*, although such a union is not specifically mentioned in the ancient sources.

*Zabinas* enjoyed a friendly and peaceful relationship with the Hasmonaeans (Jos., *Ant.* 13.269); it was therefore during his reign that *Hyrcanus* was able to begin demonstrating his independence from the Seleucids and struck his own coins, with the 'A' (= the Greek alpha) at the head of the Hebrew inscription on *TJC*'s A-series of the coins issued in the name of 'Yehokhanan' (= 'John') probably standing for Alexander *Zabinas*.[13] Several scholars are of the opinion that this series marks the beginning of Hasmonaean coinage, although, in his final verdict, Y. Meshorer is not so sure, and leaves open the possibility that the first 'Yehokhanan' coins – by implication, another series in his classification – may have been struck slightly earlier under Demetrius II, towards the end of his second reign in 128 BCE.[14] The choice of the filleted pair of cornucopias on the first Hasmonaean issue would then reflect *Hyrcanus*' close relationship with *Zabinas* and probably with his Ptolemaic allies. The conjoined cornucopias on his coins actually echo the intertwined pair on an issue of *Zabinas*; see **Fig. 4(b)**. By the time conjoined cornucopias were adopted by the Hasmonaeans, in what amounted to their heraldic device,[15] the Horn of Plenty had evidently lost its specifically pagan associations and came to generally represent "the prosperity which divine rule (or the divine king) brought to men".[16]

As regards the pomegranate, this fruit had religious significance for both the Greeks and the Jews. The pomegranate was sacred to Demeter and Persephone and was connected with the symbolism of death and resurrection in certain Greek mystery cults.[17] We are informed by the 2nd century CE Greek writer, Pausanias that the famous cult statue of Hera in her temple at Argos, fashioned using ivory and gold by the renowned Polykleitos, who was active four centuries earlier, held a sceptre in one hand and a pomegranate, in the other (Paus. 2.17, 4). A pomegranate features regularly on the coins of Side (meaning pomegranate in Greek) in Pamphylia from the 5th century BCE through to the 3rd century CE.[18]

The pomegranate also had a special place in Jewish religious tradition. According to the Book of Deuteronomy, it was one of seven kinds of agricultural produce with which the Promised Land was blessed (Deut 8:8). It was ordained that the ceremonial robe of the Jewish High Priest was to be bordered with embroidered pomegranates alternating with gold bells (Exod 28:33-34). Moreover, the pair of bronze pillars, known as Yakhin and Boaz, set up in front of the Sanctuary of the First Temple attributed to Solomon had capitals decorated with pomegranates (1 Kgs 7:16-21). The pomegranate maintained its importance to Jews into the classical period and a pomegranate motif occupies pride of place on the reverse of the silver sheqels and half sheqels struck by the Jewish authorities in the First Jewish War against Rome;[19] see **Fig. 5**.

It is generally assumed that the pomegranate in the Hasmonean motif was chosen for its biblical connotations. At any rate, after the overthrow of the Hasmonaean dynasty, Herod saw fit to exchange it for a more conspicuously pagan symbol, the caduceus of Mercury, between the cornucopias, thereby aligning his device with that used by Mark Antony.

---

[13] *Pace* Meshorer (*TJC*, p. 42). This possibility was first suggested by F. de Saulcy (1854, 99-102), but he considered that it could stand for Antiochus VII. In their turn, Barag and Qedar (1980, 17-18) supposed that these coins were struck under either Alexander II *Zabinas* or Antiochus VIII *Gryphus* (126/5 - 97/6 BCE).

[14] *TJC*, p. 31.
[15] *TJC*, pp. 33-34.
[16] Goodenough 1958, 106-114
[17] Pollitt 1990, 78.
[18] See, e.g., *BMC Lycia, etc.*, Side 1-83.
[19] *TJC* 183-191, 193-195, 202-203, 207-209 and 215-216.

**Fig. 5:** Jerusalem (67-68 CE). AR Sheqel (23 mm). Chalice with rim of bead decoration; above it, the date Sh. B (year 2), with inscr.: Sheqel Yisra'el, (Shekel of Israel) / Sprig of three pomegranates; inscr: Yerushalayim haqadoshah (Jerusalem the Holy [City]). *TJC* 193. Photograph courtesy of David Hendin.

## 2. The Significance of the Cornucopias and Caduceus Motif

### 2.1 The cornucopia(e)

The cornucopia as a symbol of prosperity and abundance has already been touched on.

Germane to this discussion is the adoption of the cornucopia as the emblem of 'good fortune' (Agathê Tychê). Hellenistic rulers were much concerned about Tychê, or fortune, especially the sudden changes in fate that could either elevate them or bring about their demise. Classical authors had previously remarked on Tychê's fickle ways but this issue was thrown into sharp relief by the shifting political allegiances in Hellenistic society, which meant that neither birth nor virtue could assure success.[20] In the first half of the 4th century Tychê assumed the status of a significant female deity and was the recipient of dedications and sacrifices.[21] One of the principal intellectual figures of the period, the Athenian orator and statesman, Demetrius of Phalerum (c. 350-280 BCE), devoted a treatise to Tychê, which is now lost, but quoted by the historian Polybius (29.21), who remarked that in that treatise, Demetrius wished "to provide men with a vivid reminder of her mutability", illustrating this point with examples from recent history.

The popular manifestation of the personification of 'fortune' was her beneficial aspect, associated with supplications to Tychê for happy outcomes, and most commonly appears in the guise as protector of the city. It is recorded that the famous sculptor, Praxiteles, made a figure of Agathê Tychê for Athens which was later transported to the Capitol in Rome (Ael., *VH* 9.39; Plin., *HN* 36.4.23). However, the city goddess of fortune achieved an iconic form in the celebrated public sculpture of the Tychê of Antioch by Eutychides of Sicyon, a pupil of Lysippus, in about 300 BCE (Paus. 6.2.7).[22] The goddess is rendered with a mural crown, the mark of her status as the patron deity of cities, seated on a rock and holding a palm branch with the personification of the River Orontes at her feet. This famous composite sculpture is known from numerous Roman copies and on coin representations. Another well-represented Tychê type, with an equally respectable Hellenistic pedigree, has the goddess in a standing position and holding a cornucopia, the horn of plenty, and often accompanied by a ship's rudder to signify her role in charting the course of human affairs. It was the version that was most widely adopted by the Romans for Fortuna, their goddess of good fortune, luck and success;[23] see **Fig. 6**.

---

[20] Rausa 1997, 125-41.
[21] Pollitt 1986, 2-4.
[22] cf. Smith 1991, 76-77.

[23] Rausa 1997, 128-131, 139 and nos. 39-86, 94-101; Graf 2004, cols. 506-509.

**Fig. 6:** Claudius (41-54 CE). AR Cistophoric tetradrachm (26 mm). Ephesus mint; struck AD 41-42. Bust of Claudius, r.; inscr.: TI CLAVD CAES·AVG / Temple of Rome and Augustus with cult statues of the Emperor being crowned by Dea Roma in the guise of Fortuna holding a cornucopia in her left hand; inscr.: COM ASI in field, and . ROM ET AVG on temple entablature. *RIC* I², Claudius 120; *RPC* I 2221. Classical Numismatic Group, Mail Bid Auction 69 (08.06.2005), Lot 1529. Courtesy of Classical Numismatic Group, Inc.

## 2.2 The caduceus

*The Dictionary of Roman Coins* succinctly expounds on the caduceus (*kerykeion* in Greek), as follows:[24]

Caduceus, or Caduceum, a wand or rod, entwined at one end by two serpents, each of whose bodies folds again in the form of two half-circles, whilst the head passes above the wand. It was an attribute peculiar to Mercury. Prudence is generally supposed to be represented by these two serpents, and the wings which are sometimes added to the Caduceus, are the symbols of diligence, both needful qualities in the pursuit of trade and commerce, which Mercury patronized. It was also the symbol of peace and concord, which that deity is related to have received from Apollo in return for the lyre.

Here it should be mentioned that the Romans identified Mercury, their patron deity of merchants (the very name is connected with *merx* and *mercari*) with the Greek Hermes, and consequently these deities shared the same attributes (see, e.g. Hor. *Carm.* 1.10). While it can be readily appreciated that the attribute of the messenger god is connected with social intercourse and trade, it is less obvious to see what he has to do with concord (Concordia). The link is referred to in the *Dictionary* entry cited above. The specific episode referred to is first described in the Homeric Hymn to Hermes (*Hymn. Hom. Merc.* 490-539). There it is related that Hermes mischievously stole 50 cows belonging to Apollo, making them walk backwards into a cave so that they shouldn't be traced. When this deed was relayed to Apollo by an old man, he approached Hermes in a rage, and the former mollified him with the gift of the lyre that he had invented. Apollo reciprocated by giving Hermes a gold wand of wealth and fortune (i.e. the caduceus). Horace (*Carm.* 1.10.17-20) commends Mercury as a conciliator of gods and men.

The Romans assigned the caduceus of Mercury also to personify the various virtuous qualities that the deity embodied. These particularly included Felicitas the personification of good luck and enduring success – financial and otherwise. Felicitas appears to be a specifically Italic deity.[25] Her first temple in Rome was built with the booty from the Spanish campaign

---

[24] Stevenson, Smith and Madden 1889, 149.

[25] Champeaux 1987, 216–236; Schaffner 2004

in 146 BCE (Dio Cass. (22).76.2; 43.21.1; Suet., *Iul*. 37). She was reputed to favour Roman commanders with military accomplishments and the latter, including Julius Caesar, devoted temples to Felicitas (Dio Cass. 44.5.2).[26]

Just as the caduceus, the potent symbol of Mercury becomes linked with Felicitas, on account of their shared reputations as bringers of good fortune so too, Roman representations of Pax, Concordia and Ceres on Roman coins are sometimes accompanied by a caduceus. As B. S. Spaeth observes, "Pax represents an end to war; Concordia, harmony among the people of the Empire; and Ceres fertility nourished by Peace".[27] In other words, there developed a tendency for the one-time exclusive symbol of a deity to represent a virtuous quality that might be associated with any one of them. This blending and blurring of attributes of Ceres and Pax in the Augustan poetry of Tibullus and Ovid and has been pointed out by Spaeth.[28] It is noteworthy that the state of harmony characterised by the merging of divine duties and attributions is credited, particularly by Ovid and Horace, to a peace-making leader, in this case Caesar (Octavian), at the helm.[29] A similar development is observed in coin types, exemplified by the representation of a female figure holding a caduceus and corn ears on coins struck in 68-69 CE. It is only the coin legend that enables us to distinguish her as either Ceres or Pax.[30]

### 2.3 The cornucopia(s) and caduceus

Being so close in their scope, and in view of the trend described above, it is quite logical that the personification of Felicitas should have been melded with that of Tychê/Fortuna as the hybid Fortuna Felicitas, literally 'good fortune' and, to all intents and purposes, equivalent to the Greek Agathê Tychê. She is represented as a female goddess accompanied by both one or two cornucopias (of Fortuna) and the caduceus (of Felicitas). Images of Fortuna Felicitas personified, bearing these devices and with the accompanying legend often referring to her simply as Felicitas (or not naming her), become fairly regular on Roman Imperial coins until the end of the 3rd century CE,[31] as exemplified by **Fig. 7**.

**Fig. 7:** Commodus (178-193 CE). AV Aureus (21 mm). Rome mint; struck in 189 CE. Draped, cuirassed bust of Commodus, r.; inscr. M·COMM·ANT·P·FEL·AVG·BRIT·P·P·/ Fortuna Felicitas, l., holding caduceus and cornucopia, with foot on a prow; inscr. FOR·FEL·P·M·TR·P·XIIII·COS·V DES·VI. (previously unrecorded in gold; similar to *BMCRE* IV, Commodus 262 and Pl. 97.12 = *RIC* III Commodus 186 [denarius]). UBS Gold & Numismatics, Auction 75 (22.01.2008), Lot 1067. Courtesy of UBS AG.

---

[26] cf. Schaffner 2004.
[27] Spaeth 1994, 93-94.
[28] *Ibid.*, 91. Examples given by her include Tibullus 1.10.45-50, 67-68; Ovid, *Fasti* 1.697-704.
[29] See, for example, Ovid, *Fasti* 4.407-408, Hor., *Car.* 4.15.4-5, 16-19.
[30] The pieces in question are *RIC* I², Galba 291, 324-326 (Ceres); Civil Wars 114-115 (Pax).
[31] For the numerous examples, see *RIC* II-V, listed under 'Felicitas standing (or seated), holding caduceus and cornucopias' in the index of 'Types' in each volume or part.

It follows from what was said in the previous section that all the positive qualities encompassed by Mercury and Fortuna were enshrined by the goddess holding a caduceus and cornucopia(s) and any one or both of these could be featured by her or, for that matter, by the combined symbols alone. So we should not be surprised to encounter a goddess with these accoutrements on Roman coins representing Pax and Concordia in addition to (Fortuna) Felicitas;[32] see, for example, **Fig. 8**.

**Fig. 8:** Crispus Caesar ( 316-326 CE). AV Solidus (24 mm), Ticinium mint, struck in c. 320-321 CE. Nude and laureate bust of Crispus, l., holding spear pointing forward and shield on l. shoulder; inscr.: FL IVL CRIS – PVS NOB CAES / Concordia seated l., holding caduceus and cornucopias; inscr.: CONCOR – D – I – A AVGG N N; in exergue, SNT. *RIC* VII Constantine 103. Numismatica Ars Classica, Auction 27 (12.05.2004), Lot 513. Courtesy of Numismatica Ars Classica NAC AG.

Among the coin types represented on the issues struck during the Civil Wars of 68-69 CE, two denarii bearing the legend PAX depict clasped hands holding a caduceus between crossed cornucopias.[33]

We also find representations of Tychê, the cornucopias of Fortuna and caduceus of Felicitas linked together in the same coin series as an affirmation of their close association and, indeed, overlap of their physical attributes, according to the Graeco-Roman belief system. Such occurrences characterise the coinage of Gadara, one of the cities of the Decapolis, in the 1st century CE. The three bronze denominations struck there in the years 92, 108 and 114 of that city's era (28/9 CE, 44/5 CE and 50/1 CE, respectively) depict the head of the reigning emperor on the obverse and veiled head of Tychê, crossed cornucopias and caduceus (in the order of decreasing size).[34]

The juxtaposition of the caduceus with a cornucopia in a single motif is first encountered on east Greek coinage. A listed example is a bronze piece from Laodiceia in Phrygia dated to 88-67 BCE; see **Fig. 9**. There is also a bronze coin from Lamos in Cilicia, which carries a winged caduceus between crossed cornucopias.[35] Unfortunately, there are doubts about its date, which may be any time between the 2nd and 1st century BCE.

---

[32] A goddess shown holding a caduceus and cornucopia on dupondii of Galba is titled PAX (*RIC* I², Galba 285 and 371) or FELICITAS (*ibid*. 411-412). There are other dupondii in this series where Pax is represented either holding a caduceus (*ibid*. 281-284, 319-323, 413 and 415) or a cornucopia (*ibid*. 273, 277-280, 368-370 and 414). On two of the Galba dupondii, Felicitas holds a cornucopia and a patera but no caduceus (*ibid*. 273 and 361-362).

[33] *RIC* I², Civil Wars 103 and 113.

[34] *RPC* I 4812-4814 (year 92 = 28/9 CE; Tiberius), 4816-4818 (year 108 = 44/5 CE; Claudius); 4819-4821 (year 114 = 50/1 CE; Claudius).

[35] *SNG Levante Suppl*. 96; Classical Numismatic Group, Mail Bid Auction (19.05.2004), Lot 550.

# THE SIGNIFICANCE OF THE CADUCEUS BETWEEN FACING CORNUCOPIAS IN HERODIAN AND ROMAN COINAGE

**Fig. 9:** Phrygia, Laodikeia (c. 88-67 BCE). Æ 20 mm. Draped bust of Laodike, r. / ΛΑΟΔΙ-ΚΕΩΝ Conjoined filleted cornucopia and winged(?) caduceus. *SNG von Aulock* 3804, *SNG Copenhagen* 501-2.

The earliest, firmly dated appearance of the conjoined pair of cornucopias with a caduceus in between, as a motif in its own right, is on an issue struck by Mark Antony in 40 BCE (*RRC* 520/1; see **Fig. 10**). In that rendering, the cornucopias and caduceus are mounted on a globe and M. H. Crawford interprets this composite motif as representing the "domination of Rome over the world and the restoration of commerce (caduceus) and plenty (cornucopiae)".[36]

**Fig. 10:** Antony, 40 BCE. AR denarius (21 mm). Corcyra (?) mint. Bust of Antony, with Lituus behind / Winged caduceus on a globe between two cornucopias; inscr.: M ANT·IMP (above), III·VIR·R·P·C· (below). *RRC* 520/1; Künker Auction 115 (25.09.2006), Lot 358. Courtesy of Fritz Rudolf Künker GmbH & Co. KG, Osnabrück, and Lübke & Wiedemann, Stuttgart.

Mark Antony and his officials may well have taken the idea of the conjoined cornucopias and caduceus motif from Asia Minor, while that triumvir was governing the eastern provinces from 42 BCE. They may have been aware of the fine series of tetradrachms minted by Lebedus in southern Ionia in the mid-2nd century BCE; see **Fig. 11**.

**Fig. 11:** Lebedus, southern Ionia, Apollodotos, magistrate (c. 160-140 BCE). AR tetradrachm (30 mm). Helmeted head of Athena, r.; inscr. ΛΕΒΕΔΙΩΝ (above) ΑΠΟΛΛΟΔΟΤΟΣ / Owl standing right, head facing, on club between conjoined, filleted cornucopias, within wreath. Amandry 1988, p. 3, group IV, 17 (D2/R13). Classical Numismatic Group, Mail Bid Auction 76 (12.09.2007), Lot 715. Courtesy of Classical Numismatic Group, Inc.

[36] *RRC*, p. 527.

The conjoined cornucopias on this attractive issue may have been a nod to the Ptolemies, under whose control Lebedus had fallen in the 3rd century BCE suzerainty.[37] Whereas W. W. Tarn had supposed that the pair of conjoined cornucopias and caduceus on the denarius of Mark Antony referred to the marriage between Antony and Octavia the Younger, the sister of Caesar Octavian, as part of the reconciliation between the two triumvirs at Brundisium, late in 40 BCE,[38] Crawford takes the view that this issue dates to earlier that year. He reasoned that the style of portraiture on the piece coupled with the smallness of the issue linked it to the sequence of coins struck for Antony by Cn. Domitius Ahenobarbus and L. Plancus earlier that year.[39] While Crawford's reasoning might be correct, it would not rule out this issue being minted in anticipation of his reconciliation with Octavian. Indeed, what other reason could there have been for issuing a coin with such a buoyant theme? That this is the most likely motivation for this issue is reinforced by the presence of the caduceus, the symbol of concord, on a series of coins that are certainly connected with the reconciliation at Brundisium (*RRC* 529/2-4). One of these, a quinarius of 39 BCE, bears an especially emphatic reference to this event, a motif of two hands clasped together around a caduceus (*RRC* 529/4a&b; see **Fig. 12**).

**Fig. 12:** Octavian and Mark Antony, 39 BCE. Quinarius (15 mm). Mint moving with Octavian. Diademed head of Concordia, r.; inscr.: III·VIR·R·P·C / Two hands clasped around caduceus; inscr.: M ANTON·C·CAESAR. *RRC* 529/4b. Numismatica Ars Classica, Auction 46 (02.04.2008), Lot 949. Courtesy of Numismatica Ars Classica NAC AG.

Herod found himself to be a major beneficiary of this act of reconciliation between Rome's supreme leaders. His appointment as King of Judaea towards the end of 40 BCE was one of the few recorded by-products calculated to further stabilise Rome's authority. It was agreed by the two triumvirs and commemorated by a procession to the Capitol in which Herod was accompanied by Antony and Octavian, culminating in a sacrifice to Jupiter in the venerable Roman sanctuary, which was referred to in the introduction.

It is against this backdrop that Herod's choice of the cornucopias and caduceus motif ought to be considered. The ideological message conveyed by this hybrid device, as understood at Rome and by the Empire's Judaean allies, and which also accounts for its popularity on Imperial coinage, will now be examined.

## 3. The Ideological Use of the Pair of Cornucopias and Caduceus Motif
### 3.1 In the service of Herod

Herod's adoption of the pair of conjoined cornucopias and caduceus on his most common coin is pregnant with political meaning. At once it refers to his appointment as client king by Antony

---

[37] Stillwell *et al* 1976, 492-93.
[38] Tarn 1932, 157
[39] *RRC*, pp. 100 and 742-3.

and Octavian, noted above.⁴⁰ Then, again, as observed by Meshorer, by employing symbols used by his Hasmonaean predecessors, an anchor surrounded by Herod's name and title on the obverse and the pair of cornucopias in the same configuration on the reverse, he was surely emphasising the legitimacy of his kingship as successor to the Hasmonaeans.⁴¹ He had therefore managed to choose a convenient emblem for himself from the repertoire of those previously used by his first important Roman patron and one that offered a convenient and meaningful twist. The 'neutral' pomegranate between the pair of cornucopias in the old Hasmonaean 'logo' was replaced by a caduceus, an unambiguous pagan symbol. That pointed modification emphasised the dynastic and ideological change that had taken place in Judaea. It advertised Herod's ties to Rome, with a possible added acknowledgement of Augustus' patronage of the cult of Mercury.⁴²

### 3.2 In the service of the Roman Principate

From its low-key initial appearance on the denarius of limited issue struck for Mark Antony, the crossed cornucopias (i.e. often not joined at the tips) and caduceus motif rapidly became a prominent Roman icon. These attributes of Fortuna Felicitas were morphed into a cipher of commitment to the enduring success and prosperity of the Roman Empire.

The display of this hybrid symbol of Fortuna Felicitas on mosaics at Pompeii and on the front of an altar at Bologna dated to the reign of Augustus demonstrates that it had taken root in Italy by then.⁴³ It also appears intermittently on the coins of Rome and its provinces until the end of the 2nd century CE,⁴⁴ although, as mentioned earlier, the representation of (Fortuna) Felicitas holding a caduceus and cornucopia(e) run on to the early 4th century CE.⁴⁵

An early instance of the crossed cornucopias and caduceus motif on coins from Rome is on a sestertius commemorating the birth of twin sons to the only child of the emperor Tiberius, Nero Claudius Drusus Caesar and his wife Livia Drusilla (Livilla) in 19 CE; see **Fig. 13**. The draped busts of the twins are shown held in each horn, separated by a winged caduceus. Tiberius was overjoyed by this event and was reported to boast that no such good fortune had ever befallen a Roman of his rank (Tac. *Ann.* 3.56-57). The crossed cornucopias and caduceus on this coin are clearly meant to represent 'happy fortune'.

---

⁴⁰ Noting the thematic connection between this coin of Herod and the one of Mark Antony bearing the cornucopias and caduceus, Meshorer (1991, 67) saw this as evidence of "a connection [of the former] with his Roman patron" but he does not elaborate. It should be mentioned, however, that there is strong circumstantial evidence, including archaeological, that Herod's anchor / twin cornucopias and caduceus coin type was minted towards the end of his reign: see Ariel 2000-2, 109, 119 and 122; *RPC* I, p. 678.
⁴¹ *TJC*, p. 67.
⁴² Combet Farnoux 1981.
⁴³ See Jones and Robinson 2007, p. 399, Fig. 25.10 (mosaic in the Vicolo di Narciso atrium of the Casa delle Vestali [vi.1.7]); Flohr 2008, 9 -10 and Figs. 21-22 (mosaic in Shop 21, House VI.14, 21.22); Lehmann-Hartleben 1927, Scott 1935 (altar at Bologna).
⁴⁴ Some of the last examples struck by the Roman imperial minting authorities, in gold, silver and bronze, date to the final years of the reign of Commodus (177-192 CE; *RIC* III, Commodus 209, 214, 565 and 566). Roman Imperial coins of the crossed cornucopias and caduceus type up to the death of Domitian in 96 CE are represented in *RIC* by Tiberius 42, 89, 90; Vespasian 756-64, 767, 902, 1016-1019, 1095 and 1508; Titus 253. Additional provincial issues not included in *RIC* and listed in *RPC* are – Vol I: nos, 4910 (Judaea, Herod the Great; see **Fig. 1**), 4912 (Judaea, Archelaus), 4960 (Judaea, Valerius Gratus), 4991 (Judaea, Agrippa II, dated 'year 6 also 11' = 65/66 CE [the reverse type is incorrectly described in *RPC* I]; for the dating of Agrippa II's coins, see **n. 51** below), 2132 (Sinope, Claudius), 4751 (Ptolemais, Nero?; see **Fig. 15**); 4849 (Sepphoris, Nero; see **Fig. 16**) – Vol. II: 708 (Bithynia, Vespasian), 2271 (Agrippa II, Judaea; see **Fig. 14**), 27-28 (Koinon of Crete, Domitian), 1747 (Anazarbus, Domitian). There are also the examples mentioned earlier from autonomous Ascalon (late 1st century BCE?; *BMC Palestine*, Ascalon no. 45 [p. 111]), the kingdom of Nabataea (Aretas IV; *ANS Arabia, Nabataea* 2010.55.92), the client monarchy of Mauretania (Ptolemy; Mazard 1955, nos. 484-486; Salzman 1974, no. 47.2; *SNG Copenhagen, N. Africa* 642).
⁴⁵ Ganschow 1997, 586-87, nos. 7-19.

**Fig. 13:** Tiberius (14-37 CE). Æ Sestertius (34 mm), Rome mint; struck 22-23 CE. Crossed cornucopias, each surmounted by the bust of a little boy, with a winged caduceus between / Large S C surrounded by inscr.: DRVSVS·CAESAR TI AVG F DIVI AVG N PONT·TR· POT·II. RIC I² Tiberius 42. Classical Numismatic Group, Mail Bid Auction 73 (13.09.2006), Lot 833. Courtesy of Classical Numismatic Group, Inc.

Continuing Herod's favour of this device, it occurs among the coin types of the small bronzes of Herod's son Archelaus (4 BCE – 6 CE) and the Roman prefect of Judaea, Valerius Gratus in 16 CE and again on one of the later issues of Herod's great-grandson, Agrippa II;[46] see **Fig. 14**. Not involving the representation of the human form, the device was employed in preference to images of Fortuna Felicitas personified on coins that were intended for circulation among the Jewish population of Judaea, for whom 'graven images' were anathema. The autonomous coastal town of Ascalon, which has been closely linked to Herod's ancestry,[47] also struck a small bronze coin with the double cornucopias and caduceus motif on its reverse.[48] A related piece has a beardless male bust, presumably representing Augustus, with a caduceus behind his shoulder on its obverse and the pair of cornucopias with an ear of corn between the horns on its reverse.[49] Although not yet formally part of the Roman Empire, Nabataea under Aretas IV (9 BCE – 40 CE) appears to have emulated his Judaean neighbour in issuing a bronze coin bearing the same device.[50]

---

[46] *TJC* 68, 68a-f; *RPC* I 4912 (Archelaus); *TJC* 68; *RPC* I 4960 (Valerius Gratus); *TJC* 163; *RPC* II 2271 (Agrippa II).
[47] Kokkinos 1998, 103-139.
[48] *BMC Palestine*, Ascalon no. 45.
[49] *Ibid.*, no. 41.

[50] *ANS Arabia, Nabataea* 2010.55.92 (unpublished?). The reign of Herod commenced almost three decades before that of Aretas IV and they only overlapped for about 5 years, so that Herod's coin bearing the cornucopias and caduceus motif most probably preceded that of Aretas.

# THE SIGNIFICANCE OF THE CADUCEUS BETWEEN FACING CORNUCOPIAS IN HERODIAN AND ROMAN COINAGE

**Fig. 14:** Judaea, Agrippa II (48/49 - 100 CE) Æ Semis (20 mm), Caesarea Paneas mint; year 26 = 85/6,[51] Bust of Domitian, r.; inscr.: IM CA D VES F DOM AV GER COS XII / Crossed cornucopias and winged caduceus between; inscr.: ΕΠΙ ΒΑ ΑΓΡΙ, ΕΤ Κϛ (across field), S C (below). *TJC* 163; *RPC* II 2271. Courtesy of Classical Numismatic Group, Inc. (no. 197355).

An overtly political nuance is given to the cornucopias and caduceus motif on a bronze coin issued by Ptolemais in northern Palestine after it had been reconstituted as a Roman Colonia and settled with veterans, which occurred at the end of Claudius' reign.[52] Its full title appears to have been Col(onia) Cla(udia) Stab(ilis) Germ(anica) Felix Ptol(emais), judging from coin inscriptions.[53] The coin depicts a subject that radiates imperial triumphalism, a winged victory bearing a palm branch and wreath. The reverse shows a winged caduceus between a pair of cornucopias, which projects the benevolence of *Pax Romana*, implicit also in the 'Felix' of the foundation's title; see **Fig. 15**.

**Fig. 15:** Ptolemais, reign of Nero (54-68 CE)? AE 15 mm. OVI AVGVS, Victory advancing r., with palm branch and wreath/ Winged caduceus between two crossed cornucopias; inscr.: COL COS CLA; *RPC* I 4751. Courtesy of Tom Vossen, Kerkrade, NL (no. 2856).

More poignant, still, is the appearance of this emblem on a bronze coin struck by Sepphoris, one of the major cities of Galilee, in the midst of the First Jewish War against Rome (66-73 CE). Rather than joining the bloody revolt, the inhabitants chose to open the city's gates to the Roman general, Vespasian, and it was consequently spared destruction (Jos., *War* 3.30-34]. The savage aftermath of an unsuccessful rebellion by Sepphoris following the death of Herod the Great (Jos., *War* 2.68; *Ant.* 17.289) was evidently still raw in the collective memory of its inhabitants and had clearly quenched their taste for further insurrection.

On welcoming the Roman army, Sepphoris proceeded to strike a series of two bronze coins, inscribed in Greek, according to Meshorer at the initiative of Agrippa II.[54] This series

---

[51] For the dating of Agrippa II's coins and regnal eras represented on them, see the excellent analysis in Kokkinos 2003, 174-180; *idem* 1998, 400 [table]. See also the discussion of this chronology in *RPC* II, p. 309, which unaccountably fails to mention Kokkinos' important contribution.

[52] *RPC* I, p. 659; Millar 1990, 24; Schürer 1979, 125. *RPC* suggests that this coin was struck under Nero, while Syon believes that it better suits a Jewish War victory issue and was accordingly minted under the Flavians (see D. Syon, in this volume).

[53] *Ibid.*, nos. 4749 and 4750.

[54] *RPC* I 4849 and 4850. See Meshorer 1979; *TJC*, pp. 103-105. On the inhabitants of Sepphoris as proponents of peace during the First Jewish War, see Jos., *War* 3.30.

is characterised by impoverished design and execution, including a weak strike for the most part, and the coins are highly variable in weight, all indicative of an emergency issue. At that very time, the Jewish rebels in Jerusalem were issuing a high quality and consistent coinage in both silver and bronze.

These two modest bronzes, dated 67/68 CE, bear vivid testimony to the local situation, in the midst of the Jewish War.[55] Both coins are devoid of human images, reflecting the fact that Sepphoris, at that time, was predominantly a Jewish city. Another striking feature of these coins is that they are issued by "Neronias-Sepphoris, city of peace".[56] While they bear the name of the current emperor, Nero, and give the year of his reign, it is mentioned on this pair of coins that they were issued "in the days of Vespasian", in acknowledgement of his position as governor of Judaea, under whose authority the coin was issued.[57] The prominent inclusion of the Latin letters 'S.C.', a widely used abbreviation for *senatus consultum*, on one of these coins is, in a similar vein, a gesture of submission to Roman authority, rather than denoting an actual decision of the Roman Senate.

The larger coin depicts the crossed cornucopias and caduceus; see **Fig. 16**. Here, this image was, like the 'S.C.' on the other piece, undoubtedly intended to advertise the fact that Sepphoris had decided to nail its colours to the mast of Rome, thereby demonstrating its commitment to the enduring success, peace and prosperity of the Roman Empire.[58]

**Fig. 16:** Sepphoris Æ 22 mm; struck in 67/68 CE. Legend in five lines within linear circle, all within a wreath; inscr.: L ΔI / NERΩN[O] / KΛAYΔIOY / KAICAP[O]/C (= year 14 of Nero Claudius Caesar) / Two crossed cornucopias with caduceus between them; inscr. EΠI OYECΠACIANO[Y EIPHNOΠOΛI NEPΩNIA CEΠΦΩP] (under Vespasian, of the city of peace, Neronias-Sepphoris). *RPC* I 4849; *TJC* 127.

## 4. Conclusion

Through the examination of the evolution and reproduction of the conjoined or crossed cornucopias with a caduceus in-between, on Roman and allied coins, we have shown that this compound motif was meant to symbolise Fortuna Felicitas ('good fortune'), which also bore the associated connotations of peace and concord, happy conditions that were made possible by a benevolent ruler. Accordingly, it became recognised as a cipher for commitment by Rome (and to Rome) as the standard-bearer of tranquillity, prosperity and general well-being. Nowhere is this meaning made more transparent than in a representation of this motif on a coin of Sepphoris, struck in the heat of the First Jewish War by the inhabitants of that city, mostly Jewish, affirming their steadfast loyalty to Rome and its Emperor.

---

[55] *RPC* I, p. 671.
[56] *TJC*, p. 104.
[57] Schürer 1973, 265 and n. 15.
[58] The choice of this motif may have been suggested by its use on a bronze piece of Agrippa II of struck in Paneas (*TJC* 132; cf. *idem*, p. 105; *RPC* I 4991). On its dating to 65/66 CE, *contra* Meshorer, see nn. 44 and 51 above.

## Acknowledgements

The author wishes to thank Professor Ted Buttrey and Dr Nikos Kokkinos for their helpful comments on the manuscript of this article and the auction houses, dealers and numismatists named in figure captions for permission to reproduce the respective coin images.

## Bibliography

*AJC* = *Ancient Jewish Coinage*, 2 vols., by Y. Meshorer (Dix Hills, NY: Amphora Books, 1982).

*BMC Palestine* = *A Catalogue of the Greek Coins in the British Museum 27: The Greek Coins of Palestine (Galilee, Samaria and Judaea)*, by G.F. Hill (London: Trustees of the British Museum, 1914).

*BMC Lycia etc.* = *A Catalogue of the Greek Coins in the British Museum 19: The Greek Coins of Lycia, Pamphylia and Pisidia*, by G. F. Hill (London: Trustees of the British Museum, 1897).

*BMCRE* IV = *Coins of the Roman Empire in the British Museum*, Vol. IV: *Antoninus Pius to Commodus*, by H. Mattingly (London: British Museum, 1940).

*IGRR* = *Inscriptiones graecae ad res romanas pertinentes*, ed. R. Cagnat *et al.* (Paris: E. Leroux, 1901-1927).

*LIMC* = *Lexicon Iconographicum Mythologiae Classicae* (Zürich / München: Artemis, 1981-1997).

*New Pauly* 5 = *Brill's New Pauly*, ed. H. Cancik, H., and H. Schneider, Vol. 5 (Leiden / Boston: Brill, 2004).

*OGIS* = *Orientis graeci inscriptions selectae*, ed. W. Dittenburger (Leipzig: S. Hirzel, 1903-1095), 2 vols.

*RIC* I$^2$ = *The Roman Imperial Coinage*, Vol. I: *From 31 BC to AD 69* (revised 2$^{nd}$ edn.), ed. C. H. V. Sutherland and R. A. G. Carson (London: Spink and Son, 1984).

*RIC* II.1$^2$ = *The Roman Imperial Coinage*, Vol. II.1: *From AD 69 -96, Vespasian to Domitian* (revised 2$^{nd}$ edn.), by I. A. Carradice and T. V. Buttrey (London: Spink and Son, 2007).

*RIC* III = *The Roman Imperial Coinage*, Vol. III: *Antoninus Pius to Commodus*, by H. Mattingly and E. A. Sydenham (London: Spink and Son, 1930).

*RIC* VII = *The Roman Imperial Coinage*, Vol. VII: *Constantine and Licinius, AD 313-317*, by P. Bruun (London: Spink and Son, 1966).

*RPC* I = *Roman Provincial Coinage*, Vol. I (in 2 parts): *From the Death of Caesar to the Death of Vitellius (44 BC – AD 69)*, by A. Burnett, M. Amandry and P. Ripollès (London: British Museum Press / Paris: Bibliothèque nationale de France, 1992).

*RPC* II = *Roman Provincial Coinage*, Vol. II (in 2 parts): *From Vespasian to Domitian (AD 69 – 96)*, by A. Burnett, M. Amandry and I. Carradice (London: British Museum Press / Paris : Bibliothèque nationale de France, 1999).

*RRC* = *Roman Republican Coinage*, by M. H. Crawford (Cambridge: Cambridge University Press, 1974).

*SC* II = *Seleucid Coins: A Comprehensive Catalogue*, Part II (in 2 vols.): Seleucus IV through Antiochus XIII, by A. Houghton, C. Lorber and O. Hoover (American Numismatic Society / Classical Numismatic Group: New York / Lancaster NY and London, 2008).

*SNG Copenhagen, Phrygia 2* = *Sylloge Nummorum Graecorum, The Royal Collection of Coins and Medals, Danish National Museum; Phrygia Pt. II, Grimenothyrae – Trajanopolis*, (Copenhagen: Einar Munksgaard, 1948).

*SNG Copenhagen, N. Africa* = *Sylloge Nummorum Graecorum, The Royal Collection of Coins and Medals, Danish National Museum; North Africa. Syrtica –Mauretania*, ed. G. K. Jenkins (Copenhagen: Einar Munksgaard, 1969).
*SNG Levante* Suppl. 1 = *Sylloge Nummorum Graecorum, Switzerland; Levante – Cilicia*, Supplement I (Zürich: Numismatica Ars Cassica, 1993).
*SNG von Aulock, Phrygia (3329-4040)* = *Sylloge Nummorum Graecorum, Deutschland, Sammlung v. Aulock; Phrygien 3329-4040* (Berlin: Gebr. Mann, 1964).
*Svoronos (Ptolemaion)* = Svoronos, J. N., *Ta Nomismata tou Kratous ton Ptolemaion (Ptolemaic Coinage)* (Athens: Sakellariou, 1904).
*TJC* = *A Treasury of Jewish Coins from the Persian Period to Bar Kokhba*, by Y. Meshorer (Nyack, NY: Amphora Books, 2001).


Amandry, M., 1988. 'Les tétradrachmes à la couronne de feuillage frappés à Lébédos (Ionie)', in *Kraay-Mørkholm Essays. Numismatic Studies in Memory of C.M. Kraay and O. Mørkholm*, ed. G. Le Rider *et. al.* (Louvain-la-Neuve: Institut supérieur d'archéologie et d'histoire de l'art, Séminaire de numismatique Marcel Hoc), 1-7.
Ariel, D. T., 2000-2. 'The Jerusalem Mint of Herod the Great: A Relative Chronology', *INJ* 14, 99-124.
Barag, D., and Qedar, S., 1980. 'The Beginning of Hasmonean Coinage', *INJ* 4, 8-21.
Cavedoni, C., 1850. *Numismatica biblica, o sia Dichiarazione delle monete antiche memorate nelle sante Scritture* (Modena: eredi Soliani).
Champeaux, J., 1987. *Fortuna. Recherches sur le culte de la Fortune à Rome et dans le monde romain des origines à la mort de César. II Les Transformations de Fortuna sous le République* (Rome: Ecole Française de Rome).
Combet Farnoux, B., 1981. 'Mercure romain, les "Mercuriales" et l'institution du culte imperial sous le Principat augusteen', *ANRW* II 17.1, 457-501.
Flohr, M., 2008. 'Cleaning the Laundries II. Report of the 2007 Campaign', *Fasti Online Documents and Research* 111, 13 pp.; see www.fastionline.org/docs/FOLDER-it-2008-111.pdf.
Fuks, G., 2002. 'Josephus on Herod's Attitude towards the Jewish Religion: The Darker Side', *JJS* 53/2, 238-245.
Ganschow, T., 1997. 'Felicitas', *LIMC* Vol. VIII.1, 585-591.
Goodenough, E. R., 1958. *Jewish Symbols in the Greco-Roman Period*, Vol. 8 (New York: Pantheon Books).
Graf, F., 2004. 'Fortuna', in *New Pauly* 5, cols. 506-509.
Henig, M., 1981. 'Amaltheia', *LIMC* Vol. I.1, 125-141.
Jacobson, D. M., 1986. 'A New Interpretation of the Reverse of Herod's Largest Coin', *ANSMN* 31, 145–165.
Jacobson, D. M., 1993/4. 'King Herod, Roman Citizen and Benefactor of Kos', *Bulletin of the Anglo-Israel Archaeological Society* 13, 31-35.
Jacobson, D. M., 2007. 'Military Helmet or Dioscuri Motif on Herod the Great's Largest Coin', *Israel Numismatic Research* 2, 93-101.
Jones, R., and Robinson, D., 2007. 'Intensification, Heterogeneity and Power in the Development of Insula VI.1', in J. J. Dobbins and P. W. Foss (eds.), *The World of Pompeii* (London / New York: Routledge), 389-406.
Kokkinos, N., 1998. *The Herodian Dynasty: Origins, Role in Society and Eclipse* (Sheffield: Sheffield Academic Press).

Kokkinos, N., 2003. 'Justus, Josephus, Agrippa II and his Coins', *Scripta Classica Israelica* 22, 163-180.
Lehmann-Hartleben, K., 1927. 'Ein Altar in Bologna', *MDAI(R)* 42, 163-176.
Madden, F. W., 1864. *History of Jewish Coinage, and of Money in the Old and New Testament* (London: Bernard Quaritch).
Mazard, J., 1955. *Corpus Nummorum Numidiae Mauritaniaeque* (Paris: Arts et métiers graphiques).
Meshorer, Y., 1979. 'Sepphoris and Rome', in O. Morkholm and N. M. Waggoner (eds.), *Greek Numismatics and Archaeology. Essays in Honor of Margaret Thompson* (Wetteren: NR), 159-171.
Millar, F., 1990. 'The Roman *Coloniae* of the Near East: A Study of Cultural Relations', in H. Solin and M. Kajava (eds.), *Roman Eastern Policy and Other Studies in Roman History* (Helsinki: Societas Scientiarum Fennica), 7-58.
Netzer, E., 2006. *The Architecture of Herod, the Great Builder* (Tübingen: Mohr Siebeck).
Pollitt, J. J., 1986. *Art in the Hellenistic Age* (Cambridge: Cambridge University Press).
---1990. *The Art of Ancient Greece: Sources and Documents*, 2nd edn. (Cambridge: Cambridge University Press).
Rausa, F., 1997. 'Tyche / Fortuna', *LIMC* Vol. VIII.1, 125-141.
Rice, E. E., 1983. *The Grand Procession of Ptolemy Philadelphus* (Oxford: Oxford University Press).
Romanoff, P., 1944. *Jewish Symbols on Ancient Jewish Coins* (Philadelphia: Dropsie College for Hebrew and Cognate Learning).
Salzmann, D., 1974. 'Zur Münzprägung der mauretanischen Könige Juba II und Ptolemaos,' *MDAI(M)* 15, 174-83.
de Saulcy, F., 1854. *Recherches sur la numismatique judaïque* (Paris: Didot Frères).
Schaffner, B., 2004. 'Felicitas', in *New Pauly* 5, cols. 377-378.
Schürer, E., 1973. *The History of the Jewish People in the Age of Jesus Christ (175 B.C. - A.D. 135)*, rev. and ed. by G. Vermes, F. Millar and M. Black, Vol. 1 (Edinburgh: T & T Clark).
Schürer, E., 1979. As above, Vol. 2.
Scott, K., 1935. 'Mercury on the Bologna Altar', *MDAI(R)* 50, 225-230.
Smith, R. R. R., 1991. *Hellenistic Sculpture: A Handbook* (London: Thames and Hudson).
Spaeth, B. S., 1994. 'The Goddess Ceres in the Ara Pacis Augustae and the Carthage Relief', *AJA* 98.1, 65-100.
Stevenson, S. W., Smith, C. R., and Madden, F. W., 1889. *The Dictionary of Roman Coins* (London: George Bell and Sons).
Stillwell, R., *et al.*, 1976. *The Princeton Encyclopedia of Classical Sites* (Princeton, NJ: Princeton University Press).
Tarn, W. W., 1932. 'Alexander, Helios and the Golden Age', *JRS* 22, 135-160.

# VESPASIAN'S ROMAN ORICHALCUM: AN UNRECOGNISED CELEBRATORY COINAGE

## Ted V. Buttrey

### 1. The Flavian Orichalcum Issue

The latest edition of the Roman coinage of the Flavians, *RIC* II.1², includes an issue of orichalcum which until recently has been attributed elsewhere, to Commagene, then to Antioch in Syria. It occurs in 4 modules, which for convenience we call dupondius, as, semis and quadrans.[1] The obverses bear a portrait of Vespasian, Titus or Domitian.

### 1.1 Dupondii

Fig. 1: *RPC* II 1983/3; *RIC* II Vesp. 498(b); *RIC* II.1² Vesp. 757.
British Museum AN638166001.

*Obv.*   Laureate head of Vespasian, r. or l.
         IMP CAESAR VESPASIAN(VS) AVG
*Rev.*   Winged caduceus between two crossed cornuacopiae
         PON MAX TR POT P P COS V CENS **Fig. 1**
         (Cohen Vespasian 376-378; *BMCRE* II 886-890; *RPC* II 1982-1983; *RIC* II.1² Vesp. 756-759)

---

[1] Weighing approximately 10, 5, 3.5, and 2.5 scruples (13, 6.5, 4.5 and 3.35 gm; 1 scruple = 1.296 gm) for the dupondius, as, semis and quadrans respectively. The proportionately heavier weight of the smaller coins probably reflects the difficulty in producing them. The same phenomenon can be seen much earlier in the Republican bronze, where the smallest denominations are regularly heavier than the As-standard. In *BMCRE* II and *RIC* II Mattingly gathered the dupondius, as and quadrans as a set of three denominations (designating the last of these a "semis"). He omitted the semis included here below, presumably taking it to be a separate Roman Provincial issue – it had already been so published in *BMC Galatia*, "Antioch" 222-223 (Vespasian), 238 (Titus), 254 (Domitian).

*Obv.*     Laureate head of Titus, r. or l.
           T CAESAR IMP PONT
*Rev.*     Winged caduceus between two crossed cornuacopiae
           TR POT COS III CENSOR
                (Cohen Titus 325-327; *BMCRE* II Vesp. 891; *RPC* II 1991-1992; *RIC* II Vesp. 813 (a)-(c); *RIC* II.1² Vesp. 761-762)

*Obv.*     Laureate head of Domitian, l.
           CAESAR AVGVSTI F
*Rev.*     Winged caduceus between two crossed cornuacopiae
           DOMITIANVS COS II
                (Cohen Domitian 97; *BMCRE* II Vesp. 883; *RPC* II 2001; *RIC* II Vesp. 816; *RIC* II.1² Vesp. 764)

*Orichalcum 25-26 mm*

These differ from the usual Roman product in that the consular dates fall on the reverse – on the contemporary, proper Roman bronzes it is always the obverse that is dated -- while also on the reverse the conventional S C is absent. The heads are never radiate but the denomination is taken conventionally to be a dupondius.

*Date*: 74 CE, when Vespasian was COS V and Titus COS III.

The dupondii were assigned in *BMCRE* to 73 (Domitian COS II), 74 (Vespasian COS V, Titus COS III), and 76 (Titus COS V). Both the first and the last dates are incorrect.

Not 73 CE:     Mattingly attributed the pieces portraying Domitian to 73, on the grounds that COS II was valid only for that year, his COS III falling in 74. Since then that consular dating has been corrected: Domitian's COS III actually fell in 75, so that COS II, held as an office in 73, was repeated in the regular way as a commemorative title throughout 74.[2] Consequently there is no problem in dating his dupondii to 74 along with the other Flavians.

Not 76 CE:     Types of Titus and Vespasian as above;
              T CAES IMP PONT
              PON MAX TR POT P P COS V CENS
                  (Cohen Titus 155; *BMCRE* II p. 220†; *RPC* II 1994; *RIC* II. Vesp 814; *RIC* II.1² Vesp. 763)

Titus' COS V did fall in 76, but he could not have been PON MAX. The coin is a mule of Titus's portrait obverse with a dated reverse of Vespasian, COS V, therefore 74. (b) A contrary mule is also known, composed of a Vespasian obverse portrait die and a reverse of Titus reading COS III.[3]

No proper die links among the three Flavians are possible, since each had his own combination of obverse and reverse. Therefore these mules guarantee their contemporaneity. All of the cornuacopiae dupondii are one coherent issue, datable to 74.

---

[2] Buttrey 1980, 33.
[3] *RIC* II.1² Vesp. 760. Another example in Ohlendorf list 3 [n.d.] 117.

*Mint:* In *BMCRE* II and *RIC* II (first edition) the Vespasianic dupondii were assigned to a mint in Commagene. The source of this attribution was Mowat, who was primarily interested in an issue of Tiberius.[4]

### I. Tiberius, dupondii

**Fig. 2:** *RPC* I 3868 or 69; *RIC* I² Tib. 89-90.
British Museum AN636414001.

*Obv.*  Laureate head of Tiberius, r.
        TI CAESAR DIVI AVGVSTI F AVGVSTVS
*Rev.*  Winged caduceus between two crossed cornuacopiae
        PONT MAXIM COS III IMP VII TR POT XXI or XXII **Fig. 2**
        (*BMCRE* I Tib. 174; *RPC* I 3868-69; *RIC* I Tib. 43; *RIC* I² Tib. 89-90)

*Orichalcum 28 mm*

Date: 19-20 CE

*Mint*:
a. Commagene
    The issue is plainly non-Roman. Some examples carry an Eastern countermark, KOB or PRO, the latter assigned by Howgego to Antioch).[5] Nothing of the types or the legends reveals the issuing mint, but Mowat was struck by the similarity of the reverse type to that of issues of Antiochus IV, and his sons Epiphanes and Callinicus, of Commagene (72 CE).[6] He therefore attributed the Tiberian coinage to that kingdom.
    Mowat's attribution was followed without query by Mattingly in *BMCRE*, and Mattingly and Sydenham *RIC* I; and was retained in Sutherland *RIC* I². In *RPC* I the problem of its mint is left unresolved, although attribution to "Commagene (?)" is reported in *RPC* II, p. 284.

b. Not Commagene
    "[I]n 19-20 dupondii were issued with a reverse type common in that district [*sc.* Commagene]". This is far from true. The reverse types of the Commagene issue which

---

[4] Mowat 1911
[5] Howgego 1985, 548, 600.

[6] *BMC Galatia*, Commagene, Antiochus IV 16-18; Epiphanes and Callinicus 8.

Mowat cited, as an analogy to the Tiberian, are in fact *not* the same: crossed cornuacopiae only, without caduceus; and crossed cornuacopiae crowned by busts, imposed on anchor. Of the cornuacopiae with caduceus there is no sign. And in any case the coinage of Antiochus IV was struck later than the Tiberian, by twenty years or more, so that there was neither antecedent nor parallel in Commagene at the time of the Tiberian issue.

c. Antioch

Howgego's attribution to Antioch of countermarks on the Tiberian dupondii is perhaps suggestive of the issue of the coins themselves at that city. Two examples occurred in the earlier Antioch excavations (Waage 1952, 1008).

d. Not Antioch

The more recent studies of that mint do not place them there: Butcher 2004, for whose discussion see his p. 332; and McAlee 2007 who does not discuss them at all. At this point the Tiberian mint city is simply unknown.

## II. Vespasian, dupondii

The reluctance to ascribe the dupondii to the Rome mint springs from several easy observations: the coin is a dupondius, yet the emperor's head is not radiate; the coin is dated on the reverse, rather than on the obverse which is regular throughout Vespasian's reign; the reverse lacks the customary *aes* indication of S C; the reverse type is like nothing to be found at Rome; and finally, while the orichalcum alloy is usual for the dupondius at Rome, the three smaller denominations ought to have been struck in copper. Therefore we look elsewhere for the mint of this series.

a. Commagene

Mowat's primary interest was in the Tiberian issue, but because of the similarity of their reverse types he was led to address Vespasian's orichalcum dupondii as well – which he then attributed to Commagene as a kind of accidental by-product. That attribution was accepted in *RIC* II and *BMCRE* II: "The most characteristic type, caduceus and crossed cornuacopiae, is native to that country and recalls the issues of Tiberius, also attributed to the same place",[7] suggesting that reference to Commagene at this time had to do with Vespasian's annexation of the kingdom. Mowat rightly saw that the Flavian type of caduceus standing proud between crossed cornuacopiae is uncommon (as against simple crossed cornuacopiae), which led him to posit the same mint for the Flavian issue as for the Tiberian, there being really no other Roman Provincial comparanda in style and fabric.

b. Not Commagene

As already noted, the type of the Flavian dupondii is actually not found in Commagene. Just as Mowat's attribution of the Tiberian bronze to Commagene is baseless, so is the similar attribution of the dupondii.

c. Antioch

That the mint of Vespasian's orichalcum *aes* was in any case not Rome was inferred from its types, uncharacteristic of Vespasian's regular *aes*; and from the orichalcum alloy of the 3 smaller denominations which would have been anomalous at Rome. In *RPC* II all four denominations

---

[7] *BMCRE* II, p. lxviii.

were retained as Eastern, suggesting uncertainly the possibility of "an official branch mint" at Antioch,[8] although this solution still leaves the fabric of the coins in question.

d. Not Antioch

However Butcher does not include Vespasian's orichalcum coins in his catalogue of Antiochene issues, simply remarking that they had "usually been attributed to Commagene",[9] while citing the work of Carradice and Cowell who noted similarities of fabric and die position with issues of the Rome mint proper — "technically, stylistically and metallurgically".[10]

e. Rome

For his part, McAlee 2007 accepted the implications of the observations of Carradice and Cowell: "The likelihood that these coins were minted in Rome was established by Carradice and Cowell".[11] The conclusion is stated baldly on p.170, "Orichalcum struck at Rome for use in Syria", without corroborating evidence. *RPC* II allowed the possibility of production in Rome for circulation in Syria;[12]

Actually the evidence for coinage at Rome has been to hand for years but no-one has recognized it, in the muling of orichalcum dies with Rome mint dies. We have already seen above how, in a cycle of untidy production, obverse and reverse dies of the orichalcum dupondii have been confused between father and son. Here, worse, dies of father and son from the orichalcum series have been mixed up with reverses of regular Roman production.

**Fig. 3:** *BMCRE* II, Vesp. 748A; *RIC* II² Vesp. 766.
British Museum AN637954001.

1. The unique, undated As of Vespasian, head 1, in the British Museum, first published and illustrated in *BMCRE* II Vesp. 748A. In that text it is segregated from all the other bronze of Vespasian struck at Rome precisely because it is undated, hence undatable. But it is illustrated: it is actually the product of an orichalcum dupondius obverse die of 74 CE, undated as usual, used with a regular Rome mint As reverse die, undated as usual (see **Fig. 3**).

---

[8] *RPC* II, p. 284.
[9] Butcher 2004, 34.
[10] Carradice and Cowell 1987.
[11] McAlee 2007, 161. Not quite: "…Rome, or a strictly-organized eastern branch mint of Rome" (Carradice and Cowell 1987, 46).
[12] *RPC* II, p. 284.

**Fig. 4:** *RIC* II² Vesp. 765.
Fitzwilliam Museum, Cambridge.

2. A second undated As of the same reverse type, muled with a different orichalcum dupondius obverse die with Vespasian, head r., has recently been acquired by the Fitzwilliam Museum, Cambridge (*RIC* II.1² Vesp. 765).[13] **Fig. 4.**

3. Contrarily, a third example of muling, known in several examples, bears too many dates, COS III on both faces. Here an obverse As die of Titus from the regular dated series has been mated with an orichalcum dupondius reverse die of cornucopiae type, dated as usual.[14]

The final attribution of the orichalcum dupondii is proved by the mules. Without any doubt their mint was the Mint of Rome itself.

It is worth recalling the objections to this attribution, as outlined above; each of them was correct, but the inference drawn from them as a whole was wrong. The problem lay not with the coins, but with our own Method: where regular repetition obtains, we treat the irregular as intrusive and try to divert it elsewhere. Even in *RIC* II.1², where the orichalcum series is correctly attributed to Rome, its intended circulation outside Rome or Italy is suggested. This may not have been the case at all.

This leads to the other denominations of the series.

---

[13] Gift of Walter Holt.
[14] *BMCRE* II Vesp. 892 (= *RPC* II 1993); *RIC* II Vesp. 813 (d); RIC II.1² Vesp. 767.

## 1.2 Asses, Semisses, and Quadrantes

### 1.2.1 As

Fig. 5: *RPC* II 1984; *RIC* II Vesp 796; *RIC* II.1² Vesp. 1565.
CNG e-Auction 71 (20.08.2003), Lot 75.
Courtesy of Classical Numismatic Group, Inc., Lancaster PA.

*Obv.* Laureate head of Vespasian, r. or l. **Fig. 5.**
IMP CAESAR VESP AVG or
IMP VESP AVG P M TR P
(*RPC* II 1984-1986; *RIC* II Vesp. 796; *RIC* II.1² Vesp. 1564-1566)
Laureate head of Titus, r.
T CAES IMP TR POT or
T CAESAR IMP PON TR POT
(*RPC* II 1995-1996; *RIC* II Vesp. 804-806; *RIC* II.1² Vesp. 1572-1573)
Laureate head of Domitian, r. or l.
CAESAR DOMIT COS II
(*RPC* II 2002-2003; *RIC* II Vesp. 817; *RIC* II.1² Vesp. 1578-1579)

*Rev.* S C in wreath[15]
*Orichalcum 20-22 mm*

### 1.2.2 Semis

Fig. 6: *RPC* II 1988; *RIC* II.1² Vesp. 1568.
Helios Numismatik Auction 5 (25.06.2011), Lot 1115.
Courtesy of Helios Numismatik, München.

---

[15] Although only Domitian's As bears a date, McAlee (1996-1997, 129 fn. 44) has shown that reverse die links connect the three obverses and establishes their contemporaneity.

*Obv.*   Laureate head of Vespasian, r. or l.
              IMP VESP AVG P M T P **Fig. 6.**
                 (*RPC* II 1987-1988; *RIC* II.1² Vesp. 1567-1568)
         Laureate head of Titus, r.
              T CAES IMP TR POT
                 (*RPC* II 1997; *RIC* II.1² Vesp. 1574)
         Laureate head of Domitian, l.
              CAESAR DOMIT COS II
                 (*RPC* II 2004; *RIC* II.1² Vesp. 1580)
*Rev.*   Turreted head of city Tyche, r.; ANTIOCHIA
*Orichalcum 19-20 mm*


### 1.2.3 Quadrans

**Fig. 7:** *RPC* II 1989; *RIC* II Vesp. 794; *RIC* II.1² Vesp. 1569.
CNG Mail Bid Auction 70 (21.09.2005), Lot 899.
Courtesy of Classical Numismatic Group, Inc., Lancaster PA.

*Obv.*   Laureate head of Vespasian, l.
              IMP VESP AVG / P M TR POT P P
                 (*RPC* II 1989; *RIC* II Vesp. 794; *RIC* II.1² Vesp. 1569-1570)
         Laureate head of Titus, r.
              T CAES IMP / PON TR POT or VESP PON TR P
                 (*RPC* II 1998-1999; *RIC* II Vesp. 807-808; *RIC* II.1² Vesp. 1575-1576)
         Laureate head of Domitian, l.
              CAES AVG F / DOMIT COS II **Fig. 7.**
                 (*RPC* II 2005; *RIC* II Vesp. 818; *RIC* II.1² Vesp. 1581)
*Rev.*   Winged Caduceus
*Orichalcum 14-18 mm*

*Date*: 74 CE, by Domitian's COS II, as with the dupondii.

*Mint*:
a: Antioch
   The typology of the orichalcum might appear to support attribution to a Syrian mint, as suggested in *RPC*. The As reminds us of the very common Antiochene bronze with S C in a wreath as the reverse type, from Augustus to well into the 3rd century CE. The semis bears a turreted head, the common city Tyche of the region, here plainly identified as ANTIOCHIA. The caduceus of the quadrans was also common enough in the East.

### b: Rome

However the criteria advanced by Carradice and Cowell concerning the orichalcum dupondii, noted above, are as valid here: physically the three lesser denominations are in every respect comparable with the dupondii, now fixed at Rome. McAlee is determined: "struck at Rome for use in Syria",[16] as now *RIC* II.1² 1564-1581.

As additional evidence should be noted mint sloppiness in the mating of dies. We have already seen the muling of incommensurate obverses and reverses of the orichalcum dupondii, and of orichalcum dupondii dies with regular Roman As dies. A third instance is to be found in the mixing of quadrantes dies —

1. Laureate head of Vespasian, l. / Titus reverse legend
   IMP VESP AVG / VESP PON TR P
   (*RPC* II 1990; *RIC* II.1² Vesp. 1571)
2. Laureate head of Titus, r. / Vespasian reverse legend
   T CAESAR IMP / P M TR POT P P
   (*RPC* II 2000; *RIC* II.1² Vesp. 1577)

The conclusion is inevitable: All four orichalcum denominations must constitute a single issue, produced at Rome in 74 CE.[17]

Nonetheless, in *RIC* II.1² the entries for this issue are divided into two distinct swatches, Vesp. 756-764, "Irregular dupondii, minted in association with 'for Syria bronzes [*sc*. orichalcum]'"; and Vesp. 1564-1581, "Orichalcum coins minted in Rome predominantly for Syria", notionally on the basis of their differing areas of circulation.

## 2. Circulation

### 2.1 Dupondii

The most obvious explanation of a series of evidently Eastern types, and the absence of Rome markings (radiate crown, persistent SC on reverse), is that the series was produced at Rome to be distributed in the East. Thus Carradice and Cowell on the dupondii: "Finds point to an Eastern region".[18]

In fact this is not the case at all for the dupondii.

(a) Of the 51 pieces cited in *RPC* II not one derives from an Eastern collection (as against some of the orichalcum fractions, for which see below). Yet the dupondii are very common coins: a full survey of the auction catalogues would produce many more than are listed in *RPC*.

(b) More to the point is the find evidence. In the *East* two of the dupondii were discovered at Masada; a third, now in Paris, was acquired in Antioch.

---

[16] McAlee 2007, 170.

[17] In fact, the period late-73/74 was a terrible time at the mint of Rome for die control. For numbers of improper mules within the regular Roman coinage see *RIC* II.1² Vesp.573-755.

[18] Carradice and Cowell 1987, 46. This is not at all the same as reliance on the *types* to suggest their purpose, as e.g. *RPC* II, "... reverse types which identify the coins for their intended area of circulation" (*ibid.*, 284). We shall come to the types below.

Antioch: 1 dupondius (Vespasian)
> J.-B. Giard, *Monnaies de l'Empire romain III* (Paris, 1998) Vespasian 906, bought at Antioch by Seyrig (this piece not in *RPC* II)

Masada Excavations: 1 dupondius (Titus), 1 dupondius (uncertain Flavian)
> Ya'acov Meshorer, 'The Coins of Masada', in *Masada I. The Yigael Yadin Excavations 1963-1965. Final Reports* (Jerusalem, 1989), 126, nos. 3825-3826.

Even allowing that evidence for Eastern circulation is more difficult to obtain than for Western, what is here is hardly impressive. It is striking that no example of the dupondii was found in the Antioch excavations, which produced for that mint a total of 23 Flavian coins.[19]

In sharp contradistinction, the dupondii are found in the *West* in abundance.

## In Northern Italy and Gaul:

Aquileia (Udine): 2 dupondii (Vespasian)
> *AIIN* 15 1968, 179, nos. 65, 67, acquired by the local Museo Nazionale, 1960-1968, with much random material, obviously local finds.

Vittorio Veneto (Treviso): 1 dupondius (Vespasian)
> *Ritrovamenti monetali de età romana nel Veneto* II/I (Padova, 1995), 440 no. 129, a surface find.

'Territorio Altinate' (Venezia): 1 dupondius (Vespasian)
> *Ritrovamenti monetali de età romana nel Veneto* VI/I (Padova, 1999), 381 no. 419.

Valle d'Aosta (Aosta): 1 dupondius (Vespasian)
> *AIIN* 26 1979, 219 no. 76.

Grenoble (Isère): 4 dupondii (Vespasian); 1 dupondius (Titus)
> B. Rémy, J. Dutel and F. Thomé, *Grenoble: Bibliothèque Municipale d'Étude et d'Information. Catalogue des monnaies* II.3 (Milan, 1999), 55 nos. 282-285, 287.

Quercy (Lot/Tarn et Garonne): 1 dupondius (Vespasian)
> G. Depeyrot, *Les découvertes de monnaies romaines imperials en Quercy d'après Raymond de Fouilhac* (Cahors-Luzech, 1975), 32 no. 246, out of 12 dupondii and asses.

Bordeaux (Gironde): 1 dupondius (Vespasian)
> R. Étienne and M. Rachet, *Le Trésor de Garonne* (Bordeaux, 1984), 56 no. 140, one of 15 dupondii of Vespasian altogether.

Condé-sur-Aisne (Aisne): 1 dupondius (Domitian)
> J.-B. Giard, 'Le Pèlerinage Gallo-romain de Condé-sur-Aisne et ses Monnaies', *RN* 6th ser. X (1968), 130 no. 2837.

## In Switzerland:

Avenches: 1 dupondius (Vespasian)
> H.-M. von Kaenel, "Die Fundmünzen aus Avenches. 1. Teil", in *Sch. Num. Rundschau* 31 (1972), 47-128, at 91 no 657.

## In Germany:

Starnberg: 1 dupondius (Vespasian)
> *Fundmünzen der Römischen Zeit in Deutschland* I.1 (Bavaria), 284 no. 19.

---

[19] Waage 1952, 36-37.

Eining: 1 dupondius (Vespasian)
> *Fundmünzen der Römischen Zeit in Deutschland* I.2 (Bavaria), 72 no. 18.

Günzberg: 1 dupondius (Vespasian)
> *Fundmünzen der Römischen Zeit in Deutschland* I.7 (Bavaria), 184 no 53.

Kempten: 1 dupondius (Titus)
> *Fundmünzen der Römischen Zeit in Deutschland* I.7 (Bavaria), 268 no. 733.

Gegenbach (Offenburg): 1 dupondius (Vespasian)
> *Fundmünzen der Römischen Zeit in Deutschland* II.2 (Baden-Württemberg), 160 no. 36.

Sulz am Necker: 1 dupondius (Vespasian)
> *Fundmünzen der Römischen Zeit in Deutschland* II.3 (Baden-Württemberg), Nachtrag I, 26 no. 40.

Rottweil: 1 dupondius (Vespasian)
> *Fundmünzen der Römischen Zeit in Deutschland* II.3 (Baden-Württemberg), Nachtrag I, 87 no. 123.

Rottweil: 1 dupondius (Vespasian)
> *Fundmünzen der Römischen Zeit in Deutschland* II.3 (Baden-Württemberg), Nachtrag I, 165 no. 101.

Rottweil: 1 dupondius (Vespasian)
> *Fundmünzen der Römischen Zeit in Deutschland* II.3 (Baden-Württemberg), Nachtrag I, 191 no.1.

Esslingen: 1 dupondius (Vespasian)
> *Fundmünzen der Römischen Zeit in Deutschland* II.4 (Baden-Württemberg), 73 no.23.

Wiesbaden: 1 dupondius (Vespasian)
> *Fundmünzen der Römischen Zeit in Deutschland* V.1,2 (Hessen), 416 no. 5.

Butzbach: 1 dupondius (Titus)
> *Fundmünzen der Römischen Zeit in Deutschland* V.2,1 (Hessen), 162 no.29.

Heldenbergen: 1 dupondius (Vespasian)
> *Fundmünzen der Römischen Zeit in Deutschland* V.2,1 (Hessen), 221 no.8.

Frankfurt-NIDA: 1 dupondius (Vespasian)
> *Fundmünzen der Römischen Zeit in Deutschland* V.2,2 (Hessen) 147 no.9.

In addition, an ancient cast fake –

Bad Homburg [Kastell Saalburg]: 1 dupondius (Vespasian)
> *Fundmünzen der Römischen Zeit in Deutschland* V.1,1 (Hessen). 355 no.72.

**In the area of Yugoslavia:**

Podgrad: 1 dupondius (Titus)
> *Fundmünzen der Römischen Zeit in Slowenien* I, 78 no. 1.

Ljubljana: 1 dupondius (Vespasian)
> *Fundmünzen der Römischen Zeit in Slowenien* I, 210 no. 10.

Ptuj: 1 dupondius (Titus)
> *Fundmünzen der Römischen Zeit in Slowenien* III, 525 no. 8 ["Rom" but *RIC* 813a, "Commagene"].

Ptuj: 1 dupondius (Titus)
> *Fundmünzen der Römischen Zeit in Slowenien* III, 574 no. 3.

Krsko: 1 dupondius (Vespasian)
> *Fundmünzen der Römischen Zeit in Slowenien* IV, 323 no. 3.

Istria: 1 dupondius (Titus)
> *Fundmünzen der Römischen Zeit in Kroatien* XVIII, 55, a grave find.

### In Austria and Hungary:
Wels, Städtischhes Museum: 1 dupondius (Flavian)
> *Fundmünzen der Römischen Zeit in Österreich* IV.1, 68 no. 90 [= Klaus Vondrovec, *Die antiken Fundmünzen von Ovilavis/Wels* (Vienna, 2003)]

Gyor Museum; 1 dupondius (Titus)
> *Fundmünzen der Römischen Zeit in Ungarn* II, 156 no. 451.

Pannonhalma: 1 dupondius (Vespasian)
> *Fundmünzen der Römischen Zeit in Ungarn* II, 336 no. 627.

### In Italy (I):
Rome: 1 dupondius (Domitian)
> Univ. of Illinois excavations on the Palatine, to be published. The site stands just above the Meta Sudans, within a few hundred meters of the ancient mint. This was the only coin of Vespasian found in the excavation.

Minturnae (Latina): 1 dupondius (Titus)
> I. Ben-Dor, 'Coins', in J. Johnson, *Excavations at Minturnae vol. I. Monuments of the Republican Forum* (Philadelphia, 1935), 99 no. 149, from a total of 2 dupondii and 3 asses of Vespasian.

Ugento (Lecce): 3 dupondii (Vespasian)
> A. Travaglini, *Inventario dei rinvenimenti monetali del Salento* (Rome, 1982), 108, 283-285, of a total of 5 dupondii of Vespasian.

Cisternino (Brindisi): 1 dupondius (Vespasian)
> G. L. Mangieri, "Rinvenimenti monetali a Cisternino e in Valle d'Itria", in *Riflessioni – Umanesimo della Pietra* (Martina Franca, July 2001), the only Flavian piece of a total of 17 Roman imperial coins, 1$^{st}$ - 4$^{th}$ centuries CE.

Mesagne (Brindisi): 1 dupondius (Vespasian)
> *AIIN* 23/24 (1976/77), 294 no. 1, a local find.

Mesagne (Brindisi): 1 dupondius (Vespasian)
> *AIIN* 37 (1990), 291 no. 50, a local find acquired by the Museo Civico 1978-1987.

### Finally, in Italy (II), Campania:
Oplontis (Napoli): 1 dupondius (Titus)
> V. C. Morelli, 'Un gruzzolo dalla stanza degli "Orti de Oplontis"', in *Rivista di Studi Pompeiani* 11 (2000) 187-234, at p. 223 no. 390, sealed by the eruption of Vesuvius in 79 CE.

Pompeii, Thermopolium: 15 dupondii (14 Vespasian, 1 Titus)
> D. Castiello and S. Oliviero, 'Il Ripostiglio del Termopolio I, 8, 8 di Pompei', in *AIIN* 44 (1997), 93-205, sealed in 79 CE.

This last is a wonderful find, the cashbox of the Thermopolion (the Cookshop) composed of 1611 *aes* coins [today 1385][20] – sestertii, dupondii, asses and (very few) quadrantes – dating from the Republic through to Vespasian COS VIII, 77/78 CE. (There were no coins of 79 – presumably they had not yet percolated into circulation at Pompeii.) This was an open find, not a burial, though it can hardly have been sitting on the counter: the original body would have weighed about 20 kilos. It could well have been used to provide change, the proprietor

---

[20] The hoard shrank while in the custody of the Italian archaeological service.

casting in whatever he did not need for immediate transactions.[21]

The orichalcum dupondii were gathered in with the rest of the coins as usable money. The total of dupondii dating to 74 CE (both regular issue and cornuacopiae type) is 71 pieces, so that the 15 cornuacopiae pieces are fully 20% of that total – perfectly ordinary currency. It is not possible to believe that their presence is accidental, that is, that originally the issue had been shipped out to the East, after which some individual specimens had somehow leaked back to Pompeii (let alone Gaul and Germany), and in this quantity, for burial there in 79.

**Area of circulation: dupondius**

|         | Vespasian | Titus | Domitian | (uncertain) |
|---------|-----------|-------|----------|-------------|
| Eastern | 1         | 1     |          | 1           |
| Western | 47        | 11    | 2        | 1           |

The find evidence is perfectly clear: the major circulation area of the orichalcum dupondii was the West (95%), not the East (5%); see **Map 1**.

### 2.2 Asses, Semisses, and Quadrantes

For the *Eastern* circulation of the orichalcum fractions *RPC* cites only the collection of the Studium Biblicum Franciscanum in Jerusalem — presumably local finds:

4 asses (3 Vespasian, 1 Domitian)
3 semisses (1 Vespasian, 2 Titus)

A bit of excavation information is also available:

Antioch excavations,

4 asses (1 Vespasian, 1 Titus, 2 Domitian, nos. 366, 368-369)
1 quadrans (Vespasian, no. 1012, "Commagene");
    see Dorothy B. Waage, *Greek, Roman, Byzantine and Crusaders' Coins* (*Antioch-on-the-Orontes* IV.2 [Princeton, 1952])

Dura excavations,

1 semis (Titus);
    see A. R. Bellinger, *The Coins. Excavations at Dura-Europos vol. VI* (New Haven, 1949), no. 1618.

---

[21] In one regard the hoard cannot have been – or perhaps better, the hoard as it stands today cannot be – a mirror of the small change in circulation at Pompeii: there were only 3 quadrantes of Augustus, and nothing smaller than the As thereafter. Quadrantes had been in enormous supply since Augustus and Tiberius; semisses, less abundant, since Nero. But the proprietor did not save them, or else they have been removed since discovery. They must have been available. King's accumulation of coin find reports from Pompeii shows more quadrantes there than sesterces, 1,827 pieces as against 1,098 (King 1975, 77). See her article for a discussion of the general problem of small change in the 1st and 2nd centuries.

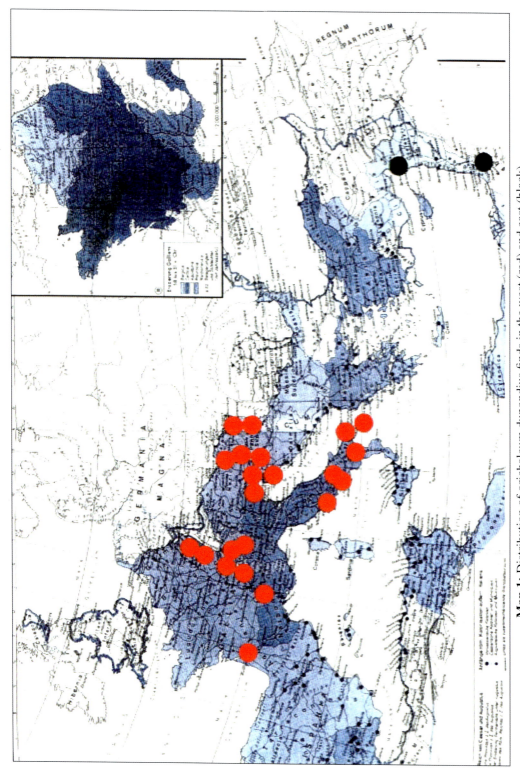

**Map 1:** Distribution of orichalcum dupondius finds in the west (red) and east (black).
Map courtesy of F. W. Putzger, *Historischer Weltatlas*, 91st edition (Velhagen & Klasing: Bielefeld/Berlin/Hannover (1969)), pp. 26-27.

## Eastern circulation: As, semis and quadrans

|  | **Vespasian** | **Titus** | **Domitian** |
|---|---|---|---|
| **as** | 1 Antioch<br>3 Jerusalem | 1 Antioch<br>– | 2 Antioch<br>1 Jerusalem |
| **semis** | 1 Jerusalem | 1 Dura<br>3 Jerusalem | – |
| **quadrans** | 1 Antioch | – | – |

These are few in number but do provide a good spread and suggest a general Syrian circulation.

However, there is also evidence for the circulation of these orichalcum fractions in the *West*. Most of the citations in *RPC* are drawn from Western collections and reveal nothing of the coins' original sources. But a few Western finds are known:

Grenoble (Isère): 1 as (Vespasian) — presumably a local find
    B. Rémy, J. Dutel and F. Thomé, *Grenoble: Bibliothèque Municipale d'Étude et d'Information. Catalogue des monnaies* II.3 (Milan, 1999), 55 no. 286.
Walheim: 1 as (Titus)
    *Fundmünzen der Römischen Zeit in Deutschland* II.4 (Baden-Württemburg), Nachtrag I, 163 no. 11, "semis". T CAESAR IMP PON TR POT / S C in a wreath.
Bingen: 2 asses (Vespasian)
    *Fundmünzen der Römischen Zeit in Deutschland* IV.1 (Rheinland-Pfalz), 106, 68-69. IMP VESP AVG P M TR P / S C in a wreath.

The semisses and quadrantes seem not to have been found so far. King, speaking of quadrantes in general, observes that they circulated primarily in Italy; the German camps did not normally attract denominations this small. "In Germany site finds of quadrantes ... with a Roman provenance are so few by comparison with the occurrence of the larger bronze denominations as to be negligible:"[22] so too elsewhere in the West outside Italy.

Overall the find evidence is thin, but in number and geographical scattering the fractions look to have circulated basically in the East. Attested finds in the West are few, but it is difficult to assume that such as have been discovered in Gaul and Germany were accidental, scattered returns from the other ends of the empire. Again the Western citations gathered in *RPC* might include local finds now impossible to identify as such. It is a pity that a complete listing of the Thermopolion hoard was not made before it was rifled, for no-one can say what has been lost; see **Map 2.**

---

[22] King 1975, 77-79.

### The Western finds together include

|  | Vespasian | Titus | Domitian | (uncertain) |
|---|---|---|---|---|
| **dupondius**[23] | 47[24] | 11 | 2 | 1 |
| as | 3 | 1 | – | – |

Thus the orichalcum was available in both the West and the East, but not evenly with respect to denomination. Even then the find evidence is perplexing: if the fractions were intended primarily for the East, why did the ANTIOCHIA semis not show up in Syria?

In sum, the largest denomination, the dupondii, circulated primarily in the West. The fractions were apparently more commonly used in the East, but asses are known in the West. That this division was deliberate from the beginning is not yet established, *contra RIC* II.1², 179. In either case the find evidence suggests that the issue may have been intended as military pay (although the coins were used in civic circulation, as Nero's orichalcum had been). Thus the intensity of dupondius finds in southern Germany suggests military usage, and some of the finds come directly from military camps. Of the 11 specimens of the relatively uncommon variety in the name of Titus, 4 occur in Slovenia and Croatia, suggesting that a packet was sent from the mint in that direction. Three pieces of Vespasian were found at Rottweil in Germany, and a fourth just ten miles distant at Sulz am Neckar – again suggesting a consolidated shipment from the mint. The best explanation is that the coins were sent out with, or to, the army.

The distribution of the dupondii in Italy might then be explained in the same way: the finds in the northern Adriatic representing e.g. pay for the fleet at Ravenna, the Campanian finds reflecting the fleet at Misenum, and the relatively rich finds in the south-east deriving from the great military staging port of Brundisium (3 pieces from the province of Brindisi; 3 from Ugento in a total of 5 Vespasianic dupondii).[25]

Military usage could also explain the discovery of two dupondii, of only three so far attested from the East, at Masada, where a Roman military camp was based from after the siege into the 2nd century CE.

---

[23] The totals in *RPC* II for the dupondii are Vesp 31, Titus 15, Domitian 5. Even given that its major sources, the museum collections, are likely to be skewed away from the commonest toward the rarest, there is still a nice correlation of significantly descending importance of Vespasian > Titus > Domitian both in *RPC*'s survey of the collection material and in the find material gathered here.

[24] Not including the ancient cast.

[25] Note however that the publications of finds are themselves very incomplete. If the equivalent of the *Ritrovamenti monetali de età romana nel Veneto* were available for the whole of Italy the orichalcum finds would certainly be more abundant, and possibly more generally spread.

# VESPASIAN'S ROMAN ORICHALCUM: AN UNRECOGNISED CELEBRATORY COINAGE

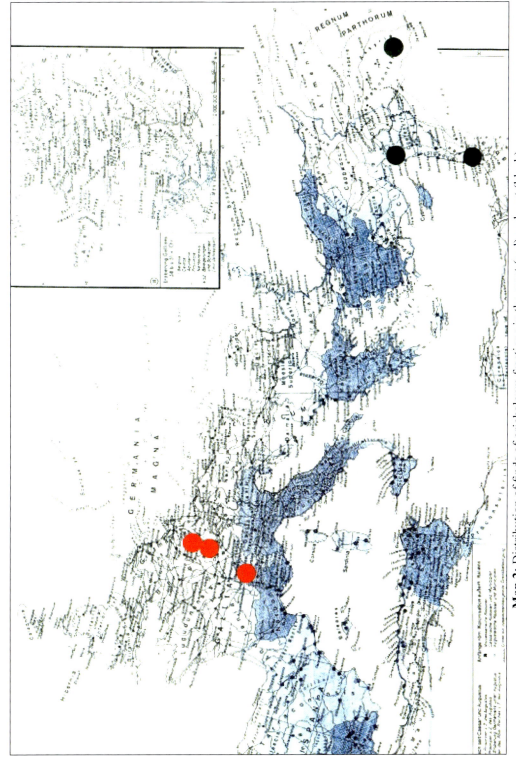

**Map 2:** Distribution of finds of orichalcum fractions in the west (red) and east (black). Map courtesy of F. W. Putzger, *Historischer Weltatlas*, 91st edition (Velhagen & Klasing: Bielefeld/Berlin/Hannover (1969)), pp. 26-27.

## 3. The Reverse Types

dupondius   *Winged caduceus between two crossed cornuacopiae*
On the reverse type, its probable Eastern origins, history and significance, see the full discussion by David Jacobson in this volume ('The Significance of the Caduceus between Facing Cornucopias in Herodian and Roman Coinage').

as   *S C in wreath*
The usual reverse type of Antiochene asses since Augustus.

semis   *Turreted head of city Tyche, r.;* ANTIOCHIA
The type, with Greek legend ANTIOXEΩN, had been struck on civic bronzes of this module in 55-58, 65-66 CE, under Nero.[26]

quadrans   *Winged caduceus*
This is obviously an element of the dupondius type, having also appeared independently under Tiberius and Claudius at Damascus and Gadara.[27]

As already remarked, the four types taken together, along with the other peculiarities of this issue — the curious alloy, the omission of Roman SC throughout, the dupondius without radiate crown — would instantly suggest an issue struck (no matter where) for circulation in the East. Yet we have seen that for the dupondius, the major denomination, this was not the case.

Further, as to the semis, if intended for Antioch it is peculiar that its type is accompanied by the place-name in Latin and in the nominative, *modo Romano*, rather than with the customary Greek genitive plural of the ethnic. The original, a civic issue of Antioch, had borne the Greek ethnic ANTIOXEΩN; and there was no barrier in imperial times to the use on Antiochene bronze of Latin legends on the obverse, Greek on the reverse.[28] Why then the Latin legend on Vespasian's Roman orichalcum? ANTIOCHIA is certainly not a mintmark. Rather it is an identification of the type itself: compare the identifications of the various figures serving as provincial geographical types on coins of Hadrian, struck at Rome and circulating at Rome.

Finally, three of the orichalcum types were actually taken over by Vespasian's mint for use on properly Roman issues. In 74, the year of the orichalcum issue, the winged caduceus appeared by itself on Roman denarii, probably the commonest denarius type of the year (*RIC* II.1² Vesp. 684, 686, 693-694, 703, 706) yet on silver uniquely for the reign. It was also used on the revived bronze quadrans (Vesp. 736) – i.e. the identical type employed simultaneously for both the smallest of the regular bronze denominations and the smallest of the orichalcum denominations. The caduceus was used again on quadrantes of 75 (Vesp. 825-826). In 76 it was combined with the type of the orichalcum As, S C in wreath (Vesp. 902). In 77-78 the crossed cornuacopiae with caduceus type was added, so that now three of the four orichalcum types were being struck on properly Roman bronze (Vesp. 1015-1020).[29] **Fig. 8.**

---

[26] McAlee 2007, 101-103, 110.
[27] *RPC* I 4799, 4802, 4814, 4818, 4821.
[28] McAlee 2007, 244 [Claudius], 284 [Nero], 365 [Vespasian].

[29] The Roman quadrans of 77-78 is attributed unnecessarily to Antioch by J.-B. Giard (1998, Vespasian 900), presumably on account of its types.

**Fig. 8:** AE quadrans.
*Obv.* Winged caduceus between two crossed cornuacopiae; *rev.* S C in a wreath
(*BMCRE* II, p. 175, 741; *RPC* II Vesp. 802 ("Commagene"); *RIC* II.1² Vesp. 1017).
British Museum AN637939001.

Now in general Roman imperial coin types are to be explained as referring in some way, directly or indirectly, to the emperor: his person, his virtues, his accomplishments, his capacities and his care vis-à-vis the state and the Roman people. It is hardly possible to explain the variety of types of Vespasian's Roman quadrantes as representing independent Eastern references: they would be completely out of place. They are to be understood rather as referring directly to Vespasian. The whole repertory of the Rome coinage types is aimed at the promotion of Vespasian's figure and government: the inventive orichalcum types reflect his career.

(a) We know independently of Vespasian's interest in Roman coin types as such, his own including references back to earlier coinages, Republican and Julio-Claudian.[30] In fact he struck the first restitution denarius, Sol / Vespasian standing.[31] This innovation has gone unrecognized because the (unique) coin does not announce itself, and combines two references, to originals of the Republic and of Octavian. But he was followed by Titus, and then Domitian, who openly produced restitution issues so marked.

(b) In 74 Vespasian celebrated the fifth year of his rise to imperial power, a rise that had begun with the eastern command entrusted to him by Nero. In the East he held the governorship of Syria, whose capital was Antioch.[32] The types of his orichalcum issue can be seen in that context, as a recognition and celebration of his rule – at the mint emblematically, by calling up examples of Eastern coin types appropriate to the time and place of Vespasian's governorship of Syria. The As and the semis reproduce types of Antioch; while the caduceus had been used in Syria at Damascus and Gadara, characteristically on the smallest denomination.[33]

But it is the major type, the dupondius' winged caduceus between two crossed cornuacopiae, which has the greatest resonance; for this was a type with which Vespasian himself was personally associated in his Eastern days.

---

[30] Buttrey 1972.
[31] *RIC* II.1² Vesp. 689, British Museum
[32] On the uncertain evidence for Vespasian's status under Nero as general in the East, see Levick, 1999, 29. However, when he was appointed to take command of the campaign against the Jewish insurgents, Vespasian was also probably considered as Roman governor of Judaea (Schürer 1973, 265 and n. 15). This supposition is consistent with the inscription which includes the words EPI OUESPASIANOU on a pair of coins struck in 67/68 CE at Sepphoris in Galilee (*RPC* I 4849 and 4850) and Caesarea Maritima (*RPC* I 4865); see below, including Fig. 9.
[33] In that regard, the caduceus appears only once on the Roman coinage of Domitian, on a quinarius, the smallest denomination in silver (*RIC* II.1² Dom. 160).

**Fig. 9:** Sepphoris (Judaea), 67-68 CE, AE 22 mm.
*RPC* I 4849; *TJC*, 104-105 and 233, no 127.
Courtesy of David M. Jacobson.

Sepphoris (Judaea), 67-68 CE. Struck in the name of Nero but under the authority of Agrippa II.[34]

*Obv.*  Wreath, within which
L ΔΙ / ΝΕΡΩΝΟ / ΚΛΑΥΔΙΟΥ / ΚΑΙCΑΡΟ / C
*Rev.*  Winged caduceus standing proud between two crossed cornuacopiae
ΕΠΙ ΟΥΕCΠΑCΙΑΝΟΥ ΕΙΡΗΝΟΠΟΛΙ ΝΕΡΩΝΙΑ CΕΠΦΟΡ **Fig. 9.**
(*RPC* I 4849; *TJC*, 104-105 and 233, no 127)

The coin is not uncommon today. Its type, on an extraordinary local coin of dupondius module, precedes Vespasian's orichalcum dupondius and ties it to his career.[35]

A second piece from Sepphoris, the half-unit, is part of the same issue and bears the same legends as the first:

*Obv.*  Wreath, within which
L ΔΙ / ΝΕΡΩΝΟ / ΚΛΑΥΔΙΟΥ / ΚΑΙCΑΡΟ / C
*Rev.*  S C; around and in field,
ΕΠΙ ΟΥΕCΠΑCΙΑΝΟΥ ΕΙΡΗΝΟΠΟΛΙ ΝΕΡΩΝΙΑ CΕΠΦΟΡ
(*RPC* I 4850; *TJC*, 104-105 and 233, no. 128).

The weights of both denominations are irregular, but in module they approximate to the Roman dupondius and As. The second piece is rather in the manner of the Augustan *aes*, S C surrounded by legend. For Vespasian's orichalcum the Antiochene As was preferred as the model.

---

[34] The attribution to Agrippa II is confirmed by the simultaneous appearance of the same reverse type on a smaller bronze bearing his own name:
*Obv.* Head of Tyche, r. ΚΑΙCΑΡΙΑ ΤΗ ΚΑΙ ΝΕΡΩΝΙΑΔΙ
*Rev.* Winged caduceus between two crossed cornucopiae ΒΑC ΑΓΡ ΕΤΟΥC ΑΙ ΤΟΥ ΚΑΙ ζ 65/66 CE (*TJC*, 105 and 233, no. 132; see *RPC* II 309 for the eras used by Agrippa II). Thus the rare type of caduceus with crossed cornucopiae has a real home at this time in the area of Judaea. The two types of Vespasian were repeated by Agrippa once later, under Domitian and with Domitian's portrait (*RPC* II 2271-2272). Otherwise they did not form part of his repertory of types. They may have been perceived as particularly Flavian.

[35] On the importance of Sepphoris to Vespasian as a city at peace with the Romans, see Meshorer 1979.

## 4. Orichalcum

A final objection to the position that Vespasian's orichalcum coin was intended for anything other than Eastern circulation lies in its metal, not otherwise struck by Vespasian as properly Roman for the As and its fractions. But the production of orichalcum in the smaller *aes* denominations, though uncommon at Rome, was not unprecedented, and does not count against such coins being produced for general circulation. Just a decade earlier Nero had produced a considerable quantity of asses, semisses and quadrantes in that metal, coins which must still have been in circulation when Vespasian added to them. That they circulated freely along with the bronze coins of the same denominations is proved by the finds of both metals, finds both extensive and plentiful.[36]

Why Vespasian's mint chose to produce orichalcum denominations at the same time as copper is not known. Perhaps it was simply to emphasize the peculiarity of this limited issue. Or, if they were intended essentially for military pay, the use of orichalcum, producing lighter coins *per* nominal value, might have been a partial solution to the practical problem of transporting masses of heavy metal to many different sites remote from Rome.

## 5. Conclusion

Vespasian's orichalcum coinage, originally given to "Commagene", was struck at Rome. It is unnecessary, and I believe misleading, to find specifically Eastern meaning in it, and then to impose Eastern circulation on it. Neither the types, although of Eastern origin, nor the coins themselves, have to do specifically with the East.[37] They are a series of reminiscences of Vespasian's service in the Levant and the coins which he met there, and, in the case of the dupondius, signed there. If we see the reverses not as simply carrying Eastern coin types, but as reflecting the actual coins which Vespasian met in the East, then the absence of S C itself is part of their reproduction. They circulated at both ends of the realm, the dupondii almost exclusively in Italy, Gaul and Germany.

Finally, we might well see in these reminiscent issues the origin of the Restoration coinages. We have already mentioned the unique denarius of Vespasian which melds a Republican type with one of Octavian, but unfortunately has no context. However the subsequent issues of Titus enlarged on the idea of looking back to earlier coinages by restoring a politically tasteful assortment of Julio-Claudian and Galban bronze, coins which in each case bear a legend identifying Titus as the agent of their resurrection. But he did not omit his father: under Titus, Divus Vespasian, dead and deified, appeared on aurei, denarii and all three regular denominations of bronze, coins which we tend to classify with Titus' regular issues (*RIC* II.1² 356-384) because they do not bear the restoration legend. But in content they are restoration issues: except for the type of Column topped by urn (356-357), which is obviously funereal, all the other reverse types of the Divus Vespasianus coinage are either a replica or a variation of a type that had appeared on Vespasian's coins in his lifetime.

---

[36] Some examples in MacDowall 1979, 85.

[37] That Vespasian's orichalcum types were not seen as strictly Eastern in their reference is shown also in the fact that three of them became part of the typological repertoire of the Rome mint. The caduceus was continued immediately as a reverse of Nerva's quadrantes (*BMCRE* III 147-148). SC in a wreath was used by Trajan on orichalcum asses (*Ibid*. 1075, 1090-1099) or semisses (*Ibid*. 1099*-1100), subsequently by Hadrian (*Ibid*. 1618-1620). The crossed cornucopiae with caduceus later appeared on both denarii and asses of Antoninus Pius (*BMCRE* IV 489, 501-502 and 1380-1385), and again on denarii of Commodus (*Ibid*. 282-284).

Regarded in that context, Vespasian's orichalcum issue can be seen as the first spark of an idea, originating with him, of historically reminiscent numismatic typology which was to enliven the coinage at Rome for another century and more.

### Addenda (to the Western orichalcum finds)

Since the list of finds above was completed for publication another twelve examples of the orichalcum coinage have been attested as having been found in Britain, Germany and Austria.

### In Britain
Newport (Wales): 1 dupondius (Vespasian)
        Portable Antiquities Scheme IARCW-63DAE272AD

### In Germany
Köngen: 1 dupondius (Vespasian)
        *Fundmünzen der Römischen Zeit in Deutschland* II.4 (Baden-Württemberg) Nachtrag I p.45 no.24
Walheim: 1 as (Titus)
        *Fundmünzen der Römischen Zeit in Deutschland* II.4 (Baden-Württemberg) Nachtrag I p.163 no.11
Trier: 1 dupondius (Vespasian)
        *Fundmünzen der Römischen Zeit in Deutschland* IV.3 (Rheinland-Pfalz) p.44 no.631

### In Austria[1]
Schützen am Gebirge: 1 dupondius (Vespasian)
        *Fundmünzen der Römischen Zeit in Österreich* I.2 (Burgenland) p.117 no.40
Zollfeld (*Virinum*): 1 dupondius (Titus)
        *Fundmünzen der Römischen Zeit in Österreich* II.3 (Kärnten) p.94 no.150
Carnuntum: Siedlungsfunde: 1 dupondius (Vespasian)
        *Fundmünzen der Römischen Zeit in Österreich* III.1 (Carnuntum) p.37 no.604
Carnuntum: Pfaffenberg: 1 dupondius (Vespasian)
        *Fundmünzen der Römischen Zeit in Österreich* no. 3712/1654
Carnuntum: Zivilstadt (coll. Weber): 1 dupondius (Vespasian)
        *Fundmünzen der Römischen Zeit in Österreich* no. 14709/1652
Eisenstadt (Niederösterreich): 1 dupondius (Vespasian)
Zwentendorf (Tulln, Niederösterreich): 1 dupondius [Flavian]
Wels (Oberösterreich): 1 dupondius (Vespasian)

---

[1] Kalsdorf (Graz-Umgebung): "semis" [2.32g] (Vespasian) Ursula Schachinger, Die Antike Münzlauf in der Steiermark (Vienna, 2006) = *Fundmünzen der Römischen Zeit in Österreich* VI (Steiermark), p. 18 no. 386. Identified as of Commagene, but in the orichalcum issue the type of SC in laurel wreath is appropriate to the *as*, impossible at this low weight. The coin must be a regular quadrans of the Rome mint, *RIC* II².1, Vespasian 902-903, etc.

## Acknowledgement

My thanks go to David Jacobson for his helpful corrections and editing.

## Bibliography

*BMC Galatia* = *A Catalogue of the Greek Coins in the British Museum 21: The Greek Coins of Galatia, Cappadocia, and Syria*, by Warwick Wroth (London: Trustees of the British Museum, 1899).

*BMCRE* I = *Coins of the Roman Empire in the British Museum*, Vol. I: *Augustus to Vitellius*, by H. Mattingly (London: British Museum, 1923).

*BMCRE* II = *Coins of the Roman Empire in the British Museum*, Vol. II: *Vespasian to Domitian*, by H. Mattingly (London: British Museum, 1930).

*BMCRE* III = *Coins of the Roman Empire in the British Museum*, Vol. III: *Nerva to Hadrian*, by H. Mattingly (London: British Museum, 1936).

*BMCRE* IV = *Coins of the Roman Empire in the British Museum*, Vol. IV: *Antoninus Pius to Commodus*, by H. Mattingly (London: British Museum, 1940).

*RIC* I = *The Roman Imperial Coinage*, Vol. I: Augustus to Vitellius, by H. Mattingly and E. A. Sutherland (London: Spink and Son, 1923).

*RIC* I$^2$ = *The Roman Imperial Coinage*, Vol. I: *From 31 BC to AD 69* (revised 2$^{nd}$ edn.), ed. C. H. V. Sutherland and R. A. G. Carson (London: Spink and Son, 1984).

*RIC* II = *The Roman Imperial Coinage*, Vol. II: *Vespasian to Hadrian*, by H. Mattingly and E. A. Sutherland (London: Spink and Son, 1926).

*RIC* II.1$^2$ = *The Roman Imperial Coinage*, Vol. II.1: *From AD 69 -96, Vespasian to Domitian* (revised 2$^{nd}$ edn.), by I. A. Carradice and T. V. Buttrey (London: Spink and Son, 2007).

*RPC* I = *Roman Provincial Coinage*, Vol. I (in 2 parts): *From the Death of Caesar to the Death of Vitellius (44 BC – AD 69)*, by A. Burnett, M. Amandry and P. Ripollès (London: British Museum Press / Paris: Bibliothèque nationale de France, 1992).

*RPC* II = *Roman Provincial Coinage*, Vol. II (in 2 parts): *From Vespasian to Domitian (AD 69 – 96)*, by A. Burnett, M. Amandry and I. Carradice (London: British Museum Press / Paris : Bibliothèque nationale de France, 1999).

*TJC* = *A Treasury of Jewish Coins from the Persian Period to Bar Kokhba*, by Y. Meshorer (Nyack, NY: Amphora Books, 2001).

Butcher, K., 2004. *Coinage in Roman Syria* (London: Royal Numismatic Society, Special Publications 34).

Buttrey, T.V., 1972. 'Vespasian as Moneyer', in *NC* 7$^{th}$ ser. XII, 89-109.

Buttrey, T.V., 1980. *Documentary Evidence for the Chronology of the Flavian Titulature* (Meissenhein am Glan: Beiträge zur Klassischen Philologie, 112).

Carradice, I., and Cowell, M., 1987. 'The Minting of Roman Imperial Bronze Coins for Circulation in the East. Vespasian to Trajan', *NC* 1987, 26-50.

Cohen, H., 1880. *Description historique des Monnaies frappées sous l'Empire Romain* I (Paris: Rollin & Feuardent)

Giard, J.-B., 1998. *Monnaies de l'Empire romain* III: Du soulèvement de 68 après J.-C. à Nerva (Paris: Bibliothèque nationale de France)

Howgego, C.J., 1985. *Greek Imperial Countermarks* (London: Royal Numismatic Society, Special Publications 17).

King, C.E., 1975. 'Quadrantes from the River Tiber', *NC* 7th ser. XV, 56-90.

Levick, B, 1999. *Vespasian* (London: Routledge)

McAlee, R.G., 1995-1996. 'Vespasian's Syrian Provincial Coinage', *AJN* 2nd ser. 7-8, 113-143.

McAlee, R.G., 2007. *The Coins of Roman Antioch* (Lancaster/London: Classical Numismatic Group).

MacDowall, D.W., 1979. *The Western Coinages of Nero* (New York, 1979) [= Numismatic Notes and Monographs, no. 161]

Meshorer, Y., 1979. "Sepphoris and Rome", in O. Mørkholm and N.M. Waggoner (eds.), *Greek Numismatics and Archaeology. Essays in Honor of Margaret Thompson*, (Wetteren: NR), 159-171.

Mowat, R., 1911. 'Bronzes remarquables de Tibère – Atelier indeterminé de Commagène', *RN* 4th ser. XV, 423-426.

Schürer, E., 1973. *The History of the Jewish People in the Age of Jesus Christ (175 B.C. - A.D. 135)*, rev. and ed. by G. Vermes, F. Millar and M. Black, Vol. 1 (Edinburgh: T & T Clark).

Waage, D.B., 1952. *Greek, Roman, Byzantine and Crusaders' Coins* [= Antioch-on-the-Orontes IV.2] (Princeton, NJ: Princeton University Press)

# THE INTERPRETATION AND WIDER CONTEXT OF NERVA'S FISCUS JUDAICUS SESTERTIUS

Marius Heemstra

**Fig. 1:** Sestertius of the emperor Nerva, 96 CE (RIC II 58).
*Obv.* IMP NERVA CAES AVG P M TR P COS II PP;
*Rev.* FISCI IVDAICI CALVMNIA SVBLATA S C, around a palm tree.

## Nerva's Sestertius

Two recent articles in the *Biblical Archaeology Review* paid attention to a sestertius that was issued by the Roman emperor Nerva (96-98) in the years 96 and 97 CE (**Fig. 1**).[1] The legend on the reverse of the coin reads FISCI IVDAICI CALVMNIA SVBLATA, which is translated in the article by Moussaieff as "the embarrassment of the Jewish Tax is removed." He assumes that the Jewish tax, which had been introduced by Vespasian after the destruction of the temple in Jerusalem, was repealed by Nerva "in whole or in part."[2] In this article I will give a completely different interpretation of Nerva's sestertius and I will explain why I think that the tax was not repealed at all and why the translation of the coin's legend should be: "the removal of the wrongful accusation of the Fiscus Judaicus."[3]

In order to understand what message Nerva wanted to communicate by issuing this type of coin, one needs to find out what went wrong under his predecessor Domitian with regard to this *fiscus* (what, in particular, does CALVMNIA refer to in this context?). So, after looking back to the emperor Vespasian (69-79) and his introduction of the Jewish tax,

---

[1] For Nerva's coin, see *RIC* II 58, 72, 82; for the *BAR* articles, see Moussaieff 2010; Shanks 2010. The latter also refers to an earlier *BAR* article (Lehmann 1993). Lehmann suggests that in Nerva's days it was discovered that Jews had continued to collect the half-shekel tax even after the destruction of the Jerusalem Temple. In his opinion Nerva ended this collection (a *calumnia* in Roman eyes) and confiscated the money. This hypothesis is not supported by any clear evidence. The present paper will remain close to the literary sources with regard to Nerva's measures, especially to the account of Cassius Dio.

[2] Moussaieff 2010, 48.

[3] The present paper is largely based on my dissertation (Heemstra 2009), and its slightly adapted publication (Heemstra 2010). On the Fiscus Judaicus, see also Smallwood 1956; 1976; Hemer 1973; Keresztes 1973; Thompson 1982; Stenger 1988; Goodman 1989; 1990; 2005a; 2007a; Williams 1990; Foster 2007.

which was supposed to be collected by the Roman tax collecting agency Fiscus Judaicus, I will look at the sources that give information about the situation during the reign of his second son Domitian (81-96). Then the focus will shift back to Nerva's coin and it will be investigated what measures Nerva took to end the problems that originated during Domitian's reign. The second part of this article will deal with the impact that Nerva's measures very likely had on the 'Parting of the Ways' between Judaism and Christianity. I will explain why I think Nerva's short reign constitutes a very important milestone in this respect, which so far has not been sufficiently recognised.

## The Introduction of the Jewish Tax under Vespasian

The first source that mentions the introduction of a special tax to be paid only by Jews in the Roman Empire after the destruction of the temple in Jerusalem is Josephus. In his *Jewish War* (7.218) he says:

> On all Jews, wherever they lived, he [Vespasian] imposed a tax (*phoron*), ordering each one of them (*ekaston*) to bring two drachms every year into the Capitol, as previously (*proteron*) contributed by them to the Temple at Jerusalem.

Cassius Dio is the second source that mentions the introduction of this specific tax by Vespasian. In his *Roman History* (65.7.2) he says:

> Thus was Jerusalem destroyed on the very day of Cronus (Saturn), the day which even now the Jews reverence most. From that time forth it was ordered that the Jews who continued to observe their ancestral customs (*tous ta patria autôn peristellontas*) should pay an annual tribute of two drachms to Capitoline Zeus (Jupiter Capitolinus).

One of the main questions which arise after reading these two passages, concerns the different definitions of the tax payer that these ancient historians seem to give. I will come back to the fact that Josephus mentions "each one" of the Jews as a tax payer and Dio states that "Jews who continued to observe their ancestral customs" should pay the tax.

In Egypt a number of papyri and ostraca have been preserved, which give us more information about the payment of the Jewish tax in this Roman province.[4] In Edfu some 70 ostraca have been found that were given as receipts to Jews who had paid the tax. They can be dated to the reigns of the emperors Vespasian, Titus, Domitian and Trajan (between the years 71 and 116 CE). It is apparent from this evidence that not only Jewish men between the ages of 20 and 50, who previously had paid the Jewish Temple Tax, had to pay this new Roman tax, but also women, children, freedmen and slaves, so all members of a Jewish *familia*.[5] From these sources we can conclude that the original name of the tax probably was "the price of two *denarii* of the Jews" (*timê dênariôn dyo Ioudaiôn* in Greek or *duo denarii Judaeorum* in Latin), but also "Jewish payment" (*Ioudaïkon telesma*) is used.[6] Furthermore, there is no apparent break between Domitian

---

[4] Receipts: *CPJ* 160-229; *SB* 18.14009; *SB* 12.15509; other documents *CPJ* 421, 460; *SB* 26.16697. Also, see Hemer 1973; Salvaterra 2000 (on *SB* 26.16697); Heemstra 2010, 13-20.

[5] Heemstra 2010, 13-4. But note that the Mishnah (*Shekalim* 1.5), states that the half-shekel tax is also accepted if paid by women, slaves and minors. Roman tax authorities may have used this wider Jewish definition of tax payers, stretching it to its limits, or they may have found these categories in existing Jewish tax registers with regard to the Temple tax.

[6] *CPJ* 2, 113. Heemstra 2010, 14-5.

and Trajan in the ostraca archive, despite the fact that no receipts dating from Nerva's short reign have been preserved.⁷

Local synagogues played a prominent role in the collection of the temple tax before 70, so the assumption that these became the most important sources of information for the tax collectors of the Jewish tax does not seem unfounded.⁸ This is also the opinion of L.A. Thompson:

> The original tax-lists can hardly have been compiled without the co-operation (perhaps even as publicly avowed intermediaries) of the leaders of the various Jewish communities who must have provided the *fiscus* with lists of payers of the temple-dues.⁹

Contacting the local synagogue would also have been the easiest and quickest way for *fiscus* officials in order to obtain the information for the yearly update (*epikrisis*) with regard to the Jewish men, women, children, freedmen and slaves who were liable for the tax.¹⁰ This is something that will have to be kept in mind when I now turn to the reign of Domitian and his alleged harsh administration of the Fiscus Judaicus.

## What went wrong under Domitian?

Our most important source regarding the status of the Fiscus Judaicus under Domitian is a passage by Suetonius (*Dom.* 12.1-2), which is actually the only other ancient source to mention the Fiscus Judaicus explicitly, besides Nerva's coin. I will quote the extended passage in order to give the full context:

> Reduced to financial straits by the cost of his buildings and shows, as well as by the additions which he [Domitian] had made to the pay of the soldiers, he tried to lighten the military expenses by diminishing the number of his troops; but perceiving that in this way he exposed himself to the attacks of the barbarians, and nevertheless had difficulty in easing his burdens, he had no hesitation in resorting to every sort of robbery. The property of the living and the dead was seized everywhere on any charge brought by any accuser (*nihil pensi habuit quin praedaretur omni modo. Bona vivorum ac mortuorum usquequaque quolibet et accusatore et crimine corripiebantur*). It was enough to allege any action or word derogatory to the majesty of the prince. Estates of those in no way connected with him were confiscated, if but one man came forward to declare that he had heard from the deceased during his lifetime that Caesar was his heir. Besides other taxes, that on the Jews was levied with the utmost rigour, and those were prosecuted who lived a Jewish life without publicly acknowledging that fact, as well as those who concealed their origin and did not pay the tribute levied upon their people. I recall being present in my youth when the person of a man ninety years old was examined before the procurator and a very crowded court, to see whether he was circumcised. (*Praeter ceteros Iudaicus fiscus acerbissime actus est; ad quem deferebantur, qui vel inprofessi Iudaicam viverent vitam, vel dissimulata origine imposita genti tributa non pependissent. Interfuisse me adulescentulum memini, cum a procuratore frequentissimoque consilio inspiceretur nonagenarius senex an circumsectus esset*).

---

⁷ As noticed by Hemer (1973, 9): "there is apparent continuity between Domitian and Trajan." But note that Goodman (2007a, 81-9; 2007b, 469-75) and Richardson and Shukster (1983, 42-4), have argued that this may be proof that Nerva (temporarily) abolished the Jewish Tax. Also, see Heemstra 2010, 19-20 and 73-4.
⁸ Heemstra 2010, 21-3.
⁹ Thompson 1982, 333.
¹⁰ An example of such an update is *CPJ* 421.

Financial difficulties constituted the reason why Domitian around 85 CE started to use these strategies to increase his income, and confiscating the property of such victims was a quick way of obtaining money.[11] Usually these people were brought to trial by informers (*delatores*) who also received a part of the proceeds after a successful court case.[12] With regard to the Fiscus Judaicus, there seem to have been two categories of victims: non-Jews who "lived a Jewish life without publicly acknowledging that fact" (*inprofessi Iudaicam viverent vitam*),[13] and Jews who "concealed their origin and did not pay the tribute levied upon their people" (*dissimulata origine imposita genti tributa non pependissent*). Apparently the main punishment in these cases was confiscation of property, and from this it can be concluded that people who were targeted were mainly those who had enough possessions to make a court case worthwhile for both informer (*delator*) and *fiscus*.

A second source in Dio (67.14.1-2) is relevant here:

And the same year [95 CE] Domitian slew, along with many others, Flavius Clemens the consul, although he was a cousin and had to wife Flavia Domitilla, who was also a relative of the emperor's. The charge brought against them both was that of atheism (*egklêma atheotêtos*), a charge on which many others who drifted into Jewish ways (*es ta tôn Ioudaiôn êthê exokellontes*) were condemned. Some of these were put to death, and the rest were at least deprived of their property. Domitilla was merely banished to Pandateria.

From this report one can conclude that during this episode in the reign of Domitian non-Jews who "drifted into Jewish ways" (which seems to correspond to Suetonius' "living a Jewish life") could also be executed after their possessions had been confiscated. Apparently the underlying crime committed by these people was being "atheists", by which the Romans usually meant people who did not recognise the traditional Roman gods or traditional religions in general. Moreover, high-ranking Romans could also become the victims of the Fiscus Judaicus, either because of political reasons, instigated by the emperor himself, or because any affiliation with Judaism, however small, could lead to a conviction in these days.[14]

The main question is of course: who were the possible victims that Suetonius may have referred to in his account about the administration of the Fiscus Judaicus under Domitian? In the scholarly literature on this issue different categories of people have been pointed out that may have been reported to the officials of the Fiscus Judaicus, based on the two different legal categories as mentioned by Suetonius.[15] I will list the main victims per category: (A) Jews; and (B) non-Jews:

(A) "Those who concealed their origin and did not pay the tribute levied upon their people" (*qui [...] dissimulata origine imposita genti tributa non pependissent*):
- apostate Jews
- Jewish Christians

---

[11] See, for example, Jones 1993, 77: "the confiscations began as early as 85 (...)".

[12] See Rutledge 2001, 9-16 on the *delatores* (informants) in the early Roman Empire.

[13] I think the translation of *qui (...) inprofessi Iudaicam viverent vitam*, is better rendered by "those who lived a Jewish life without publicly acknowledging that fact", than by "those who lived a Jewish life without publicly acknowledging that faith", as given in Heemstra 2010. Religious beliefs formed an important and essential part of "living a Jewish life", but the translation should not be limited to this aspect of a Jewish life.

[14] Goodman (2005a, 173) asks "how likely it was that any non-Jew in the city of Rome under Domitian would be attracted to a cult at such a low ebb in its fortunes". Goodman seems to be in agreement with Williams (1990, 208 ff.), when they both stress the fact that these accusations against people so close to the emperor were extraordinary affairs and politically inspired; also Rutledge 2001, 155, incl. note 98; and most recently Cook 2010, 117-31.

[15] For an extensive overview see Heemstra 2010, 32-66.

(B) "Those who led a Jewish life without publicly acknowledging that fact" (*qui* [...] *inprofessi Iudaicam viverent vitam*):
- God-fearers (including other sympathisers with Judaism)
- Gentile Christians as a distinct class of sympathisers with Judaism;

The first two categories mentioned above (apostate Jews and Jewish Christians) would have 'passed' the circumcision test and, if missing from the tax registers, would have been suspected of evading the Jewish Tax that they were supposed to pay to the Fiscus Judaicus. It is highly plausible that apostate Jews were not registered for the Jewish Tax and it is also likely that Jewish Christians were missing from the tax registers. Their estrangement from their former synagogues in the days of Domitian is supported by earlier testimonies in the New Testament. Already from the time Paul, there were strong tensions between Jewish Christians and the local Jewish communities in the Graeco-Roman cities of the Diaspora.[16]

If a circumcision test was used in all cases to make a legal distinction between circumcised and uncircumcised men (Jews and non-Jews), like the one Suetonius witnessed, the other two categories, God-fearers and Gentile Christians, would have been exposed as uncircumcised. These could subsequently have been suspected of leading a Jewish life *inprofessi*, of which the decisive characteristic from a Roman perspective would be their "atheism". A sacrifice test may well have been used to prove or disprove atheism (like the one used by Pliny not much later or the one that can be found in the Book of Revelation), and as a consequence some of the God-fearers, and in theory all of the Gentile Christians, may have been exposed as "uncircumcised atheists" – but only if they held on to their exclusive monotheistic beliefs by fully rejecting polytheism and idolatry (Pliny, *Ep*. 10.96; Rev 13:15; 20:4).[17] The punishment on conviction was confiscation of their property and possibly execution. In view of the severity of the punishment, one may expect that some of the accused decided to sacrifice under this pressure and thereby save their properties and their lives, if this was a possible way out.[18]

It must be stressed that the latter two categories were not made liable for the Jewish Tax, but were "discovered" during the proceedings of the Fiscus Judaicus and could also be prosecuted to raise the revenue of the *fiscus* by means of the confiscations. They were not charged with tax evasion, but another "crime" was detected of which they could be found guilty: "atheism". As a consequence the proceeds of these convictions also went to the Fiscus Judaicus. This is most probably the abusive situation that Domitian created, because it could be argued that this procedure lacked a legal basis. A tax collector like the Fiscus Judaicus could prosecute tax evasion by Jews, but the charge of "living a Jewish life" was a different accusation directed at non-Jews. Moreover, this specific accusation seems to have become an easy way to target high-ranking Romans towards the end of Domitian's reign, based on the report by Dio about the execution of Flavius Clemens. It is highly plausible that this charge of leading a Jewish life *inprofessus* and the "atheism" connected to it, as prosecuted by the officials of the Fiscus Judaicus under Domitian, is the *calumnia* ("wrongful accusation") that his successor Nerva removed. This will be discussed in the next paragraph.

Looking at these results, one of the most important conclusions should be that the wealthier members of mixed Christian communities (consisting of Jews and non-Jews) were at a great

---

[16] For example, see Van der Horst 1993, 366: "The New Testament also makes clear that measures such as punishment of Christians by Jews in the synagogues, persecution, and excommunication, measures that are mentioned not only by John but also by other New Testament authors (e.g., Mk 13:9; Lk 6:22; Acts 22:19 and 26:11; 2 Cor 11:24; 1 Thess 2:14; etc) were taken on a larger scale and more consistently than is usually assumed."

[17] Heemstra 2010, 31.

[18] See, for example, Pliny's letter to Trajan (*Ep*. 10.96) about people who had apostatised from Christianity, "a few as much as twenty-five years ago" (that is to say in the late eighties of the first century, during Domitian's reign).

risk to fall into the hands of the Fiscus Judaicus and be convicted after denunciation by *delatores*. In fact they must have presented the officials of the *fiscus* with a confusing picture. They were brought forward as members of one community, some of the men of which were circumcised Jews and others were not. The circumcised men (legally still Jews in Roman eyes at this moment in time) could be prosecuted as tax evaders. The others (non-Jews) were found to be close to Judaism by having given up their ancestral religious traditions in favour of the god of the Jews, so that they could be charged with living a Jewish life *inprofessi*. The element of atheism could even be punished by the death penalty.

Following from this, another important conclusion can be drawn concerning the alleged persecution of Christians by Domitian. In modern scholarship there is a tendency to downplay this persecution or even deny it.[19] Cook has recently concluded: "We can dispense with Domitian's persecution (…)", mainly paying attention to the persecutions under Nero and Trajan.[20] However, the reports about the persecution of Christians by Domitian, which can be found in early Christian historiography (e.g., Eusebius), can very well be explained by the harsh administration of the Fiscus Judaicus. Christian communities still consisted of Jews and non-Jews, who could be charged with different crimes and were punished accordingly. In the context of the Fiscus Judaicus it made no sense to prosecute them as 'Christians', because they were not the only victims and the relevant criterion in this case was whether they belonged to the *gens* or *ethnos* of the Jews or not.

## Nerva's Measures

When Nerva came to power in September 96 CE, after the assassination of Domitian by members of his own court, he immediately took a number of measures to end some of the abusive situations that had grown under his predecessor. To avoid the eventuality of informers starting court cases that ended in a verdict by which the property of their victims was confiscated, Nerva apparently took one general measure that would improve the judicial system, mainly in favour of the senatorial and equestrian classes. He decided that disputes between Roman citizens and the *fiscus* ('the treasury of the emperor') were transferred from judgement by a *procurator* to one by a newly instituted *praetor*.[21] Domitian's strategy of 'unleashing the informers' had been followed before in a similar way by the emperors Tiberius and Nero. But the chances for success of this strategy probably decreased substantially after Nerva appointed the new praetor, which meant that informers would run a higher risk of being themselves accused of *calumnia* ("wrongful accusation"), if their accusation failed.

According to Dio (68.1.2), the new emperor also took the following measures:

> Nerva also released all who were on trial for impiety (*asebeia*) and restored the exiles; moreover, he put to death all the slaves and the freedmen who had conspired against their masters and allowed that class of persons to lodge no complaint whatever against their

---

[19] See, for example, Yarbro Collins 1984, 73; Thompson 1990, 95, 116-32, 175; Aune 1997, lxiv-lxix; Carter 2008, esp. 39, 69-72.

[20] Cook 2010, 10; also see his Chapter 3 ("Domitian and the Christians"), especially its conclusion (136-7). Cook does pay attention to the passage about the Fiscus Judaicus by Suetonius (122-125), but he does not relate this to Christian communities. This is also the reason why Barnes (2010, 37), is able to conclude: "the 'persecution of Domitian', though widely accepted as historical by later writers both ancient and modern, is not attested by any reliable evidence at all." In contrast to these views it has become impossible for me to imagine how relatively well-to-do members of Christian communities could have escaped the *delatores* and Fiscus Judaicus under Domitian.

[21] *Digest* I.2.2.32 (Pomponius): *et adiecit divus Nerva qui inter fiscum et privatos ius diceret* ("and the deified Nerva added [one praetor] who exercised jurisdiction between *fiscus* and private citizens.") See also Grainger 2004, 53.

masters; and no persons were permitted to accuse anybody of impiety or of a Jewish life (*tois de dê allois out' asebeias out' Ioudaïkou biou kataitiasthai tinas sunechôrêse*). Many of those who had been informers were condemned to death...

With regard to the Fiscus Judaicus in particular, apparently two measures were taken, one of which can be found in the account above. The accusation of "living a Jewish life" was no longer permitted and this was explicitly stated. This accusation thus became a "wrongful accusation" for which the technical term in Latin is *calumnia*. It is only a small step to connect Nerva's sestertius to this passage by Dio.[22] By issuing this sestertius slaves and freedmen, e.g., were warned that they could no longer use this accusation against their masters and their masters were reassured that they could no longer become the easy victims of the Fiscus Judaicus, like, e.g., Flavius Clemens. This explanation is conceivably more straightforward than the usual one which stresses that Nerva ended the harsh treatment of the victims of the Fiscus Judaicus, as reflected in the eyewitness account that Suetonius gives about the ninety year old man being inspected.[23] The more recent suggestion by Martin Goodman (and Moussaieff, as noted in the introduction) that the coin is proof of the fact that the Jewish Tax was temporarily abolished by Nerva is not convincing.[24] In this case the tax as introduced by Vespasian would have been labelled as a *calumnia* by Nerva, which seems deeply implausible.[25] Furthermore, this particular sestertius was part of Nerva's first issue, which means it is reflecting a measure that was taken immediately after his coming to power, suggesting that this was primarily meant as a message to Romans, not to Jews.[26]

The second measure that was very likely taken with regard to the Fiscus Judaicus should be considered in connection with the second accusation as mentioned by Suetonius: that of tax evasion by Jews. With regard to the definition of the Jewish tax payer, the striking difference between the descriptions of the Jewish tax by (1) Josephus and Suetonius, and (2) Dio, will now be addressed.

---

[22] The first issue of this sestertius (*RIC* II 58) can be recognised by the obverse legend IMP NERVA CAES AVG P M TR P COS II PP (Imperator Nerva Caesar Augustus, Pontifex Maximus, Tribunicia Potestas, Consul II, Pater Patriae). When the second issue (*RIC* II 72) started to be struck is not exactly clear. Coins from this issue have the obverse legend IMP NERVA CAES AVG P M TR P COS II DESIGN III PP, which tells us that Nerva was consul designate for 97. Some scholars claim these coins were already issued after six weeks into his reign (which means early November 96; so Merlin 1906, 75, and Grainger 2004, 47), others think they were not issued before December 96 (e.g., Shotter 1983, 217). The third issue (*RIC* II 82 = January-September 97), has IMP NERVA CAES AVG P M TR P COS III PP. A possible specimen from the fourth issue is unlisted, but turned up in an auction (Numismatica Ars Classica, Auction 51 [March 2009], Lot 251); this coin has the obverse legend IMP NERVA CAES AVG P M TR P II COS III PP and is wrongly labelled *RIC* II 82. The catalogue notes that the coin has been "heavily tooled", but the TR P II looks genuine. This is also the opinion of David Hendin, who has studied this coin extensively and kindly informed me about his findings at the conference in London and later in an email. Nerva's coin is Hendin 797 (*RIC* II 82) in the 4th edition of his *Guide to Biblical Coins* and Hendin 1603 in the recent 5th edition. Besides *RIC* II 58, 72 and 82, Hendin also mentions a specimen from Nerva's sixth issue (COS IIII), but this is probably not right, since this coin should also read TR P II, which is not the case. This latter listing should probably be replaced by the coin from the fourth issue, as mentioned above.

[23] See, for example, Hemer 1973, 11; Keresztes 1973, 6; Williams 1990, 202; Jones 1993, 118.

[24] First suggested in Goodman 2005a, 176; further developed in Goodman 2007a, 81-89; also in Goodman 2007b, 469-75. Further, see Richardson and Shukster 1983.

[25] For example, Stenger (1988, 110) commenting on earlier ideas that Nerva's coin was proof of the abolition of the tax itself, says: "Es ist [...] kaum anzunehmen, dass Nerva eine von Vespasian geschaffene kaiserliche Behörde als 'Schurkerei' bezeichnet hätte".

[26] David Vagi, whose comment on this coin has appeared in a number of catalogues issued by the auction firm Numismatica Ars Classica, rightly stresses the fact that this coin does not represent a Roman apology to a conquered people (for Vagi's alternative theory, see Hendin 2010, 458).

(1) Josephus and Suetonius (the latter with regard to the situation under Domitian) state in general that the tax was meant to be paid by all Jews in the empire, providing us with a strong ethnic accent. In this respect it need not surprise us that the informers of the Fiscus Judaicus under Domitian were convinced that members of Christian communities also needed to pay the Jewish tax or could be prosecuted in relation to it. During the prosecutions it turned out that Christian communities consisted of circumcised Jewish men and their families, who should pay the tax as members of the Jewish *gens* or *ethnos*, and non-Jewish men (including their families) who had given up their own traditional gods for the Jewish exclusivist monotheism, even though they were not circumcised. This latter group could be successfully prosecuted before *fiscus* officials on the charge of "living a Jewish life". Their "atheism" could even lead to the death penalty under Domitian.

(2) Turning to the report by Dio, one finds a more pointed definition of the taxpayers (when compared to Josephus and Suetonius), which could well be a reflection of a decision made by Nerva. According to Dio, the tax was meant to be paid by Jews "who remained faithful to the customs of their forefathers" (*tous ta patria autôn ethê peristellontas*), changing the definition of 'Jew' from an ethnic into a religious one, as has already been suggested by Goodman in 1989.[27] The consequence of this measure would have been that apostate Jews were no longer regarded as taxpayers (being part of the *gens* of the Jews was no longer the criterion), but also Jewish Christians could be set apart from Judaism in this way. Many Jewish Christians did not meet the criterion of remaining "faithful to the customs of their forefathers" in Roman (and Jewish) eyes. They appeared to Romans more and more as members of a separate religion (despite firm Jewish roots), which had a missionary tendency leading to the spread of atheism or contempt of the traditional gods in the Roman Empire.

After Nerva Roman authorities are not found to make any distinction between Jewish and Gentile Christians, as they very likely did under Domitian without using the term 'Christian'. This is clear from the letter from Pliny to Trajan, in which the only distinction made is the one between Christians who were Roman citizens and those who were not. Christians with Roman citizenship were sent to Rome to be tried (and most likely executed, judging from Ignatius' case), the others were killed immediately, their only crime "being Christians" (Pliny, *Ep.* 10.96).

So, summarising, there seem to have been three measures that Nerva took to end the general abuse under Domitian and the problems relating to the Fiscus Judaicus:

(A) The abuse that was felt to exist with regard to the ease with which court cases were decided in favour of the imperial treasury, was greatly relieved by appointing an extra *praetor* who needed to look into cases between Roman citizens and the *fiscus* (as found in the Digest).

(B) To end the possibility of reporting people to the Fiscus Judaicus on the accusation of "living a Jewish life", this accusation was explicitly forbidden (Nerva's coin and Dio).

---

[27] Goodman 1989.

These two measures were mainly to the benefit of the wealthier classes within the Roman Empire at that moment in time.

(C) To end the uncertainty about who was supposed to pay the Jewish Tax, Nerva very likely changed the definition of the tax payer from "each one of the Jews" (Josephus) or those belonging to the Jewish *gens* (Suetonius) to those Jews "who continued to observe their ancestral customs" (the definition as used by Dio, which he wrongly backdates to the introduction of the tax by Vespasian). By doing this, Nerva changed the Roman definition of 'Jew' from an ethnic into a religious one.

## 'Parting of the Ways' Between Judaism and Christianity[28]

For all parties concerned Nerva seems to have created legal clarity with regard to the confusing picture presented by Judaism and related movements that also involved non-Jews. Apostate Jews were exempted from the Jewish tax and were no longer regarded as Jews. Jewish Christians (and in this case we should probably primarily think of those who were members of mixed communities) were also no longer regarded as Jews by the Romans, if they were not registered for the Jewish Tax, and in the eyes of other Jews they were probably heretics, no longer 'real' Jews, as it will be explained below. As a consequence they ran the same risk of persecution by Roman authorities as Gentile Christians, because they could also be regarded as illegal "atheists" from that moment on. The charges against members of Christian communities thus changed from "tax evaders of the Jewish Tax" (directed at Jewish Christians) and "living a Jewish life *inprofessi*" (directed at Gentile Christians) under Domitian to 'being Christians' for both groups under Trajan and subsequent emperors. This was in fact the clear cut between a legal religion (Judaism) and an illegal superstition (Christianity) from a Roman perspective.[29]

## Jewish Legal Perspective in the New Testament

Corroborating evidence for an important change in the legal status of Jewish Christians, which as has been suggested was brought about on the Roman side by Nerva's decision to redefine the tax payers to the Fiscus Judaicus, can be found in the New Testament and the Talmud. This will be argued in the following two sections. First the focus will be on the Jewish perspective.

In a legal sense there is a fundamental difference in the status of Jewish Christians reflected in most of the New Testament writings on the one hand and the Gospel of John on the other.

---

[28] For the discussion about the 'parting of the ways' between Judaism and Christianity, see Heemstra 2010 (Chapter 8). Without having been able to use the latter work on the influence of the Fiscus Judaicus on this parting, Carleton Paget (2010, 3-24) gives a very useful overview of the *status quaestionis*. Other important contributions are: Dunn 1991; 1992; Becker and Reed 2003, Boyarin 2004; Katz 1984; 2006; Robinson 2009; Schiffmann 1981; Schremer 2010; Wander 1997; Wilson 1995.

[29] The importance of the Roman perspective is also stressed by Schremer (2010, 96): "Already by the early second century C.E., Christianity was recognized by *Roman officials* as a distinct religion, distinguished from Judaism, as one can infer both from Pliny the Younger and from Tacitus. It is difficult to imagine that an imperial discourse that distinguished Christians from Jews had no effect on Jews and Christians themselves." (italics Schremer). Carleton Paget (2010, 9-11 and 18) also highlights the relevance of the "pagan evidence" (including Fiscus Judaicus) with regard to the issue of "the parting of the ways".

Based on passages in the letters of Paul, the synoptic Gospels (Mark, Matthew and Luke), and the Acts of the Apostles, it is evident that Jewish Christians could be prosecuted by local synagogues. This means that they were still considered to be Jews by other Jews. From Paul's own writings one learns that he had been punished in Diaspora synagogues: "five times I have received from the Jews the forty lashes minus one" (2 Cor. 11:4).[30] This remark clearly relates to floggings that only Jews could be subjected to in synagogues, which followed from the Jewish privilege of organising their own courts of law. When we find a number of warnings by Jesus in the synoptic gospels, including the prediction that people will be judged and flogged in synagogues, it can be concluded that these are also messages that can only have been addressed to Jewish Christians by the gospel writers (Mt. 10:17; 23:24; Mk 13:9; Lk. 12:11; 21:12). These punishments could not have been applied to non-Jewish Christians (or God-fearers or any other sympathisers with Judaism for that matter). It is safe to conclude, that all these cases refer to a moment in time when Jewish Christians were still considered to fall under the jurisdiction of the synagogues, which could and did punish them. At the same time this evidence may show that there was already a social separation between synagogues and Jewish Christians.[31] This is an important observation when looking at the context of the Fiscus Judaicus under Vespasian and Domitian, indicating that they were probably no longer full members of these synagogues when the Jewish Tax was introduced; they were not officially registered for the tax and thus could be prosecuted as Jewish tax evaders under Domitian.

Around the time they lost their legal status of Jews within the Roman Empire under Nerva, they probably lost their legal status within Judaism as well. This seems to be reflected in the Gospel of John (9:22; 12:42; 16:2), in which Jesus no longer warns his followers that they will be flogged in the synagogues, but now warns them that they will be put out of the synagogue (made into *aposynagogoi*), which is more like excommunication: they are no longer punished, but are considered to be no longer part of 'Israel' by mainstream Judaism (see below). Although it is often assumed that we should think of a local issue between John's Christian community and the local Jewish community, it is much better to interpret this in a general way.[32]

The latter has already been put forward more than 40 years ago by Martyn, who suggested that we should see the *aposynagogos*-passages in the Gospel of John in connection with the traditional date of the introduction of the *birkat ha-minim* around the year 90 CE.[33] Although this view of Martyn has been strongly challenged over the years, it is strongly reinforced when the Fiscus Judaicus is added to this context.[34]

---

[30] See also Goodman 2005b.

[31] For example, Carter (2001, 133) concludes with regard to the gospel of Matthew that "Matthew's community (…) has probably separated from the synagogue." His conclusion that Mt. 17.24-27 (Jesus and Peter paying the temple tax) relates to the Jewish tax and tells its readers to pay this new tax to the Romans, is less convincing. For the audience of Matthew's Gospel, it is obvious that this is a story about the temple tax, since the Jewish tax did not exist in Jesus' days. This pericope could also be interpreted as downplaying the importance of the Temple tax, in which case paying a Roman tax should certainly be refused. For example, also see Tellbe's (2005, 43) conclusion regarding Christian communities and the temple tax: "further away from Jerusalem the fidelity to this custom declined locally some time before 70 CE."

Further, see Mandell 1984 and Foster 2007, 312-5.

[32] See Heemstra 2010 (Chapter 7). With regard to the *birkat ha-minim* also see: Horbury 1982; Kimelman 1981; Marcus 2009; Teppler 2007; Van der Horst 1993.

[33] Martyn 1968; see also the essay in the third edition of Martyn's book (2003, 1-19) about the influence of this theory on the study of the Gospel of John by D. Moody Smith.

[34] More recently, Marcus (2008, 537) has also defended the basics of Martyn's reconstruction, concluding: "(...) the Jewish Christians emerge as the most prominent candidates for *min* status in the earliest strata of rabbinic literature." This conclusion with regard to Jewish Christians is also supported by Schremer (2010, 98): "the discourse that emerges from the early rabbinic material is that of *exclusion*." (italics Schremer).

## Jewish Legal Perspective in the Mishnah

If the Gospel of John is reflecting a new phase in the legal relations between Jewish Christians and mainstream Judaism, and if we were to look for a corresponding passage in the Rabbinical literature, the best candidate is *m.Sanh.* 10.1, which is the *locus classicus* for the definition of heresy in Tannaitic Judaism.[35] After it has been stated that "all Israel (*kol jisraeel*) has a portion in the world to come", we read:

> The following are those who do not have a portion in the world to come: the one who says there is no resurrection of the dead, (the one who says) the Torah is not from Heaven, and the *apiqoros*.

Although the term *minim* is not found in this passage, there are a few reasons why this description seems to give an early definition of those who are excluded from mainstream Judaism, those who apparently do not belong to "all Israel" any longer.[36] First it clearly refers to the Sadducees ("the one who says there is no resurrection of the dead"), who probably disappeared relatively quickly after the destruction of their power base in 70 CE (the Jerusalem Temple). Furthermore, immediately following the quote from *m.Sanh.* 10.1, an addition by Rabbi Akiba is found in the text, which would be in line with a date in the late first century for the original description of "those who do not have a portion in the world to come".

The first and third descriptions of these three categories of heretics can probably be recognised relatively quickly. The first (as already noted) is most likely referring to the Sadducees, who apparently did not believe in the concept of resurrection in contrast to Pharisees and of course Jewish Christians. This Sadducee characteristic is found in many first century sources (Mk 12:18; Acts 23:8; Jos., *Ant.* 18.16-7; *War* 2.164-5). The third description of a heretic most probably refers to strongly Hellenised Jews (the word *apiqoros* is considered to be related to the name of the Greek philosopher Epicurus and seems to be a corruption of his name). One may assume that these were mainly apostate Jews.

It could very well be defended that the second description: "(the one who says) the Torah is not from Heaven" refers to Jewish Christians, especially to those who embraced the increasingly 'high' Christology that was to become central to mainstream Christianity. This high Christology (which one could describe as "the Messiah is from Heaven") is arguably the main theme in the Gospel of John and the Letter to the Hebrews, which explicitly value the Messiah higher than the Mosaic Law. In the first chapters of the Letter to the Hebrews, it is made clear that the revelation in Christ (Messiah) had come from God in a more direct way than the revelation under the old covenant, which was mediated by angels according to the writer of this letter.[37] It is not hard to see how this Jewish Christian perspective could have been interpreted by mainstream Judaism as stating: "the Torah is not from Heaven".

Other Jewish groups that could be labelled as Christians, e.g., the Ebionites, apparently remained faithful to keeping the Jewish Law in combination with a 'low' Christology. This may have meant for their position within Judaism that they were not (yet) considered to be heretics by other Jews. The criterion of "Torah from Heaven" was sufficiently clear to make the distinction between different Jewish Christian groups.

---

[35] In the context of this Mishnaic tractate, which is concerned with courts of justice, their composition, rules about trials, arbitration and judicial procedure in monetary and capital cases, it makes sense to be describing those Jews who are considered to fall under rabbinical jurisdiction and, more specifically, those who do not. In any case, it is clearly drawing religious boundaries within Judaism ("Israel").

[36] For example, see Schiffman 1981.

[37] See also Heemstra 2010 (Chapter 6).

## Conclusion

Within fifteen years after the introduction of the Jewish Tax by the Roman emperor Vespasian the issue of Jewish identity and semi-Jewish identity became all important. Under his second son Domitian apparently both Jews and non-Jews could be reported to the Fiscus Judaicus: tax evading Jews could be robbed of their possessions after having been found guilty and the possessions of non-Jews could also be confiscated by the Fiscus Judaicus after having been found guilty of "living a Jewish life". The underlying crime in this latter case was apparently "atheism", for which they could subsequently be executed as well.

Nerva's coin, in close connection with the report by Dio, is very plausibly evidence for the fact that the new emperor no longer permitted people to be accused of living a Jewish life. This specific accusation became a "wrongful accusation" (*calumnia*). Since this coin illustrates the first specific measure that Nerva took, solving this issue must have been very urgent. This was probably the case because towards the end of Domitian's reign also high-ranking Romans could be accused of "drifting into Jewish ways" or "living a Jewish life" (even by their freedmen and slaves), their property could be confiscated and they could even end up being executed. This situation must have had a disruptive effect on Roman society, especially in Rome itself.

It is highly plausible that at the same time it was felt necessary to change the definition of the tax payer. Instead of "each one of the Jews" (Josephus), the definition was very likely changed to those Jews "who continued to observe their ancestral customs" (Dio), because in practice these were the Jews that had been paying the tax since its introduction in the first place. The legal distinction that was thus made by Roman authorities between Jewish Christians (primarily those who were members of mixed Christian communities) and practicing Jews seems to be mirrored by the change in legal status of these Jewish Christians in relation to mainstream Judaism. In this case they went from a situation in which they could be punished by the synagogues, to a situation of excommunication. In this way the Roman and Jewish definitions of 'Jews' were harmonised under Nerva, which solved many or even all of the problems that had come to the surface under Domitian. Both Romans and Jews adopted a definition of 'Jews' along religious lines ("those who remain faithful to the customs of their forefathers"; "those who say that the Torah is from Heaven"), thus excluding apostate Jews and a highly important group of Jewish Christians. The end result was a clear legal distinction between Judaism and Christianity, between an ancient religion accepted within the empire and a relatively new illegal "superstition".

## Bibliography

The following abbreviations (other than journal) are used in this paper:

*CPJ* = *Corpus Papyrorum Judaicorum*, vols. 1-3, ed. by V. A. Tcherikover, A. Fuks, and M. Stern (Cambridge, MA: Harvard University Press, 1957-1964); *RIC II* = H. Mattingly and E.A. Sydenham (eds.), *The Roman Imperial Coinage 2. Vespasian to Hadrian* (London: Spink, 1926); *SB* = *Sammelbuch griechischer Urkunden aus Ägypten* (Strassburg/Berlin/Wiesbaden: O.Harrassowitz, 1915– )

Aune, D. E., 1997. *Revelation 1-5* (Word Biblical Commentary 52A; Nashville, TN: Thomas Nelson).
Barnes, T. D., 2010. *Early Christian Hagiography and Roman History* (Tübingen: Mohr Siebeck).

Becker, A. H. and Reed, A. Y. (eds.), 2003. *The Ways that Never Parted. Jews and Christians in Late Antiquity and the Early Middle Ages* (Texts & Studies in Ancient Judaism, 95; Tübingen: Mohr Siebeck).

Boyarin, D., 2004. *Border Lines: The Partition of Judeao-Christianity* (Philadelphia, PA: University of Pennsylvania Press).

Carleton Paget, J., 2010. *Jews, Christians and Jewish Christians in Antiquity* (WUNT 251; Tübingen: Mohr Siebeck).

Carter, W., 2001. *Matthew and Empire. Initial Explorations* (Harrisburg, PA: Trinity Press International).

Carter, W., 2008. *John and Empire. Initial Explorations* (New York/London: T&T Clark).

Cook, J. G., 2010. *Roman Attitudes Toward the Christians. From Claudius to Hadrian* (WUNT 261; Tübingen: Mohr Siebeck).

Dunn, J. D. G., 1991. *The Partings of the Ways: Between Christianity and Judaism and their Significance for the Character of Christianity* (London: SCM Press) – reprinted 2006.

Dunn, J. D. G. (ed.), 1992. *Jews and Christians. The Parting of the Ways A.D. 70 to 135* (WUNT I 66; Tübingen: Mohr).

Foster, P., 2007. 'Vespasian, Nerva, Jesus, and the *Fiscus Judaicus*', in D. B. Capes, A. D. DeConick, H. K. Bond and T. A. Miller (eds.), *Israel's God and Rebecca's Children. Christology and Community in Early Judaism and Christianity. Essays in Honor of Larry W. Hurtado and Alan F. Segal* (Waco, TX: Baylor University Press), 303–320.

Goodman, M., 1989. 'Nerva, the *Fiscus Judaicus* and Jewish Identity', *JRS* 79, 40–44.

Goodman, M., 1990. 'Identity and Authority in Ancient Judaism', *Judaism* 39, 192–201; reprinted in M. Goodman, *Judaism in the Roman World. Collected Essays* (Ancient Judaism and Early Christianity, vol. 66; Leiden/Boston, MA: Brill, 2007) 21–32.

Goodman, M., 2005a. 'The *Fiscus Iudaicus* and Gentile Attitudes to Judaism in Flavian Rome', in J.

Edmondson, S. Mason and J. Rives (eds.), *Flavius Josephus and Flavian Rome* (Oxford: Oxford University Press) 167–177.

Goodman, M., 2005b. 'The Persecution of Paul by Diaspora Jews', in J. Pastor and M. Mor (eds.), *The Beginnings of Christianity: A Collection of Articles* (Jerusalem: Yad Ben-Zvi Press), 379-387; reprinted in M. Goodman, *Judaism in the Roman World. Collected Essays* (Ancient Judaism and Early Christianity, vol. 66; Leiden/Boston, MA: Brill, 2007), 145–152.

Goodman, M., 2007a. 'The Meaning of 'Fisci Iudaici Calumnia Sublata' on the Coinage of Nerva', in S. J. D. Cohen and J. J. Schwartz (eds.), *Studies in Josephus and the Varieties of Ancient Judaism. Louis H. Feldman Jubilee Volume* (Ancient Judaism and Early Christianity, vol. 67; Leiden/Boston, MA: Brill) 81–89.

Goodman, M., 2007b. *Rome & Jerusalem. The Clash of Ancient Civilizations* (London: Allen Lane).

Grainger, J. D., 2004. *Nerva and the Roman Succession Crisis of AD 96-99* (London/New York: Routledge).

Heemstra, M., 2009. *How Rome's Administration of the* Fiscus Judaicus *Accelerated the Parting of the Ways between Judaism and Christianity. Re-reading 1 Peter, Revelation, the Letter to the Hebrews and the Gospel of John in Their Roman and Jewish Contexts* (Diss. University of Groningen).

Heemstra, M., 2010. *The* Fiscus Judaicus *and the Parting of the Ways* (WUNT II 277; Tübingen: Mohr Siebeck).

Hemer, C. J., 1973. 'The Edfu *Ostraka* and the Jewish Tax', *PEQ* 105, 6–12.

Hendin, D., 2001. *Guide to Biblical Coins* (4th ed.; New York: Amphora).
Hendin, D., 2010. *Guide to Biblical Coins* (5th ed.; New York: Amphora).
Horbury, W., 1982. 'The Benediction of the *Minim* and Early Jewish-Christian Controversy', *JTS* 33, 19–61.
Jones, B. W., 1993. *The Emperor Domitian* (London/New York : Routledge).
Katz, S. T., 1984. 'Issues in the Separation of Judaism and Christianity after 70 C.E.: A Reconsideration', *JBL* 103, 43–76.
Katz, S. T., 2006. 'The Rabbinic Response to Christianity', in S. T. Katz (ed.), *The Cambridge History of Judaism, Vol. 4: The Late Roman-Rabbinic Period* (Cambridge: Cambridge University Press), 259–298.
Keresztes, P., 1973. 'The Jews, the Christians, and Emperor Domitian', *VigChr* 27, 1–28.
Kimelman, R., 1981. '*Birkat Ha-Minim* and the Lack of Evidence for an Anti-Christian Jewish Prayer in Late Antiquity', in E. P. Sanders (ed.), *Jewish and Christian Self-Definition. Vol. II. Aspects of Judaism in the Graeco-Roman Period* (London: SCM Press), 226–244.
Lehmann, M. R., 1993. 'Where the Temple Tax was Buried", *BAR* 19:6, 38–43.
Mandell, S., 1984. 'Who Paid the Temple Tax When the Jews Were under Roman Rule?', *HTR* 77, 223–232.
Marcus, J., 2009. '*Birkat ha-minim* Revisited', *NTS* 55, 523–551.
Martyn, J. L. (ed.), 1968. *History and Theology in the Fourth Gospel* (New Testament Library; Louisville, KY/London: Westminster John Knox Press) – reprinted 1979 and 2003.
Merlin, A., 1906. *Les revers monétaires de l'empereur Nerva (18 Septembre 96–27 Janvier 97)* (Paris: Fontemoing).
Moussaieff, S., 2010. 'The "New Cleopatra" and the Jewish Tax', *BAR* 36:1, 47–49.
Richardson, P. and Shukster, M. B., 1983. 'Barnabas, Nerva, and the Yavnean Rabbis', *JTS* 34, 31–55.
Robinson, T. A., 2009. *Ignatius of Antioch and the Parting of the Ways. Early Jewish-Christian Relations* (Peabody, MA: Hendrickson Publishers).
Rutledge, S. H., 2001. *Imperial Inquisitions. Prosecutors and Informants from Tiberius to Domitian* (London/New York: Routledge).
Salvaterra, C., 2000. 'L'amministrazione fiscale in una società multietnica. Un esempio dall'Egitto romano sulla base di P. Carlsberg 421', in L. Mooren (ed.), *Politics, Administration and Society in the Hellenistic and Roman World. Proceedings of the International Colloquium, Bertinoro 19-24 July 1997* (Studia Hellenistica 36; Leuven: Peeters, 2000), 287–348.
Schiffman, L. H. 1981. 'At the Crossroads: Tannaitic Perspectives on the Jewish-Christian Schism', in E. P. Sanders (ed.), *Jewish and Christian Self-Definition. Vol. II. Aspects of Judaism in the Graeco-Roman Period* (London: SCM Press), 115–156.
Schremer, A., 2010. *Brothers Estranged. Heresy, Christianity, and Jewish Identity in Late Antiquity* (Oxford: University Press).
Shanks, H., 2010. 'Adding Insult to Victory', *BAR* 36:3, 20.
Shotter, D. C. A., 1983. 'The Principate of Nerva: Some Observations on the Coin Evidence", *Historia* 32, 215–226.
Smallwood, E. M., 1956. 'Domitian's Attitude Toward the Jews and Judaism', *CP* 51, 1–13.
Smallwood, E. M. 1976. *The Jews under Roman Rule from Pompey to Diocletian: A Study in Political Relations* (Leiden/Boston, MA: Brill) – reprinted 1981 and 2001.
Stenger, W., 1988. "*Gebt dem Kaiser, was des Kaisers ist...!" Eine Sozialgeschichtliche Untersuchung zur Besteuerung Palästinas in neutestamentlicher Zeit* (Athenäums Monografien, Theologie, Bonner biblische Beiträge LXVIII; Frankfurt am Main: Athenäum).

Tellbe, M., 2005. 'The Temple Tax as a Pre-70 CE Identity Marker', in J. Ådna (ed.), *The Formation of the Early Church* (WUNT 183; Tübingen: Mohr Siebeck).

Teppler, Y. Y., 2007. *Birkat haMinim. Jews and Christians in Conflict in the Ancient World* (Texts and Studies in Ancient Judaism, 120; Tübingen: Mohr Siebeck).

Thompson, L. A., 1982. 'Domitian and the Jewish Tax', *Historia* 31, 329–342.

Thompson, L. L., 1990. *The Book of Revelation. Apocalypse and Empire* (New York/Oxford: Oxford University Press).

Van der Horst, P. W., 1993. 'The Birkat ha-Minim in Recent Research', *The Expository Times* 105, 363–368; reprinted in P. W. van der Horst, *Hellenism –Judaism –Christianity. Essays on Their Interaction* (Kampen: Kok Pharos Publishing House, 1994), 99–111.

Wander, B., 1997. *Trennungsprozesse zwischen frühem Christentum und Judentum im 1. Jarhundert n. Chr. Datierbare Abfolgen zwischen der Hinrichtung Jesu und der Zerstörung des Jerusalemer Tempels* (Tübingen/Basel: Francke Verlag).

Williams, M. H., 1990. 'Domitian, the Jews and the "Judaizers" – A Simple Matter of *cupiditas* and *maiestas*?', *Historia* 39, 196–211.

Wilson, S. G., 1995. *Related Strangers. Jews and Christians 70 – 170 C.E* (Minneapolis, MN: Fortress Press).

Yarbro Collins, A., 1984. *Crisis and Catharsis: The Power of the Apocalypse* (Philadelphia, PA: Westminster Press).

# THE SILVER COINAGE OF ROMAN ARABIA

## Kevin Butcher

A paper on the Roman silver coinage of the *provincia Arabia* might seem out of place in a volume devoted to Judaea and Rome. However, the coins in question certainly circulated in Judaea and, as will be explained below, some of the coinage in question has strong connections with Rome, so it is not wholly inappropriate for such a venue.

The coins were all produced in the reign of a single emperor, Trajan, under whom the kingdom of the Nabataeans was annexed as the province of Arabia in 106 CE. The attribution of this coinage to the newly-created Arabian province was for a long time obscured by the fact that the coins were commonly assigned to an entirely different province, Cappadocia. They were catalogued as products of the mint of Caesarea in Cappadocia by Warwick Wroth in the British Museum Catalogue (1899)[1] and included by Edward Sydenham in his standard work *The Coinage of Caesarea in Cappadocia* (1933). There they stayed until 1975, when William E. Metcalf demonstrated that they were likely to be Arabian and not from Caesarea in Cappadocia. That they circulated in Arabia and the southern Levant and not in central Anatolia can be demonstrated from hoards.[2] Although the coins give no indication of their mint of origin, the north Arabian city of Bostra has been posited as the mint for at least some of them.[3]

Despite the fact that several of the types implicitly refer to Arabia, the earlier attribution of Trajan's Arabian silver coinage to Caesarea was not wholly capricious. Stylistically most of the Arabian coins of Trajan look like the coins of Caesarea. Indeed, they look like a whole group of provincial silver coinages produced under Trajan, and this is because these stylistically-similar coins, or the dies used to strike them, were probably all produced centrally at a single mint, which was not located in the eastern Mediterranean at all.

Only one Arabian silver issue of Trajan does not conform to this pattern, but there are reasons for believing that this, too, was not minted in the province of Arabia, even if at least some of it was made by overstriking on old Nabataean silver coins.[4] Thus the province of Arabia has an extensive silver coinage under Trajan, but it is possible to argue that none of it was actually made in the province of Arabia.

Trajan's Arabian coinage is not very complex, and there is not much variety; but type-content is not the only point of interest here. Indeed, the coins are a subject of some considerable interest to those interested in the organisation of production of coinage in the Roman world, and they can be best understood by looking at the broader picture of minting in the eastern Roman Empire and minting in the empire as a whole.

There are six main varieties of Arabian silver coinage issued under Trajan. One was issued at some point during the period between Trajan's fifth and sixth consulship, 103-112 CE, and the other five varieties in the period between his sixth consulship and his death, 112-117 CE. Two of the varieties share the same reverse type, whose association with Arabia is not in doubt. Another also has clear associations with desert places. Two of the others are not very specific at all (their designs do not link them to any specific place), and the last has no obvious association with Arabia, but as we will see, does seem to have associations with the Roman province of Asia in western Anatolia. It is perhaps not surprising, then, that some of these coinages were originally thought to have been produced for circulation elsewhere than in Arabia, because they seem not to have any obvious iconographic link with Arabia or Nabataeans.

[1] Wroth 1899, 54-7.
[2] Metcalf 1975; Spijkerman 1978, 32-4.
[3] Kindler 1983, 95-9.
[4] Spijkerman 1978, 32-4.

Fig. 1

**Coins of Trajan's Fifth Consulship**

The coinage referring to Trajan's fifth consulship consists of a single denomination and type (**Fig. 1**). Although Trajan held his fifth consulship in 103 CE and did not hold another until 112 CE, it is likely that this issue belongs closer to 112 than the annexation of Arabia in 106.[5]

The denomination is a tetradrachm, a four-drachm piece. It is sometimes referred to as a tridrachm,[6] because it is lighter, thinner and slightly smaller in diameter than the contemporary tetradrachms of neighbouring Syria. Indeed, it weighs about three-quarters the weight of contemporary Syrian tetradrachms, but its silver content is equal to the Syrian tetradrachms.[7] Another good reason for believing it is a tetradrachm and not a tridrachm will be explained below.

Fig. 2

The significance of the reverse type can be explained by reference to contemporary Roman coinage, where the same design appears (**Fig. 2**).[8] There is a female figure holding a branch and some other uncertain object (some say a bundle of cinnamon sticks), with a little camel at her feet,[9] and on the Roman imperial issues this design is often accompanied by the inscription ARAB ADQ(VISIT) for *Arabia adquisita* (rather than *Arabia capta*). While the Roman coinage is explicit, the Arabian tetradrachms do not give the figure any label, but there can be no serious doubt that the same personification of Arabia is intended.

If one compares the style of the denarii and other Roman imperial coins with the Arabian tetradrachms, one can see a clear similarity between them. This raises questions about the origin of the Arabian tetradrachms, and whether they can be assigned credibly

---

[5] The reverse type is identical to one found on regular Roman coinage dated to ca. 110-111 CE: Woytek 2010a, 125; 131-5.
[6] E.g. Sydenham 1933, 63, no. 182; Kindler 1983, 97.
[7] Butcher and Ponting 1998.
[8] Woytek 2010a, 336, no. 285; 340, no. 290; 377-8, nos. 362-5; 379, 370; 386, nos. 385-7.
[9] Some gold coins show the animal in its entirety (Woytek 2010a, 340, no. 290) and it is clearly a single-humped dromedary. In some older catalogues the animal is mis-described as an ostrich (see comment in Kindler 1983, 154, n. 3). This identification goes back at least as far as the sixteenth century. Sebastiano Erizzo, in the *Dichiaratione* of his *Discorso* (1559, 230-1), illustrated an Arabia adquisita coin and described the ostrich as a symbol of Arabia, even though the accompanying woodcut illustration clearly shows a camel.

to a mint city in Arabia, as has sometimes been suggested.[10] If one compares the style of these coins with the civic coinages of the region it is clear that these silver coins have little in common with locally-produced issues. What should one make of this? In recent years it has become apparent that the mint of Rome was involved in some way in the production of certain provincial coinages,[11] and these Arabian tetradrachms look like they too belong in such a category. As we will see below, Arabia was only one of a number of regions that was receiving Rome-style provincial coinage. One thing that all of these coinages have in common is that they bear no reference to an issuing city, and in most cases the only authority to which the inscriptions refer is the emperor himself.

Two main possibilities present themselves: that the dies were made in Rome and shipped to the east, where the coins were struck; or the coins themselves were made in Rome and shipped to the east.[12] The idea that they might have been produced at Rome and transported to the province could seem improbable, but given what we know about the integration of the Roman economy, it is in fact not particularly surprising that a commodity was manufactured in one place and transported an enormous distance to a market in another place. Marble columns and sarcophagi, brick and tile, everyday household pottery – all sorts of goods in the Roman Empire were manufactured in large production centres and distributed to other regions,[13] so why not coins? It might seem easier and more secure to ship the dies instead, although a provincial mint would then have to have a strategy to cope with dies breaking or becoming faulty before the production cycle was complete.[14] Presumably requesting replacement dies from the mint at Rome was not an option, unless the authorities were prepared to wait. Finally, where we have reliable sets of metallurgical analyses,[15] these often point to the metal originating in Rome, as well as the dies. These factors tend to favour the production at Rome of the coins themselves rather than just the dies, but both modes of production (of coins or dies at Rome) are possible.

The phenomenon of Rome-style provincial coinages, of which the Arabian silver seems to be a part, can be first detected about thirty years earlier under the Emperor Vespasian,[16] and reaches its zenith under Trajan, although it continued down to the mid third century CE.[17] Many of Trajan's provincial silver coinages, and at least two base metal coinages, appear to have been struck at Rome. The Italian origin of these coins (or at the very least, their dies) could not be guessed from their reverse types, each of which is specific to a particular region: Lycian drachms with their characteristic lyre reverses; Cappadocian silver coins with Mount Argaeus; Tarsus tetradrachms with the city's Tyche; brass and copper coins of Cyprus with the temple at Paphos or Zeus Salaminios; base metal coins of Syria in the name of the provincial koinon; silver tetradrachms of Syria with the Tyrian god Melkart; and drachms and hemidrachms of Cyrenaica with Zeus Ammon.[18] This list is not exhaustive, but it is clear that the Arabian silver fits the pattern.

---

[10] Kindler 1983, 95-100.
[11] Walker 1978, 159; Carradice and Cowell 1987; Butcher and Ponting 1995.
[12] As noted above, a mint in Arabia has been suggested (e.g. Kindler 1983).
[13] Ward-Perkins 1992; Parkins and Smith 1998; Mattingly and Salmon 2001.
[14] I owe this point to a discussion with Terence Cheeseman.
[15] Carradice and Cowell 1987; Butcher and Ponting 1995; 1998.
[16] Carradice and Cowell 1987; Butcher and Ponting 1995; 1998.
[17] Baldus 1969; Burnett and Craddock 1983.
[18] Butcher 2004, 82-7.

Fig. 3

Fig. 6

Fig. 4

Fig. 7

Fig. 5

Fig. 8

**Coins of Trajan's Sixth Consulship**

Once again, the Arabian coinage includes tetradrachms. There were three types, though this time the figure of Arabia is absent.[19]

   1) A bundle of corn ears (**Fig. 3**)
   2) A legionary eagle and standards (**Fig. 4**)
   3) A temple containing a cult image (**Fig. 5**)

Parallels for these types can be found easily, but not in Arabia. They are common types on earlier tetradrachms (of similar size to, but slightly higher weight than, the Arabian coins) from the province of Asia in what is now western Turkey, issued during Trajan's second consulship (98-99 CE) and bearing Latin, rather than Greek, inscriptions (**Figs 6-8**).[20] These Asian tetradrachms are conventionally called *cistophori*. Though not exactly the same in every detail, the similarities are striking.[21]

While the first two types could be regarded as appropriate to any province or region of the Roman Empire,[22] the third is rather more difficult to comprehend in an Arabian context if, as

---

[19] For a more detailed consideration of these tetradrachms, see now Woytek 2010b, 111-20.
[20] Woytek 2010b.
[21] On the differences, see Woytek 2010b, 114. The Trajanic cistophori have two further types, absent from the Arabian tetradrachms: the cult image of Artemis of Perge (without the temple) and a temple of Rome and Augustus.
[22] Note that a bundle of corn ears is carried by the Tyche of Bostra on early civic bronze issues of that city, and the bundle appears independently as a type on small denominations (Kindler 1983, 105, no. 2; 107, no. 8; 108, no. 11; 112, no. 23).

Fig. 9 Fig. 10

Fig. 11

is usually assumed, the cult image is Artemis of Perge. The cistophori of Asia of the second consulship leave one in no doubt: the temple is explicitly labeled DIANA PERG, i.e. Diana Pergaea. In Asia the type would be appropriate: the Diana or Artemis of Perge in Pamphylia was one of the distinctive cult images of that province. Its relevance for Arabia is less clear, and this fact might have led to Kindler's decision to exclude all three tetradrachm types from his catalogue of Arabian coins.[23] It is always possible that the identification of the cult image on the Arabian coin is wrong, however, and that some other, local or regional, deity was intended, despite its similarity to the images of Artemis of Perge found on cistophori. While the resemblance cannot be ignored, the cult image on the Arabian coins also has more than a passing resemblance to busts of local deities depicted on coins of Near Eastern cities (**Fig. 9**). These busts, which are occasionally shown in profile, sometimes rest on a rectangular base or plinth (**Fig. 10**), very much like the bust on the Arabian tetradrachms. A base also appears on the Asian coins, but its shape varies; most commonly it seems to taper. Therefore a case might be made for the deity being other than Artemis of Perge, although there are no obvious parallels among the civic coinages of Arabia itself.

Once again the tetradrachms are Roman in style,[24] and resembling a whole group of eastern provincial coinages that might well have been produced at Rome (see below).

Accompanying the tetradrachms, and equally Roman in style, is a drachm with the reverse type showing a Bactrian camel (**Fig. 11**). The denomination is interesting in the wider context of provincial silver coinage: drachms were not normally produced by Levantine mints, and so in the context of Roman provincial silver from the region they appear as something of an anomaly. But as a continuation of Nabataean coinage they do not seem out of place: the Nabataeans also had a preference for small silver coins like these. In the Arabian context, it is the tetradrachms that could be viewed as unusual.

These drachms look very much like contemporary denarii, although the camel reverse type is not found on denarii. Indeed, the reverse type is curious: a two-humped Bactrian camel rather than a one-humped Arabian dromedary. Elsewhere I have argued that, because this issue was probably made at Rome, the die engravers or the official responsible for the issue simply made a mistake in choosing a Bactrian camel for the type.[25] Though Bactrian camels may have been present in Arabia for breeding purposes in the Roman period,[26] it seems unlikely

---

[23] Kindler 1983, 97.
[24] Walker 1978, 159; Woytek 2010b, 115-6.
[25] Butcher 1995/6.
[26] Potts 2004; Graf 2007.

that this animal would have been chosen to symbolise the province. When camels do appear on coins that are unquestionably of Arabian origin, on issues of civic coinage at Bostra, they are all dromedaries.[27]

The weight and fineness of the Bactrian camel drachms is also of interest. Although they weigh a third the weight of the Arabian tetradrachms (which might suggest that the tetradrachms are really tridrachms), they contain a quarter of the silver. The tetradrachms are struck on a standard of 2/3rds silver to 1/3rd copper, whereas the drachms are struck on ½ silver ½ copper standard.[28] It offers clear proof that the tetradrachms are really tetradrachms and not tridrachms.

Why the use of two standards of fineness? Part of the answer to that may lie in the study of the final type of Arabian coinage that we have not yet considered.

Fig. 12            Fig. 13

The final group of sixth consulship coins is not in the Rome style (**Fig. 12**). It is composed of drachms, and unlike the previous Rome style coins they are dated by Trajan's tribunician power which, unlike consulships, was renewed annually and allows us to date the group precisely, beginning with his sixteenth renewal of tribunician power in 111/112 CE (although the drachms must start in 112 alone, because that was the year in which Trajan entered his sixth consulship) and ending with the eighteenth in 113/114 CE.

These drachms all have the standing Arabia type, similar to the tetradrachms of the fifth consulship, but they are of quite different style to the products of Rome. Another mint seems likely. The drachms are also of the same weight and fineness as the Bactrian camel drachms of the Rome style. They are commonly overstruck on earlier Nabataean silver drachms.[29] The Nabataean drachms were struck on the ½ silver ½ copper standard,[30] so it would seem that the succeeding Roman drachms maintained the same standard – in this case simply by using Nabataean drachms as the raw material for the Roman ones. This may explain why the 50:50 silver/copper alloy standard was chosen for the drachms rather than the 2/3rds silver and 1/3rd copper of the tetradrachms: it was the traditional standard.

Even though they were overstruck on Nabataean drachms, they were not necessarily produced in Arabia. The style is not unique to the Arabian drachms, and some other major provincial silver issues are clearly the work of the same die engravers.[31] The most obvious comparison to make is with contemporary Syrian tetradrachms which are also dated by consulship and tribunician power. Not only are these very similar in style; they are also made from a 50:50 silver/copper alloy standard (**Fig. 13**). There are also some minor provincial silver coinages in the same style, including some tetradrachms with Asian cistophorus types, dated by Trajan's seventeenth

---

[27] Kindler 1983, 58.
[28] Butcher and Ponting 1998.
[29] The traces of the Nabataean designs can sometimes be seen under the later type (Negev 1971; Metcalf 1975, 95; Weder 1977; Spijkerman 1978, 32-5; Kindler 1983, 98).
[30] Schmitt-Korte and Cowell 1989.
[31] Weder 1977; Kindler 1983, 98; Butcher 2004, 87-92.

renewal of tribunician power (112-113 CE), and undated drachms of the island of Crete.[32]

The largest group of coins in this style is the Syrian tetradrachms, suggesting that wherever they were produced was also the mint (or at least the workshop producing the dies) for the other coinages, including the Arabian drachms. If one searches for stylistic parallels among the bronze coinages of the Near East, the closest are a few issues of Antioch,[33] although a case has also been made for these tetradrachms being made at Tyre,[34] even though there are no contemporary Tyrian civic bronzes with imperial portraits, making it rather hard to argue a case based on any comparisons.

So there appear to be two centres for the production of this Arabian coinage. One mint, Rome, made all the tetradrachms, and one issue of drachms, or the dies for them; and the other, probably Antioch but perhaps another eastern mint, made an issue of drachms or the dies for drachms, part or all of which was made by overstriking Nabataean drachms. There are no direct stylistic links to the civic coinages made in the *provincia Arabia* itself.

Inevitably there are complications to a relatively simple picture. In his study of the coinage of Bostra, Kindler mentioned a Bactrian camel drachm 'which bears clear traces of overstriking on a Nabataean coin', though he did not illustrate it.[35] It would be easy to dismiss this as an error of identification, but that would be mistaken. Examination of the coin in question leaves no doubt that it is overstruck on a Nabataean drachm.[36] At present it appears to be the only known example, but it is nonetheless extremely important. It could be seen as undermining the case for the production of these drachms at Rome; after all, why would the authorities go to the trouble of sending old coins (in this case Nabataean drachms) all the way to Rome for re-minting, and then for the Roman mint to ship the re-minted coins all the way back to Arabia? The weight of this counter-argument diminishes somewhat when one realises that the mint of Rome must have been constantly receiving shipments of denarii from distant provinces, re-minting them, and sending them out again. A consignment of Nabataean drachms could have been sent to Rome utilising existing arrangements for transfers of coin.

Thus one could make the same argument for the fineness of the camel drachms as for the standing Arabia drachms: the 50:50 silver/copper alloy standard was chosen because at least part of both types of drachm issue were struck using Nabataean 50:50 silver copper alloy drachms as blanks.

We still have not considered why the Arabian tetradrachms are issued at a rather higher fineness than the 50:50 silver/copper alloy standard of the drachms, so that they contained four times as much silver as the drachms but weighed only three times as much. Why were they not struck at four times the weight, with a fineness of 50%? One potential motive is that the authorities did not want the Arabian tetradrachms confused with Syrian tetradrachms, so they made them lighter and smaller than the latter. It is possible to imagine reasons why they did not want this confusion (though these must remain speculative, given the paucity of the evidence). The meagre hoard evidence could be taken to show that Syrian and Arabian tetradrachms commonly circulated together in Arabia and Palestine, but it could be the case that only Syrian tetradrachms commonly circulated in the north.[37] If this evidence reflects reality (and currently there is no certain indication that it does), then

---

[32] Butcher 2004, 88 and 91, fig. 26, nos. 6 and 8. For a full discussion of the tetradrachms with cistophorus types, see Woytek 2010b, 121-4. McAlee (2007, 194) includes these tetradrachms as issues of Arabia accompanying the standing camel drachms.

[33] Weder 1977; Butcher 2004.

[34] McAlee 2007, 189.

[35] Kindler 1983, 96.

[36] A fuller discussion of this coin, and its implications, will be published by Bernhard Woytek and myself.

[37] The evidence from northern Syria for this period is so poor that new hoards may challenge this insecure claim, however. Note three Arabian tetradrachms in a Severan hoard from Nineveh (Butcher 2004, 274, no. 36), though considering that Nineveh lay outside the Roman empire this hardly qualifies as 'northern Syria'. The hoard included 92 Parthian drachms and 121 Syrian tetradrachms of the first century BCE.

some kind of differential selection must have prevented the Arabian tetradrachms circulating in the north. It clearly was not the case of one being more valuable than the other, because the Arabian and Syrian tetradrachms contain more or less the same amount of silver.[38] Whatever the reasons for the apparent rarity of the Arabian coins in the north, by making the Arabian coins different the authorities would have enabled people to discriminate between the two coinages easily, simply according to size and weight. Drachms on the other hand were not a normal coinage for Syria, so the Arabian ones could not be confused with anything else (except perhaps Roman imperial denarii).

## Conclusions

It would therefore seem to be the case that during Trajan's fifth and sixth consulships hardly any eastern provincial silver was produced locally, and most of it was produced in two centres: Rome; and an eastern mint which is probably Antioch. The Arabian coinage was a typical product of this system. It might be described as a system of co-operation between major mints for the provision of silver (and some base metal) coinage, but it is difficult to see any clear pattern in the minting activity (why does 'Antioch' make coins for Crete and Rome make coins for Syria?), or to guess who was organising the co-operation. Did provincial authorities, or even individual cities, commission the mints to produce coins, and did they provide the old coins or bullion, with the mint taking its cut? Or was it co-ordinated centrally, using imperial bullion supplies or tax coins?

Central co-ordination could help to explain why the apparently inappropriate type of Artemis of Perge (if this identification is correct) ended up in Arabia. The three types typical of Asian cistophori may have been intended for Asia, but for some (perhaps purely bureaucratic) reason they were diverted to Arabia. At the moment the evidence from Asia is so poor that we do not know if any of these particular tetradrachms circulated there as well, but there are certainly no hints that they did. Differences in weight and fineness between the Arabian tetradrachms and the cistophori and the use of Greek rather than Latin might speak against such reasoning.[39] Furthermore, if a case can be made for the types being pertinent to Arabia then this speculative scenario is quite unnecessary, and this support for central co-ordination evaporates. Whether any of the Arabian coins ended up in Asia or not, it would seem that at about the same time the eastern production centre (Antioch?) produced its own version of Asian cistophori, with specifically Asian types.[40] Where they circulated is not known.

Until better evidence is made available, whether one favours central co-ordination or individual political entities placing orders with the mints is probably a matter of personal taste. Some features look more like a centralised, top-down arrangement (the same or similar standards of fineness, the use of a few important mints); others more resemble a bottom-up arrangement (no apparent logic to the pattern of minting). The two positions are not necessarily incompatible: in Medieval Europe and in the Ottoman Empire the state normally dictated the location of the mints and the types, weights and finenesses of each denomination, while the quantity of coin produced was in large part decided by private individuals who commissioned the mint to produce it from privately-held supplies of raw materials.[41] While the Arabian coinage provides some important clues about the organisation of minting it is clear that more work needs to be done on the general organisation of minting of provincial coinage in this period.

---

[38] Butcher and Ponting 1998.
[39] Woytek 2010b, 116-7.
[40] The types include a *cista mystica* and snakes (Woytek 2010b, 122, Typ 4; Sydenham 1933, 64, no. 186) and Artemis of Ephesus (Woytek 2010b, 121, Typ 3; Sydenham 1933, 65, no. 188).
[41] Pamuk 2000, 34-6.

**Fig. 14**  **Fig. 15**  **Fig. 16**

Thus far nothing has been said about the historical context for the Arabian silver coinage. It looks as if there was an attempt to create a distinctive provincial coinage for Arabia, but minting did not survive the reign of Trajan. Some might see the timing of the issues as significant: rather than coinciding with the annexation of the Nabataean kingdom in 106 CE, the period of issue, ca. 112-114, falls just before and during the Emperor's campaigns in Armenia and northern Mesopotamia.[42] The evidence for circulation does not support the minting of the Arabian coinage to pay soldiers on campaign (since most of the coins appear to have stayed in the vicinity of Arabia), so any association with the war must have been indirect, and has to be open to question.[43] Perhaps it was simply an exercise in recycling Nabataean drachms and silver bullion from the Nabataean royal treasury, and once that had been achieved, no further coinage was necessary. The coins enjoyed a fairly long life, however, and hoard evidence such as the finds from Mampsis and 'Tell Kalak' indicates that the tetradrachms and drachms continued to circulate down to Severan times.[44]

However, the story of the Arabian silver coinage does not quite end with Trajan. Although no further tetradrachms were produced, the Arabian tradition for drachms found its last expression in the early third century, under the Severans.

A small and rare group of drachms, probably also on the 50:50 silver/copper alloy standard, were issued between c. 208 and 211 CE, a century after Trajan's coins, for the emperors Septimius Severus, Caracalla, Geta, and the Empress Julia Domna (**Figs 14-16**).[45] Again the mint city is not indicated, but the reverse type is fairly explicit: a standing or seated Tyche holding a small lump (thought to be a cult stone) and carrying a military trophy over her shoulder. The type is otherwise known only on the civic coins of Petra. The style of contemporary bronze civic coins of Petra is exactly the same as the silver drachms, and there can be little doubt that Petra is the place of production. Unlike under Trajan, where the Arabian coinage points to mints outside Arabia, here we have something that appears to be locally made. If so, the issues of Septimius Severus and his family would be Arabia's only homegrown silver coinage of the Roman period. Again, this is not surprising, given the wider context: this time there is a profusion of local production, with many mints producing silver coinages under Caracalla, rather than centralised production at a few mints. Perhaps we might see in this last silver coinage of Roman Arabia a distant echo of the Nabataean preference for drachms, via the Bactrian camel and standing Arabia drachms of Trajan, issued a century earlier.

---

[42] Butcher 2004, 45.

[43] Some *might* have gone with soldiers on campaign, though explicit associations linking coins from archaeological contexts with Trajan's Parthian war are lacking. Apart from the three Arabian tetradrachms in the Nineveh hoard, concealed in Severan times (see above, note 37), there was one standing Arabia drachm at Dura (Bellinger 1949, 100, no. 2067). This was a stray find rather than a coin from a hoard, and there is no indication of when it arrived at Dura. If it arrived in Severan times its silver fineness would have been about the same as contemporary denarii (Butcher, Ponting and Chandler 1997).

[44] Butcher 2004, 275, nos. 36, 38, 38a, 40b.

[45] Walker 1978, 104; Butcher 1989. For the drachm of Geta, see *Classical Numismatic Group*, Auction 60 (May 22, 2002), lot 1407. I am grateful to Terence Cheeseman for drawing my attention to the drachm of Septimius Severus, which appeared in an on line H. D. Rauch sale. It is dated to Severus' third consulship, 202-211 CE. The drachms of Caracalla also refer to a third consulship (208-212 CE).

**Acknowledgements**

The author would like to thank Classical Numismatic Group, Inc. (www.cngcoins.com), and private collectors, for images of the coins.

**Bibliography**

Baldus, H. R.. 1969. *MON(eta) URB(is) – ANTIOXIA: Rom und Antiochia als Prägestätten syrischer Tetradrachmen des Philippus Arabs* (Frankfurt am Main: Busso Peus).
Bellinger, A. R., 1949. *The Excavations at Dura-Europos. Final Report VI. The Coins* (New Haven: Yale University Press).
Burnett, A. and Craddock, P., 1983. 'Rome and Alexandria: the Minting of Egyptian Tetradrachms under Severus Alexander', *ANSMN* 28, 109-118.
Butcher, K., 1989. 'Two Notes on Syrian Silver of the Third Century AD', *NC* 149, 169-172.
Butcher, K., 1995/6. 'Bactrian Camels in Roman Arabia', *Berytus* 42, 113-116.
Butcher, K., 2004. *Coinage in Roman Syria. Northern Syria, 64 BC – AD 253* (London: Royal Numismatic Society).
Butcher, K. and Ponting, M., 1995. 'Rome and the East: Production of Roman Provincial Silver Coinage for Caesarea in Cappadocia under Vespasian, AD 69-79', *OJA* 14, 63-78.
Butcher, K. and Ponting, M., 1998 'Atomic Absorption Spectrometry and Roman Silver Coins', in A. Oddy, M. Cowell (eds.), *Metallurgy in Numismatics*, vol. 4 (RNS Special Publication no. 30; London: Royal Numismatic Society), 308-334.
Butcher, K., Ponting, M., and Chandler, G., 1997. 'A Study of the Chemical Composition of Roman Silver Coinage, AD 196-197', *AJN* 9: 17-36.
Carradice, I. and Cowell, M., 1987. 'The Minting of Roman Imperial Bronze Coins for Circulation in the East: Vespasian to Trajan', *NC* 147, 26-50.
Erizzo, S., 1559. *Discorso di M. Sebastiano Erizzo, sopra le medaglie antiche, con la particular dichiaratione di molti riversi, nuovamente mandato in luce* (Venice: Bottega Valgrisiana).
Graf, D., 2007. 'Two-Humped Camel Drachms: Trajanic Propaganda or Reality?', in al-Khraysheh *et al*. (eds.), *Studies in the History and Archaeology of Jordan IX* (Amman: Department of Antiquities), 439-450.
Kindler, A., 1983. *The Coinage of Bostra* (Warminster: Aris and Phillips).
Mattingly, D. J. and Salmon J. (eds.), 2001. *Economies Beyond Agriculture in the Classical World* (London: Routledge).
McAlee, R., 2007. *The Coins of Roman Antioch* (Lancaster, PA: Classical Numismatic Group, Inc.).
Metcalf, W. E., 1975. 'The Tell Kalak Hoard and Trajan's Arabian Mint', *ANSMN* 20, 87-108.
Negev, A., 1971. 'Notes on the Trajanic Drachms from the Mampsis Hoard', *JNG* 21, 115-120.
Pamuk, Ş., 2000. *A Monetary History of the Ottoman Empire* (Cambridge: Cambridge University Press).
Parkins, H. and Smith, C. (eds.), 1998. *Trade, Traders and the Ancient City* (London/ New York: Routledge).
Potts, D., 2004. 'Camel Hybridization and the Role of Camelus Bactrianus in the Ancient Near East', *JESHO* 47, 143-165.
Schmitt-Korte, K. and Cowell, M., 'Nabataean Coinage – Part I. The Silver Content Measured by X-ray Fluorescence Analysis', *NC* 149, 33-58.
Spijkerman, A., 1978. *The Coins of the Decapolis and Povincia Arabia* (Jerusalem: Franciscan Printing Press).

Sydenham, E. A., 1933. *The Coinage of Caesarea in Cappadocia* (London: Spink).
Walker, D. R., 1978. *The Metrology of the Roman Silver Coinage. Part III, from Pertinax to Uranius Antoninus* (Oxford: British Archaeological Reports).
Ward-Perkins, J. B., 1992. *Marble in Antiquity. Collected Papers of J.B. Ward-Perkins* (London: British School at Rome).
Weder, M., 1977. 'Zu den Arabia-Drachmen Trajans', *SM* 107, 57-61.
Woytek, B., 2010a. *Die Reichsprägung des Kaisers Traianus (98-117)* (Moneta Imperii Romani, Band 14; Vienna: Verlag der Österreichischen Akademie der Wissenschaften).
Woytek, B., 2010b. 'Die Cistophore der Kaiser Nerva und Traian (mit einem systematischen Anhang zu typologisch verwandtem traianischem Provinzialsilber)', *Revue Suisse de Numismatique* 89, 69-143.
Wroth, W., 1899. *A Catalogue of the Greek Coins in The British Museum: Galatia, Cappadocia, and Syria* (London: British Museum Publications).

# FURTHER REMARKS ON COINS IN CIRCULATION DURING THE BAR KOKHBA WAR: TE'OMIM CAVE AND HORVAT 'ETHRI COIN HOARDS

Boaz Zissu and David Hendin

## 1. Introduction

Leo Mildenberg noted in 1984 that although there has never been a hoard in which the coins of the Jewish War and the Bar Kokhba Revolt are found together, "this in no way precludes the possibility that Bar Kosiba's men knew of the rebel coins from the Bellum Judaicum or even that they had seen such coins."[1]

Mildenberg's discussion of the similarities between the coins of the two Jewish Wars has now been completed, since one of the three coin hoards found by Zissu *et al.* in the Te'omim Cave in the western Jerusalem hills revealed a Jewish War shekel together with Bar Kokhba silver coins.[2]

Here we offer a numismatic discussion to supplement the original report of the archaeological excavations of the Te'omim Cave[3] and the earlier numismatic report.[4] For readers who may not have ready access, we briefly summarize the description and history of research of this cave.

Me'arat Ha-Te'omim — Te'omim Cave ("Cave of the Twins") — is a karst cave on the northern bank of Nahal Hame'ara (coordinates 152049/126028), on the western edge of the Jerusalem hills. The first comprehensive study of this cave was carried out by Conder and Kitchener in 1873.[5] They found a deep pit at the northern tip of the entrance hall. They did not enter it, or notice the continuation of the cave to the north. Late in the 1920s, Neuville excavated the bottom of the cave's entrance hall and found ceramic, wooden, and stone vessels from the Neolithic and Chalcolithic (Ghassulian) Ages, Early Bronze Age I(?), Middle Bronze Age II(?), Iron Age, and Roman and Byzantine periods.[6] Between 1970 and 1974 Gideon Mann studied this cave and entered the deep pit, where he discovered natural passages leading to two inner chambers. He mapped the section and found pottery from the time of the Bar Kokhba Revolt.[7] Zissu *et al.* studied the cave and prepared a new plan of it (**Fig. 1**) during the summer and fall of 2009, in which they discovered the three hoards of coins discussed here.[8]

Hoard A was discovered inside a hole in the rock on the southern edge of the chamber; nearby were large fragments of storage jars. These coins were found as a clump, probably

---

[1] Mildenberg 1984, 68.
[2] Zissu *et al.* 2010.
[3] Zissu *et al.* in press.
[4] Zissu et al 2010.
[5] Conder and Kitchener 1883, 148–149.
[6] Neuville 1930, 65. Uri Davidovich referred us to this publication and helped analyze and summarize the findings of Neuville's excavations.
[7] Mann 1978, 161–164. We thank Prof. Amos Kloner, who in November 2009 reexamined the pottery found by Mann. The pottery is in the collections of the State of Israel (IAA storage facilities, Beit Shemesh).
[8] The survey was carried out by B. Zissu, R. Porat, B. Langford and A. Frumkin (permit S-133/2009) on behalf of the Department of Land of Israel Studies and Archaeology at Bar-Ilan University together with the Cave Research Unit at the Hebrew University of Jerusalem, with assistance from the Jeselsohn Epigraphic Center of Jewish History, the Israel Nature and Parks Authority (INPA) and the participation of Vladimir Buslov, Mika Ullman, Uri Davidovich, and Yonathan Goldsmith. The coins and metal objects were cleaned by Marina Rassovsky in the Israel Museum laboratories. The pottery was restored by Andrei Weiner of the Israel Museum laboratories. The coin plates were prepared by Doody Evan. We are grateful to the late Prof. Hanan Eshel, Dr. Zvika Tsuk, Menachem Fried, and Onn Valency of the INPA and to Dr. Zvi Greenhut of the Israel Antiquities Authority for their help. Dudi Mevorach, Daniel Ein-Mor, Yinon Shivtiel, Amos Kloner, and Nili Graicer also provided assistance.

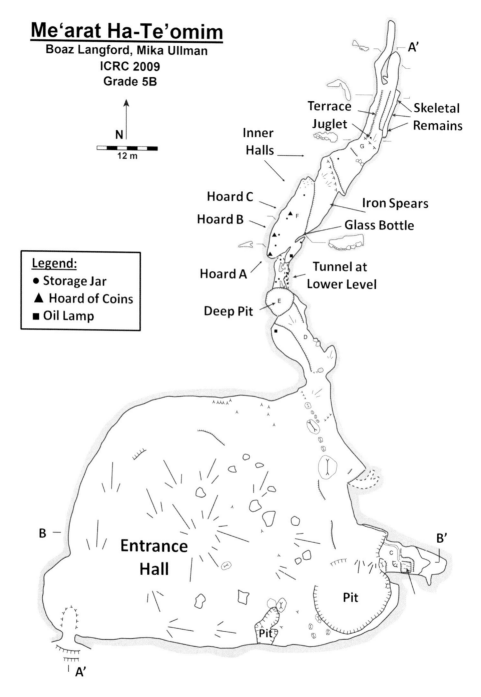

**Fig. 1a:** Te'omim Cave - Plan

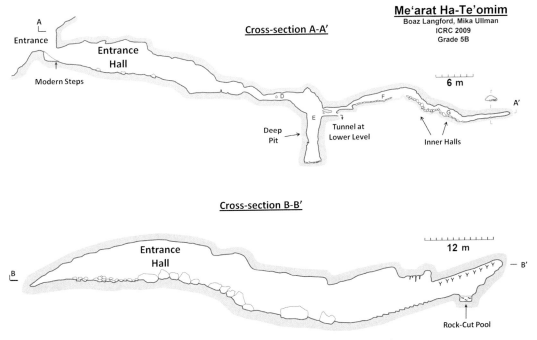

Fig. 1b: Te'omim Cave - Cross-sections 2 and 3

because they had been kept in a pocket or sack made from organic material, which disintegrated (**Fig. 2**). The group consists of 83 Bar Kokhba silver coins, 20 sela'im (tetradrachms) and 53 zuzim (denarii),[9] and a piece of a silver earring (**Fig. 3**).[10] Nearby, on a storage jar fragment, a bronze coin of Ascalon was discovered. About two meters north of this spot, Hoard B, consisting of another group of ten coins and a bronze needle, was found. This is the group that contained a Jewish War shekel, Bar Kokhba zuzim, and a Hasmonaean bronze (**Figs 4** and **5**). Hoard C consists of another group of 24 coins, including five Roman gold coins, fifteen silver coins (two of them Bar Kokhba zuzim), four bronze coins and an iron needle, which were found *in situ* next to fragments of a storage jar (**Figs 6** and **7**).

These three coin hoards apparently belong to three separate families or individuals, and it seems likely that they were hiding themselves and their stores of wealth in dire circumstances, near the end of the war. These hoards seem not only to be a stash of personal wealth, but they show that people sometimes also held old coins that the owners may have saved because they were meaningful.

The value of Hoard A was 153 zuzim. Hoard A is the largest Bar Kokhba silver coin hoard discovered to this time in recorded, licensed archaeological excavations. Undoubtedly other hoards have been discovered in illegal excavations. Our comments on these intact hoards should provide sufficient information to further establish the importance of maintaining the integrity of coin hoards, and discovering them in a scientific setting. The true story of a hoard

---

[9] Zuz is the Mishnaic name for this coin, although the same denomination Roman denarii or Roman provincial drachms are the very coins overstruck to create them.

[10] The earring fragment found together with coins illustrates the continuation of the tradition of the use of weighed metal currency alongside coinage in the ancient Near East well into the second century. This phenomenon is generally discussed by Schaps 2004 and by Stern 1982 regarding the Persian Period, but the tradition continued well into the Roman period or later.

**Fig. 2:** Te'omim Cave - Hoard A
in situ

**Fig. 3:** Te'omim Cave - Hoard A
after cleaning

**Fig. 4:** Te'omim Cave - Hoard B
in situ, partly covered with dirt

**Fig. 5:** Te'omim Cave - Hoard B
after cleaning

**Fig. 6:** Te'omim Cave - Hoard C
in situ

**Fig. 7:** Te'omim Cave - Hoard C
after cleaning

cannot be known from its individual, separated parts, nor can it ever be understood without knowing the context in which it was buried. Mildenberg cites two hoards resembling Hoard A that were discovered by antiquity thieves in 1976 in Beit 'Umar and in 1980 near Dahariyeh,[11] but their completeness or archaeological contexts are not known.

We also find of significance that Hoard A provides three examples of a Bar Kokhba sela' (Nos. A16, A17, A18) that has been struck by a pair of "irregular"[12] dies previously unrecorded by Mildenberg[13] or Kaufman.[14] This is the first documented Bar Kokhba hoard that proves irregular silver coins circulated side-by-side with standard issues. Unlike virtually all other coins, the Bar Kokhba issues—standard or irregular—had no value added (fiduciary value) when they were created from bullion at the mint.[15] Since the coins circulated together, this constitutes proof that the Bar Kokhba irregular coins were accepted currency. This provides additional validity to Barag's theory that both bronze and silver Bar Kokhba coins were struck officially and contemporaneously at two separate mints.[16]

We can further suggest that Bar Kokhba's two mints may reflect similarities to earlier coin production during the Second Temple Period. All of the coin series—from Yehud to the Jewish War—contain irregular issues. Previous discussions of these irregular issues invariably speculate on the possibilities that they were contemporary forgeries or simply 'irregular' issues from unskilled workers. Physical appearance of the flans and manufacturing of both regular and irregular Judaean coins, including those of Bar Kokhba, are similar. The principal difference is the crude, almost child-like style of the die engraving. The flans used to strike the Bar Kokhba irregular coins were coins already in circulation, just as with the regular Bar Kokhba issues.

The value of Hoard B was at least 14 zuzim and one prutah and consisted of two Bar Kokhba zuzim, one Roman provincial tridrachm, five Roman denarii or drachms, one Jewish War shekel and a Hasmonaean prutah. This is the hoard that completes Mildenberg's discussion of differences and similarities between coins of the Jewish War and the Bar Kokhba Revolt.[17] There is an undeniable similarity of script and slogans between the coins of the two Jewish wars, although the production qualities and motifs are quite different.

The presence of the Jewish War (year 2) shekel was cited in the excavation report as an example of Gresham's Law, in which "good money" drives out "bad money."[18] There is no doubt that from the standpoint of silver content, the Jewish War coin is better quality, with silver around 98 wt.% pure, according to Deutsch.[19] The Roman denarii were approximately 90 wt.%[20] silver and many of the Roman provincial silver coins were further debased. The Jewish War shekel had been saved for some 64 years, well beyond the time it had been invalidated by the Flavian victory and destruction of Jerusalem. Invalidated or not, the Jewish War shekels were 14 grams of nearly pure silver and had significant bullion value even if they were not valid as coins. This situation is similar to an American in 2012 saving "silver dollars"

---

[11] Mildenberg 1984, 56–57. Although Mildenberg believed that all the hoards had been found in the Judean Hills, it seems that some of them were found in the Shephelah (in rock-cut hideouts located underneath Jewish villages and systematically looted between 1967 and 1984). It turns out that antiquities dealers told Mildenberg that the hoards had been found near the antiquity thieves' villages, and that the thieves had kept the exact location of the discovery a secret. See Mildenberg (ibid.), 54–57.

[12] These coins have erroneously been tagged "barbaric" for years, although Mildenberg spurned that adjective in favor of "irregular" (Mildenberg 1983, 22) and Barag noted that from the perspective of the Greeks and the Romans "all Jewish coinage was no doubt considered 'barbaric coinage'"(Barag 2000-2002, 155).

[13] Mildenberg 1984.
[14] Kaufman 2000-2002; idem 2007-2008.
[15] Hendin 2011.
[16] Barag 2000-2002.
[17] Mildenberg 1983, 68
[18] Hayek 1978, 41-43
[19] Deutsch 2009a.
[20] Burnett 1987, 48-49

that were inherited or received as a child. The United States stopped striking silver dollars in 1935. Thus these minimum 77-year-old dollars are nice mementos of an earlier time. It does not damage the "saver" that, based on current silver values, each silver dollar is worth more than 20 times its face value. Needless to say this "good money" is no longer in circulation, but was melted or sits in hoards and collections around the world.

Since Hoard B also contains a virtually valueless 240-year-old prutah of Hyrcanus I (134-104 BCE), we must consider the possibility that this family's savings also constitutes something of a collection.[21] Hendin previously published an unprovenanced Bar Kokhba hoard found in an Herodian oil lamp that was buried no earlier than 151/152 CE,[22] but contained a neatly collected set of Bar Kokhba bronze coins which had long been invalidated and retained no commercial value after the war; see **Fig. 12**.[23] Meshorer also observed that Bar Kokhba coins were sometimes perforated and used as jewelry.[24]

Hoard C had a value of 150 zuzim, and consisted of five gold aureii,[25] eight Roman denarii, five Roman provincial tetradrachms, two Bar Kokhba zuzim, and four bronze coins of Ascalon. The gold aureii were struck under Tiberius, Nero (2), Vitellius, and Vespasian, and the dating of these coins suggest that this hoard is a clear example of a multi-generational family savings.

It is, of course, possible that the owners of Hoard A deliberately converted all of their money into Bar Kokhba coins for nationalistic reasons. If that was the case, then one might suggest that the owners of Hoards B and C were more cautious, and deliberately retained some of their savings in Roman and provincial coinage which, presumably, could be traded more easily with non-Judaean merchants. In other words, the overstriking of the Bar Kokhba coins was probably a large-scale administrative issue, and not a matter of individual families taking coins to be re-struck by the rebels' mint.

## 2. Horvat 'Ethri

Another coin assemblage not yet fully discussed was found in Horvat 'Ethri in the Judaean Shephelah (**Fig. 8**).[26] This residential complex was founded at the end of the Persian Period and reached its largest during the first century CE when it covered some 12 dunams. Based on finds of at least four ritual baths (miqva'ot), stone vessels, and the coins, its inhabitants were most likely Jewish. The village was abandoned after the Jewish War (66-70 CE) and partly rebuilt by Jews in the interval between the two Jewish Wars. The people of Horvat 'Ethri participated in the Bar Kokhba Revolt and the village was violently destroyed.

Beneath the village's residential buildings, underground complexes were cut in the bedrock. These include burrows, chambers, and connections to existing water cisterns. The presence of typical datable finds suggests that these systems were used as hideouts for the residents during the Bar Kokhba Revolt.

---

[21] Hasmonaean prutot continued to circulate through the fourth century as small change. For excavation data on this topic see, for example, Ariel 2002, 281-305; Bijovsky 2000, 155-189, and Bijovsky 2000-2002.

[22] Hendin 2000-2002

[23] Meshorer 1967, 99-100. In this context, Meshorer quoted the Jerusalem Talmud: "With regard to a coin which was invalidated but is accepted by the government, R. Yose in the name of R. Yonatan (said): 'It is like a blank'. R. Hiyya in the name of R. Yonatan (said): 'It is like a coin of the former kings.' Should it be accepted as currency because it bears a recognizable design, (the second tithe) is exchanged for it, but if not, (the second tithe) is not exchanged for it. *(The second tithe) is not exchanged for a coin issued by one who rebelled, such as Ben Koziva.*" (y. M. Sh. 1, 2).

[24] Meshorer 2001, 162. He noted that "Only the coins hidden by their owners during the war and not removed from the hiding place, either because the owners were killed or taken captive, sold as slaves, and sent to foreign countries, did not undergo the process of invalidation or being fashioned into jewelry."

[25] Each gold aureus had a value of 25 denarii, drachms, or zuzim.

[26] Zissu and Ganor 2009.

**Fig. 8a:** Horvat 'Ethri – General plan

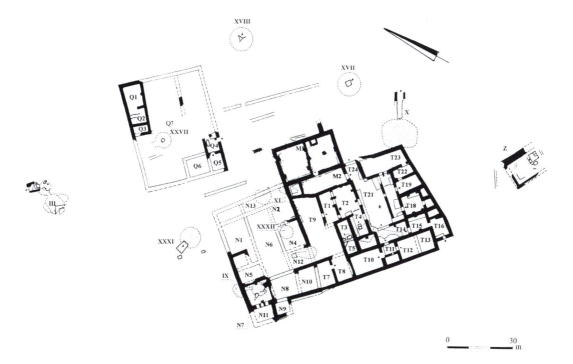

**Fig. 8b:** Horvat 'Ethri – Plan during the period 70-135 CE

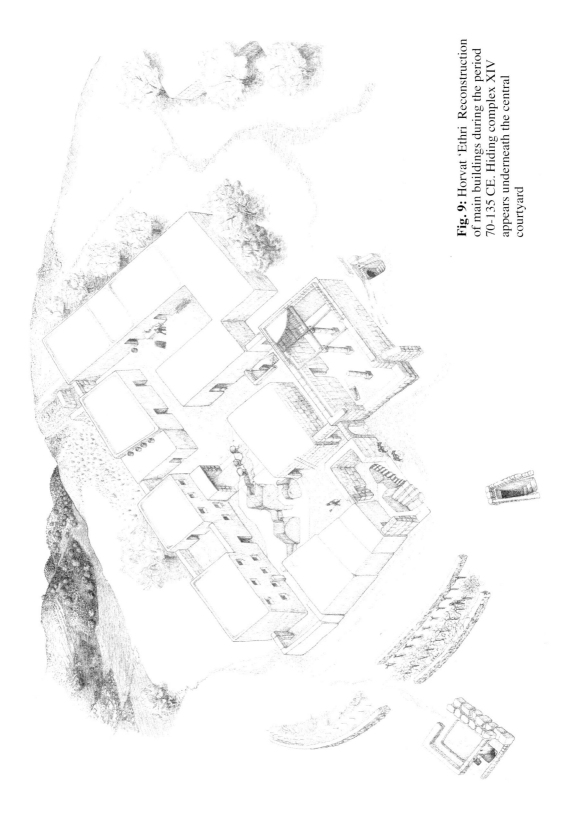

**Fig. 9:** Horvat 'Ethri Reconstruction of main buildings during the period 70-135 CE. Hiding complex XIV appears underneath the central courtyard

Some of the systems, such as the large complex XV, were looted before Zissu and Ganor's excavation. A smaller complex (XIV) was reopened during the Late Roman period and remained subsequently sealed (**Fig. 9**). It contained a typical assemblage of finds from the Bar Kokhba Revolt, including Judaean (Darom) oil lamps, Roman and provincial coins, and three bronze coins minted by the Bar Kokhba administration (**Fig. 10**). We call special attention to a silver half-shekel of the Jewish War dated 'year 3' (**Fig. 11**). The context of this coin, hidden in the floor of one of the underground chambers, suggests that like the shekel in Hoard B of the Te'omim Cave, it had been in the possession of Bar Kokhba followers.

**Fig. 9b:** Photograph inside hiding complex XIV showing typical burrow

**Fig. 10:** Bar Kokhba bronze coin from the first year of the revolt, found in complex XIV, obverse and reverse

**Fig. 11:** Silver half-shekel of the Jewish War dated 'year 3', found in complex XIV, obverse and reverse

## 3. Discussion and Conclusion

The finds from the Te'omim Cave and Horvat 'Ethri add to the numismatic evidence of the Bar Kokhba Revolt and raise a number of interesting questions for further study and discussion:

1. Not a single Bar Kokhba bronze coin was found in the three hoards of the Te'omim Cave, even though several provincial bronze coins were found there. This is a bit mysterious, especially when one notes that until now Bar Kokhba hoards or assemblages seem to contain either Bar Kokhba bronze or silver coins, but not both. For example, Fr. Spijkerman reported on hundreds of Bar Kokhba coins of many types found at Herodium—all of them bronze.[27] Porat *et. al.* reported on two groups of Bar Kokhba coins from Ein Gedi; the first group from the Har Yshai Cave consisted of 11 Bar Kokhba bronze coins, the second group, from the Zabar Cave consisted of nine silver coins, three of which were Bar Kokhba coins.[28] Bijovsky published two hoards from Khirbet Badd 'Isa: "Group B", concealed in a crevice underneath the floor of one of the houses, included 43 bronze coins and a tetradrachm of Vespasian from Tyre. The latest coin was of Hadrian, and it points to the date of deposition – the Bar Kokhba revolt, despite the absence of coins overstruck by the rebels. "Group C", buried on the bedrock in one of the enclosures, included 144 silver coins and two aurei of Vespasian and Trajan. The latest coins included in this hoard were from the days of Hadrian, pointing to the date of its burial. This hoard lacks coins minted by the rebels.[29] The same phenomenon was identified by Bijovsky in "Group C" at Horvat Zalit[30] and by Eshel and Zissu in the silver hoard found in the Cave of the Sandal at Ketef Yeriho.[31] In the Hiding Complex of Ar-Ras in the foothills of the mountains of Samaria, Janai reported on one grouping from a hiding complex that contained five coins, all bronze with two Bar Kokhba coins.[32] This separation of Bar Kokhba bronze and silver coins may simply result from the relative wealth of the original owners of the coins, but is interesting nevertheless.

2. Did Jews of the Bar Kokhba period save or collect earlier Judaean coins for nationalistic reasons? This theory is supported by Hoard B, the Bar Kokhba Lamp Hoard,[33] and re-use of Bar Kokhba zuzim as jewelry, discussed above. Future discoveries in archaeological context may reveal more information about this phenomenon.

3. Bar Kokhba coin hoards or assemblages discovered so far consist either purely of Bar Kokhba coins or Bar Kokhba coins together with other contemporaneous circulating coins. Because of the nature of the Bar Kokhba revolt, it seems a fair assumption to assume that the Bar Kokhba coins were not valid currency outside of Bar Kokhba's territories.[34] But the question of whether Roman and Roman provincial coins, as well as earlier issues, circulated together with the Bar Kokhba coins within Judaea remains unanswered at this time.

## Bibliography

Ariel, D., 2002. 'The Coins from the Surveys and Excavations of Caves in the Northern Judaean Desert', *Atiqot* 41.2, 281-304.
Barag, D., 2000-02. 'The Two Mints of the Bar Kokhba War', *INJ* 14, 153-156.
Bijovsky, G., 2000. 'The Coins from Horbat Zalit', *'Atiqot* 39, 155-189.
Bijovsky, G., 2000-2002. 'The Currency of the Fifth Century CE in Palestine: Some Reflections in Light of the Numismatic Evidence', *INJ* 14, 196-210.

---

[27] Spijkerman 1972.
[28] Porat *et. al.* 2003-2006, 79-86.
[29] Bijovsky 2004, 244-248, 271-300.
[30] Bijovsky 2000, 163-169.
[31] Eshel and Zissu 1994-99.
[32] Janai 1994-1999, 78-82.
[33] Hendin 2000-2002.
[34] See discussion by Eshel (1995).

Bijovsky, G., 2004. 'The Coins from Khirbet Badd 'Isa—Qiryat Sefer, Isolated Coins and Two Hoards Dated to the Bar Kokhba Revolt', in Y. Magen, D. T. Ariel, G. Bijovsky, Y. Tzionit and O. Sirkis, *The Land of Benjamin* (Jerusalem: SOA and IAA),243-300.

Burnett, A., 1987. *Coinage in the Roman World* (London: Seaby).

Conder, C. R., and Kitchener, H. H., 1883. *The Survey of Western Palestine: Memoirs*, vol. 3: *Judaea* (London: Palestine Exploration Fund), 1883.

Deutsch, R., 2009. *The Jewish Coinage During the First Revolt Against Rome, 66-73 CE*, Unpublished Ph.D. dissertation submitted to Tel Aviv University.

Deutsch, R., 2009a. English summary of Deutsch 2009.

Eshel, H., 1995. 'The Policy of Overstriking Roman Coins during the Bar Kokhba Revolt in the Light of Finds from the Judean Desert', in Y. Eshel (ed.), *Judea and Samaria Research Studies*, vol. 5, 173–182 (Kedumim-Ariel: Eretz) (Hebrew);

Eshel, H., and Zissu, B., 1994-1999. 'Roman Coins from the 'Cave of the Sandal' West of Jericho', *INJ* 13, 70-77.

Hayek, F. A., 1978. *Denationalization of Money: The Argument Refined. An Analysis of the Theory and Practice of Concurrent Currencies* (London: Institute of Economic Affairs).

Hendin, D., 2011. 'Jewish Coins of the Two Wars: Aims and Meaning' (in this volume).

Hendin, D., 2010. *Guide to Biblical Coins, 5$^{th}$ Edition* (Nyack, NY: Amphora).

Hendin, D., 2000-2002. 'A Bar Kokhba Lamp Hoard Collection', *INJ* 14, 180-184.

Janai, J., 1994-1999. 'A Find of Bar Kokhba Coins from the Al Midya Ar-Ras Area', *INJ* 13, 78-82.

Kaufman, J. C., 2000-2002. 'Additions to Leo Mildenberg's Corpus of The Coinage of the Bar Kokhba War', *INJ* 14, 129-152.

Kaufman, J. C., 2007-2008. 'Additions to the Corpus of Leo Mildenberg's Coinage of the Bar Kokhba War', *INJ* 16, 136-139.

Mann, G., 1978. 'On a Rope — Into the Pit of Me'arat Ha'Teomim,' *Teva Va-Aretz* 20, 161–164 (Hebrew).

Mazar, B., 1975. *The Mountain of the Lord: Excavating in Jerusalem* (New York: Doubleday).

Meshorer, Y., 1967. *Jewish Coins of the Second Temple Period* (Tel Aviv: Am Hassefer).

Meshorer, Y., 1982. *Ancient Jewish Coinage* I and II (Nyack, NY: Amphora).

Meshorer, Y., 2001. *A Treasury of Jewish Coins* (Nyack, NY: Amphora).

Mildenberg, L., 1984. *The Coinage of the Bar Kokhba War* (Salzburg and Aarau: Verlag Sauerlaender).

Neuville, R., 1930. 'Notes de préhistoire palestinienne: La grotte d'et-Taouamin', *JPOS* 10, 65.

Porat, R., Eshel, H., and Frumkin, A. 2003-2006. 'Bar Kokhba Coins from Ein Gedi', *INJ* 15, 79-86.

Schaps, D., 2004. *The Invention of Coinage and the Monetization of Ancient Greece* (Ann Arbor, MI: Michigan University Press).

Spijkerman, A., 1972. *Herodion: Catalogo delle monete* (Jerusalem: Studium Biblicum Franciscanum).

Stern, E., 1982. *Material Culture of the Land of the Bible in the Persian Period 538-332 BC* (Jerusalem: Israel Exploration Society).

Zissu, B., and Ganor, A., 2009. 'Horvat 'Ethri – A Jewish Village from the Second Temple Period and the Bar Kokhba Revolt in the Judean Foothills', *Journal of Jewish Studies* 60, 90-136.

Zissu, B., Eshel, H., Langford, B., and Frumkin, A., 2009-2010. 'Coins from the Bar-Kokhba Revolt Hidden in Me'arat Ha-Teomim (Mŭghâret Umm et Tûeimîn), Western Jerusalem Hills', *INJ* 17, 113-147.

Zissu, B., Porat, R., Langford B., and Frumkin, A., in press. 'Archaeological Remains of the Bar Kokhba Revolt in the Te'omim Cave (Mŭghâret Umm et Tûeimîn), Western Jerusalem Hills', *Journal of Jewish Studies*.

**Fig. 12:** The Bar Kokhba lamp hoard

# HADRIAN AS NERO *REDIVIVUS*:
# SOME SUPPORTING EVIDENCE FROM CORINTH

## Larry J. Kreitzer

In my book *Striking New Images* (1996), which contained a series of studies on Roman Imperial coinage and the light it sheds on the New Testament world, a chapter was included on 'Hadrian and the Nero *Redivivus* myth'. This explored how the imagery surrounding the expected return of the wicked emperor Nero became applied to the emperor Hadrian by Jewish writers who were seeking to make sense of the disaster of the so-called Second Jewish Revolt (132-135 CE). It is generally acknowledged that both Jewish and Christian writers of late 1st and early 2nd centuries viewed the conflict with Rome through the interpretative lens of such apocalyptic imagery. The best example of this within the New Testament occurs in the Book of Revelation, where the Nero *Redivivus* myth is applied to the review of Roman Imperial history contained in chapters 13 and 17, specifically as it relates to the seven-headed beast. It is generally agreed that this beast imagery represents the Imperial cultus, particularly as it was practised in Asia Minor and the eastern half of the Empire.[1] The identification of the beast as a symbol of the Roman emperor Nero, is confirmed via the use of *gematria* in the form of the number 666, 'the number of the beast' in Revelation (13:18).[2] The number is derived by taking the Greek characters of ΝΕΡΩΝ ΚΑΙΣΑΡ, and then transliterating them into their Hebrew equivalents.[3] The numerical values of the Hebrew characters yield the total of 666. This suggestion is well supported by the fact that Irenaeus (*Haer.* 5.30.1) mentions a variant reading of 616 in Rev 13:18 within some Latin manuscripts. In the Latinised spelling of ΝΕΡΩΝ the final Ν would be dropped, thus reducing the total of the equivalent Hebrew characters to 616.[4]

Further, it seems clear from surviving documents that ancient Jewish and Christian authors were able to find new and creative means of applying the Nero *Redivivus* mythology to their own situations. It is part of the power of such mythological constructs that they survive by being eminently adaptable to different times and varying contexts. Indeed, there is some evidence for the association of the emperor Hadrian with the figure of Nero *Redivivus* within select Jewish documents generally dated to Hadrian's reign. I suggested in my 1996 book that it is possible to trace a development of the association of the emperor Hadrian with the prevailing mythological expectations about the return of Nero which run through the *Sibylline Oracles*. This connection starts in Book 5, where there is an indirect association between the two rulers, continues in Book 8, where there is a direct association between them, and concludes in Book 12, where the connection

---

[1] Friesen (2001) offers an excellent study along these lines.
[2] On the whole issue, see Collins [A. Y.] 1984; Aune 1998, 769-73. Barnes (2010, 37-40) dates the Book of Revelation to the autumn of 68 CE; Bell (1978) dates it to 68-69 CE in the turmoil following the death of Nero; Sanford (1937, 99) suggests 70 CE, citing traditions of Nero's flight to the Parthians in the East as a catalyst for Rev 13.
[3] Hillers (1963) gives details of an Aramaic scroll dated to the second year of the emperor Nero (55/56 CE) which employs the appropriate transliteration. The document from Murabba'at is *DJD* II, no. 18, 100-4 and pl. XXIX. Lehman (1963/4, 56-7) suggested that it belongs to a year earlier, 54/55 CE
[4] The issue has been recently revived by the publication in 2007 of a 3rd-4th century Greek papyrus ($P^{115}$) of the Book of Revelation first discovered when Bernard Grenfell and Arthur Hunt began their excavations at Oxyrhynchus in Egypt in 1896; the papyrus has only recently been digitally photographed and re-assessed. Interestingly, this is one of the oldest extant manuscripts of Revelation, and it gives the number of Nero the beast as 616. Elliott (2000) and Parker (2000) discuss the papyrus.

between the two emperors no longer pertains and the descriptions of Nero (and Hadrian!) are simply part of an historical survey.

Moreover, it is possible to detect a chronological sequence with the various Books of the *Sibylline Oracles* which helps explain why the Nero *Redivivus* myth becomes relevant and applicable to Hadrian. Book 5 probably dates to about 130 CE, that is to say, *prior* to the outbreak of the Second Jewish Revolt, although important echoes of the First Revolt are contained in the work.[5] The bulk of Book 8, on the other hand, probably dates to 132-135 CE, and was thus compiled during the Revolt itself, which helps explain the negative depiction of Hadrian as a wicked ruler and the re-incarnation of Nero, under whom the First Jewish Revolt began some 65 years before. Book 12 probably dates to 235 CE, during the reign of Severus Alexander, when sufficient time had passed to remove Hadrian from active consideration as a focal point of mythological interest. In fact, the presentation of Hadrian here is quite a positive one, markedly different from that contained in Book 8, where there is a close identification of Hadrian and the Nero *Redivivus* figure.

In this paper I do not intend to rehearse the arguments I proposed for suggesting that Hadrian was viewed as a Nero *Redivivus* figure within sections of the *Sibylline Oracles*. What I would like to do is to build upon that suggestion by appealing to some numismatic evidence which supports a close connection between Nero and Hadrian and helps us understand how a later mythological identification of the two could easily be made. In fact, there are some intriguing similarities between provincial coins of Corinth issued during the reigns of Nero and Hadrian which illustrate this. No doubt the impetus to produce such coinage was conditioned in part by the fact that Nero and Hadrian had much in common, particularly when it came to an interest in, and commitment to, the Eastern half of the Empire. Hadrian's activities among the eastern provinces, particularly Greece (where he enrolled in the Eleusinian mysteries), is well documented and is reflected in both *Sib. Or.* 8.50-6 and 12.164-74:

> But when, luxurious one, you have had fifteen kings Who enslaved the world from east to west, There will be a gray-haired prince with the name of a nearby sea, inspecting the world with polluted foot, giving gifts. Having abundant gold, he will also gather more silver from his enemies and strip and undo them. He will participate in all the mysteries of magic shrines. (8.50-6)

> A silver-headed man. He will have the name of a sea presenting the beginning of the alphabet, an Ares of four syllables. He will also dedicate temples in all cities, inspecting the world on his own foot, bringing gifts. God and much alloy he will give to many. He will also master all the mysteries of the magic shrines. Indeed the thunderbolt will give a much better ruler to men. There will be a long peace when this prince will be. He will also be a singer of splendid voice, sharer in lawful things, and just legislator. (12.164-74)

Not since the time of Nero had such care and attention been showered on the East by a Roman emperor. As C. E. Manning has commented:

> Though he was considerably older, there was much about Hadrian that was

---

[5] See 5.397-413 which describes the destruction of the temple of Jerusalem by Titus. Interestingly, Nero's hand in the destruction of the Jewish Temple is mentioned in 5.150-1: He seized the divinely-built Temple and burned the citizens and peoples who went into it; no doubt this recalls the fact that the first two years of the Jewish Revolt were fought while Nero was still on the throne.

reminiscent of Nero. There was the same philhellenism, the same lavish generosity in giving shows and building theatres, the same interest in unorthodox innovation in architecture and engineering. Like Nero, his literary studies and in particular his poetic ambitions were of an extent and type that the senate considered unsuitable for the princeps.[6]

Nero and Hadrian shared an abiding passion for Greece and its contributions to civilization.[7] Both had interests in philosophy, religion, art, literature and music; both were renowned as travellers who had journeyed extensively around the empire; and both were known to have made Corinth an important stopping point in their travels. Most scholars agree that Nero visited Greece from the autumn of 66 CE to December of 67 CE, and stayed in Corinth for most of his time in the province.[8] Hadrian, on the other hand, is known to have made two different trips to Corinth. His initial visit to Corinth took place in 124 CE, as part of his first extensive journey around the Empire which lasted from 121-125 CE. A second visit to Corinth was made in the spring of 134 CE during Hadrian's second major tour of the Empire, which lasted from 128-134 CE and was commemorated in an extensive series of coins produced by the mint in Rome between 134-138 CE.[9] The series included an issue in gold, silver and bronze with a reverse type depicting the female personification of the province of Achaia, draped and kneeling before the standing figure of Hadrian on the right. The emperor is dressed in a toga and extends his right hand to the personification of Achaia in a gesture of goodwill, intending to raise her to her feet. Between the two figures is a Greek-style vase or amphora which contains a palm branch; surrounding the scene is an inscription proclaiming RESTITUTORI ACHAIAE (**Fig. 1**).

**Fig. 1:** Sestertius of Hadrian issued in 134-138 CE

Interestingly, Nero's visit to Corinth is closely connected in our surviving sources with his attempt to construct a canal across the Corinthian isthmus, an undertaking which was frequently seen as an act of hubris that was an affront to the gods.[10] Occasionally, details of the construction attempt of the canal can be gleaned from available sources. For example,

---

[6] Manning 1975, 173.

[7] Spawforth 2012, 233-70, discusses the reliance of both upon an Augustan model of Roman imperial statecraft for their Greek benefactions.

[8] Kokkinos (1998, 388-9) suggests that Nero's arrival in Greece may have taken place as early as late spring or early summer of 66 CE. The major sources for Nero's trip to Greece are Cassius Dio (62) and Suetonius (*Nero* 19-24).

[9] For more on the series, see Kreitzer 1996, 146-86. Danziger & Purcell (2006, 129-138) offers a recent discussion of Hadrian's journeys.

[10] The Corinthian canal project of Nero is also mentioned by Philostratus (*Vit. Ap.* 4.24; 5.7), Dio (62.16.1-2), Pausanias (2.1.5), Suetonius (*Nero* 19.2), Pseudo-Lucian (*Nero* 2-4), and Pliny (*N.H.* 4.4.10), who describes it as an 'impious act' (*nefasto incepto*). Suetonius specifically mentions Nero's part in the opening ceremony of the construction of the canal; he also notes (*Caes.* 54:3) that Julius Caesar at one time also proposed to cut a canal across the Corinthian isthmus. Alcock (1994, 101-3) discusses the mixed review that Nero's project received within the ancient sources.

Josephus (*War* 3.540) records that following the battle of Tarichaea[11] in 67 CE, Vespasian sent some Jews who had been captured to work on the construction of the canal at Corinth:

> He (Vespasian) then gave orders for the execution of the old and unservicable, to the number of twelve hundred; from the youths he selected six thousand of the most robust and sent them to Nero at the isthmus.

It seems that Vespasian had accompanied the emperor Nero on his visit to Corinth the year before (66 CE), so the emperor's interest in building a canal would have been known to him.

The cutting of a canal across the Corinthian isthmus is mentioned at three points within *Sib. Or.* 5, once in *Sib. Or.* 8 and once in *Sib. Or.* 12:

> He will also cut the mountain between two seas and defile it with gore (5.32).

> The poets will bewail thrice-wretched Greece when a great king of great Rome, a godlike man from Italy, will cut the ridge of the isthmus (5.137-9).

> You, too, Corinth, bewail the mournful destruction within you. For when the three sister Fates, spinning with twisted threads, lead the one who is (now) fleeing deceitfully beyond the bank of the isthmus on high so that all may see him,
> who formerly cut out the rock with ductile bronze, he will destroy and ravage your land also, as is decreed. (5.214-9)

> Alas for me, thrice-wretched one, when will I see that day, destructive indeed to you, Rome, and especially to all Latins? Celebrate, if you wish, the man of secret birth, riding a Trojan chariot from the land of Asia with the spirit of fire. But when he cuts through the isthmus glancing about, going against everyone, having crossed the sea, then dark blood will pursue the great beast. (8.151-7)

> Another man of the number fifty will come again, terrible and frightful. He will destroy many who are outstanding in wealth from all the cities, a terrible snake, breathing grievous war, who one day will lay hands on his own family and kill them and perform many things as athlete, charioteer, murderer, one who dares ten thousand things. He will also cut the mountain between two seas and will defile it with gore. (12.78-84).[12]

What is perhaps most intriguing is that all five passages occur in sections specifically given over to the depiction of Nero or Nero *Redivivus*. In effect, the attempt to build the Corinthian canal becomes one of the identifying characteristics of the Nero *Redivivus* figure.

It seems then that the presence of the emperor in Corinth in order to build the Corinthian canal was an integral element within the mythological presentation of the Nero *Redivivus* figure, but what numismatic evidence is there of Nero being in Corinth? This question invites a careful examination of the coins of Corinth to see if there are any parallels between the

---

[11] Kokkinos (2010) discusses the location of the city in Galilee, as well as some intriguing Imperial coinage issues celebrating a naval victory over the Jews on the Sea of Galilee.

[12] Collins [J. J.] 1983, 394, 396, 398, 421 and 447.

issues relating to the reign of Nero and those from the reign of Hadrian. Similarities might suggest that the moneyers of Hadrian were deliberately appropriating coin types from the reign of Nero and presenting him as a reincarnation of Nero who had reappeared in Corinth. Such coinage would establish a pattern that could be potentially picked up by others who later wrote about Hadrian, including the writer(s) of the *Sibylline Oracles*. In effect, numismatics would effectively be establishing a pattern that literary efforts could follow later. However, there is a note of caution which must be sounded here, for there are no coins that depict Hadrian as Nero *Redivivus* as such. The coin issues of Corinth by their very nature present *positive* images of the emperor and his connection with the city, and in this sense are not going to match the *negative* presentation of Hadrian as a wicked Nero *Redivivus* figure. Rather, the coins of Hadrian were intended deliberately to evoke memory of Nero's visit to Corinth nearly sixty years before, and to associate Hadrian with the glory days of Nero from a by gone era. Nevertheless, such an association in the coin issues of Corinth could be taken as analogous to what we see happening in the *Sibylline Oracles*, and thus legitimately regarded as a parallel phenomenon. Fortunately, there are some interesting coins which were produced in connection with the Imperial visits to Corinth which bear investigation in this regard.

**Fig. 2:** Bronze coin of Corinth issued under Nero in 66/67 CE

**Fig. 3:** Bronze coin of Corinth issued under Nero in 66/67 CE

**Fig. 4:** Bronze coin of Corinth issued under Nero in 66/67 CE

The Corinthian quinquennial duovirs for the year 66-67 CE, L. Rutilius Piso and P. Memmius Cleander, were responsible for two coin issues which were linked to Nero's presence in the province. The first of the two issues has a lauretted (or crowned) head of Nero and a surrounding inscription NERO CAESAR AVG(ustus) IMP(erator) on its obverse. The reverse depicts a galley and rowers, and the abbreviated words ADVE(ntus) AUG(usti) in the field are generally taken to commemorate the arrival of Nero in the province of Achaia in the autumn of 66 CE.[13] The reverses of the coins have a surrounding inscription of the abbreviated name and office of the duovirs, either L R T PISONE IIV(iro) QVI(nquennali) COR(inthi) (**Fig. 2**) or P M CLEANDRO IIV(iro) QVI(nquennali) COR(inthi) (**Fig. 3**). The reverse of the second coin from these duovirs of Corinth depicts the emperor Nero, wearing a toga and standing on a platform with his right arm raised and holding a scroll in his left hand (**Fig. 4**).[14] In the field are the abbbreviated words ADLO(cutio) AVG(usti), a powerful image of his action in proclaiming the liberation of Greece while he was attending the panhellenic games

---

[13] Amandry 1988, Issue XXII, nos. 1-28.

[14] Amandry 1988, Issue XXII, nos. 29-34.

at Isthmia.[15] Nero's activities in Greece were published widely throughout the empire, and are even recorded on an interesting series of billon tetradrachma from Alexandria. One reverse type, effectively an equivalent to the ADVENTUS AUGUSTI coin of Corinth mentioned above, depicts a galley sailing to the right with two dolphins beneath and has a surrounding inscription which reads ΣΕΒΑΣΤΟΦΟΡΟΣ ('The Emperor-Carrier');[16] the obverse has a bust of Nero wearing a radiate crown, facing left, with a surrounding inscription ΝΕΡΩ[Ν] ΚΛΑΥ[ΔΙΟΣ] ΚΑΙΣ[ΑΡ] ΣΕΒ[ΑΣΤΟΣ] ΓΕΡ[ΜΑΝΙΚΟΣ] ΑΥ[ΤΟΚΡΑΤΩΡ] and the date symbol LIΓ in the field which dates the coin to year 13 of the emperor's reign (66/67 CE) (**Fig. 5**).[17] A related tetradrachma from the series has the same obverse bust and inscription but has the date symbol LIΔ in the field which dates the coin to year 14 (67/68 CE). The reverse type on this coin depicts a bust of the god Poseidon wearing a crown and facing right, a trident visible behind his shoulder, while the surrounding inscription reads ΠΟΣΕΙΔΩΝ ΙΣΘΜΙΟΣ, referring to the Isthmian games in honour of Poseidon (**Fig. 6**).[18]

**Fig. 5**: Billon tetradrachma of Alexandria issued under Nero in 66/67 CE

**Fig. 6**: Billon tetradrachma of Alexandria issued under Nero in 67/68 CE

**Fig. 7**: Bronze coin of Corinth issued under Hadrian in 124 CE

Corresponding to these Neronic coin issues, there is an early coin of the emperor Hadrian issued by the city of Corinth which adapts the Corinthian galley reverse type of Nero and depicts a galley and rowers on its reverse, probably a reference to Hadrian's first visit to the city in 124 CE (**Fig. 7**). The inscription above the galley is COL(onia) L(aus) IVL(ia) COR(inthiensis) AD(ventus) AVG(usti), an abbreviated version of the Latin name of the city together with an announcement of the arrival of the emperor.[19] Interestingly, while he was in Corinth Hadrian granted the city freedom from taxation, no doubt recalling Nero's

---

[15] There is some scholarly debate about which year Nero delivered his speech proclaiming the freedom of Greece: was it in November of 66 or 67 CE? See Warmington 1969, 117-20; Grant 1970, 231-2; Bradley 1978; Gallivan 1973; Levy 1984; 1989; 1991; Howgego 1989. The speech is preserved on an inscription from Acraephis in Boeotia; the Greek text can be found in Charlesworth (1939, 32-3); an English translation is provided by Braund (1985, 102-3).

[16] Levy (1982/3) discusses this unusual reverse type.

[17] *RPC* 1.5296.

[18] *RPC* 1.5300. Similar coins were issued celebrating the Pythian and Actian games in honour of Apollo, the Heraian games in honour of Hera, and the Nemean and Olympian games in honour of Zeus (see Kennell 1988). Nero's manipulation of the calendar schedule of the games, coupled with his decision to enter himself as a competitor within them, created a scandal (Suet., *Nero* 23.1; 25.2; Dio 62.8.3; 62.9.1-6; 62.10.1; 62.14.1-4; 62.20.3-5). Juvenal (*Sat.* 8.226) sarcastically remarked that Nero loved winning Greek parsley-wreaths (*Graiaeque apium meruisse coronae*). Dio 62.21.1 says that Nero returned from Greece to Rome with 1808 crowns.

[19] *SNG* 12.1, no. 453.

proclamation of the liberty of the province of Achaia in 67 CE.[20] Clearly the ADVENTUS AUGUSTI coin is an adaptation of the coin issued by the moneyers of Nero nearly sixty years before, and was deliberately intended by the later moneyers to invite a comparison between Hadrian with his imperial predecessor.

However, unlike Nero for whom the arrival in Corinth and the attempt to cut the canal across the Corinthian isthmus are virtually synonymous, Hadrian is never recorded as having attempted to complete Nero's bold ambition of cutting a canal. As far as we are aware he never seriously considered the task. But, that is not so say that the idea died with Nero. There is one tantalysing discussion of it within Philostratus *Lives of the Sophists* which is worth noting, for it relates to the philosopher and benefactor Herodes Atticus (c.100-c.177 CE), who was once a member of Hadrian's court. Philostratus (*Vit. Sop.* 551) records that Herodes considered all of his great building works in Athens and throughout Greece as unimportant because he had not cut through the isthmus of Corinth:

> For he regarded it as a really brilliant achievement to cut away the mainland to join two seas, and to contract lengths of sea into a voyage of twenty-six stades. This he longed to do, but he never had the courage to ask the Emperor to grant him permission, lest he should be accused of grasping at an ambitious plan to which not even Nero had proved himself equal.[21]

Clearly the memory of Nero's ambitious project across the Corinthian isthmus lingered on into the time of Hadrian, even if this was an aspect of Nero's reign that Hadrian chose not to emulate.

The surviving Corinthian coinage of Hadrian indicates that his moneyers, like Nero's, took a great interest in the importance of the mythological history and geography of Corinth, as well as the city's close connection with the Isthmian games, and that they incorporated features of these within provincial coinage bearing his image. Is there other evidence that in so doing Hadrian's moneyers made use of reverse types which first appeared in Nero's Corinthian coinage? If so, the coins would reinforce the idea that Hadrian was being styled as a second Nero.

In fact, there are two other coin issues with reverse types that make their first appearance during the reign of Nero which were later taken up and used by Hadrian's minters in the city. Both were issued initially by the duovirs Ti. Claudius Optatus and C. Julius Polyaenus, who held office in 57/58 or 58/59 CE. The first issue demonstrates a renewed interest in the Isthmian games by the city of Corinth. The coins have on their obverse a youthful portrait of a bare-headed Nero with a surrounding inscription NERO CLAUD(ius) CAES(ar) AVG(ustus). The reverses of the issue depict a victor's crown of celery surrounding the word ISTHMIA together with a surrounding inscription of the abbreviated name and office of the duovirs, either TI(berio) CLAVD(io) OPTATO IIVIR(o) COR(inthi) (**Fig. 8**) or C[aio] IVLIO POLYAENO IIVIR(o) COR(inthi) (**Fig. 9**).[22] The wreath reverse motif was a long-established one within Corinthian coinage, and was used by several duovirs of Augustus between 17-16 BCE and 4-5 CE before being taken up by Nero's minters.[23] It seems that these coins were issued as part of

---

[20] Walbank (2003, 342) argues that Hadrian granted immunity from taxation in 124 CE during his *first* visit to Greece.
[21] This story is undated, but it probably comes from the time of Marcus Aurelius (161-180 CE).
[22] Amandry 1988, Issue XXI, nos. 19-33; *RPC* 1. 1202.
[23] Amandry 1988, Issues IX, XI, XII, XIII.

the celebrations surrounding the re-establishment of the Isthmian games in 59 CE.[24] In some respects these are the most interesting coins from the time of Nero as far as the New Testament is concerned, for there may be an echo of the Isthmian games underlying the athletic imagery contained in 1 Cor 9:24-27. Here the apostle Paul contrasts the glory of a perishable crown, like the Isthmian athlete's celery crown, with that of the imperishable crown of Christian salvation.[25] Underlying the use of such athletic imagery is a clash between the values and ideals of Nero's imperial world, and those contained within the world of Christian belief. It is but a small step from this to later Christian interpretations of Nero as the archetypal Antichrist figure. It only takes Nero's maniacal persecution of Christians in connection with the great fire of Rome in 64 CE to set things heading in this direction.

**Fig. 8:** Bronze coin of Corinth issued under Nero in 57/58 or 58/59 CE

**Fig. 9:** Bronze coin of Corinth issued under Nero in 57/58 or 58/59 CE

**Fig. 10:** Bronze coin of Corinth issued under Domitian in 87 CE

**Fig. 11:** Bronze coin of Corinth issued under Hadrian in 134-138 CE

The reverse type depicting a victory wreath surrounding the word ISTHMIA was clearly a popular one among Corinth's moneyers, for it appears again in two later issues, one from the reign of Domitian and one from the reign of Hadrian.[26] The Domitian coin shows a laureate head of Domitian facing to the right with the inscription IMP(erator) CAES(ar) DOMITIAN(us) AVG(ustus) GERM(anicus) P(ater) P(atriae) COS XIII; the reference to the thirteenth consulship of Domitian allows the coin issue to be dated to 87 CE (**Fig. 10**).[27] The Hadrian coin issue similarly shows a laureate head of Hadrian facing to the right with an inscription [Imperator] CAESAR TRAIANUS HADRIANUS [Augustus] (**Fig. 11**). The reverse victory wreath on both coins is slightly different from those from Nero's reign in that they look to be made of pine rather than celery, but otherwise the central image is the same.[28]

What about other points of similarity between Corinthian coinage of Nero and Hadrian? Another coin issue containing a reverse type that makes its first appearance during the reign of Nero, and then later reappears on coins issued during Hadrian's reign, involves one of

---

[24] Gebhard (1991, 56) discusses the coin and its connection with the revival of the games by Nero.
[25] Broneer 1951; 1962a, 17. Garrison (1997, 95-104) discusses Paul's athletic imagery and the connection with the Isthmian Games, but does not mention the coins from Corinth.
[26] The reverse type also appears in coins from the reigns of Antoninus Pius (138-161 CE), Marcus Aurelius (161-180 CE) and Commodus (177-192 CE).
[27] *RPC* 2.111.
[28] Broneer (1962b) discusses the depiction of the wreaths on Corinthian coins.

the foundational myths of the city of Corinth: the story of Bellerophon and Pegasus. In a recent study of Corinthian coinage of the late 1st and early 2nd centuries, Mary Walbank has argued that during the 2nd century the city of Corinth made a conscious decision to emphasise its Classical past, while at the same time promote its position as a thriving Roman colony. This represented something of a change of emphasis from Corinthian coinage of the first century, which concentrated more overtly on the Roman imperial family and their interests. In particular, she has argued that in the reign of Hadrian there was

> an increasing emphasis on myths and legends connecting Roman Corinth with is Greek predecessor. The most popular theme on the Hadrianic coinage is the foundation myth of Bellerophon taming Pegasos... The winged horse was, of course, the obverse type on the famous staters of Greek Corinth. It was taken over by the Roman colonists, but throughout the 2nd century Pegasos, usually with Bellerophon, appears far more frequently than previously.[29]

The image of Bellerophon taming Pegasus and bringing him to drink at the Fountain of Peirene in Corinth constitutes a second reverse type issued in 57/58 or 58/59 CE by the duovirs Ti. Claudius Optatus and C. Julius Polyaenus. The obverse of the issue has the same portrait noted above, a youthful portrait of a bare-headed Nero with a surrounding inscription NERO CLAUD(ius) CAES(ar) AVG(ustus). The reverse depicts an image of a naked Bellerophon with a shield on his left arm advancing to the left and holding in his right hand the bridle of the horse Pegasus, who stands behind.[30] Surrounding this scene are the inscriptions of the names of the duovirs, either TI CLAVD OPTATO IIVIR COR (**Fig. 12**) or C IVLIO POLYAENO IIVIR COR (**Fig. 13**).[31]

**Fig. 12:** Bronze coin of Corinth issued under Nero in 57/8 or 58/59 CE

**Fig. 13:** Bronze coin of Corinth issued under Nero in 57/58 or 58/59 CE

**Fig. 14:** Bronze coin of Corinth issued under Domitian in 87 CE

Like the ISTHMIA coin reverse discussed above, this second reverse type also reappears in two later issues, one from the reign of Domitian and one from the reign of Hadrian. The

---

[29] Walbank 2003, 345.
[30] There is a related image of Bellerophon and Pegasus which appears on the obverse of a coin issued by the duovirs P. Tadius Chilo and C. Iulius Nicephorus in 43 or 42 BCE (*RPC* 1.1117). It shows Bellerophon leading Pegasus to a fountain porch, but the scene has them moving to the right rather than the left. Robinson (2005, 125-7) discusses the importance of the story for Roman Corinth.
[31] Amandry 1988, Issue XXI, nos. 1-18; *RPC* 1.1201.

Domitian coin shows a laureate head of Domitian facing to the right with the inscription IMP(erator) CAES(ar) DOMITIANVS AVG(ustus) GERM(anicus) P(ater) P(atriae) (**Fig. 14**).[32] The reverse image of Bellerophon taming Pegasus has a surrounding inscription COL(onia) IOVL(ia) FL(avia) AVG(usta) COR(inthiensis), the official name of the colony as altered by Vespasian.[33] The Hadrian coin issue similarly shows a laureate head of Hadrian facing to the right with an inscription IMP(erator) CAE(sar) TRAIANU(S) HADRIAN(us). The reverse image of Bellerophon and Pegasus has a surrounding inscription COL(onia) L(aus) IUL(ia) COR(inthiensis), an abbreviated form of the official name of the colony which is typically found on coins of Hadrian minted after 124 CE, allowing us to date the issue to this period.

Lastly, we turn to one final aspect of the presentation of Hadrian within the *Sibylline Oracles* which is relevant to our concerns. It is worth noting that the reference to Hadrian's own participation in the Eleusinian Mysteries in *Sib. Or.* 8.56 is immediately followed by a reference to his propagation of the cult of Antinous in 8.57-8:

He will display a child as god, and undo all objects of reverence. From the beginning he will open up the mysteries of error to all

Antinous was, of course, Hadrian's beloved companion who died tragically by drowning in the Nile in 130 CE during the emperor's second tour of the east.[34] Hadrian sought to honour his deceased lover by enrolling him among the gods and setting up temples dedicated to his name. Numerous heroic busts, in both marble and bronze have been uncovered throughout the empire, and dozens of temple remains as well as coins and medallions testify to the great popularity of the cult of Antinous.

We noted above that one of the historical features used to identify the Nero *Redivivus* figure was his claim to be god (as in *Sib. Or.* 5.34 and 12.86). In all likelihood this is a veiled reference to Nero's construction of the Domus Aureus and the huge 120-foot high bronze statue of himself that adorned its entrance. We know that the statue caused quite a stir when it was erected in Rome itself and it is usually pointed to as evidence of Nero's increasing megalomania (Suet. *Nero* 31.1-2). Miriam T. Griffin has commented:

There had long been statues of the emperor and members of his family set up in Rome, but the size of this monument clearly made a different impact, for colossal statues were traditionally reserved for the gods.[35]

Could it be that Hadrian's attempt to propagate a cult of Antinous is being deliberately mentioned by the Jewish author of *Sib. Or.* 8, having in mind the memory of Nero's religious arrogance? After all, Aelius Spartianus mentions that Hadrian re-erected the Colossus of Nero, moved it to another site and re-dedicated it to the Sun god, 'after removing the features of Nero, to whom it had previously been dedicated'.[36] It may well be that the attempt to propagate a cult of Antinous by Hadrian was seen as a repeat of a similar move by Nero a generation earlier. If so, we have once again an instance where the author of *Sib. Or.* 8 is re-applying aspects of the

---

[32] *RPC* 2.119.
[33] Walbank 2002.
[34] Dio 69.11.2-4 and Aelius Spartianus *L.H.* 14.5.
[35] Griffin 1984, 131. It is open to question whether a religiously sensitive Jew, such as the author of *Sib. Or.* 8, would have maintained this distinction between human portrait/representation of a god. To his mind, the whole episode would probably have smacked of idolatry.
[36] Aelius Spartianus *L.H.* 19.12-3.

Nero *Redivivus* myth to Hadrian, based on historical parallels between Hadrian's and Nero's reigns, and is thus speaking to his own historical situation. Interestingly, the writer of *Sib. Or.* 12 does *not* include any reference to the propagation of the cult of Antinous, although, as we noted above, he does make reference to Hadrian's initiation into the Eleusinian Mysteries (12.169-70). In this sense, a more positive picture of Hadrian is presented, and the connection with Nero, who did dare to make himself equal to God (12.86), is broken.

**Fig. 15:** Bronze medallion of Corinth issued under Hadrian in 134 CE

At this point Corinthian coinage once again contributes to the discussion, for the city was one of the important sites for the propagation of the cult of Antinous.[37] Some extremely rare bronze medallions approximately 40mm in diameter are extant, including one which depicts a bare-headed and draped bust of Antinous facing right on its obverse with a surrounding inscription in Greek which reads ΟϹΤΙΛΙΟϹ ΜΑΡΚΕΛΛΟϹ Ο ΙΕΡΕΥϹ ΤΟΥ ΑΝΤΙΝΟΟΥ ('Hostilius Marcellus, the priest of Antinous').[38] The reverse is a reworking of the image of Bellerophon taming Pegasus discussed above, an image which we noted first appeared on coinage from the reign of Nero. Once again we see the figure of Antinous in the guise of a naked Bellerophon standing and facing left, restraining the rearing Pegasus by holding the horse's bridle in his right hand; a large round shield is on his left arm. The scene has a surrounding inscription in Greek which reads ΑΝΕΘΗΚΕ ΚΟΡΙΝΘΙΟΙϹ ('Dedicated to the Corinthians') (**Fig. 15**). The bronze medallion was issued by Hostilius Marcellus, probably in 134 CE.[39] Clearly Hostilius Marcellus struck the medallions in his capacity as regional priest of the cult of Antinous in Corinth, but it is not certain precisely what occasioned their production. They were probably commemorative pieces, with a limited number being struck (only two or three examples have come up for sale in recent years).[40]

It is possible that this image of Bellerophon and Pegasus was based on a statue which stood near a fountain in Corinth, probably the fountain of Eurykles on the Lechaion road.[41] Pausanias (2,3.5) tells of such a statue, suggesting that it may have been publicly erected, or remodelled, by Hadrian:

> Corinth has plenty of baths, some publicly constructed and one put up by the emperor Hadrian. The best known of them is near Poseidon. It was built by a Spartan, Eurykles,[42]

---

[37] Lambert (1984, 238-43), discusses the coins and gems which depict Antinous. He suggests that there were thirty-one cities or confederations which produced 143 different issues; Corinth was one of six cities on the mainland of Greece which contributed to the cult of Antinous in this way.

[38] Hostilius Marcellus was one of thirteen moneyers responsible for producing coins of Antinous who allowed their names to appear on the coinage (see Lambert 1984, 238-9).

[39] On the date of the medallion, see Walbank 2010, 180-1.

[40] One specimen was sold by Classical Numismatic Group, Inc. in June of 2005 for $15,000 (Sale 69, Lot 951); another was sold by Fritz Rudolf Künker Gmbh & Co in March 2010 for 1500 EUR (Auction 168, Lot 7762).

[41] C. Julius Eurykles Heraclanus was a well-connected Spartan who served as a Roman senator during the reigns of Trajan and Hadrian; he died sometime after 130 CE.

[42] See comment by P. Levi in his Penguin translation of Pausanias (p. 138, n. 24). Imhoor-Blumer (1887, 13, 24) discusses the passage from Pausanias and the statue's location near one of the fountains of Corinth. For more on Eurycles, see Bowersock 1961.

and among his ornamental stonework he used the stone they quarry at Krokeai in Sparta. Poseidon with a hunting Artemis beside him stands on the left of the entrance. A great number of public fountains have been constructed all over the city, as they have abundant streams and also Hadrian's aqueduct from Stymphalos; the best fountain to see is by the statue of Artemis: Bellerophon stands over it and the water comes rushing through the hoof of Pegasos.

In any event, it seems clear that this image of Bellerophon taming Pegasus, which was first introduced on coinage of Corinth during the reign of Nero, was once again used by the moneyers of Hadrian in about 134 CE. A related issue was also produced by Hostilius Marcellus at the same time. It has the same basic obverse of a bust of Antinous with the same surrounding inscription in Greek. The reverse depicts Antinous in the guise of the god Poseidon, enthroned and facing left, holding a patera and a trident, with two dolphins at his feet; the scene has the same surrounding inscription in Greek as appears on the Bellerophon and Pegasus reverse.[43]

Perhaps the medallions of Hostilius Marcellus were struck as part of the celebrations surrounding the unveiling of new statues commissioned by Hadrian to honour his beloved Antinous. Indeed, the medallions suggest that the heads of Bellerophon and Poseidon, gods intimately connected with the mythological story of Corinth, were replaced by the image of Antinous. More to the point, it seems that the reverse type of a coin which first appeared in the time of Nero served as the model for the new statue of Bellerophon and Pegasus during the reign of Hadrian. A fresh association between the two rulers, Nero and Hadrian, one responsible for the outbreak of the First Jewish Revolt and the other responsible for the outbreak of the Second, was being forged. Perhaps it is not surprising that this takes place at precisely the same time that the anonymous Jewish writer of *Sib. Or.* 8 interpreted the disaster that was befalling his people in Jerusalem as the work of a Nero *Redivivus* figure operating in the form of the emperor Hadrian.

## Bibliography

Translations of classical texts cited are those of the Loeb Classical Library (Josephus' *War*; Philostratus' *Lives of the Sophists*; Aelius Spartianus' *Life of Hadrian* in *Scriptores Historiae Augustae*) and of the Penguin Books (Juvenal' *The Sixteen Satires*; Pausanias' *Guide to Greece*). The translation of the *Sibylline Oracles* is that found in Collins [J. J.], 1983.

The following abbreviations (other than journal) are used in this paper:

*DJD* = *Discoveries in the Judaean Desert II: Les grottes de Murabba'at,* 2 vols., ed. by P. Benoit, J. T. Milik and R. de Vaux (Oxford: Clarendon Press, 1961); *RPC 1* = *Roman Provincial Coinage: From the Death of Caesar to the Death of Vitellius, 44 BC-AD 69*, vol. 1, ed. by A. Burnett, M. Amandry and P. Pau Ripollès (London/Paris: The British Museum Press/Bibliothéque Nationale de France, 1992); *RPC 2* = *Roman Provincial Coinage: From Vespasian to Domitian (AD 69-96),* vol. 2, ed. by A. Burnett, M. Amandry and I. Carradice

---

[43] One example was sold by Monnaies et Médailles of Basel in June 1975 for SF3000 (Auction 52, Lot 634); another was sold by Numismatik Lanz München in November of 2001 for DM4800 (Auction 105, Lot 648); a third was sold by Classical Numismatic Group Inc. for $3250 in January 2004 (Triton VII, Lot 720).

(London/Paris: The British Museum Press/Bibliothéque Nationale de France, 1999); *SNG* 12.1 = *Sylloge Nummorum Graecorum Volume XII – The Hunterian Museum, University of Glasgow. Part I. Roman Provincial Coins. Spain – Kingdoms of Asia Minor*, ed. by J. Goddard (London/Oxford: The British Academy/Oxford University Press and Spink and Son Limited, 2004).


Alcock, S. E., 1994. 'Nero at Play? The Emperor's Grecian Odyssey', in J. Elsner and J. Masters (eds.), *Reflections of Nero: Culture, History and Representation* (London: Duckworth), 98–111.
Amandry, M., 1988. *Le Monnayage Des Duovirs Corinthiens* (Athens: Ecole Francaise D'Athenes).
Aune, D. E., 1998. *Revelation 6-16* (Word Biblical Commentary, no. 52B; Nashville, TN: Thomas Nelson Publishers).
Barnes, T. D., 2010. *Early Christian Hagiography and Roman History* (Tübingen: Mohr Siebeck).
Bell, A. A., 1978. 'The Date of John's Apocalypse: The Evidence of Some Roman Historians Reconsidered', *NTS* 25, 93–102.
Bowersock, G.W., 1961. 'Eurycles of Sparta', *JRS* 51, 112–118.
Bradley, K. R., 1978. 'The Chronology of Nero's Visit to Greece AD 66/67', *Latomus* 37, 61–72.
Braund, D. C., 1985. *From Augustus to Nero: A Sourcebook on Roman History, 31 BC-AD 68* (London: Croom Helm).
Broneer, O., 1951. 'Corinth: Center of St Paul's Missionary Work in Greece', *BA* 14, 95–96.
Broneer, O., 1962a. 'The Apostle Paul and the Isthmian Games', *BA* 25, 2–31.
Broneer, O., 1962b. 'The Isthmian Victory Crown', *AJA* 66, 259-263.
Charlesworth, M. P., 1939. *Documents Illustrating the Reigns of Claudius and Nero* (Cambridge: Cambridge University Press).
Collins, A. Y., 1984. 'Numerical Symbolism in Jewish and Early Christian Apocalyptic Literature', in W. Haase (ed.), *Aufstieg und Niedergang der römischen Welt* II 21.2 (Berlin: Walter de Gruyter), 1221-1287.
Collins, J. J., 1983. 'Sibylline Oracles (Second Century BC-Seventh Century AD)', in J. H. Charlesworth (ed.), *The Old Testament Pseudepigrapha, Volume 1, Apocalyptic Literature and Testaments* (London: Darton, Longman & Todd), 317–472.
Danziger, D. and Purcell, N., 2006. *Hadrian's Empire: When Rome Ruled the World* (London: Hodder & Stoughton).
Elliott, J. K., 2000. 'Seven Recently Published New Testament Fragments from Oxyrhynchus', *NovT* 42, 209–213.
Friesen, S. J., 2001. *Imperial Cults and the Apocalypse of John: Reading Revelation in the Ruins* (Oxford: Oxford University Press).
Gallivan, P., 1973. 'Nero's Liberation of Greece', *Hermes* 101, 230–234.
Garrison R., 1997. *The Graeco-Roman Context of Early Christian Literature* (JSNTS no. 127; Sheffield: Sheffield Academic Press).
Gebhard, E. R., 1991. 'The Isthmian Games and the Sanctuary of Poseidon in the Early Empire', in T. E. Gregory (ed.), *The Corinthia in the Roman Period* (Ann Arbor, MI: The University of Michigan).
Grant, M., 1970. *Nero: Emperor in Revolt* (New York: American Heritage Press).
Griffin, M. T., 1984. *Nero: The End of a Dynasty* (London: B. T. Batsford, Ltd).
Hillers, D. R., 1963. 'Revelation 13:18 and a Scroll from Murabba'at', *BASOR* 170, 65.

Howgego, C. J., 1989. 'After the Colt has Bolted: A Review of Amandry on Roman Corinth', *NC* 149, 206–208.

Imhoor-Blumer, F. and Gardner, P., 1887. *A Numismatic Commentary on Pausanias* (London: Richard Clay and Sons).

Kennell, N. M., 1988. 'ΝΕΡΩΝ ΠΕΡΙΟΔΟΝΙΚΗΣ', *AJP* 109, 239–251.

Kokkinos, N., 1998. *The Herodian Dynasty: Origins, Role in Society and Eclipse* (JSPSS, no 30; Sheffield: Sheffield Academic Press).

Kokkinos, N., 2010. 'The Location of Tarichaea: North or South of Tiberias?', *PEQ* 142, 7–23.

Kreitzer, L. J., 1996. *Striking New Images: Roman Imperial Coinage and the New Testament World* (JSNTS, no. 134; Sheffield: Sheffield Academic Press).

Lambert, R., 1984. *Beloved and God: The Story of Hadrian and Antinous* (London: Weidenfeld and Nicholson).

Lehman, M. R., 1963/4. 'Studies in the Murabba'at and Nahal Hever Documents', *Revue de Qumran* 4, 53–81.

Levy, B. E., 1982/3. 'Kaisar Epibaterios: A Seafarers' Cult at Alexander', *INJ* 6, 102–117 (Pls. 18–20).

Levy, B. E., 1984. 'Nero's Liberation of Achaea: Some Numismatic Evidence from Patrae', in W. Heckel and R. Sullivan (eds.), *Nickle Numismatic Papers* (Waterloo, Ontario: Wilfred Laurier University Press), 167–185.

Levy, B. E., 1989. 'Nero's "Apollonia" Series: the Achaean Context', *NC* 149, 58–68.

Levy, B. E., 1991. 'When Did Nero Liberate Achaea – And Why', in A. D. Rizakis (ed.), *Achaia und Elis in der Antike: Akten des 1. Internationalen Symposiums, Athens, 19-21 May 1989* (Athens: Institut für Griechische und Römische Antike), 189–194.

Manning, C. E., 1975. 'Acting and Nero's Conception of the Principate', *Greece and Rome* 22, 163–175.

Parker, D. C., 2000. 'A New Oxyrhynchus Papyrus of Revelation: $P^{115}$ (P.Oxy. 4499)', *NTS* 46, 159–174.

Robinson, B., A., 2005. 'Fountains and the Formation of Cultural Identity at Roman Corinth', in D. N. Showalter and S. J. Friesen (eds.), *Urban Religion in Roman Corinth: Interdisciplinary Approaches* (Cambridge, MA: Harvard University Press), 111-140.

Sanford, E. Matthews, 1937. 'Nero and the East', *HSCPh* 48, 75-103.

Spawforth, A. J. S., 2012. *Greece and the Augustan Revolution* (Cambridge: Cambridge University Press).

Walbank, M. E. Hoskins, 2002. 'What's in a Name? Corinth Under the Flavians', *ZPE* 139, 251-264.

Walbank, M. E. Hoskins, 2003. 'Aspects of Corinthian Coinage in the Late 1st and Early 2nd Centuries AC', in *Corinth: Results of Excavations Conducted by the American School of Classical Studies at Athens, Volume 20. Corinth, The Centenary, 1896-1996* (Athens: American School of Classical Studies), 337–349.

Walbank, M. E. Hoskins, 2010. 'Image and Cult: The Coinage of Roman Corinth', in S. J. Friesen, D. N. Showalter, and J. C. Walters (eds.), *Corinth in Context: Comparative Studies on Religion and Society* (Supp. to *NovT*, no. 134; Leiden: E. J. Brill), 151–197.

Warmington, B. H., 1969. *Nero: Reality and Legend* (New York: W. W. Norton & Company).

# LIST OF CONTRIBUTORS

Dr Rachel Barkay is Curator of Ancient Coins in the Bank of Israel, Jerusalem.
rachel.barkay@boi.org.il

Robert Bracey is Project Curator of Kushan Coins in the Department of Coins and Medals, British Museum, London.
rbracey@thebritishmuseum.ac.uk

Dr Andrew Burnett is Deputy Director of the British Museum, London.
aburnett@thebritishmuseum.ac.uk

Professor Kevin Butcher is Head of the Department of Classics and Ancient History, University of Warwick.
k.e.t.butcher@warwick.ac.uk

Professor Ted V. Buttrey is Honorary Keeper of Ancient Coins, Department of Coins and Medals, Fitzwilliam Museum, Cambridge.
tvb1@hermes.cam.ac.uk

Robert Deutsch is a doctoral candidate in the Department of Classics at Tel Aviv University
rd@robert-deutsch.com

Dr Marius Heemstra received his doctorate from Groningen University.
m.heemstra@alumnus.rug.nl

David Hendin is Adjunct Curator, American Numismatic Society, New York.
amphoracoins@gmail.com

Professor David M. Jacobson is Honorary Fellow in the Department of Hebrew and Jewish Studies, University College London, and Editor of *PEQ*.
jacobson.d.m@gmail.com

Dr Nikos Kokkinos is Honorary Fellow in the Department of Hebrew and Jewish Studies, University College London.
nikos@kokkinos.co.uk

Revd Dr Larry J. Kreitzer is Tutorial Fellow in New Testament and Tutor for Graduates in the Regent's Park College, Oxford University.
larry.kreitzer@regents.ox.ac.uk

Anne Lykke is a doctoral candidate in the Department of Classical Archaeology, University of Vienna.
anne.lykke@univie.ac.at

Dr Danny Syon is Head of the Scholarly Assessment Branch, Israel Antiquities Authority, Jerusalem.
dsyon@israntique.org.il

Professor Boaz Zissu is in the Martin (Szusz) Department of Land of Israel Studies and Archaeology, Bar-Ilan University, Ramat Gan.
bzissu@gmail.com

Participants at the International Conference, September 2010